S0-DMV-164

The Golden Thread

By

Keith Walker

To Brian + Teresa
Sort of "neighbors"
all the best
Keith Walker

GOLDEN DOOR PRESS

Santa Rosa, California

2004

ALSO BY KEITH WALKER

"A Trail of Corn"

"The Escape"

"How to Survive Financially During Hard Times"

"The Dilapidated Dragon"

The Golden Thread

THE GOLDEN THREAD

Copyright 2003 Keith Walker

All rights reserved. No portion of this book may be reproduced in any form, except for brief quotations in reviews, without permission in writing from the publisher. Published by Golden Door Press, 6450 Stone Bridge Road, Santa Rosa, Ca., 95409, (707) 538-5018.

Library of Congress Control No. 2003092767

Walker, Keith.
The Golden Thread/by Keith Walker--1st ed. p. cm.
ISBN 1-885793-04-9
1. Iowa history 2. California history. 3. Salvation Army.
4. Biography--George A. Tallmon I.Title.
2003092767

Manufactured in the United States of America

First edition, January, 2004

To Moremama

1.

Giant paddles bit into the cold waters of the Mississippi River as, quietly, a chugging steamboat made its way northward.

Behind lay the battlefields of the South, drenched with the red blood of Union and Confederate soldiers. Ahead lay the bustling cities and green farms of the North and Midwest.

Little boys played happily along the river bank. Trees dipped to the water's edge. How could either of them be aware that peace had been declared, four years after the Slaveholders' Rebellion had broken out?

On board the round white boat was much rejoicing. Everyone was looking forward to reaching homes and loved ones. They cherished returning to the peaceful life they had longed for during many, many months and years.

A group of ladies sat at the captain's table as honored guests after tea, playing a little game of sucher with the weathered skipper.

Some of them were wives of officers or ministers, returning from the South at the end of the Great War. Some were teachers who had taught "contraband slaves" in goverment schools or aid society schools.

They were accustomed to good society, expecting deference and able to demand it.

Nearby sat other women--poor men's wives, just work-a-day women who had married some soldier after he enlisted, perhaps, and never had had a real home. Ivy-like women, helpless and timid, they had not been happy with their life "from pillar to post."

Off by themselves were the Southern women, most of them nervous but lady-like sisters from the South, perhaps coming north to meet a promised husband.

But one--and what a hag yellow fever had left her--felt no misgivings about being on a former enemy boat. She boasted how she had kept rid of Northern teachers--"nigger teachers"--by telling them that she could not attend to them and cholera at the same time.

"Had you cholera?" asked a gentleman.

"Noos," she laughed. "Were we not full of contempt?"

Over to one side, next to the windows, sat a young woman, quite pretty, with brown hair made into ringlets. A tiny baby girl lay asleep in her arms. A partially-opened book lay beside her.

She watched the other women as they pursued their social status. She heard the Southern woman speak--and recalled that she herself had been one of those government teachers.

When bluecoated soldiers drank wine at the table, she looked her disapproval. When the colored stewardess said they had been rude to her she raged impotently, quietly, to herself.

She looked out the window at the passing river bank. There was no fear of enemy bullets now, as there had been when she went south little more than a year before--with another baby in her arms.

Now passenger boats ran frequently if not regularly, though telegraphic communication was still not available between New Orleans and Cairo.

Her husband was with his regiment in Washington, D.C., being mustered out. Soon they would be home together in Iowa, ready to start the life they had never realized because of the war.

One time earlier, she was headed for Iowa in similar manner. Her thoughts drifted back to those days.

But I was not so anxious to get there, she recalled. I was 13, leaving the beautiful home in New York I had known all my life.

Her family--parents and brothers and sisters as well as herself--was headed toward the prairie lands of the west to make "a new start."

Behind lay the lands where parents and grandparents and great grandparents had lived since Revolutionary War days.

She remembered the numerous uncles and aunts and cousins; the genial help both in and out of doors; the individual animals, some of which were almost like personal friends.

And there was Grandma Cheseboro, who lived in the house built of bricks brought from Holland. Grandma Cheseboro was almost blind, yet always cheerful and agreeable to those around her.

The old fashioned house, with main hall from front to rear and fireplaces in many rooms; the outdoor oven; the immense barns and sheds where children loved to swing and play and hunt for eggs--all brought a host of memories flooding back on her.

But all that had been left behind. Her carefree life as a child was left with it.

Her father, John Carhartt, crippled since birth, had never been able to do hard manual labor. He worked first as a tanner at Bridgeport, near the Erie Canal, and that was where she had been born.

The tannery with its strong smell of tan bark could never be forgotten. She recalled how her brother, Albert, fell into a vat one day and was fished out before the tanning solution caused him any harm.

And, oh, yes. Edward fell into the fresh water vat one Sunday when the tannery was idle and Mother and Father were away. But the children fished him out, drenched as a soaked rat, gasping for breath. By the time the parents arrived home, he was tucked snugly in bed.

Later, they moved to Guilderland, and Father taught school for $32 a month. That wasn't much, and often the family had nothing for dinner but corn meal mush with a little molasses for flavoring.

The apples, cakes and pies carried to school by other children looked wonderfully good, and fruit was a real treat.

Maybe in Iowa things would be better.

But they weren't. The $2,000 her father brought from New York soon vanished to pay for the farm, house and horses.

Breaking the land and supplies for the stock and family soon put him heavily in debt. Then the Panic of 1857 and poor crops combined to make him nearly lose the place.

The women were kept indoors, cooking for gangs of men, while the men worked outside from dawn until late at night.

If Father happened to find Susan out-of-doors with a hammer or hoe or pet animal, he was more than likely to tell her, "Your place is in the house with Mother--you can find enough there to employ your time, if you try."

Their house was built of rough barn boards set on end and battened with one-by-two-inch strips. The roof boards were slabs two inches apart, and for a long time the house was not plastered. Snow drifted in quite freely.

Many a time the children made tracks in the snow indoors as they made their way to the head of the stairs on a winter's morning.

Except for the garret where the men and boys slept, the house consisted of one room. Susan slept in a trundle bed which was pushed under her parents' bed during the day.

She had no privacy. She never could be assured that her papers or writing or letters would be her own personal property. She never could call anything her own.

If she wanted to read or write in her journal, she had to sit up nights after her parents went to bed and try to work by candlelight. She almost ruined her eyes that way.

She felt doomed to a life of hateful drudgery. But for very self-pity she dared not openly complain, and instead brooded over her plight with sullen discontent and self-imposed unhappiness.

Her parents were honest, conscientious, God-fearing people, but austere and strict in family government. The boys often felt the whip.

An unnatural reserve brooded over all home affairs, and confidential communications were few.

Susan recalled the Great Revival of January, 1858, when nearly 40 persons were converted. Some of the cases were truly remarkable.

Her brother Edward was among the shouting converts (he had been in danger of sliding the other way until then), and her sister Melissa was definitely converted.

Susan felt a more or less intelligent tug toward a new spiritual beginning, although she had been a Christian, as far as a young girl can be, all her life. Often when her mother read an inspiring story or article, her soul rose within her and she vowed secretly to be good and do her part to make the world a better place.

But her faith was more of the quiet kind, and she wondered sometimes if she really was religious. Yet she felt she was.

When 15, she started writing a voluminous diary, because she felt the need for a friend. The diary was very morbid in tone, yet true to the highest standards of life.

On the day she began her journal, she started to attend a school whose teacher was a young man of 20. During the first month every entry had some reference to him, and he impressed her so much she resolved to try to make his time pleasant.

He seemed to enjoy her company, too, and soon began paying visits to her house, and sitting with her in church. He marked his name in her Methodist hymnal to show his requests for certain hymns.

In between school, prayer meetings, writing essary and letters, they had long confidential talks. Her mother, listening to these talks, told her to be more prudent.

All these things, and more, were duly recorded in her journal.

She recorded how she thought she ought to talk in meeting (at church), but felt she had a backwardness that she was sure was pure sinfulness.

And how she was unable to shed tears over her guilt, when she approached the mourner's bench (a sort of altar confessional at which sins were acknowledged), and how she concluded that her heart was dreadfully hard.

And how she received attentions and freedoms from her teacher, recording simply and faithfully that during a conversation "he then kissed me and went into the house."

The teacher came to see her more often--and before he left for college to study to become a minister, he held her tightly and told her that he loved her.

She remembered how, in all her maiden delicacy, she quietly whispered in return, "I do love you."

He left then, but they wrote faithfully, their letters full of love and trust in God.

His letters were beautiful and thrilling, and three times each day--as they had promised--she knelt and prayed for him, as he had said he would do for her.

Then, in May, he came to visit for a weekend, and again in June.

Her heart beat quickly as they met, and they spent happy hours talking over the past and future, and all of their hopes and expectations.

She longed for the future--hoping for grace to do duty when she could be a minister's wife.

But then came the dread announcement. That fall, the trustees of Iowa College decided to move from Davenport to Grinnell. Davenport was only 10 miles from her home in Amity, but Grinnell was 125 miles away.

George came for one last visit--and how hard it was to part! She clung to his hand, and wished he didn't have to go.

But then came a letter. George said he would be teaching in Linn Grove, much closer than Grinnell, instead, that winter-- the school where they had met. They would see each other at least every two weeks!

But, he warned, his college career would be delayed. What should he do?

"Do just as you think best, Dear George," she wrote back.

When he came to visit a few days later, he could hardly wait to get her alone.

"I will teach!" he announced.

"Oh, George!" she exclaimed breathlessly.

And he swept her into his arms and whispered to her: "Oh, my love, how near and dear you are to me. I love you more every day. I know I do. Dearest, sweetest, loveliest, charming girl!"

"I love you, too," she replied.

"It has been less than a year since I first met you," he said, "and only eight months since I first called you mine, and yet you are nearer to me and dearer far than any sister. And I seem to know you better than I know either of my sisters."

And she smiled and hugged him back and returned his kiss.

"I wouldn't exchange your simple, pure, unalloyed affection for the love of all other women in the world!" he vowed.

And then they knelt together and thanked God for their lives.

2.

George came even more often to see her after that--until one day her mother said perhaps it would be best if he didn't come so often--"it wouldn't look good."

Susan reluctantly agreed to tell George not to come for two or three weeks. He was disturbed, but understanding.

A week later he was back again.

Not that he entirely planned it that way. He was "just in the neighborhood" to visit the local school teacher, Mr. Gorton. If she had heard he was there and hadn't stopped, she might wonder why. He would only stay a little while.

But he stayed two hours--two short hours that seemed like only moments. They sent up a prayer together in their own behalf, and finally, at one o'clock, he tore himself away and went home.

Susan's mother wanted him to stay for the night for fear of suspicions, but he said he got home and went to his room without anyone knowing where he was or when he got there.

The next weekend he visited again--and stayed overnight, because it got too late to see Mr. Gorton.

Susan and George talked until one o'clock, which they knew was not right. But when they were in each other's company, it seemed as if they couldn't leave.

Next morning her mother said again she thought George came too often. He was goodnatured about it, and agreed to stay away for four weeks.

He pressed Susan tight when he left, and bid her a long, long farewell. Four weeks seemed like forever!

Then, a few days later, two letters came that showed Susan he really was a little bitter. Not that the letter said so. One only apologized to Mother for coming so often. But the other one, to Susan, said he probably would not see her even in four weeks. She didn't know when she would see him again--maybe never.

She knew Mother was concerned only because her daughter was so young--only 16. But it seemed so hard. Maybe they weren't meant to be married. She tossed on her pillow, and cried herself to sleep.

Before the four weeks were up, she did see him--at school when he brought a group of students for a surprise contest with Mr. Gorton's pupils. He took her hand, but wouldn't look into her face. She could see he was troubled, though glad to see her.

She hoped to see him again at a Christmas party at the school two weeks later. But he wasn't there. She wondered why --then decided maybe he had stopped at her home instead.

As soon as she could, she persuaded her brothers, Richard and Albert, to go home with her. As they rushed through the darkness, she noticed someone coming the other way. Her heart almost stopped! It was George!

"Good evening!" he said, when he recognized them.

She grasped his hand and laughed happily.

"Oh, George!" she exclaimed. "We were at the party. . . "

Then she realized something was wrong. George didn't seem pleased to see her. He didn't squeeze her hand as warmly as he always did.

She remained silent for a moment, then asked him to go back with them.

"No," George replied. "I promised to meet Mr. Gorton at 8 o'clock. It's almost that now."

"But you can go part way . . . " she insisted.

He hesitated, then agreed, and they walked along together. The boys had already gone ahead.

He said nothing.

After some time passed in silence, she finally stopped and demanded, "What's the matter, George?"

"Nothing," he said.

"But you don't act like you usually do."

"I guess it's because I have a slight cold."

They went on, and he talked some. But whenever she asked a leading question, he shied away from answering it.

Really, she knew what was wrong. But she couldn't get him to tell her, as he always did. And at the gate bars, he left her, unhappy and alone, as he hurried off through the darkness.

She ran home, feeling more blue than ever in her life. Her whole world had collapsed about her. The tears rushed uncontrollably down her cheeks. She tried to hide them, but Mother saw her. She rushed into her room and threw herself on the bed. Mother came in after her, and Susan sobbed out her story.

The next day, George came to return some books to Father. As he was hitching his horse, Mother went out, whether on purpose or for something else, Susan didn't know. She spoke to George.

Susan could tell she was urging him to put his horse in the stable and stay all night. He shook his head.

But when Mother told him Susan wanted to see him, he quickly changed his mind and eagerly followed her into the house.

She met him at the door, and he shook hands with her. And he quickly followed her into the little room, for their business was with each other.

He let the curtain drop, and she discovered that he was his old self again--and that he realized he was now welcome to come--anytime and as often as he wished.

They spent a happy hour or two--they took no notice of time--until finally George said he had to leave to keep his date with Mr. Gorton. He promised faithfully to return as soon as he could and spend the evening with her.

He did, and they spent two of the happiest hours of their lives. All else was forgotten; they lived only for each other.

They knelt together at a mercy seat, and raised their hearts in prayer to God. They thanked Him for past blessings, and asked Him to take care of them in the future, to prepare them for His service, and for Heaven.

They rose, and George pressed Susan to his beating heart, and kissed her fondly; then returned her low good night, said goodbye, and mounted his horse and rode away into the night.

Her heart sang as she undressed and climbed into bed.

Next day Mother wrote to George to say his visit on the next Friday --New Year's Eve--would be agreeable.

And he came, and they spent the time together when the old year, 1858, went out and the new year, 1859, came in. The last thing they did in the old year was to pray together, and the first thing in the new year was to kiss each other.

Those were happy days--but before long, George's school term was over and he returned to college--this time to Beloit College in Wisconsin.

Before he left, they talked of their affections for each other, and the possibility of their changing during the long period they must necessarily be apart.

He argued that, considering their youth, as their minds became more and more developed, their affections, too, might change. But she argued that, if they lived only for the Glory of God, their love could only grow stronger.

He went off to school, and she lived each day for his letters. When he could, he visited her, sometimes staying for as long as two weeks.

She decided to go on to school while she waited, and that fall entered Cornell College in Mt. Vernon, Iowa.

Then came national events that changed their lives. As the winter drew toward spring, the air was full of rumors of war. Then rebel guns fired on government troops at Fort Sumter and the War Between the States was on. But at first, the fighting seemed far off.

One day, while riding home from college in a conveyance, Susan saw a "boy in blue" leave a house, mount his horse and ride after the carriage, evidently going to camp at Davenport. He rode beside them for awhile, chatting pleasantly with the driver.

Susan kept thinking, "If he were my cousin or schoolmate--going into danger, temptation and suffering--does he have the guidance and comforts a faith in God can give? Oh, if only I could do something!"

Then she took a little book of Bible texts from her satchel and asked the driver to give them to the soldier, who restrained his horse to thank her and ask her name.

The soldier rode away, and Susan never knew if she ever heard from him again. Was he a brave, true man? Did he return alive to his friends, to be a good citizen in peace?

Did he save her little book, and did it perhaps, in a hospital or prison, remind him of a woman at home who prayed for the cause, for his safety, as well as of the One who died to save us all?

George and Susan were married on March 2, 1862, and for a short time enjoyed the wonders and joy of being newlyweds.

But when a call came for 75,000 volunteers, George felt that he must go. He argued he could leave Susan with her mother during his absence.

Susan wasn't at all anxious for him to go. She remembered telling him, if he felt it was his duty, she would not say anything against it--although she didn't feel it was his duty.

She lived in a bedroom George had added to her father's house, and there their little baby Grace was born the following Jan. 13. George obtained a furlough while she was still in bed, but he only could stay a few days.

A year went by, and Susan waited and yearned for the husband and marriage and joy she had tasted for only a short period of time.

Then came word that George had been placed in charge of a plantation near Baton Rouge, La., where "contraband" negroes --those who had followed the Union army--had been sent. The Aid Society had started a school for colored refugees, with three or four northern women as teachers.

George sent for Susan to come and be a teacher, even though it meant a long, hard journey into enemy territory.

Her mother thought she was only joking when she first began to talk of going. When she realized Susan was serious, she cried all night.

Her brother, Albert, a lad of 17, felt responsible for her going, believing that it would be better for him to go and for her to remain in safety on the Iowa farm.

Not that he could have prevented her going; besides, he had duties at home that restrained him. And Susan, being married, felt she must obey, not her mother, but her husband.

The neighbor men scolded, the women bit their lips as if afraid of speaking too harshly, the young women wished that they could go with her--the young men had already gone.

The doctor said the baby should not go, and Mother begged to leave the child with her. But Susan was adamant about taking little Grace with her.

To George, his wife wrote: "My feelings remain unchanged about coming to you. I desire to come if you think best. I would like to be your housekeeper (jailer?) but will agree to teach if I may keep Grace with me when you cannot keep her.

"Mother has many and very good objections to my going, but I think I have better answers . . . Mother says I will be in 'a fix' by next winter. Well, we shall see. I did not mean to write the last . . . 'I wish somebody'd come' near enough to let me kiss him . . . "

Poor Mother! You know what she did--objected and cried, but helped all she could to get ready for the journey.

She and Albert took Susan and the baby to a railroad town, and left her with friends, who were to take her to the train station at the proper time.

On the way to the depot, the friend's husband gave Susan a fatherly lecture about making acquaintance with men, but especially warned her to beware of friendly soldiers.

She replied that her husband had said officers of the road were there on purpose to help travelers, and she should always apply to them for help.

When the friend had chosen her a seat and arranged her bundles, he turned and asked someone behind her to take care of her.

She looked back. It was a soldier.

During the several hours that followed, the soldier brought the fretful baby frequent drinks of water as kindly and quietly as if he had not worn army blue.

When his road led away from hers and she had to change cars, and a train had been delayed, she was glad to accept help from two other passengers, whom she instinctively recognized as college professors.

As she drew near the enemy lines, she felt that people were less friendly. One loud-voiced woman wore the Confederate colors in three large flowers in her bonnet.

There was a feverish uneasiness about almost everyone. Other women and children, wishing to go south, were inquiring for boats and discussing chances. Though boats made trips, it was not safe to do so because the enemy held much of the country. Each agent represented his own boat only, and none went below Memphis.

Her instructions had been to get a "through boat," so she went to a hotel. Hotel fare and drayage seemed very costly, she recalled, and her baby was evidently sick and rather tyranical if not unreasonable, she thought.

She saw one woman with children shed tears, but she would not do that!

Day after day she saw the government boat at the wharf, but was always assured it would be sent north.

At last, carrying her pretty baby, whom she instinctively felt to be her best protection and advocate, she walked to the wharf where men in blue were carrying boxes of provisions to the steamer, and asked where she could see the captain.

There was an army captain as well as a boat captain. She couldn't remember which she saw--both, probably--but she saw such sympathy in the silent soldiers' faces when they heard her asking if she might go with them to her soldier husband in the south that she secretly vowed she would always love soldiers.

She was told, of course, that it was not a passenger boat, that it carried stores and men, that she would not be pleasantly circumstanced, etc., "but if it depended only on me," each said, "you shall go."

She returned to the hotel and waited. After a few hours she remembered receiving word that the boat was about to leave, and she might go aboard. Who sent the word to the hotel, she never knew.

At last she was seated in the after cabin, removing her hat and her baby's cloak. Two ladies came delightedly to meet and welcome her. One was a nurse. She realized then that she was on a hospital boat, returning soldiers to duty after sick leave.

Many of the soldiers were very young. She could recall one face that was even childish, as a soldier leaned into the after cabin, vainly coaxing her fretful little one to come and play with him.

Older children ran freely where they chose. Her baby played with a box of books, tiny volumes of Scott or translations from Herodotus, prepared for use of convalescent soldiers.

For once in her life, she was too nervous to read. It was not a pleasure trip.

Sometimes the boat had to be tied up and its boiler cleaned. To choose a place where the Confederates would not attack was a difficult matter.

One evening when she had retired early, because her baby was fretting, there came a sudden loud alarm by boat whistles; and soon the vessel seemed emtpied of men, the last one clanging after him his sword and scabbard as he hurried out.

She could not leave her child, who was coughing violently, but how her ears opened to the orders she heard! How her eyes strained at the light of a burning barge of hay started downstream by the enemy, in hopes that the current would carry it among the Union boats.

All of the boats that could, immediately got up steam and, by going out farther into the river, escaped danger.

The vessel she was on was helpless and, for all they knew, powder or bombs might be buried in that blazing hay. The barge came closer and closer, headed right for their boat.

As it came alongside, the fire blazing brightly, the fire-hot, sweaty men, working feverishly, used long poles to hold the front away from the side of the boat.

With great effort, the men diverted the burning barge away from the main part of the boat, and then the stern was pushed aside.

A great cry went up from the boat. As they watched, the barge floated by harmlessly. Then it was lost, still glowing, in the distance and the night. Such was Susan's remembrance of Memphis.

At last they reached the city of her destination. A messenger went at once to the provost marshal's office to inquire about her husband. It would have been more kind to tell her what they learned, than to only advise her to go to a hotel. For he had been sent some miles away.

But she didn't go to the hotel right away. She was confident he would be at the landing in a few minutes. Had he not written that he had met every boat?

An hour passed, and she felt she shouldn't keep all those people waiting. Finally, although she knew her husband would be disappointed, she consented to follow their advice.

After a long time, notwithstanding her own agitation, she succeeded in getting her baby to sleep and in bed, and then wrote her husband a note. Finding the hotelkeeper in the hall (there didn't seem to be any servants about), she asked him to send a messenger at once to the camp of Freedmen, where her husband was employed.

Her request seemed very amusing to Boniface. He "could not do it."

"Why not?" she asked, increduously.

"Because the city is under martial rule, and no one can go out of doors after 8 o'clock without a permit."

She reluctantly retraced her steps to her room.

At least twice in the night she recognized her husband's step on the sidewalk. But the next day she learned her ears had deceived her.

At daybreak her impatience was beyond all bounds. Taking her baby, speaking to no one, she started out in quest of State Prison Buildings, where the contraband camp was located.

She asked directions from a Negro man and a refined looking mulatto woman, and finally reached the end of the walk "tired almost to death."

She stood before a large arched doorway, and tried to speak to several old negresses who were busy about a large black kettle, inside. They scattered like leaves in the wind.

Then came a white man in army blue, and an old Oriental woman, one smiling faintly and saying the lieutenant was away, the other crying out and rejoicing to see the baby and wife, of whom she had heard so often.

They made Susan and the baby feel at home. They asked her if she would like breakfast. They were having cornbread, bacon and coffee. No butter, vegetables or milk.

Baby Grace reached eagerly for the cup and was quite indignant to find no milk in it. Susan ate a taste of the hard bread but no more.

Aunt Marie, whom Susan had known through letters, talked constantly. While they were sitting at the table, Susan's note arrived from the hotel, and soon after her husband, to whom it was addressed.

"George!" she exclaimed when she saw him. Elation welled up inside of her. It had been such an arduous trip, such a long time since she had seen him!

"Susan, darling!" he replied, then hugged her tight and gave her a kiss she would never forget. How good it was to be together! How wonderful it was to be in each other's arms again!

They had much to talk about, and many lost moments to make up for. It was like a wonderful honeymoon all over again.

But their joy was short-lived.

Little Grace wasn't well.

Her whooping cough didn't seem to go away. Her eyes were red, her nose runny, and she seemed to be developing a fever.

Then one morning she awoke with pink spots around the ears. They spread gradually over her face, becoming bigger and darker. Her cough was more and more insistent, and she wouldn't eat.

Susan soon realized the truth. She had the measles. She had caught it from someone on the boat--possibly the young fellow who tried to coax her to come to him.

They watched over her day and night, doing everything they could to ease the burning fever. But that dreadful coughing continued, and she grew weaker and weaker.

Then, one night, she closed her eyes and opened them no more.

Susan's whole world crashed about her. Her own little Grace, her bright-eyed little daughter who had meant so much to her--gone from her arms and never to return again. The pain returned to her in her memories.

Her only consolation was the knowledge that little Grace was with Jesus, and someday she would see her again--in Heaven.

Jack Coffin dug a little grave beside a pear tree on the deserted plantation, and George and Susan laid their little baby to rest. She was only 14 months old.

Susan recalled the beautiful place where the grave was. No one in all the world could care for that little spot as she did. But she was now powerless to take care of it.

She thought: Does some old Negro still keep a little watch of it for my sake? I hope so! Someday I will return--as I promised.

When she left the baby's sick room and began to note her surroundings, the season was already far advanced. She could go but little out-of-doors.

Flowers--especially roses--bloomed in greatest profusion. The heat was extreme. Visiting the little grave in the garden was done only when the blazing sun would permit.

George soon was ordered back to his regiment, leaving her to serve as one of the "government teachers" who taught escaped slaves to read and write.

They lived in one of the deserted plantations outside the Union lines. It served as living quarters and school combined.

The house showed the signs of the war which had swept over it. Broken blinds and shattered windows lined the handsome hall doors. Inside, the rooms were stripped of almost all furniture.

A hole was stamped through the lower hall floor. Timbers under the parlor floor were cracked, so that it sagged to one side. Some of the rails were missing. Plaster was broken from the great brick pillars that supported the porch roof.

On the wall were two portraits, cut and punched by bayonets.

The stable had been burned. The sugar house stood, though the shutters were broken, its engine crippled, and its heavy sugar troughs torn up and made into schoolroom benches.

They were in constant danger of attack by rebel forces. Their concern was increased by tales of a woman teacher who died at her schoolroom door, and of another who "nearly starved to death" in a rebel prison.

Then one cloudy evening a soldier rushed up the back stairway of the plantation house and gave the captain hasty word that the pickets half a mile away had been firing.

Without a word or one backward look the officer ran out to his men. The soldier stayed long enough to tell the captain's wife to turn down her lamp, throw water on the fire in the hearth, and call the other four women.

She went first to the room of the lieutenant's bride, who had sent her husband away with a kiss "to his possible death," as she said. Then the two wives came to warn the others, returned to their own rooms for a moment, and soon all five women stole downstairs and outside. A weedy spot on the plantation beyond the kitchen garden was their destination.

They waited anxiously, but there was no further alarm. A couple of hours later, they were re-assembled in the teachers' room talking over their "scare." They were all still a little hysterical.

Susan was surprised to see her hat which she could not find when she left, and emptied her pockets of the treasures she had gathered to save: an autograph album, pictures in heavy cases and a large flannel penwiper   . . .

Susan Tallmon was ripped from her thoughts about her past life just then, and her attention returned to the captain's quarters where she sat by the window on the boat heading north.

Her little tow-headed child, born in the Southland, roused up from sleep.

A passing steamer decorated with many flags and streamers, caught her eye.

It must be a great victory for the Union. But where? Might not her brothers and cousins been at the place and been killed?

And why was that flag at half-staff in the city she was approaching?

Some general must be dead.

Before the boat reached the wharf, a small active man boarded the vessel.

He goes all over the boat. He talks to everyone. He is crowded and questioned.

He says President Lincoln is dead!

Men are crying and women are terrified.

Will it all have to be fought over again, as the man is saying?

Susan resolved to keep away from him.

Pull your satchel into your stateroom, and hug baby in your arms. If Lincoln is dead there will be time to cry tomorrow, and the next day. Guard yourself from this dreadful man!

Meanwhile, who wants any food? Only the poor little senseless baby!

Soon the boat reached a city near home, and mother and baby went to the office of a friend.

Other friends came in and smiled, and yet as at a funeral. For it is true, too true. Our Lincoln--our dear President!

To the lonely farm they went. Susan's mother came wonderingly to the lumber wagon. Her eyes were red because of the news she had heard.

She looked up at the veiled woman, not knowing who it can be. A little baby was held down for her to take.

Then she knew: her daughter's child, of which she had never heard.

Later someone asked her, "Didn't you faint?"

"What, faint," she answered, "and drop that dear little one?"

3.

George Washington Tallmon was going to be a minister. He went to Beloit College in Wisconsin with that in mind. His wife, Susan, looked forward to a life as a preacher's wife.

But when George returned from the war, the idea of being a minister was gone. He was going to get rich. Besides, he had a family to support.

So he took advantage of a government offer to veterans, and homesteaded a farm in Scott County, Iowa, not far from his wife's folks' place. Susan called it "Wild Rose Farm."

It was wonderful new land, and he worked hard. He accomplished more than two men, and gloried in it. He had a half-day's work done before breakfast, changed teams, worked until noon, then changed teams again and worked until night. Then he did the chores and milking.

And he loved it. He enjoyed fixing up the new place, planting a garden, and growing bumper crops.

But his wife didn't.

To her, farm life was a lot of hard work. She hated the inconvenience, the drudgery, the dirt and grime.

She went out and worked on the reaper when she shouldn't. George expected her to work hard, and she couldn't.

And a bad case of intermittent fever during the first summer made her even more unhappy.

Late that fall, soon after she got up from the fever, they moved into a new house only partly plastered--and the wet plaster had frozen.

The ground was flat and low; the cellar hole was shallow and open, with water often standing in it.

The corn in the rail crib was often disturbed by the neighbor's cattle during the winter and she, with leaky shoes, had to drive them away through wet and snow.

The new plaster stayed frozen until spring. Even the following year, they slept in an unheated room, for although she owned a small heating stove, there was not enough pipe to reach the chimney. Her husband did not approve of spending money for more. Wanting to keep her promise to obey, she submitted to his decision in silence.

She suffered severely from headaches and toothaches, spending many sleepless nights because of them. Some entire nights were devoted to pain. Though a pillow covered her head, she couldn't get it warm.

The days were spent in a small and very hot kitchen, without ventilation except by drafts.

The next autumn her hands and wrists were weak and painful, and she doctored for sprains and wore rubber bands for "weeping sinew." She had several teeth pulled.

Her feet hurt, and she had to rest one foot on the rung of a chair while doing the washing.

Feeding the hired help also was a trying experience for the young woman who loved fancy and dainty things.

During harvest time, George hired a large crew. As was the custom, the hired hands ate at their employer's table. And Susan set the table with care--preserves, jellies, jams, bread, cornbread, butter in pats, little decorations, as well as main course dishes such as many of those men seldom had.

The first day, one of the hunkies on the crew, before George's lengthy grace was said, and before anyone else sat down, seated himself in front of the butter plate.

This uncouth member of the crew, unshaven and maybe not washed --at any rate he was still pretty dirty--reached out and scooped up a pat of butter with his thumb.

As he placed it in his mouth, he remarked, "By gum, I'm going to have my share of the knick knacks!"

Susan was mortified, horrified, and ran off to the kitchen, hiding her tears. She felt like her whole world was collapsing. How could she stand it? But she didn't say anything. She must be supportive of George.

So life continued, but gradually, after much work and sacrifice, they began to get the farm in shape. It was becoming a home--a place to live. George made good money on his crops, and times seemed to be getting better.

Then, one day, late in the summer of 1868, George came rushing into the house, rattling money in his pocket.

"Sold my farm!" he exclaimed.

"You what?"

"Sold my farm. Sold my farm. A man offered me $2,000. That's enough to buy two more farms. And then we . . ."

"When do we have to move?" Susan asked, cautiously.

"October 1."

"George, you know I am going to be confined the first of October."

George hadn't thought of that. He hesitated, then said, "I guess we can arrange to stay a little longer."

He did, and they moved in late November, after another little girl, Clara, joined their household.

Susan never felt quite sure of a home after that, always afraid George might sell their property once again without her knowledge nor consent.

George used the money to buy two farms in central Iowa, one four or five miles south of Gilman, the other on the Iowa River several miles away. He bought both because he did not know which was better--and for speculative purposes.

Later he sold the Iowa River farm and with the money bought more land north of the Gilman farm, increasing it in size to 320 acres.

He with his family lived at his wife's folks' farm at Circle Grove for a year, then moved onto the new place--quickly named Wild Rose Farm II.

There was no house, and they lived in the unplastered, barren toolhouse for three years while George worked on the house evenings and rainy days.

The farm, too, was undeveloped, and George worked early and late to get it into shape. He made ditches and hauled stone and built a great barn and granary. He was determined to improve the farm.

One evening all his hard work almost went up in flames. A neighbor came rushing up the driveway.

"A prairie fire is heading this way," he warned.

George ran outside and looked. Sure enough, the whole southern sky was ablaze. He hurriedly harnessed up the team of horses that had been working all day, hitched on the plow, and headed for the fire line.

Before he left, he told his wife to bring as many gunny sacks as she could find, and wet them at the pond.

Other farmers gathered. Quickly, they began plowing furrows across the prairie in the face of the flames. Soon several teams were working, staggered one behind the other, widening the band of safety.

But they weren't quite fast enough. The flames, when they arrived, swept around the end of the fire trail, and went on.

Another fire trail was started. But, again it was breached.

Finally, desperately, a line was formed at the very front gate of the Tallmon farm. A narrow furrow was plowed--there wasn't time for more--and a back fire ignited to meet the oncoming flames.

It was just in time. The two fires came together. The aggressor fire was badly beaten--but managed to cross the fire line in several places.

Everyone grabbed wet gunny sacks--including Susan--and beat desperately at the intruder. Black forms of the people against the leaping flames could be seen by the frightened children waiting on the porch.

The fire was stopped--and next morning the children went down to see how, in just a few places, it had crossed the line. The road was lined with dead prairie chickens, killed by the blaze.

The family was extra fire conscious after that.

One Sunday, on the way home from church, as the mules plodded along, Susan noticed a pall of black smoke in the eastern sky, way off in the distance.

"What's that?" she asked.

Her husband looked.

"It's not a prairie fire or a timber fire," he replied. "It looks like something big--maybe a whole city ablaze--perhaps Iowa City or Davenport."

Later they found out what it was--it was Chicago ablaze-- the famous fire of Oct. 8, 1871, when the entire city was burned to the ground and more than 300 people killed--one of the worst fires in the history of the world.

The Iowa Central Railroad was built across the edge of the Tallmon farm soon after they moved there. The track made a curve, ran through a cut, and then onto a fill where it crossed the farm.

The family was eating dinner one day when suddenly they heard a big crash. They were petrified. Rushing to the window, they saw two trains that had come together. Most of the cars had stayed on the tracks, but the front ends of the engines had raised up together to form a huge inverted "V," then fell over. They rushed over to the crash scene to help. Several people had been killed.

Little Clara and her Papa went over to see the wreck the next day, and Papa hired a man they found sitting on a box. Papa needed someone to help in the haying and harvest. Clara's Mamma wasn't at all happy about having a "tramp" in the house.

The farming country was still new, and one day a deer came across the prairie near the farm.

Some of the neighbors tried to catch it, and Papa got on his horse and followed it for eight or ten miles before giving up.

While he was gone, little 4-year-old Angie exclaimed, "I do hope Papa gets it because then we can have roast crimson for dinner!"

4.

Come with me to a quiet farm neighborhood close to the center of Iowa in the year 1871.

It is May, and the green corn shoots are already through the ground.

Follow a dirt lane, lined with willow trees and osage orange hedges, and turn where you see red barns, a white gate and a long driveway up a hill.

The house isn't finished yet, but the barns are in good repair, and farm animals of all kinds are plentiful. A neatly-kept garden is located close by, just beginning to grow, and little plum trees some day will grow into an abundant orchard.

Chickens scatter as we approach the small, one-room wooden building, set up on stones, which is the Tallmons' temporary home. Later it will be the shop building, after the house is finished.

We enter to find a single, unplastered room, with rough wooden floor. There is an air of expectancy. The father is busy heating water on the stove and caring for his wife, who lies in bed. She groans as the pains come on strongly, then recede.

"It probably will be a girl," the father says, as he takes supper to his wife. "Doesn't seem we can have anything else."

Their four older children had all been females.

In time, the pains grow stronger and more frequent. Mamma groans as her body draws up tight.

Papa brings water and washes her, and puts a warm moist cloth across her forehead. She sighs and thanks him.

Another labor pain presses down on her body. She holds her husband's hand, then squeezes hard and grimaces and cries out as the pain bears down. In a short time, she relaxes.

"That was a hard one, wasn't it?" he asks, as the pain recedes.

"Oh, yes!" she murmurs, her forehead glistening with beads of perspiration.

Papa wipes them away, pats her reassuringly, and comforts her.

Another pain arises in her body, starting high and moving downward.

"Push, now," he says. "Push! Push hard!"

She cries out and grimaces and pushes.

"I see the head!" Papa exclaims.

Mamma responds with the next wave of contractions, and then Papa announces: "Here it comes!"

With an extra hard push, Mamma cries out in anguish, and the baby comes forth into the great strange world that lies ahead.

Papa takes the very little red thing into his two big hands, carries it to the kitchen where warm water is heating on the wood stove, washes it off, and wraps it in a tiny flannel blanket.

Then he returns to the bedroom and lays the precious bundle in Mamma's arms. She looks down into the very red, wrinkled little face, and her heart is filled with great joy and thanksgiving.

But when the wail of a baby's new voice is heard, it is not that of a girl. It is a little boy--and is he hairy! "The missing link," his father dubs him.

His official name, however, would be George Albert Tallmon--after his father, but with a different middle name. His birthdate: May 13, 1871, in Jasper County, Iowa.

It was some time before Mamma felt better. She was plagued with dispepsia, palpitations, lame arms and shoulders, and she had no appetite.

Little George grew fast, and was already crawling when the family moved into the new house, still under construction. The frame was finished, and Papa added the partitions, lathing and plastering, as he had time, on rainy days and evenings.

Then came a close call that made Mamma shudder.

Papa had plowed for a garden on the west side of the house, leaving only a few feet between. The spring weather turned very hot, and Mamma opened the west door, which was seldom used. The older girls were off playing.

Mamma was busy ironing and didn't notice that baby Georgie and 3 1/2-year-old Clara had gone out onto the plowing, until she suddenly realized they were making a lot of noise out there.

Going out to investigate, she was dismayed to find Georgie within a few feet of a coiled rattlesnake and Clara throwing clods at it.

Mamma snatched the unperturbed children away, and quickly killed the hissing snake with a hoe.

Having three little sisters in one household kept the place lively.

Eldest was Ada, Mamma's little helper. She rocked baby and picked up play things, told stories to the little ones and heard their prayers.

She dusted and swept, and asked questions and gave good advice. She never wilfully disobeyed her mother nor struck a younger child nor engaged in a single quarrel.

Angie, next eldest, began her regular lessons when she was four. Ada had taught her the letters by rote. But when Papa skipped around while reciting with her, Angie got mixed up and couldn't tell half of them. Papa, being a school teacher, started the lessons young.

"Mamma," she ventured one day, while watching some fence posts being piled in the yard, "can't we have a 'post' office now?" She knew Papa had a long ways to go to the post office, especially in stormy weather.

Ada, when her Sunday shoes were missing, "Mustn't we be kind to those who treat us bad, so they will be good?" It seemed she had given the shoes to her special enemy.

In summer, each little girl had her own garden bed. The bugs and flies held great interest for little Clara. She had quite a collection in the fall--all pinned to a smoothly papered board. But in trying to "fix them better" she broke them all to pieces-- "lady bird, bumblebee, mosquito and flea."

That was the day she brought a botfly and yellow-jacketed hornet home to Mamma in her fat little hands.

Nothing animate was repulsive to her. Perhaps she would confidently present you with her treasures--an angleworm or a young mouse.

Blue-eyed, round-faced, wide awake little girls--in winter they wore copper-toed shoes, woolen dresses and gingham sack-aprons; in summer they rejoiced in barefeet and ragged sunbonnets that served by spells for dolly's bed or kitty's jacket.

They did the dishes twice a day, to earn a cent to subscribe to The Corporal children's magazine. But they amused the baby for love because, as Addie explained to Angie, "Mamma has more love than money."

One day Mamma was reading one of her old essays about subjecting order to comfort in the home. Ada had neglected to sweep under the stove and sewing machine.

Looking in her mother's face with earnest eyes, she asked, in all seriousness:

"Mamma, don't you think that a little--just a little--dirt around a room makes it more pleasant?"

One day, Mamma found Angie sitting on a box in the closet.

"What are you doing here?"

"I asked God for a little girl," Angie explained, "and I'm waiting for him to put one in my arms." She had often expressed the desire for a little girl of her own.

She didn't get one, of course--at least not right then. But she did suggest to Papa that a wax doll would be very acceptable for her birthday, which was approaching.

"Oh, you don't want a wax doll," he bantered with her. "How could you care for such a frail thing?"

"I'll be very, very careful," Angie assured him, and somehow she felt he had put the word "doll" down in his memory. She also prayed that he would not forget.

A few days later, Papa went to town, three miles away, to visit the store and post office. How little Angie studied every bundle when he returned!

Next morning Angie awoke before daylight and wondered how soon she could go downstairs and see the dolly, for it was her birthday.

The stair-door opened, and a low voice called: "Is there a birthday girl up there who is awake?"

"Yes, Papa," she answered.

"Want to come down? I have a nice fire in the sitting room."

As she hastened down to the pleasant warmth and light, her father said: "Now dress your feet and put on your clothes. I'll help with the buttons when I come in. See how much you can do before I get Snowball milked. Then, you'll see!"

And he went out with the milk pails and lantern.

Angie managed all her buttons and washed her face, even brushed her brown locks, and then climbed on a chair to wait for the blissful moment when Papa should have the milk strained and could turn his attention to her.

"Seems to me," he remarked, "I heard a little girl say she wanted a wax doll. Do you remember any such girl?"

"I did!" Angie exclaimed breathlessly, claspy her hands tightly.

"Well," he said judicially, "how would it do if, instead of a doll, you should have a real live baby sister?"

Angie considered.

"Could I have her for all my very own?"

"Yes, all your own," Papa replied.

"Well, then, I'd rather have the little sister."

Her father disappeared into Mamma's room and soon returned with a little red flannel bundle in his arms. Such a tiny little bundle!

He laid it in her arms, and she saw among the red folds a wee face and a little fist and the very brightest little eyes, and dimples.

"Oh, darling, sweet baby sister!" Angie cried.

"Time to take her back to her Mamma now," said Papa.

The nicest part was that Susan Barbara was born on Angie's birthday. Well, it might have been a little before midnight, but those old clocks weren't too accurate, so they called it Angie's birthday, anyway.

After that, Angie always called Susie hers.

With a new arrival in the house, little George was no longer "the baby."

He had a pet bottle, and loved to play with it. Someone warmed the baby's feet at the stove, and he came and warmed "Bottle's" feet, too. He was just beginning to talk.

As he grew, his world broadened. He was a "big boy" now. He enjoyed playing with the cat out in the grass on a sunny day, or following Papa to the barn to do the chores or milk the cow.

And being the only brother in a family of sisters didn't seem to bother him. He enjoyed playing their games and entering their fun.

His oldest sisters, Addie and Angie, took care of him as much as his mother.

One wintry day, Mamma was putting the washboiler filled with snow on the kitchen stove, and called to Addie:

"Hurry and get your lessons, for I want you to amuse the little children in the other room today. I must churn and wash, and they will catch cold out here. I have made a fire for you, and you may have your playhouse, and play anything you please."

Addie called, "Come," to Clara and George, who were both on one chair by the stove, slying eating snow from the boiler.

They came, and Mamma carried the baby into the next room. They were satisfied for a while, amusing themselves by looking at pictures, examining the clock and rocking in the big rocking chair which had an inclination to go over backwards.

"Now, will you please help me move my playhouse, Mamma?" asked Addie.

Of course. Her mamma wiped the suds from her hands, and carried the heavy end of the box that Addie called a playhouse--a small cupboard with two shelves.

Mamma went to a trunk and brought out a yard of pink calico which she placed on the table, and putting Georgie on a chair behind it, said to Ada:

"Miss Tallmon, your brother has a nice tablespread in his store; if I were you, I should buy it." Here was a hint she knew the children would not disregard.

They soon transferred the contents of the playhouse to the table, preparing a quantity of fractional currency, and each one played the merchant for a while.

Addie showed the baby what to do, and talked for her. Clara went shopping to spend a dime and said she wanted a comb, a "singing Bible," and the rest in candy.

George sold the tablespread for five cents and bought the scrapbook for 50 dollars.

Then Clara asked Georgie to play horse. He had no objection, so they carried all the chairs together to make a stable.

George submitted to a halter after Clara caught him with "grass in a hat" and industriously ate "make believe" oats and hay.

At his own suggestion, Clara led him out to drink. He said she must let him roll in the snow "as Pa does Prince," but as soon as she let go the halter he ran away, explaining that he was frightened at the blacksmith shop; they were romping around the room with great laughter and noise.

Mamma looked in to say she feared they would waken the baby, but the baby was sitting up in the cradle, sober and silent, and now called to be taken out.

At last the little table was set, and Ada came to the buttery for food, and gave her mother a pressing invitation to tea.

It was a great disappointment to be told not to take any bread nor cheese nor milk into the sitting room. But she agreed to use paper for pretend food.

They surrounded the little stand, Georgie and Clara on their knees in leather bottomed chairs, Ada and Angie standing up, the baby in her highchair, Mamma lending the honor of her presence.

"I can't stay long," Mamma said, "but I will take a cup of tea if you please."

After disposing of the tea, which she impolitely said tasted too strong of brown sugar, and telling them not to swallow any paper, she left them and they had a long pleasant meal.

Georgie said every time, "Please for the butter," or "Please for the meat," when he wanted something.

Evening approached before all the tiny dishes were washed and put away, and the floor swept, and Mamma came to rest until Papa should come to supper.

"What can we do now, Mamma?" asked tired little George.

"I know," said Angie, "sing!" For she saw her mother taking the carefully preserved green box that held her accordion from the clock shelf.

The children stood around her chair and sang, "O Come, Come Away," and "Home, Sweet Home," and "I Think When I Read That Sweet Story of Old."

At supper, Papa asked his wife if she had had a blue Monday.

"Addie helped me so much I thought only of my sunshine all day," Mamma replied.

"Then was it blue for Addie?" asked Papa.

Before Ada could reply, Clara said positively: "Yes, me and Addie had a bloo tablecloth."

"Somebody's education has been sadly neglected," said Papa, laughing.

Then followed a lively account of the day, though Angie thought Clara and Georgie very inaccurate in their statements.

While Mamma washed dishes, Papa and the children went into the sitting room and stirred up the fire, and the room looked very pleasant to weary Mamma when she came in.

The children, with all their energy still only slightly diminished, obtained a sack from the kitchen, and decided to play a joke on Papa.

Papa later wrote a poem about the affair:

> There came to my room, as a very good joke,
> A very small boy with head in a poke.
> Behind him there tripped a bevy of girls
> Shaking with laughter their sides and their curls.
> Now I had heard from my father of old
> "A pig in a poke is not easily sold."
> But then for a bear, for that was the guise,
> We surely might bid, while shutting our eyes.
> I therefore bid quickly a nickel, and won,
> And got for my money, my own little son.

George and Clara were very proud at being trusted to take a note to Mrs. Morgan. She lived clear across the prairie, south of their father's farm.

Down by the road stood Papa's horses, stomping their feet and swishing flies, at the gate.

Clara had been told not to go near the horses, but she was especially attracted by Fairy's colt, two or three months old, and stopped to pat her nose.

George was uneasy and begged her to "come on!"

Clara started on, but then, wanting to show she wasn't afraid, paused by the horse's heels for a final pat.

A swift kick left Clara in the dust. She screamed and cried, and Ada came running. Clara wasn't hurt, but Ada and Angie went along to deliver the note.

New babies were always very precious, very welcome, in the Tallmon family.

Although Mamma was disturbed to find out another was coming, because she was ill, she always loved them dearly when they were born. And she talked of how darling they were, and how much better looking than those of other families.

Having children she considered her duty, but, once they were born, she welcomed them. Papa also was very happy and enjoyed his children.

And, before long, another was coming. When the new little baby joined the family, it was a girl.

Georgie didn't seem too happy as he hung around Mamma's pillow.

"This is your own, precious little sister--just like Susie," Mamma explained.

Georgie held back, then bashfully replied:

"I wanted a baby brother."

"What shall we call her?" excitedly asked Ada.

"How about Mary, or Kate?" suggested Angie.

"Or Nan or May?" asked Clara.

George, gently touching and talking to the little baby, said nothing. But when asked for his suggestion, he murmured, "Lucy."

"Can we call her that, Mamma?" he asked, with earnest, pleading eyes.

And Mamma, pitying his brotherless condition, gave the baby the family name that he fancied.

5.

In those days, little boys wore dresses almost until they were old enough to go to school. Perhaps George wore them extra long, because he had plenty of sisters to hand them down to him.

Finally, though, his father decided it was time for Georgie to have his first suit.

So father, triumphantly, with his son, headed for town, in the great high old wagon, while Mamma remained behind, rather unhappy about the change.

Papa drove to the old general store and carefully picked out a suit. It fit just fine.

"He might as well wear it home," Papa said.

When Mr. Hatch, the storekeeper, started to wrap up the little dress, Georgie began to cry.

"What's the matter?" his father asked, perplexed. "Don't you like your nice new suit?"

"I want my little red dress like the other girls!" Georgie wailed.

Indians used to come to the farm sometimes to trade cloth given to them by the government and receive grain. The little girls would run and hide.

Two very fat squaws one day bought a bushel of corn in exchange for cloth, which Mamma was going to use as curtains on a bookcase. Then they wanted a chicken.

Papa pointed out a young rooster that they might have "if you can catch it."

The squaws ran, and they chased, and then ran some more. Papa laughed. When they were out of breath, they implored:

"Goody white man catch'em! Goody white man catch'em!"

The rooster was out of breath, too, and was hiding behind a post under the corn crib. So Papa went and got it for them.

One day the children were playing dress-up in the upstairs bedroom. Susie and Lucy were big enough to get around.

Papa's double barreled shotgun was standing in the closet, and someone cocked the trigger.

The children had been instructed not to touch the gun, and Angie knew that would never do. She reprimanded the child: "You must never do that!" Carefully she put the gun back where it was.

Then she tried to uncock it, and bumped the trigger.

The resultant discharge was deafening. Papa and Mamma came dashing up the stairs.

They were relieved to find no one hurt and only the plaster damaged. As the gun leaned in the corner, the shot went up through the wall and out through the ceiling and roof above the stairway, sprinkling the steps with broken plaster.

Another time, the children were playing "grind corn" out behind the shop, in the cogs of a mowing machine. Mamma had gone across the meadow to Mr. Green's on an errand.

The children would raise the tongue to open the cogs, put in several kernels, then pull down the tongue to crush them. After brushing out the "corn meal," they did it again.

Angie was busy scraping the meal into a can when Georgie decided to climb up onto the tongue. The tongue came down, and Angie cried out in pain. The first finger of her right hand was badly crushed.

The group of children marched around and around the shop, Ada holding Angie's hand, and all were crying loudly.

Mamma was nearly home, and was badly frightened. She "fixed things," and Angie's finger healed--except that the nail had a lengthwise crack the rest of her life.

The large, rambling old barn, filled with fresh hay and alive with pigeons and swallows, was a paradise for the children.

They enjoyed exploring every bin and crib and hen's nest, making new discoveries and planning new fun. Even the pigeons had names, and every pig and lamb was a special friend.

The haymows were piled every summer with sweet fresh hay which afforded an endless source of amusement. It could be made into roofs, walls, sofas, beds or carpets.

A whole house was once dug out. It was furnished with winding passages and windows made by cracks in the outside wall of the barn.

There they could lie for an hour at a time, just paying half attention to a story being read aloud, listening to the squealing of the barn swallows as they flitted and fluttered around the eaves outside.

Way above the hay rose square beams, and one of the greatest delights was to climb to the highest and, at the command, "Jump, boy, or I fire!" spring down upon the soft hay below.

The cellar was damp and dingy and cobwebby, and full of ghostly shadows and musty corners. The ground was sloped, so that the back of the cellar opened onto the barnyard, while the front was dug out of a hill. The cellar served as a barn for pigs and calves.

The children trembled and held each other's hands tightly as they made their way between sties of eager pigs and several slimy little calves' noses.

There was a root cellar which smelled delightfully of apples and turnips, and an old deep well into which a poor animal had once fallen and been drowned. The children shivered when they thought of the poor brute's moans and struggles, as he died.

What if the ground should cave in! What if they should drop into that dreadful well! They hurried upstairs again.

Hide and seek was a favorite game--but once Georgie climbed into the cow meal bin, and somehow the lid got pushed down above him.

He was petrified, and pounded on the box and yelled until someone came and let him out. The fear he experienced he never forgot--and always was afraid of closed-in places.

Another source of amusement was following Papa around the farm, "helping" him as he worked. Maybe he was mending fences, maybe planting trees, maybe plowing. He would build a fence of cut willow trees or osage orange shoots, which would grow and then could be bent to form living fences.

Out in the fields, Papa turned the prairie sod on edge as he plowed. Clara and Georgie, who were chums, tagged after him, stepping on the sod as they went, or playing in the flowers nearby.

Sometimes they gathered flowers until their small hands were full, then carried them to the creek, where the flowers were made into fairyboats and floated down the stream; the children following until they came to the fence through which they were forbidden to go.

Other days they wandered for hours across the farm together, but Mamma did not worry if Jack was with them. Grandpa Carhartt had sent Jack in a crate from Davenport. He was a big yellow bulldog, with bobbed tail.

Jack loved to hunt snakes. He would grab one in the middle and shake and shake it until it broke to pieces.

Clara, with pink calico sunbonnet hung around her neck and her little brother tagging along behind, often headed for the bank of the creek, where they amused themselves watching the shiny, black waterbugs circle in the shade, or dangle an improvised fishing rod in the water.

They especially enjoyed hunting frogs and toads, catching the little creatures and stuffing them into their pockets.

One day they were a long ways from the house when the dinner bell rang. They couldn't bear to turn their trophies loose after working so hard to get them.

So they carried them to the barn. The most promising plan seemed to be to put them into Papa's half bushel grain measures, one turned on top of another.

The rest of the family was already at dinner, and they were sent to wash their hands.

Papa soon left to do the evening chores. Out at the barn, he noticed that the grain measures were not where they belonged.

As he stooped to pick up the top one, the prisoners all made a dash for liberty--and they were about his ears and under his feet.

The children heard about it, and Papa let them know in no undercertain terms that hereafter his grain measure was to be used only for grain.

Clara had a pretty white kitten, of which she was very fond. But it persisted in staying in the cow yard during milking time, was a hazard to purity of the milk, and so had to be removed.

Papa said he would bury it before going to work, but forgot his promise, and was gone before Clara could remind him of it.

When he returned at noon, the little ones joyfully informed him that they had buried the kitten; and took him in triumph to view their work.

He was conducted to the orchard, where, under a low spreading apple tree, he spied the grave; rounded up to a smooth mound and literally covered with flowers.

The only strange thing about it was that at the end of the grave, rising like a minute flagstaff, propped up by the earth pressed tightly around it, was poor pussy's tail!

When he inquired why the little tail had been refused burial, he was informed that it was the gravestone.

"Isn't it nice?"

Papa was always the progressive farmer. He took pride in having the tallest corn in the county or the largest garden. He practiced crop rotation, selective breeding, or other agricultural practices far ahead of his time.

One day when a man came by the farm selling Jersey cows, he couldn't resist. He was raising grade Shorthorns for beef, but these new cows with the rich, creamy milk were tempting.

Mamma noticed the long face he wore for several days and heard him complain of poor prices, poverty and expenses, and she knew what that meant.

Somehow, from some source, he would get the money. And Jersey cattle they would have--the first in Jasper County. By next year, she would be churning butter.

It wasn't long before Papa made a trip to Grinnell to purchase a Jersey cow and calf from R.M. Haines.

The older girls and Georgie went along, and coming home the girls took turns following behind the cow with the buggy whip.

The cow didn't take kindly to being tied to a lumber wagon, even though her calf was in it. It was a nine-mile trip, and the girls were pretty tired when they got about two miles from home.

They had to cross a railroad. As they mounted the rise to the tracks, the cow took that moment to decide not to go any further. She balked right on the tracks.

Angie was out with the whip. Papa suddenly yelled: "Whip her! Whip her hard!"

Angie did. The cow jerked forward.

They had just cleared the tracks when a train roared by! Calamity was missed by inches!

They reached home without further difficulties, and put the cow in the barn. In time, she became a beloved member of the family.

She gave a lot of good, rich, creamy milk, and so they named her "Nigra," from Niagara Falls. Her calf was called "Fawn," because the girls thought she looked like a deer.

One November evening, just at twilight, the children saw a traveler coming up the lane driving a large brown mule.

"Hello," he called. "Can you put me up for the night?"

Papa came from the barn and talked with the stranger. The children saw him lead the mule, buggy and all, into the granary driveway. Then the man, with Papa, came to the house.

Mr. Cammack was a jolly man and told the children lots of stories. (They loved stories.) He had driven his team of mules across the state to see his sick mother and bid her goodbye. Now he was returning to his claim near Spirit Lake where his wife and small son were bravely waiting.

One of the mules had died and the other insisted on walking in the tracks.

"That makes the buggy wheels run over the rough sides and gives me a terrific bumping. Isn't Bill William a bad old boy?"

The family soon learned what a "bad old boy" Bill William could be. For when the visitor went away, he left the mule and drove pretty Princess in his buggy while the little colt, Prince, trotted after.

Papa turned Bill William into the barnyard, where he kicked the colts, bit the hogs, nipped the cows and brought general terror.

He lifted the pigs by their tails, their hind legs just off the ground. His long ears flapping, he seemed to enjoy their squeals.

One day there was a dreadful racket out in the barnyard; cows bawled, calves bleated, hogs squealed, turkeys gobbled.

The hired men ran to see what the trouble was. There was Bill William holding a tiny calf by the nap of the neck. He was capering about on his hind feet and swinging the poor baby calf back and forth while Lilly, its mother, ran bawling around and around.

When Bill William saw Papa coming, he dropped the calf and gazed off across the orchard with an innocent stare, like a bad school boy who had passed a note. He looked at Papa in a surprised sort of way as if to say, "What are you staring at me for? What have I done?"

There was a new calf at the barn. Angie wanted to see it, but her father said she must wait until the next day, because the horses were out and she might get hurt.

The next day! She couldn't wait five minutes!

So she put on her blue cloak and little red hood and made her way to the barnyard fence to a spot nearest old Pansy and her calf.

There she knelt on the ground and, peeping through the pickets and a forest of horses' legs, she caught fascinating glimpses of a very white little calf.

Papa was milking the cow. Soon she could see the foam spilling over the side of his milk pail.

So intent was she that she did not hear a footstep. But something like a hand clutched the top of her head and the hair below, and held it very firmly.

Perhaps her sister Addie was teasing. She put up her hand.

"It's you, Addie," she cried.

But instead her hood was jerked roughly off and she fell back with a scream of pain. There in the barnyard on his hind legs danced Bill William, waving her red hood in wicked glee.

Papa came, threatened the mule with his milking stool and recovered Angie's hood.

"Here is your bonnet," he said. "Too bad! Bill William is a scalawag! Run in and tell your mother!"

And what do you suppose Mamma found inside that hood? A long curl of Angie's hair. And on her head was a red bald spot. Years later, when Angie told the story to her children, she could still show them the bald spot as evidence.

One day Mamma let Angie and Clara go coasting on their sleds in the pasture lot. They supposed Bill William was tied inside.

Snow was deep that winter. In one place it had drifted so high it reached the roof of the granary, and was hard as flour. It seemed to be a wonderful place to slide.

Angie took the first turn. She got clear up to the peak of the roof and started down. She was barely half way when here came Bill William, galloping around the corner of the barn, with ears forward and eyes sparkling.

He chased her all the way down the hill, and nearly caught up. When she reached the ditch, she scrambled into it, pulling the sled over on top of her.

Bill William stopped with a loud snort, and cautiously put his nose down to smell the trembling little girl under the sled. His eyes danced and his long ears waved.

Angie doubled up her red mittened fist and hit him on the nose. It was velvety soft.

He jerked away in alarm--and danced on his hind legs and kicked and whirled around and around. Then he came back again.

Over and over they played their little game.

Angie shook her fist and scolded. Bill William danced and capered.

It seemed hours since she had jumped into the ditch, half full of smooth ice. Wouldn't anyone come and rescue her? Would she have to stay there all night? Would she freeze to death?

Bill William seemed to forget her for a minute. He was looking toward the fence.

Angie peeped out from her shelter. There was Martin the hired man taking the cows to water.

Bill William looked at her; then he looked at the cows. He seemed to be debating. Should he stay with her, or should he go nip the cows?

Maybe she would wait until he came back.

But she didn't. As soon as Bill William was a little ways away, she jumped out of the ditch, grabbed the sled and ran as hard as she could for the fence.

"Run," yelled Martin behind her. "Run fast! He's a'coming! Run! Run!"

She ran, as she never had run before. She got to the fence and climbed over just as she heard hoof beats behind her. She was safe!

Bill William halted at the fence and waved his long ears dejectedly! Angie was sure she saw tears in his eyes.

Papa bought another mule to work with Bill William but they were poor mates. Jennie Lind was small and quick and Bill was big and lazy.

The hired man sometimes got very angry with them.

One day he hitched them to the scraper, to lift dirt out of the new barn cellar. Jennie didn't mind very quickly, so he started to spank her with a spade. It twisted sideways and cut a deep gash across her hip. The wound healed up all right, but she had a big scar.

While she was getting well, Bill William had plenty of time for mischief.

He opened doors and feed bins and ate too much oats and corn. He unfastened gates and got into the garden or orchard. Papa tried six different locks until he found one the old fellow could not manage--and this one was secured with a padlock!

The children had a playhouse in a sunny corner of the yard. The sand-tarts and mud-pies were arranged on a board to bake. A row of corn dollies, neatly dressed, sat on the wagon seat ready for lunch.

As the children played, they watched for their possible enemy. But Bill William surprised them.

Suddenly, without warning, he came galloping around the corner of the shed.

They fled, and he soon ate all their corn children and their cookies, turned over their furniture and stepped on their mud pies.

Of course they were not sorry when Papa sold him.

Mr. Cammack, the man who had previously owned Bill William, sometimes wrote to the family, saying how happy Mrs. Cammack and his son were to see him when he got home, and what a fine pony Princess was and how he had trained Prince to harness. He hoped they were as pleased with their end of the bargain!

One day Papa and Angie were driving to town and stopped to watch some house movers. The movers were placing rollers under a house, and a big brown mule was walking round and round the capstan winding up the hawser.

"Do you recognize that old fellow?" asked Papa.

"It's old Bill William!" Angie exclaimed.

Bill recognized them, too. He waved one long ear in their direction and actually winked as if to say, "Hello there! If I were not so busy wouldn't we have lots of fun?"

And Angie felt almost sorry for poor old Bill William!

He wasn't the only farm animal who scared the children.

There was Peggy, the old sow, who (it was rumored) ate her own pigs. She put her feet up on the fence when the children went by, and they were deathly afraid of her.

Peggy had a way of getting out of her pen. The gate, when opened, swung shut by the weight of a log chain fastened from a tree.

She pulled on the bottom board of the gate with her teeth, and backed off until the gate was wide open. The little pigs scrambled through, and then she ran, quick as she could, and tried to catch the gate with her nose before it swung shut.

If she didn't succeed, she tried again and again--maybe a dozen times--until she did. Then she and the little pigs headed for the corn bin.

There, she climbed up on her hind legs, and pulled ears of corn out of the bin. She carefully dropped one for each pig, and then took one more in her mouth for herself before getting down.

One day she got out of the pen, and both she and her pigs disappeared. That evening, Papa went looking for them--and finally found them, in the pasture, up against a fence.

They were resting comfortably, so Papa fixed a shelter and left them there for the night.

Next day, he told the children to "come on," and they went down to the pasture where the old sow was.

Somehow Papa managed to get Peggy's attention off her pigs and the pigs into a bushel basket. Then the children carried the basket ahead and Papa drove the sow behind.

The mother heard the pigs squealing in the basket and followed.

The children were very much afraid, and kept going faster and faster. Every so often, Papa had to call to them to wait up or come back.

They had to pass through two or three fences before they came to the sunken pen where the sow belonged. The road seemed endless.

When the children got there, they set the basket down and scrambled out, fast as they could. The sow came on in after them and Papa upset the basket, letting the pigs out.

A day or two later the children were out playing. There was a board across the pen from the corn crib to the rail.

Clara was going to show the others that she dared to walk across the board, right above the hog pen. She stepped bravely onto the board. The others stood nervously watching.

But her bravery was short-lived. Suddenly the board broke, plummeting her into the pen. She hardly touched the ground before she was up and over the fence and out.

Snowball was an old white cow with red ears. Grandpa Carhartt gave her to Mamma when she started housekeeping.

One spring day when the children helped drive the cow home from the prairie at milking time, she refused to come-- simply walked around them and went back.

Papa said, when they told him about it, "Never mind just now. After the milking is done, we'll go see if she hasn't a new calf out there."

With two or three children to help hunt, it didn't take long to find, hidden in the coarse waist-high grass, a little white calf with red ears.

Snowball paid no attention when Papa carried the calf across the flowing creek, up the road, and put it down inside the driveway gate.

"Oh," he said, "must be twins."

And sure enough. Further search disclosed another little snow-white calf with red ears, exactly like the first, hidden in the tall coarse grass quite a distance down the creek.

That, also, was carried away, and only then would Snowball follow.

One day Addie, now getting to be quite a big girl, came running into the house with tears in her eyes.

"What's the matter?" asked Mamma. For Ada was seldom unhappy.

"I dropped my pretty ring in the chicken yard," she cried, "and one of the chickens snatched it up and ate it."

"Well, that's too bad," Mamma sympathized.

Papa seemed concerned, too.

"Do you know which hen gobbled it up?" he asked.

Ada said she believed she did, and with a smile breaking through her tears, went with Papa to the chicken yard.

Next time the family had chicken for dinner, there, in its crop, was Addie's ring!

6.

Susan Carhartt Tallmon was engaged when she was a very young girl with very little experience.

She had been trained in a good, strict home where duty played a vital part. Her idea of duty was to deny herself, to forget herself, to renounce herself for others.

George Tallman was her teacher. He fell in love with her, and loved her very much.

But she did not react with the feeling of delight and hope that all women should experience, but idealized him and felt it was her duty to marry him.

When they talked of love, she replied with a surprised: "Oh, no, sir, I don't love anyone else, and if only you think me worthy to help you in working for God, and He is willing, I will marry you."

After they were married, she gave herself completely in self sacrifice to him. He was perfect, and everything he said and did was right. If she disagreed, she was wrong, not him.

He was lord and master as never was man before. She made their home as pleasant and bright and restful as she could, as far as patience and gentleness and planning could do it.

After a hard day's work he came home to eat and retire while she did up the work and shut up the house. He woke in the night perhaps and woke her for company and she did not protest. He got up in the morning and called her and she meekly obeyed.

If he reproved her for not doing more work, she said she was sorry; she asked him to forgive her and promised to do better.

He came from the field to ask if she was making his favorite dishes for dinner, and she made them. He objected to Sunday's breakfast and she dutifully prepared a better dinner than usual.

Unconsciously she came to avoid the mention of anything she wished--it only insured her disappointment. In time she ceased to name the most dear interests, the most holy feelings, the highest motives--she only subjected them to slight and insult by naming them.

It was so delightful for her husband to be master in his home--and lord of his wife--that he rested there content.

But she began to realize that he wasn't as perfect as she had thought. Their ideas on right and wrong differed; he was a good man but his beliefs were a little more worldly.

In his religion, he went by rules, whereas she tended to think every question out for herself, asking, "Am I doing right?"

Her faith in him was first shaken when, in Louisiana, she heard rumors and talk about illegal profits from contraband goods and government-issue materials. It helped explain the funds deposited into her account in the bank--higher than the pay he was receiving as an officer--and which she never touched. It was at this time that he changed his name from Tallman to Tallmon, perhaps to cover up such inconsistencies.

Her faith was further shaken when he sold their new farm, while she was pregnant, without her prior knowledge nor consent. She never felt sure of a home after that.

She began to fret and pine for a different life--for a settled, convenient and pretty home, instead of one rough, pioneer house after another.

She found her soldier, instead of needing care and petting, was rather inclined to drag her at his chariot wheels.

She didn't agree with his training of the children. He was too strict, and whipped them unmercifully for every little thing.

His unmanly treatment of them irritated her, and destroyed all her pleasure in him--and all respect.

His temper was uncontrollable, she felt, and his egotism was extreme.

He spent money foolishly, yet kept her on meager allowances and made unwise economies.

For example, he would regret spending $5 for her henhouse, but pay $500 cash for new railroad bonds. Sometimes he gave big discounts to churches and schools, while keeping his family painfully stinted.

His wife devoted herself to the babies, as they came, and felt she did all the work she could handle.

When she asked for a hired girl, he said he couldn't afford one, and promised to help in the house himself. But his help seemed so uncertain and so grudgingly given that she took no more than he insisted on giving.

There were other phases of his personality that bothered her.

He sought public praise and admiration, and couldn't stand to be surpassed in possessions, knowledge or work. He took an unusually prominent place in the church and made considerable show of his wisdom, morality and goodness.

He made a business of praising one woman's looks, another's wit, the business qualities of a third--all to his wife.

When stylish visitors came to buy or sell a farm or costly blooded hogs or cattle, he did not excuse his poor home or dirty children on the basis of poverty, but said hired girls were scarce.

His idea of superiority was standing on someone else.

At least that was the way she looked at it.

His viewpoint was different.

He was ambitious, hardworking. He wanted to get ahead, and was willing to work early and late to reach his goal.

And she, instead of helping, was a continual drag on him.

She spent much of her time writing in her journal, or doing art work, or reading, or practicing music, or fixing fancy little things for the children.

He couldn't understand how a woman could get so little done when there was so much to do. His mother used to do three times as much work. It about drove him to distraction.

The house was often untidy, and sometimes meals weren't ready when he came in.

She had a tendency to spend money on hobbies and art--more than he felt was necessary.

And she complained often about not feeling well. She doctored continually, and had many aches and pains.

She defied his orders and did what she knew he didn't want done, in an era when a man was head of the household and master of his family.

She interfered with his training of the children, especially when he set them to work--too hard, she felt.

She didn't appreciate it when he tried to help in the house to save the expense of a hired girl. Yet she wasn't satisfied with the hired girls when they did work for her, claiming they were careless and lazy.

She seemed to lack the knack of keeping the home in good spirits and everything clicking.

The mounds of unfinished work did worry her.

But it seemed she could never get it done, constantly interrupted by a baby's scratched finger, a headache, a broken machine, a smoking stove, a lot of callers, a washwoman, a cross child, a baking day, a sore eye, a lame hand, or another of the hundred and one unexpected things that delay a woman's work.

Then, there are the many different jobs a woman and mother must do--housekeeping, gardening, fruit canning, vegetable saving, sewing, knitting, teaching, visiting, washing, ironing, sweeping, and endless cooking supplemented by almost continual dishwashing.

All this on top of trying to rear a houseful of children to be well adjusted citizens with high ideals and a love for God and Jesus.

And to keep up with a steam engine husband and his demands for attention and companionship.

Sex undoubtedly entered the picture of difficulties between George and Susan Tallmon.

As the children kept coming and coming, and their mother became lamer and lamer with arthritis and felt the press of family cares, she wished for a limit to the size of her family.

Not that the children weren't loved and wanted and adored once they were born.

But she worried that she might die if she went through another confinement. And her husband, too, expressed the hope that she would not be pregnant again.

On the other hand, they had their happy side. Family fellowship was thoroughly enjoyed. Poetry, love of nature and education were considered very important.

Papa could be a very kind and gentle person, and both he and his wife loved children.

But, as a result of all the difference and difficulty between them, Mamma became more and more critical of her husband. No longer did she idealize and cater to him.

And when she openly disagreed with him, he resented it. She had trained him too long to take for granted that she would do whatever he said.

He scolded and scolded and scolded. She argued back for a while, trying to make her point, and then, when she couldn't, she shut up.

It was partly because she found, when she would fret and complain, her husband was harsh and uncharitable. He would make the children bear severe burdens and constantly criticize them to her--and her for not making them do more work or a higher quality.

Once, after an interval of several years, he read a few pages of her journal. In it she said some very hard and plain things about his temper.

He was so gravely hurt, she burned the journal and wrote no more for months, except for a few secret pages, also consigned to oblivion.

"I must have some way to express my opinions and feelings about you, when you vex me," she explained.

But he couldn't see it. It just made him angry.

When her idealism was destroyed, she stood entirely apart from her husband--her heart broken; her hope and trust gone; her home, it seemed, worse than purgatory; her marriage tie a hideous bondage.

To see her eyes criticizing his conduct, to note the hopelessness of her mouth, to see her utter distance from him to whom she had for years looked for all her earthly light and joy-- was completely frustrating to him.

True to the nature he had been forming all his life, he sought to overcome her instincts, scruples, impulses.

While she attended listlessly to her household duties, he day after day left his work and followed her from room to room, sneering, scolding, arguing.

When she left him, he followed. When she locked herself in her room, his boot heel at the catch sent the door flying open. When she would have passed him with silent indignation, he easily caught her by the shoulder and sent her headlong across the floor.

When she would have gone away with contempt, he raised his hard hand to bruise her flesh.

Suddenly, losing control of himself, he began pounding her face with his fists. Then, angrily, he slapped her on one cheek, then the other.

She stood there, accepting the punishment, saying nothing back, her eyes docile, her mouth relaxed. She stood in silent waiting, not even with contempt, waiting for wrong, wondering vaguely why he did not raise his foot and kill her unborn child.

He stopped.

"If you weren't so stubborn!" he exclaimed. "Why don't you listen to me?"

Then he stormed out of the house.

For a time he kept up his tone and air of mastership. But when the neighbors came in and gazed with wonder at his wife's face--she said nothing but made no effort to conceal her bruises-- he asked her pardon.

"I'm sorry," he said. "I shouldn't have done that. Won't you please forgive me?"

His humble repentance touched her.

"Of course," she replied, "I forgive you."

7.

Georgie, as the only boy in the family, had been with his sisters so much he seemed to have developed girlish instincts.

Quite at ease with them and Mamma, he was painfully annoyed if Papa saw him dressing.

But when Lucy came along, he faintly expressed the wish to have a brother, instead. It must have been a very strong wish, for he was a very quiet and patient little fellow.

It was partly for this reason and partly that a father is supposed to spoil an only son that Mamma prayed that her next child would be a boy.

And, sure enough, when it arrived, it was a boy!

Georgie, now a little jealous, nevertheless insisted, "Isn't he a darling?"

And Papa, Mamma and all the girls, even to Lucy, agreed.

The baby was named for Grandpa Carhartt, but Mamma was afraid joking Grandpa wouldn't like it. So at first the little boy was called Arthur. Later, it was John Arthur, and, after a year, Johnie.

Georgie was a little confused. Always before, the younger children were "Mamma's," because they needed special care. And the older children were "Papa's," so they wouldn't feel left out.

Now, with three children older than he, and three younger, where did he stand? Finally, he figured it out.

"I'm half Papa's and half Mamma's, because I'm in the middle!" he exclaimed.

Georgie was quite impressed by how close in age his two younger sisters were--one hardly more of a baby than the other.

"When they get a little older, they will be twins, won't they, Mamma?" he asked.

The farmhouse still wasn't finished, even though the family had been living there for nearly five years. Some of the plastering upstairs was still incomplete, and other finishing touches were lacking. Papa, busy elsewhere, just never got around to it.

In addition to his farm work, he taught school winters at a nearby schoolhouse.

The house still wasn't finished when he and Mamma began talking about moving to town.

"The children could receive a better education in Grinnell than in the country schools," Papa argued one evening, as the family sat around the supper table.

"Town would be an easier place to get a variety of food, fresh meat and hired girls," Mamma added.

"I could teach in the public schools," Papa enthused. "And keep the farm going on the side."

Papa bought a lot at the north edge of town. Then he discovered that the children would have to pass a saloon on their way to school. He didn't want that.

Although Grinnell was a dry town, the saloon, at the head of Main Street on Eighth Avenue, was just outside the corporation limits. There was no legal way to force the saloon out.

Papa decided to talk to the saloon keeper, Mr. Preston. Maybe he would be reasonable. But Mr. Preston stood pat. He wasn't going to move.

"All right, then," Papa told him. "I'll buy you out. How much do you want?"

Mr. Preston named a high figure.

"Sold!" Papa said. And he became owner of a saloon house, with grounds that included a barn and pasture.

Mr. Preston merely took Papa's money, bought another place a little further out, and went back into business. But Papa had achieved his purpose of keeping the children from passing a saloon every day.

When the family moved in, the children found ample evidence that the house had once served as a saloon.

"What's this?" asked Georgie, pointing to a curved fringe of paint on the diningroom floor.

"That's where the bar once stood," his father explained.

"What's a bar?"

"That's the table where the men were served drinks," Papa replied.

The girls, as they were cleaning the pantry shelves to put away the dishes, found round marks on the paint.

"What are these?" they asked.

"That's where the bottles stood," Mamma told them.

The children soon learned other things about their new home.

The ground was swampy, and the cellar was full of water when they moved in. Ada and the five older children soon learned what fun it was to climb through a hole under the porch, and walk around the edge of the cellar.

They were walking gleefully along when someone yelled: "Lucy fell into the water!"

She had tried to follow, and had slipped. Ada and Angie rushed back and pulled her out, crying, dripping wet, but otherwise unhurt.

Moving to town was a big event in Mamma's life. She had never cared for the isolated farm, was glad to leave it, and glad to live in Grinnell.

On the other hand, she was worried and shy about the new neighbors' opinion of her. During the first and second weeks of their time in town, while it rained every day, she thought she was perfectly indifferent to them.

Then, on Saturday, when of all days she expected to devote herself to work without interruption, they came--her callers.

First, leaving her dough, she let in a brisk little old woman, neat as a pin, who excused herself for calling when Mamma was in disorder. She asked the number of Mamma's children, and told the reputation and number and names of all the neighbors.

Second, the nearest neighbor's little girl brought a pretty bouquet and said if it were convenient she had permission to stay a half hour.

Mamma was afraid stepmother Grandma Amanda, next to call, would be ashamed of the dust in the corners, as Mamma was herself. But Mamma made no excuses.

Then came a formal but lady-like woman, a carpenter's wife, who stayed "nine and three-quarters minutes." The little girl who accompanied her was dressed simply, a lady-like child.

The minister came, along with his wife, who asked if Lucy, less than two years old, "went to school?"

Finally, a woman called who had moved from country to town a few months earlier. She was sufficiently polite, and dressed in modern style, but very simply. Mamma felt as if she had known and liked her for a long time. They began chatting like old friends.

"The neighbors are smiling over the great intimacy of my girl and your boy," the new friend remarked.

"I have been congratulating myself on his having a little classmate so near to be his company to school and back," Mamma replied.

George had just started to school.

One night, after they went to bed, Ada and Angie were telling three-year-old Susie of God and Christ and death and Heaven.

Their undisguised anxiety that she should choose the better part was so apparent they almost endangered the cause they had at heart.

Susie was indifferent when they told of the golden harps and crowns and city of gold and the little sister waiting. But when told she could go with Mamma and have a pretty white dress, she changed her attitude sharply. She seemed pleased to think she could wear the dress all the time and have it clean every day.

Mamma had been a Methodist all her life, and Papa was Congregational. While they lived in the country, the issue had not been a serious problem. But, in town, Papa wanted Mamma to transfer to the Congregational Church.

Mamma finally went, reluctantly, for "duty is master." A wave of the old humility she used to feel so often when she gave up her cherished wishes swept over her, but she tried to control it.

A month later the new Congregational minister came to call, and found her sewing at the machine (in clean dress and collar, fortunately!).

The hired girl was in the rocking chair, Sue and Lue bareheaded and barefoot, baby tearing paper, clean clothes piled on the lounge, mending on an armchair, and papers and books on secretary and open organ.

She made no apologies, although she knew Papa would have done so--and felt disgraced for the rest of his life by the evidence of comfortable occupation by women and children.

A few days later the five younger children brought an armful of asparagus limbs into the house and made a grove by placing them upright between the furniture.

They had just started playing happily when their father came in.

Angrily, he demanded: "What's all this litter? Throw every bit of it out the window--every scrap!"

While the children meekly obeyed, he turned on his wife.

"Why do you allow such things brought into the house?" he asked furiously.

She had been feeling glad to have so many of the children playing so pleasantly and innocently about her room. But instead of telling him so, his temper so annoyed her she made no reply.

As he stormed out, she thought of three pairs of muddied pants in a wad by his trunk and three pairs of manured boots behind the kitchen stove. She felt that innate order and neatness were not his real motive, but only his personal comfort, convenience and food for vanity.

Papa planned at first to be very sociable with the neighbors. But, as Mamma would not go with him until she had clothes "a little like other women," he soon got used to going without her.

Finally she agreed to go to an entertainment, expecting to hear essays and orations. Instead, it turned out to be an ice cream-lemonade festival.

Many townspeople were present, but only one man spoke to them. Papa, who was chief of the temperence lodge and accustomed to such social crowds, did not seem to feel out of place.

But Mamma felt very self conscious about blundering into the wrong seat, the critical glances of other women, and her husband whispering behind his hat that she ought to take off her old shawl and carry it on her arm, for which she could see no reason whatsoever.

She hurried home as soon as they could get away, and buried her troubles in her journal.

"It seems probable that for the 10th time I am pregnant and that I have been for nearly two months," she wrote. "It has the effect on my temper of producing timidity and distrust.

"I dare not look forward, and the present is viewed with a kind of subdued apathy . . . "

"In beginning a journal after an interval of months if not years I am resolved to prevent the chance of injustice to my husband, owing to my morbid state, by making no references to him, usually.

"He is in usual health, employment and spirits, and does all he can to make home pleasant to his family . . .

"I hired a girl some lately but have the usual experience of hired girls with her. Good help and ambitious and reckless of her health at first and in about a week so careless of the work--so tender of herself . . .

"I have trouble to get money of late as in the past. I go to the dry goods store and have a few things charged, and bought a bonnet for four dollars, and think I will buy some other things in the same way.

"It is certain I must go unsupplied with many things I need, otherwise, and I have a right to some of my husband's money as well as his brother's wife has, and his sister's son and the hired men and temperance, lodge and nobody knows who besides . . .

"I hire my washings done this summer though since I began to talk physiology to the girl she has developed a weak back and leaves her rinsing water for others to empty and I am afraid to pay her less than before lest she cease to come and then George would pretend to wash while the girls and I should bear the burden of it and be bossed and hustled by him in the bargain . . .

"Perhaps after worrying for a week over some debt I will learn by some accident, not through George, that it has been paid with his salary as teacher, or the price of 10 or 20 hogs or half a dozen cattle or a couple of pair of horses, or a few tons of corn.

"If it is not now time to think of my wants rather than his means, that time never will come.

"No woman I am sure could in my place have been more patient and self forgetful, and naturally the reward I get is a chance to be more patient and self denying still . . .

"Now I believe my book is balanced up to date and I can go to work at cooking and cleaning and sewing and ironing and mending . .

"P.S.   After I had written this, my husband came from downtown and spoke pleasantly to me, calling me love. I felt half sorry for what I had written . . Behind him came a man with several nice flowering plants, which I had long desired, and for which I feel grateful . .

"Thursday.   I have not been able to forget this is my birthday, for the children have kept knocking at the door to leave presents for Mamma and Mrs. Tallmon, and Papa, Grandma and Grandpa have added to my pleasures . .

"My husband took so much trouble to get the young canary bird at the right time--I felt pleased and grateful."

"July 19.   Lately George has been so kind in every possible way except the thorough control of his temper . . that it seems treason to keep such a record as the above, but I may as well keep this as write another as I fear sometime I should have to do.

"I am anxious to make it plain that he really is kind. A few days ago he said he knew it must be hard for me to love him but he loved me and wanted my love.

"It was honest in me to say I hoped we should live together many years to love very dearly and unreservedly. Life does seem weary when I am so weak and there are so many things and persons waiting on my little strength."

Susan's health, gradually declining for years, grew worse as she had more babies. To her rhumatism, augmented by cold kitchen floors and damp cellars, was added a growing weariness, weakness, dizziness and pain.

Writing and other work with her hands was increasingly difficult and painful. She gave up much of the work except tending babies.

The thought crossed her mind that she might die--and it grew and disturbed her.

She must not. She felt sure George would take the girls back to the farm and overwork and abuse them cruelly.

But she felt God was not ready to take her away from her children yet.

During the summer George concentrated on the farm, working like a slave each day, returning home at night worn in strength, endurance and nerves.

The farmhouse he rented to his younger brother, Dave, who had lived for a while with them and then married the hired girl, Ida Green.

Crops looked good, and George said he hoped to pay off all their debts. But Susan was not so optimistic. She was sure he would spend the money on some unnecessary thing.

When he began to talk of a one-horse covered buggy in which two could ride, she was more sure. What use was such a carriage to them? They had a good light wagon--best for a family.

Soon George had a horse and covered buggy--ready for his wife to ride in daily--and then Susan decided she knew why he had bought it. As far as she was concerned, a hired girl would do her 10 times as much good.

No, Mrs. Hays had a buggy and Mrs. Merrill rode every day and Mr. Craver got his wife a buggy. And, decided Susan, so did Mr. Tallmon.

She drove downtown sometimes for mail and groceries, and one day headed out to the farm. As she drove into the yard, her horse was uneasy and she could not leave it before unhitching.

After 10 minutes, perhaps, Ida looked out the door and asked: "Are you coming in, or staying out there to be by that new carriage?"

8.

Papa had promised the children a picnic for the next day. He was at the farm threshing. Mamma had gone downtown to do some last minute shopping and came home tired and weary.

Ada, always thoughtful and helpful, urged: "Go lie down, Mamma, and I'll make the fire for dinner."

She first used paper and cobs, but they wouldn't burn. So she lifted the great kerosene can which stood in the hot kitchen, and poured some into the stove.

The heat of the day apparently had caused vapors to form on the kerosene. And apparently there was a spark left on the cobs . .

Suddenly there was a bright flash and explosion, and Ada was covered with fire. Her dress, her stockings, her hair was ablaze. The room was in flames.

Her first thought was to run outdoors to the rain barrel. But Angie and Clara were playing just outside the door and baby John Arthur was crawling on the floor.

"Get Artie! Get Artie!" she cried, and, staggering back into the fire, sat down on a roll of rag carpet in the corner. The girls carried the baby out and ran across the yard to summon the neighbors.

But already carpenters from Mr. Penfield's new bouse across the street and men from the brickyard on West Street were running toward the house.

Mamma, dozing in the other room, heard the explosion and ran to the flaming kitchen. She quickly pumped water and threw it over Ada. It sizzled and evaporated into vapors.

The roaring fire surrounded the pump. Mamma found a bag to whip the fire in an attempt to reach her daughter. But the bag began to burn and she dropped it.

The neighbors were pumping and bringing water.

"Bring bedclothes," Mamma shouted, and, taking off her woolen dress, tried to put the fire out with it.

Ada stood up, flames leaping around her, then knelt in agony at her mother's feet.

Mamma could see she was doing no good, for the fire was worse and filled the room, covering the floor between them.

It was on the walls and in her face. And then Mamma ran from it and from her daughter.

Ada rose and turned about, her hands clasped on her face. She stamped and stooped, rose erect and turned again. Her body was a mass of flames.

"Is Ada dead?" the children cried.

"Oh, I'm afraid so!" Mamma exclaimed.

And Ada fell insensible on the floor.

Then, from three rods away, the water came, and men poured it over her and the room. Soon the flames were out.

The room was scorched and almost all of Ada's clothes were burned off, except the bands around her waist and the shoes on her feet.

The little children tried to press inside to see what had happened, but painters from next door pushed them out, and wouldn't let them see.

Ada lay on the charred floor, breathing painfully.

Mamma tenderly pulled off the straw hat she had worn, put something under her head, and spread the woolen dress over her almost naked body, burned in places to a black hard crust or fiery blisters.

The brickmakers went for Grandpa Carhartt, the doctor and Papa.

Others carried Ada in their arms and held her until the lounge and bedding were ready, then laid her tenderly on the makeshift bed.

When Ada began to regain consciousness, she struggled and said she could not see.

Mamma was kneeling beside her, holding Ada's scorched hair against her tear-streaked face.

"Don't try," she whispered. "It will hurt so much."

Soon the doctor arrived. He gave her morphine, cut off what was left of her burned clothes, and wrapped her in sweet oil and the cotton Mrs. Ricker brought to envelop her.

The doctor tried to console Mamma by saying, "She's not in pain."

"Yes, I am," Ada insisted.

"Where?" Mamma asked.

"My feet and in my ears."

As the painful minutes ticked by, Ada told of a premonition that she was going to die and about putting away gifts for each of the younger children. She also left messages for each of them.

Soon Papa arrived, and went into the sick room to console his wife and comfort his daughter.

"Water, water, water!" she cried. Her tongue was burned and her front teeth black.

Mamma held a glass to her parched mouth, and she tried to drink.

"Oh, is it a dream?" she exclaimed. "Wake me up! Put out the fire! Pour cold water on me! Pray the Lord to take me quick! I try to be brave! Will He take me away?"

She turned her blistered face toward her mother.

"My precious Mamma, I love you!" she cried. "I know Jesus loves me, and I love Him. He will go with me and take care of me."

Then she lifted her head and seemed to be looking about.

"Sing something," she implored. "Sing, 'There is a Happy Land.'"

Ada's Sunday school teacher was there. She sang the requested hymn.

"Sing more!" Ada pleaded. "Wake me up! Take Artie out!"

They could not understand all she said. And as the minutes and hours ticked on, Ada grew weaker. Scores of people came and offered whatever help they could. But what could anyone do?

Finally, the long waiting was over. Ada talked less and less, and then her talking ceased. She sighed. Her eyes flickered and closed.

Mamma grasped her daughter's arm, tears streaming down her face. Papa caressed the fire-blackened forehead.

The short, heavy breaths came farther and farther apart and, finally, there were no more. Ada's head lay quietly to one side, her eyes closed, her blackened face quiet.

"She is gone," the Sunday school teacher whispered. "She is with Jesus."

Mamma buried her face in her hands and knelt over her daughter, weeping and crying. Papa laid his arm across his wife's shoulders and tried to console her.

"Adie is in a happy place now," Papa assured her. "She has no more sorrow."

The doctor covered the grotesque little fire-blackened body with a blanket.

The door slowly opened into the kitchen, where the younger children were anxiously waiting. It was Papa. His eyes were sad, his jaw tight. He told them, in words they would never forget:

"You haven't any sister Adie any more."

Mamma took Ada's death very hard. She felt she was partly to blame.

"If only I had reacted differently!" she moaned, over and over again. "If only I had braved the flames to get to her! If only I had called for her to come! Maybe I could have saved her!"

Others said she had done all she could. But she replied, "If only I had not let her light the fire, it might never have happened!"

Mamma found a dress, lying just as Ada had left it-- almost finished, a large needle hanging by a doubled thread. And now her hands were still and helpless!

Her darling, her sweet girl, the kindest and best little daughter a mother ever had--was gone.

She remembered saying sometimes, "Ada, dear, can you do up this work and watch baby so I can sleep? I am not well." And Ada always cheerfully agreed, perhaps giving her a kiss as she went.

Or, "My Ada, will you get supper and let me work on this picture until dark?" Her daughter never objected. She was a wonderful helper, a little mother!

Ada had grown nearly as tall as her mother. And when people mentioned it, how she held her head up high and smiled a pleased, happy smile!

Ada could not know how Mamma's unborn child and the other children prevented her from going into the fire to help her more--and only God knew whether she could have helped by also burning.

Mamma nearly went out of her mind thinking about it.

The family tried to console her, to tell her it could not be helped--that it was an accident and she had done all she could.

They tried to keep her from dwelling on it; they encouraged her to do the shopping and meal planning, which seemed to help some.

On the doctor's advice, she took painting and music lessons from a lady in town. That helped, too.

A year later the children found Adie's burned shoes and the kerosene can in the garden.

They didn't want Mamma to see them, and hid the dread reminders in a secret place.

9.

Grandpa Carhartt moved to Grinnell the same year as the Tallmons. Grandma Carhartt had died, and Grandpa and his new wife lived in the saloon house until Mamma and Papa and family arrived, then moved into a new home one block east and half a block south.

Mamma's brothers, Albert and Lester, also moved to Grinnell, Albert and his family building a house on the lot Papa first bought before purchasing the saloon.

Papa taught fourth, fifth and sixth grades in the Grinnell School, and cared for the farm on the side.

Grandpa Carhartt and his two sons owned a lumber yard and a farm machinery business.

Papa thought his family would eventually go back to the farm to live. But Mamma never cared for the farm, and was glad to leave it. She never wanted to return.

One evening while the Tallmon children were playing in the house after supper, they heard the tap of Grandpa Carhartt's cane and a knock on the door.

They were delighted. They always liked to have Grandpa and Grandma Amanda come.

Clara ran to the door and let them in. Georgie brought Grandpa's favorite armchair to the stove, and Susie and Lucy hurried to him, crying, "Grandpa! Grandpa!"

He gave each of his "honeysuckles" a "bear hug," and then sat down. The children darted away from his chair, then got as close as they dared while he tried to catch them around the neck with the crook of his cane. Then they would dart away again. Sometimes they got caught--and that was the fun of it.

When they tired of the game, the little girls climbed up on his knee and the older children stood nearby.

Susie and Lucy asked him at once to tell a story--"a bear story."

He began to trot them very gently and said: "'She rode away to Banbury Cross, to buy the baby a plum, but when she got there, the tree wouldn't BEAR, and so she came galloping home.'"

Then he asked, "Does that suit you?"

Georgie, seeing from Grandpa's face he was talking in fun, replied quietly, but with resolve: "That wasn't a bear story, Grandpa!"

Lucy, who liked to ride better than to hear stories, gave a little spring and called "ap!" to hurry her pony.

But he did not seem to hear her, for Clara was saying she wished to hear about a "fierce animal, with black hair and paws like a cat, which could hug with its front legs."

"Well," said Grandpa, "one time two men were picking blackberries, and an old bear was out at the same time, and in the same place, picking, too.

"Now, bears like blackberries as well as men. So as the bear and the men were picking blackberries in the same place and at the same time they came together.

"The men didn't like the bear, and the bear didn't like the men. So the bear ran after the men and got quite close to one of the men, and he ran around a tree.

"The bear clapped his paws around the tree, hoping to catch the man, and the man, seeing his paws around the tree, caught hold of the paws and held the bear close to the tree on the other side.

"Now the bear was fast and could not get away. He pulled but the man held him. This man told the other man to go home quick and get a gun and shoot the bear.

"The man went and was gone a great while. When he came back with the gun, the man that held the bear said, 'I want to kill the bear--please you hold him.'

"So the other took hold of the bear, and the other took the gun, and then asked, 'Why did you stay so long?'

"'Why, dinner was most ready and I waited and ate dinner before I came back.'

"'Well,' said the other. 'I will teach you better than to stop and eat dinner when I am holding a bear. So I will go home and let you hold the bear 'til I eat my supper before I kill him.'"

Susie, quite interested, asked if that was the end of the story. Grandpa said, "Yes," and she said, "Tell another."

"Oh, I'm tired," replied Grandpa, goodnaturedly. "I should like to hear you tell a story."

Susie started to tell about the "little cub that like molasses," when there came a knock at the door, and Papa let Dr. Hodges in.

"Good evening!" said the doctor.

"We've been expecting you," Papa said.

He was there to vaccinate the children for small pox, just as Grandpa had been inoculated a few days before. A small pox scare was sweeping the community.

Dr. Hodges had visited a family with small pox--so the story went--and hung his coat in the shed when he returned home. A boy went through the pockets of the coat, and spread the small pox germs all over town. Many had it, and the boy's sister died.

The doctor laid his black bag on a chair. "Will you children line up over here?" he asked.

They all stood around the stove, while Dr. Hodges took matter out of Grandpa Carhartt's arm and scraped it onto each child's arm.

They shied away as the doctor administered the dose. The littlest ones cried and said they were scared and didn't want their arm hurt. But Papa made clear they had to accept it, and all did, albeit a bit of whimpering.

"Now," offered the doctor when all was done, "that didn't hurt too much!"

"Yes, it did!" insisted little Susie.

"Well," said the doctor, "it's better than getting small pox."

Then, with a sober, "Good evening," Dr. Hodges was gone.

The children were sent to bed, while the adults sat around and talked, Grandpa and Papa on one side of the room and Mamma and her stepmother on the other.

The women were discussing families and flowers and friends when Mamma overheard Papa and Grandpa talking about "assets" and "interest."

"What's this all about?" she asked Grandma Amanda.

"Father, Albert and Lester want George to unite with them in a banking scheme," her stepmother explained.

"I don't like that," Mamma exclaimed immediately.

"I am opposed to it, too," Grandma Amanda agreed. "It's too risky. I've tried to argue Father out of it, but he won't listen. Why don't you talk to him?"

"I can't," Mamma replied. "It's understood that I have less interest in his property than my brothers."

After Grandpa and Grandma left, Mamma told her husband what she had heard and begged, "George, I want you to keep to your land and teaching for an income."

Papa, obviously piqued by her "interference" with his business plans, replied:

"You won't go back to the farm. Tenants don't take good care of it. I might as well sell it and invest the money in something worthwhile."

Mamma, remembering how the first place was sold without her knowledge or consent, retorted:

"If you go to speculating, you must first give me a deed to this house and lot."

"Why?" Papa demanded.

"So when all else is gone, I may have shelter for my babies while I take in washing to support them."

"Well, I think I will sell the farm at the first good chance."

"Then you must give me a deed to this house."

"Well, maybe I will."

And, in silence, they went off to bed.

The banking scheme never materialized. But Papa did sell the farm --for the wonderful price of $9,000, compared to its estimated value for fire insurance purposes of $3,000.

And Mamma was not sorry, because she never wanted to return.

Papa used the money to buy two farms near Grinnell, and continued teaching for the first three years they lived in town.

Later he sold one farm and bought two more in Franklin County, then sold one of them.

He also went to work for his father-in-law, selling lumber and farm machinery, and later sold buggy tops for the Spaulding company, all in the interest of making money.

10.

Georgie came running into the house. Plopping his school books on a table, he hurried to the basement to get some apples.

Then, climbing the stairs, he marched into the sitting room and gave Mamma and each of the girls a bright red apple.

"Dogie! Dogie!" cried baby Johnie, dancing with delight to see his big brother come.

"Johnie Boy!" Georgie replied, hugging his little brother fondly. "I wish I had five brothers just like you!"

Then, sitting in a chair near the fire, George pulled Johnie up on his lap and began showing him pictures in a story book. Big brother explained the pictures while Johnie pointed his stubby finger at the book and talked happily about them.

Just then Susie came through the room, nose and cheeks swollen and eyes bloodshot.

"What's the matter?" Georgie asked.

"She cried for an hour and acted like she was sick, so I put her to bed," Mamma explained as she continued running the sewing machine.

Johnie climbed down, running off to ride on his hobby horse. Susie brought a piece of paper to Georgie, tears still rolling down her cheeks.

On the paper were pictures she had drawn. Below were letters--S, U, O, A.

"Were you trying to write names for the pictures?" Georgie asked.

Susie nodded her head. She took a book from the bookcase, and sat next to her brother.

"I want to learn to write," she pleaded.

"Well," Georgie replied, "first you must learn the alphabet. Now, say after me: A, B, C, D, E . . . as fast as you can."

"A, B, C, D, E . . . " repeated Susie, diligently saying each letter and looking around the room.

She thought she had learned to read and Georgie seemed to think the same.

Lucy, not to be left behind, went to Mamma overcome with anxiety. She made repeated efforts to tell her mother before Mamma could understand her to say: "Na (I) want to learn to wead."

When Papa was told, he took a book and named every letter to the bewildered girls, telling them exactly what they must do and what to learn--spelling out a whole lesson or two.

A few days later Papa asked Sue if she was going to learn some more letters. She promptly answered, "No." Apparently she had had all she could absorb earlier.

But Lue had an idea she could read. She lay in her crib and told Mamma that she could spell a-b-c Susie, and b-a cow, but not Cora.

Georgie, gentle and affectionate, was so reasonable about choosing his way Mamma thought him very perfect and precious.

She could hardly forgive the father who whipped him, when she in quiet gentleness could induce him to do anything she thought best.

One time, though, the older children let Lucy climb into the haymow, which had been forbidden. Mamma had to punish them.

When she came to Georgie, he hid his humbled head on her knee and asked, "Mamma, what is the use of whipping?"

"Why, dear," she replied, "to prevent your forgetting my commands next time. If you always obeyed and were a good boy I would not need to whip you."

"But whipping don't make me good--it makes me worse!" he asserted.

Mamma told him she thought he was mistaken, and at any rate she would not need to whip him while he was good and obedient. She thought later she should have taken more time to ask what he thought would make him good, but with so many children to care for, she hadn't time.

Johnie, always a cross baby, was unlike all the other children. Rather than contented, quiet and reasonable, he was mischievous, self-conscious, active and imaginative.

He often hurt Georgie at play. But Georgie was not one to resent or resist. One day when Johnie was about three years old, rushing from one place to another, he struck Georgie, who was sitting on the rocking horse.

Georgie's wrist was hurt and, still not too old to cry, he broke into tears.

Mamma said, "Johnie must kiss brother Georgie, for Johnie has hurt poor brother Georgie."

Johnie did not wish to do so, and backed into a corner, putting both hands down to protect "the place to spank," and insisted, "Me Arthur!"

Johnie's imagination was vivid.

Asked why he was on the screen door, he replied he was "climbing to the moon."

When Susie was sewing on a broken doll's leg, he fell down and said his leg was broken, and, climbing into Mamma's lap, wanted her to mend him.

He asked for an envelope and was told by Papa that he must wait until he was old enough to write. He answered: "I be big then. D'orgie be my papa, and Clara my mamma, too."

Johnie had trouble remembering his age. He was just as apt to say that George was three and he was eight as vice versa.

When he was four, his father asked his age at intervals of about six hours. To aid his memory, Papa always gave him some extra information.

"Here," Papa said, putting his finger on Johnie's plate between a piece of bread and a bit of steak--"here is the sun, and the world goes around it once a year"--rubbing the edge of the plate.

"Now, it has been around it four times, so you are four years old. And when it goes around next time you will be five years old. How old are you?"

Half understanding that the sunshine is what tans his face and that Papa's finger was on his plate and steak is good to eat and that he is responsible for the earth--which means dirt or mess--on his plate, Johnie looked at Mamma in bewilderment and says, "I don't know."

Papa began scolding him for being obstinate, believing after such a lucid explanation the child couldn't help but know his age.

Suddenly remembering something said by Georgie at the barn the day before, Johnie declared triumphantly, "I am as old as the horse's legs."

By this time, another little girl, Margaret, had joined the family, and Mamma was expecting again.

The ever-increasing burden of work was oppressing, especially since Mamma was not well. In addition to trying to keep up the day-to-day housework, she had to stay up nights with sick children. And she tried desperately to add in time for the writing, painting and music she enjoyed.

In an odd moment she jotted down the experiences of one particular day and night, typical of many.

"Had a bad headache last night, and was so weak and dull this morning that I had to submit to the indignity of having a man and little girl get the breakfast, another little girl making the beds and sweeping.

"I made a pretense of dressing and washing the little children, and when my husband kindly brought my breakfast into the sitting room, I shared it with Lue, Johnie and little Margie . .

"The house was in good order when the older children went to school, but before noon Lue had got a lot of pink, white and brown paper over the carpets, some ashes had got scattered, and Johnie had a market basket half full of building blocks and clothespins, and they were scattered, too . . .

"I picked up baby Margie and sent Sue for a wet towel to wash her little face, then shut the sewing machine I was using and started to sweep . .

"Johnie got me by the finger and led me to a chair to 'hold-a-me'; then baby being sleepy, she is jealous, and I put him in the crib to take her, and he cried.

"I gave her some bread and a drink of milk, and put her on the floor while I tried again to sweep; but before I had finished saw her nodding with sleep, took her in my arms, fixed her in the crib at Johnie's feet, and covered both with a quilt.

"Sue had gone into the study. I followed, and found her asleep on the sofa with hot cheeks and cold feet. Stirred up the fires and put her to bed . .

"Gave Lue paper and shears to keep her quiet, 'took stock' of my work; decided I must hire my dress finished and if John gets sick again must hire mending done also, and send out the washing.

"Lue, who is past four, has just had her first spell of croup, baby asthma, and a sore throat. George's nose is a great botheration, Clara has nosebleed, and Angie aches all over every day . . .

"Well, having swept and rested and thought it over--I will water my houseplants, fill the water dish on top of the stove, feel Sue's pulse, take some cough medicine myself, and then finish a letter to Aunt Isabella, or work on one of those picture frames I began before Christmas and had not time to finish . .

"I got away to see poor Addie (Lester's wife, dying of tuberculosis) for a few moments . . . While I was away my baby had been set on the floor without her socks and took cold . .

"During the early evening I wanted Angie to stay from her singing class, because her father was tending baby and could not go with her. I needed rest--indeed nature asserted herself and took rest, even though baby was fretting at the time.

"At midnight she seemed worse, and I arose, nursed her, sweat her, gave her medicine and water, and got her quiet in her crib, sending George senior and Johnie into bed. George was very sleepy, Johnie very fretful, begging to be 'rock-a-by,' for 'din,' for 'crackie,' and for 'Mamma to take.'

"I hear him thumping Papa's chest right now; and must go and see if he has kicked off the covers, and if his skin is moist. His last cough was a little too tight.

"Sue came downstairs with a stomachache, and when I nursed baby I poured little drops of peppermint into a little tea and sent her to get into the crib with Lucy, who wakes, coughs hard and cries.

"I put down baby and rub liniment on Lucy's neck; and Johnie sees me and will get up.

"For my own good I should not lift him; to let his father rest, I do, thinking to rock him to sleep. But he talks and whines me for milk, and asks for apple and cries when baby needs me--and she cries, too.

"Sue says she is too hot, and wants to go upstairs again, but I decide to keep her where she is. Lucy, who is easily crowded, doesn't like Sue's presence and gets up, and the fire gets down and so I add coal . .

"Lucy cries because I won't let her dress for the day, Johnie off the bed barefoot is taking the baby's teacup to his sleeping father, cries aloud when interrupted.

"I put the mousetrap in the study, wash hands, dress up feet for the day, go to empty some slops, fix mustard for baby's chest--poor little thing, how pitifully she cries--and get Johnie to sleep if I can."

She lay down her pen and began thinking about the life she led--so wearing on her health, declining for years.

Her hands were so crippled with arthritis she couldn't open them any more. And she was constantly plagued with headaches, colds, fevers, dizziness and indigestion.

She still tried sometimes to wash clothes, or dishes, with her lame, swollen hands. But the use of cold water--or warm on a cold day--invariably made her worse. Frequently she was so lame she could not dress her feet or comb her hair. The pain, it seemed, was in every part of her body.

Sometimes she had coughing fits, almost spasms. Often in cool weather she awoke with a feeling of cold in her lungs or a chill that ascended slowly from her feet to her chest followed by a slight fever. Often her limbs were swollen for weeks at a time.

She had to give up more and more of the housework, leaving it for Papa or the older children or the hired girl to do.

She felt so miserable she could scarcely get about the house.

One day Clara came home from school to find her sitting on a 2-by-3-foot oleander box, on the front porch.

"Oh, Clara!" she said. "Help me! I walked out and sat down here and couldn't get up. If I had been six inches closer to the post, I could have pulled myself up."

Mamma had sat there for an hour or two, just waiting for someone to come along and help her.

Finally she went to Dr. Hodges--as she had done many times before--and he advised her to go to Colfax mineral springs, famous for its healthful baths.

After some delay and hesitation, deciding she was of no use at home, she agreed to go. Grandma Amanda went along, to care for little Hester, the latest addition to the family.

Mamma was so optimistic about the results that she sat down and wrote a "farewell to rheumatism."

She stayed for two weeks, lolling in the warm baths, drinking the sulfur and iron water, and relaxing at the Colfax hotel. She met other victims of rheumatism, saw their symptoms and heard their experiences.

It seemed to do her much good, and she lengthened her stay to three weeks.

Then, in a few days, she was home, Grandma Amanda and little Hettie with her. As Papa carried the luggage up the sidewalk, the children ran out to hug and kiss her.

There was a cry, and across the yard came weeping, toddling Margaret. She had gotten wet, then sat in some coal, and her panties were all dirty.

Mamma knew she was back into the harsh realities of motherhood--in a hurry.

11.

It was a pleasant spring day on the rolling Iowa farmlands around Grinnell.

The sycamore trees were green with new leaves, and the young grass was soft along the road. A cow lazily chomped away in a field nearby.

A plain, somewhat drab-looking red schoolhouse stood where two dirt roads met. The children were at recess, and a group was watching from the window as a small, short-legged, chubby boy came running along the road toward them.

"Here comes a little kid, with his britches up, carrying a water jug," announced Burt Jones, one of the students.

The boy filled the jug at Houghton's well, then ran abck down the dusty road, as fast as his legs could carry him. He didn't waste a minute.

"That man Tallmon does work those kids," remarked the teacher.

George turned into the field at his father's farm, half a mile from the country school. Papa pulled the horses to a halt, tied the reins to the corn planter, and lifted the jug to his lips.

"You didn't fool around, did you?" he asked. "Now plant these corn seeds in hills six inches apart, five seeds to a hill."

Then, wiping the sweat from his forehead with the back of his hand, he gathered up the reins and continued on.

Georgie took a handful of seeds from the gunnysack and began planting. He knew better than to disobey.

The long day ended as the sun set in the west, leaving a red glow on the horizon. Papa drove to the end of the row, then pulled the tired horses to a halt where his small son was working steadily.

"Are you putting five seeds to a hill?" Papa asked. "Aren't you to the end of that row yet? Come on, we must get home and do the chores."

The horses' hoofs plodded along in the dust as they made their way toward Grinnell.

"What's six times seven?" asked Papa, taking advantage of the opportunity to train his son in arithmetic.

"Forty two," Georgie replied.

"Eight times nine?"

"Seventy two."

"Four times eight?"

"Thirty two."

"That's fine. What's seven times eight?"

"Fifty eight."

"No! No! Fifty six!" his father exclaimed impatiently. "You always get that wrong. If I had eight Jersey cows, and each of them gave seven pails of milk a week, how many pails of milk would I have by the end of the week?"

"Fifty six."

"Yes, fifty six. Now, don't forget, seven times eight is fifty six. Fifty six."

Papa asked some more arithmetic problems, returning occasionally to "seven times eight" to give his son extra practice on the difficult one.

Then, changing the subject, he said: "When you get older, we'll go into farming together. You can buy a farm next to mine, and by using equipment together, we can do very well. We'll use the latest agricultural methods, and grow big crops of hay and corn."

George was not sure whether he wanted to be a farmer. Especially field work. He liked the animals, but the other work was too long and too hard.

But he said nothing. He only listened to his father talk, answered questions when necessary, and tried to hold his sleepy eyelids open.

When they finally reached home, it was nearly dark. Georgie fed the pigs, threw down hay for the cows, drew water for the horses and mixed grain for the calves, while his father milked the cows.

Then, as they started into the house for supper, Papa asked him to "just run over to the neighbor's and get a piece of rawhide."

Georgie went without objection, then washed his hands and sat down to eat. Devouring a piece of bread and butter, he climbed wearily upstairs to bed.

It was still dark when Papa called him the next morning.

"Get up, son," he said. "It's almost five o'clock. We must do the chores and get out to the field."

George staggered out of bed, sleepily pulled on his clothes, and went downstairs. He passed through the livingroom, and noticed the big hand of the clock pointing to seven, the little hand to four. His father had stretched the real time.

Papa put hot rolls in the oven for breakfast. He called the older girls to take them out when they were done.

Then he and Georgie went to the barn. Georgie fed the animals, checked their water, and threw down hay while his father milked.

"Hurry and wash up for breakfast," Papa said, when the chores were done.

"Don't take too much time to eat," Papa added, as Georgie gulped down some food.

"We must get out to the farm," Papa continued, going out the door. Soon the horses were plodding down the country road again, as the sun peeked over the eastern horizon.

"If we have a good crop this year, I should be able to put away $500," Papa said. "Then maybe I can sell this farm and invest it in some enterprising business."

They reached the field while dew still hung on the grass, and soon Papa was operating the planter once again. George filled more hills with corn--five seeds to the hill.

At noon, they stopped to eat at the tenant's house on the farm. Georgie was still hungry when they left; but he thought Papa was in a hurry and so stopped before he was done.

Then came another long afternoon, another sleepy ride home, and another short night of sleep.

The heavy work continued all summer. Then threshing time arrived. Georgie's job was to drive the team of horses around and around, supplying power to the threshing machine.

The weather was hot and humid. The thresher groaned and creaked and chattered. The dust was so thick Georgie could hardly breathe.

But he had to stay. The men were there. They were receiving big wages. He couldn't stop.

The horses were attached to a beam that went around and around and turned the gears in the middle, which turned a shaft, which operated the thresher.

Sometimes Georgie rode on the end of the beam. Sometimes he had to walk. He and the horses had to step over the shaft every time they came to it.

It was against the rules to ride the horses. His father wouldn't let him. It wasn't allowed.

In the fall, he went back to school. But afternoons, evenings and Saturdays, it was work time. If Georgie played ball or kite with other boys, even in his own yard, his father called him away and set him to wheeling manure or cleaning cellar or clearing stable.

Day after day, George rode off to the farm for a load of hay, even in the bitter cold of winter. Back home, he carried coal, did chores, and studied early and late.

Mamma worried about what she considered unreasonable demands made on George by his father. Georgie seemed dissatisfied and lonesome, and yielded and yielded and yielded, not thinking of himself but serving as a constant target for his father's, in her opinion, "witty experiments."

Mamma thought he should have some things of his own, and saw to it that he received a bracket saw for Christmas.

But 10 days later, he had not cut a stroke with it. A neighbor's child had sent to New York after seeing George's and already had made something. But Georgie didn't have time.

Grandpa Carhartt offered to show George how to use the saw, and took it home to build a frame for it. But Georgie didn't go get it for months.

Finally one Saturday Mamma sent George over to Grandpa's to get the saw. It was not 10 minutes before his father came into the house asking, "Where's Georgie?"

However, his father did see to it that he had chickens and pigs and calves he could call his own. George spent many happy hours at the barn, feeding and caring for them, and watching their every movement.

Once he set a trap for a rat that was eating the feed. Next morning he rushed out to see what his luck had been. Eagerly, he peered into the bin. Then a puzzled look crossed his face.

Not only was there no rat, but even the trap was gone.

Papa laughed. "The rat must have taken the trap with him," he explained.

In school compositions, George told about the farm animals he knew and loved best.

Once he described a horse:

"The horse is a domestic quadriped. It is a useful animal. We see it on almost every farm. They are almost always gentle and kind . . .

"They have ribs hair jaws teeth bones eyes, eyebrows, eye-lids, legs heels hoofs backs backbones, sides, tail mane forelock, ears, hips, lips, stomach head body neck blood veins arteries liver lungs heart nerves muscles meat nose tongue throat knees, skin fetlocks and withers.

"They are used to haul wagons carriages cutters sleighs bobsleds buggy reaper mower thresher corn-planter headers horserakes coaches stages etc.

"They are from four to six feet high. They are used to ride in some places."

The composition was well marked in red ink, and at the end the teacher had remarked, "Punctuation poor!"

Another composition told about the new Lick Observatory in California, which brought the moon "within 40 miles."

One wintry day the skies grew dark and winds began to blow.

"Hurry!" Papa urged George. "It looks like a blizzard. We must get the cattle in the barn before it strikes!"

Father and son rushed to the fields.

"Hey, bess! Here, bess!" they shouted, herding the cows toward the buildings.

Soon soft white snow flakes began settling on their arms and in their hair. By the time they reached the barn, it was snowing in earnest, and by the time they had the animals settled in their stalls, they couldn't even see the house.

All they could see was a blinding, swirling mass of white.

They threw hay down from the loft. And then Papa tried to figure out how to get to the house.

"This is going to be dangerous," he warned. "A man can easily lose his way. You stay here and I'll try to make it."

George remained, shivering, half filled with fright, as his father disappeared into the white vastness.

Papa set out at a quarter-angle, with his arm up, figuring he would hit the clothesline. He did, it worked, and he followed the clothesline to the house.

Then he tied a rope to the house, followed the clothesline back as far as he could, and struck out for the barn to get George.

As his father's form came toward him out of the darkness, George was relieved.

He and Papa followed the rope back to the clothesline. They made their way safely to the house, where sisters, mother and a warm fire greeted them.

12.

The day was warm and somewhat humid, and the high windows in the old-fashioned Grinnell schoolhouse didn't help the circulation.

Only a week remained until summer vacation, and the sixth grade, of which George W. Tallmon was teacher, had finished its work for the day.

Half an hour was left until dismissal time, so Mr. Tallmon asked the students if they would like to learn to speak in Latin!

"Oh, yes," shouted the class--at least the more studious members. Some of the big boys in the back row showed little enthusiasm.

"Unus, duo, tres, quattuor, quinta, sex, septem, octo, novem, decem," said Mr. Tallmon, counting from one to ten in Latin.

"Unus, duo, tres, quattuor, quinta, sex, septem, octo, novem, decem," repeated the class, a little shakily but with resolution.

By the time school was dismissed, they could count in Latin quite well, and rushed home to try their new-found knowledge on their parents.

On one side of the room, a poorly-dressed girl still poured over a book, trying to master the day's lesson.

Mr. Tallmon strode rapidly to her side, snatched up the book, and rattled off an imperfect explanation of the lesson. Then he sent her home to study the lesson with the help of her mother.

Gathering up his books and tidying up the room, he left the school building and walked the few blocks home. Then, changing his clothes, he started the chores.

When he came in, supper wasn't ready. Mamma was busy doing other things, and the girls were occupied.

Deciding to eat downtown, he went to change into his good clothes, but couldn't find any clean underwear. He told Mamma, who was writing in her journal.

"Look in the drawer," she replied.

He looked again, but couldn't find any. Disgusted, he filled a tub and washed his dirty pair while Mamma kept on writing.

"Where are you going?" Mamma asked, when she noticed his preparations.

"Downtown to eat," he replied.

"The girls will fix supper," she said. "It won't take long."

"Half the time supper isn't ready when I want it."

"Well, we never know when you are coming in."

"I have to get the chores done--and often something delays me . . "

Mamma made no reply. She turned her head and ignored him.

That made him angry.

"One of these days I'm going to leave you!" he retorted. Mamma made no comment.

Among Papa's possessions were two farms in Franklin County, 80 miles north of Grinnell--a good three-and-one-half days' journey from home.

Starting in 1880, he went there each summer to tend the crops and take in the harvest. He would come home for two or three days each month, then travel back again.

The first summer, he took George along to help with the work and Clara to cook. He would have preferred to take the whole family, but Mamma wouldn't go.

The second summer, he and George were able to stay with tenants, and Clara didn't go.

Papa made arrangements with a man to milk the cow at home while he was gone. But the man went away without obtaining a substitute, and the little girls had to have milk.

So Clara, who had never milked before, went out to see what she could do.

Old Nige waited patiently an hour and a half for Clara to finish the first night. By the time the summer was over, Clara could milk pretty well, and was an old hand at caring for the cows.

Georgie's letters told about sleeping upstairs "with the sharp-toothed mice and rats," and of the "hen that crows but it lays eggs."

He also told of riding the black mule, Coe, 10 miles to town one day. She was stubborn and wouldn't go, and finally he tied her to a fence and walked the rest of the way.

He tried to catch an owl, but it flew. In the meantime Judy, the mule, ran home and he had to carry the sack of bran that slipped from her back.

When Papa returned to Grinnell in the fall, he began to talk of making a new move--farther west.

"I've been wanting to go for a long time," he said. "I'm going to sell out here, and start anew, where land is cheap. I could get a good price for my farms, and we could buy many good acres out there. Maybe we could move to Colorado--or Oregon--or California."

"I don't want to move," Mama replied, firmly. "We're settled here. I'm tired of pioneering. We're not going to move any more!"

"Yes we are," Papa declared. "And I'm going to make a trip out there to see what it's like."

He began to make preparations, feeling his way at all points, talking to the preacher, the doctor, the grocer, the merchant and washwoman, but not much at home. Mamma didn't think he was really serious.

He spoke of taking Mamma with him, but she made it clear she wasn't going.

He talked of the dangers of travel and his fear of accident, and insured his life. And he hung about the house, sitting by the stove, talking to Mamma about the trip.

Finally, the day came for him to leave.

When all the bags and suitcase were in the buggy, and train time was due, Papa went to Mamma and said: "Promise me not to speak to any man while I'm gone."

Mamma flushed, an angry look crossed her face, and she turned coldly away. Of all the asinine demands!

"Promise me or I'll never return!" Papa demanded.

Mamma continued to ignore him.

Papa looked at her with disgust, then turned, strode to the buggy, and drove away without saying goodbye.

Mamma shed many an angry, troubled tear over his having dared to leave in such an "insulting" way. But, when a letter came from Colorado telling of business as if nothing had happened, she set the whole affair aside as one of her trials in life.

A later letter said he was coming home, and in glowing terms spoke of a "big present" for Mamma.

When he arrived, he proudly displayed a big certificate saying he owned $3,000 stock in a Pike's Peak gold mine!

Mamma didn't have the least bit of faith in it. She was sure the stock would never be worth anything. It wasn't.

Papa was confident it would be. He gave the certificate to Mamma for Christmas.

He also sold part of his gold stock to a man in town. The man invited Papa and Mamma over to supper the night he and Papa closed the deal. She went.

Later the man sued Papa because the stock never paid off and he claimed Papa guaranteed that it would be good.

At the trial, the judge asked Mamma if Papa had said, "I'll guarantee the stock."

Yes, she said, after the sale was made and she and Papa had gotten into the buggy to leave he had said it was good stock-- "I'll guarantee that."

Papa won the case, and didn't have to reimburse the man. He had made no guarantee until the deal had been completed, and then only an assurance the stock was good.

But $3,000 of Papa's hard-earned money was gone. After that, the family was almost constantly in debt.

13.

It had been a hot Saturday afternoon in June in the town of Grinnell, Iowa. The intense heat weighed down on everything with a close stickiness. There was no relief, indoors or out.

Then, as evening approached, a strange stillness filled the air. It was almost uncanny, as if the whole world was awaiting some big event. Off in the northwest tiny, black clouds began to appear.

Finally, a breeze brought relief to the sweltering town, and people began to close windows in anticipation of a bad thunder storm. Others hurried downtown to complete errands delayed during the hot daytime.

The dark spots grew in size, and soon the entire northern sky was hung with downward-pointing clouds. Then the western sky turned lurid and brilliant and unearthly.

Just at dark, June 17 , 1882, the storm broke.

Clara was milking Nigra and Bonny when the first drops of rain began to fall. She heard the splashing water as she sat there on the stool, her head pressed against the cow's side.

She stripped the last drops of milk and pulled the pail from under the cow. As she stood up, she heard footsteps. It was one of the girls, carrying a welcomed umbrella. Her sister seemed breathlessly excited.

"Papa's home!" she exclaimed. "He came just after you went out to milk. Uncle Lester and his two sons came with him on the train. They are visiting Grandpa Carhartt and Grandma Amanda. Georgie stayed up there to care for the farm."

Her words fairly spilled out.

"Oh, that's wonderful!" Clara exclaimed.

Then, hesitating as she started to loosen the cows' ropes, she said, "Papa wouldn't like it, but I think I'll leave the cows tied in the barn tonight. It may mean more work for me in the morning. But I don't have the heart to turn them out into the pouring rain." Papa had frequently advised against keeping the cows in at night.

The two sisters made their way to the house, sloshing through puddles they couldn't see in the darkness. Clara carried the pail to the kitchen and started to strain the milk.

In the dining room, a happy crowd of children were gathered around their father, eating candy mice he had found in a store. It was 8 o'clock and they should have been in bed. But it was a special occasion: Papa was home!

Mamma was heating flatirons to iron a white shirt for Papa to wear the next day.

Clara, from the kitchen window, noticed a stiff young crabtree a few yards away blown first to one side and then to the other, so hard the top hit the ground. She wondered about the cause.

Then came a strange noise, and Papa went out onto the front porch to take a look at the weather. It was hailing violently, and the children begged, "Get us some hailstones, Papa!"

"Here's a big one," Papa replied, jokingly, as he threw back a white china doorknob.

A minute later he was shutting the door with considerable effort and crying, "It's a tornado--get down cellar quick!"

The children scampered for the cellar stairs in a hurry.

As the older ones paused for the little folks ahead, they heard loud bangs and thumps on the tin roof of the pantry above them.

"Those must be big hailstones," remarked Clara, through chattering teeth.

"Bricks from the chimney," grunted Papa.

Papa saw them down and went back to find Mamma. Little Margaret tagged along.

Mamma had gone to the bedroom for year-old Clover, and John followed her. Mamma feared the hot stove would set fire to things and had gotten as far from it as she could. She was kneeling at the bed when Papa found her, a child under each arm.

"Didn't I tell you to get downstairs?" he roared. "Do your praying in the cellar!"

Just then a post came flying through the bay window.

Papa rushed Hester and Margaret to the top of the stairs, then grabbed the baby and literally threw her down the steps into Clara's arms. John was able to get down by himself, and Mamma followed.

The fearful roaring and crashing was like a dozen freight trains rumbling by, and the almost constant flashes of lightning lit up the cellar with an eerie light.

Papa warned everyone to stay out of the draft between the open windows for fear they would be blown out.

They waited for what seemed like ages in the momentary expectation that the house would go to pieces over their heads.

Suddenly Papa--who could see out the north cellar window--cried, "There goes the barn!"

Clara passed the baby to someone else, and ran to look, too, groaning with remorse. "My poor cows! My poor cows!"

They huddled there, terrified, not knowing what would happen next.

After what seemed like endless time--but perhaps only about 15 minutes--Papa decided the storm had passed, and they went upstairs to survey the damage.

It was still raining violently, and every pane of glass in the north windows was blown out. Many on the west side and a few on the east were broken, also. None on the south.

Angie and Clara were trying to fasten a quilt over the north bedroom window when Papa called to them. They ran downstairs in a panic, fearing the tornado had returned. But when they got there, they found the next door neighbors standing in the parlor. They had seen their light, and had come for help.

"Our house was moved clear off its foundation," the man from next door was saying, as he stomped the mud off his feet. "One side dropped into the cellar, and you can scarcely stand up in it."

"The water was up to our knees in the road," his wife added, her clothes dripping wet.

"Well, you're more than welcome to stay here with us tonight," Papa said. "Girls, bring some bedding from upstairs."

Another knock came at the door. It was more neighbors.

"We saw your light . . . " they explained.

"Come on in," Papa invited them. "We have a fire, and you can dry yourselves."

It was a wet and weary crew that made their way into the house. Among them was a 10-year-old boy, who was hurt.

His mother seemed only barely concerned. She swept the wet plaster dust from her hair and stroked her black dress, trimmed daintily with fringe and puffed bands of the same material.

"My new dress!" she exclaimed. "I'm afraid it's ruined!"

"We're lucky we escaped with our lives," her husband reminded her. "Our house is completely gone."

Other neighbors arrived, and soon were gathered around the fire, warming themselves from its welcomed glow.

"The storm divided when it came to your house," declared one man with a gash on his cheek, speaking to Papa.

"No, it swung around north of the house, and then cut east," another neighbor replied, as Mamma brought cups of hot tea.

"I guess we were luckier than we thought," responded Papa. "My barn's flat, but otherwise we got by all right."

"Mr. Day's house was riddled by timbers from your barn," the neighbor said.

There was an insistent knock on the door.

"Someone come and help, quick!" a man was asking. "Mrs. Merrill, her mother and the children are buried under the timbers. John is almost frantic. He was downtown when the storm struck."

Several of the men left to help, while the women and Tallmon girls stayed to do what they could to help the refugees and find dry clothes for them.

Mamma caught Papa's arm as he started out the door. "I wonder about Grandpa and Grandma, Lester, and the boys . . ." she said.

"I'll go see how they are," he assured her.

Soon the men returned, carrying Mrs. Merrill's mother on a mattress. She seemed to be badly injured, and was complaining of pain.

Mrs. Merrill followed, her clothes dirty and wet, along with her daughter and son, Nettie and Walter. Nettie had just been graduated from high school the night before, and her grandparents had come from Des Moines for the occasion.

"Are you all right?" asked Mamma, earnestly.

"Oh, yes," Mrs. Merrill replied. "But John was so worried about us. He ran frantically back and forth over the very timbers under which I lay before he discovered where we were."

The men laid old Mrs. Reed in the middle of the diningroom floor on her mattress. Clara was set to watch her, with a washbowl handy--for she was nauseated.

"I shall puke!" she warned. Clara hadn't heard the word before, but she knew what it meant. She was prepared.

"Oh, look!" someone shouted, pointing out the east window. "Something's on fire. It must be the college."

A red glow filled the sky. It grew brighter by the second. Soon flames could be seen licking against the sky.

"If it is, everything's down for two blocks," replied someone else.

Mamma's heart caught--that meant Grandpa's house had been destroyed.

Soon Papa returned with word that all of Grandpa's family was safe at a neighbor's.

"Lester's boys were eating supper, and hadn't gone to bed yet," he reported. "Lester realized the danger, and hurried Eddie and Herman down cellar--Grandma ahead with the light, he following with a boy under each arm. Grandpa was in bed. Grandpa jumped up but couldn't move fast because of his lame leg. He made it to the cellar steps all right. As he stood on the landing he saw the windows, both north and south, burst outward."

"My!" exclaimed a neighbor. "That was a close call!"

"The house was torn to kindling wood over their heads," Papa continued. "It was thrown mostly to the east. When they dared leave the cellar they made for the Phelps' house half a block south. But both the roof and interior were gone. The Larrabes' house showed a light, and they went there."

"Were they hurt at all?" Mamma asked, worriedly.

"They were bruised by falling bricks and debris as they crouched in a corner of the cellar," Papa replied. "Otherwise, they weren't hurt. And it was amusing. After all the excitement,

Herman still had his silver spoon in his hand. Grandma gave it to him as a souvenir."

Papa went on.

"I also stopped by Albert's house. They were all right, except that Albert stepped on a rake outside. Grandpa and Grandma are going there to stay tomorrow."

The doctor finally arrived at the Tallmon house--after midnight, for many people were hurt.

He wished to examine Mrs. Reed, and they were going to cut her clothing off in undressing her; but she wouldn't allow it. So they had to work her sodden clothing off. Later a half brick was found under the mattress.

About 3 o'clock, when a lull came, Papa said, "Come, Clara, let's see about the cows."

Clara held the lantern and put in props while Papa used a timber as lever.

She waited breathlessly, hoping against hope that her pet cow wasn't hurt, yet fearing the worst.

When a lot of timbers had been moved, Clara's heart sank--then rose. Old Nige . . . she was alive!

Papa removed a few more boards, and Nige struggled to her feet and scrambled out, apparently unhurt.

Then they went to Bonny's stall, and dug her out. She was lame, but walked off into the orchard.

As Corny, Bonny's calf, was in the back stall, Papa feared her legs were broken "at the least," but "we better try to see."

Again Clara held the light, and put in supports as Papa worked. Finally the sill was raised enough so he could creep under.

In a few moments, he backed out, pulling the calf by its front legs. It had been lying down, and was "safe and happy, in a little warm dry nest," as the story was told for years afterward.

The calf was turned loose--and the family got no milk from Bonny the next morning!

It was a long, dismal night at the Tallmon house that night. Thirty-four drenched, exhausted people spread out on makeshift beds of pillows, quilts and blankets the full length of the study floor. No one slept much.

Next morning, the whole significance of the tornado became known. The storm had entered town at the southwest corner, cut through a curve, around the Tallmon house, and southeast through the college grounds.

About 100 people were killed, more than 200 hurt, and dozens of houses destroyed. The schoolhouse was turned into a hospital.

Many houses had been picked up like match boxes, turned around, dropped into the cellar, laid off to one side, or destroyed completely. In the short space of 20 feet, one house would be blown to the west, another to the east.

Chimneys were blown off many homes, shingles ripped off, and shutters broken. Scraps of carpets, pieces of tin roofs, dresses and hats were scattered over the ground and lodged in trees.

People who reached their cellars escaped, but those who didn't often were killed. Some houses were so badly destroyed reporters the next day missed counting them because they didn't think a house had been there.

The two college buildings were destroyed. The wind wrecked one, and chemicals set fire to the other. A bucket brigade and the fire engine, which arrived two hours late, were unable to save it.

Yet, in spite of the widespread damage, some people on the opposite side of town didn't know there had been a tornado until they went to church the next morning.

The Tallmons' house escaped serious damage. The tenement house was on its side, with one corner tipped into the cellar.

A hailstone went right through a window without breaking it, leaving a hole as sharp and clean as a bullet hole.

The hay mow and top of the barn were lifted off and laid carefully on the ground a short distance away. The rest of the barn was blown hither and yon. Some calves, left tied to a stanchion, were unhurt.

The Tallmons' pasture was as full of sticks and timbers as a pincushion of pins, all at an angle of about 45 degrees. They made a pile more than 12 feet high and 30 feet across. Mostly, they were too splintered for anything but firewood. George later built a playhouse for the girls out of the larger pieces.

Trinkets, spoons and other household articles from homes in Grinnell also were scattered across the pasture. Some had names on them. The little girls gathered them all up and took them back to the schoolhouse so people could come and claim them.

Grandpa Carhartt's house was turned completely upside down. Workers later had to pull floor carpets off the "ceiling."

The house was trimmed in robin's egg blue. Pieces of wood painted robin's egg blue were found for miles around, even in the next town.

Papa's barn had been painted red. A board painted bright red was found six miles southeast of town.

A farmer found Grandpa Carhartt's wallet in a field while plowing corn. It was returned. The wallet still had quite a bit of money in it. It had been locked in a drawer in the desk.

Little Johnie also found a wallet after the tornado.

"Did it have any money in it?" his father asked him.

"Lots of money," Johnie replied, "but it all lost out before I found it."

Many other strange things happened.

Papa found a piece of black walnut board driven into a cottonwood tree. Through the black walnut was driven a straw!

In one place a piano was in a tree. In another, a dead cow. At the corner of West Street and Sixth Avenue, a 2x8-inch plank was driven into the ground so solidly it could not be budged. It was left there for several years.

A man who was calling at Professor Chamberlain's house ran out to see about his horse, tied in front. The wind was so strong that he grabbed a tree, and was flopped up and down against the ground, until he rolled around and around the tree.

Afterwards he discovered his pockets full of corn from an overturned freight train a few rods away. His horse and buggy were carried over the train, but neither was damaged much.

A basketful of eggs was lifted from a pantry shelf and set down by the back door. Not an egg was cracked!

Mrs. Isenberg was holding her three-year-old son when the storm broke. He was blown out of her arms, and she snatched and snatched, trying to grab him back. She pulled all his clothes off trying to hang onto him--and succeeded. She kept him.

A woman was found wandering, dazed, in a field, without a stitch of clothing on.

A baby was found in a field, unhurt. Its identity was never learned; its parents probably were killed in the storm. Someone adopted it, and it was named, "Tornado."

A horse was left standing, unhurt, in a manger, while the barn around it blew away. It was so shocked it had to be put out to pasture for the rest of the summer.

On one farm, the chickens were completely cleaned of their feathers.

Soldiers were stationed around the city to prevent looting. Sightseers arrived on trains by the hundreds. They took everything they could lay their hands on for "souvenirs."

Clara was sent over to Grandpa's yard the following day to get some of Grandma's tulips, as people were digging them up.

A neighbor stopped a man leaving another neighbor's yard with both hands full of silver--old family silver. A woman sightseer opened a cupboard door in a shattered but not demolished house. In the presence of the mistress of the house, she took out a butter dish.

But perhaps the most noteworthy incident came when a woman walked into Mr. Kimball's dry good store, carrying a wall basket.

"Please wrap this up for me," she said. "It is the only relic I found worth keeping."

Mr. Kimball immediately recognized it as coming from his own home, which had been destroyed by the storm.

"My wife might also think it worth keeping," he remarked, as he laid it on the shelf to take home to its rightful owner.

14.

Young George Tallmon had a happy home life--in general. With nine brothers and sisters--little Edith was born shortly after the tornado--there was always something interesting going on.

Like little Margaret running downtown alone one day, taking it upon herself to get the mail.

She was so little, she could hardly see to the window level. But she held her head way up, and the postmaster saw her.

"What do you want, little girl?" he asked.

"I want G. Doub's (G.W. Tallmon's) mail."

She got it.

Or like Susie, age 9, writing for her mother's journal. "First I suppose I must introduce us. There are little Clover, Hetty, Margy, Johnie, Lucy, Susie, George, Clara and Angie. I don't want you to say as soon as you read this to say, 'What a large family!' It isn't any bigger than we need!"

Or like Angie and Clara getting into the green tomato pickles Uncle Dave had brought from his farm. They smelled most intriguing, and the girls kept tasting samples one after the other while getting supper.

By mealtime the level of the pickles had been lowered noticably. And when Papa came to the table and asked, "Where are the rest of them?" the girls had to admit what happened.

They felt very uncomfortable finishing the rest of the dish on Papa's orders while the other children watched enviously.

Or the time Clover was at the barn watching Nigra being milked. Mamma wanted her to come indoors. Clover didn't want to go and, pulling her thumb out of her mouth, put both arms around the cow's hind leg and clung there.

Angie was watching George load corn. Many mice were disturbed and she began to gather them into her big apron, saying, "The cats ought to be here."

George called her a "catamount" (a large, wild, cat) after that.

Susie was interested in foreign missions from the time she was very young. She also carried around an old satchel and a lot of bottles, doping people up. She was always the doctor.

One day she went to her mother with a worried look. "By the time I get grown so I can be a missionary, they won't need missionaries any more," she complained.

"I don't think you need to worry," Mamma reassured her. "As long as this world exists, I think there will be a need for missionaries."

Papa gave up locking the doors at night after a burglar broke in one time, took about $200 from Papa's trousers pocket, and left without being heard.

The burglar broke the glass in a window next to the summer kitchen door, reached in and opened the door, and walked through the summer kitchen, the kitchen, the dining room and on through the house to Papa's bedroom.

He stole money Papa had collected for selling several buggies.

When Edith was coming, Mamma said, "If I'm going to be pregnant again this summer, I'm going to be more of a lady." So she took up painting.

Lucy was chosen for the privilege of carrying Mamma's paints and supplies. They walked together downtown, past houses that had been blown down by the tornado.

By this time, Mamma's hands were so crippled with arthritis, she could not open them. Yet she did some beautiful work with a brush.

On birthdays, the honored member of the family could choose his or her own menu. Lucy always picked oysters--and it meant going to the store to buy frozen ones from Chesapeake Bay. It was a mile to the store, and the youngsters kept warm under a buffalo robe during the ride in freezing weather.

It was also the custom to have a candy treat. Papa bought 25 cents worth at the grocery--they got so much the grocer must have put in two or three times what they paid for--and it would be the honor of the person or persons whose birthday it was to divide the candy among the dishes in front of each place around the table.

Mealtime was always a special time in the Tallmon family. It was a time when all were together--and it was a time of visiting.

Sunday was also a family day. Often the family sat around, cracking hickory nuts, while someone read aloud. It wasn't necessarily a new story; often an old familiar favorite.

Sometimes they just watched the baby, and laughed at the things she did.

Not rich, they had to get along with plain, everyday things. But they enjoyed each other.

One evening, the family was sitting around the table when George and Clara decided to draw a picture of what they would look like in 50 years.

Everyone added features, including, of course, a beard and sunken cheeks.

Lucy was to keep the picture and, in 1930, 50 years later, send it to George.

In those days, people believed a person should eat charcoal in order to "purify the blood."

So George sat up to the table, eating charred corn cobs with milk and sugar, following doctor's orders.

The children had to eat mustard and molasses every spring, too. To purify the blood. Each had to eat a certain portion.

They would vie to see who would get theirs down first, as a game to help consume it.

Picnics were a great family treat. The children alone--or sometimes everyone--hitched up the horse and buggy, and drove off to a grove out in the country for an outing. They played games, picked fruit or berries, and ate lunch, then returned home at dusk.

At least once a year they made an overnight camping trip to the Iowa River. That was a longed-for occasion, and one with memories to last a lifetime.

The trip was full of hikes and cooking out-of-doors, nature study, and camping--and fishing in the early sunrise hours.

Papa was generally up before daybreak, and the children awoke to the sound of his voice: "Twenty, twenty-one, twenty-two," as he counted the fish he threw from the water.

Papa was a strict father. The children were whipped daily, often without knowing what it was for. And the whippings were not light. Often the horsewhip was used.

One of the girls received a severe horsewhipping for telling neighbors her mother was going to have a baby after being told not to.

Lucy fixed a bottle for the baby. It was too hot to hold, so she wrapped it in a blanket to take it to her little sister.

Papa waylaid her, and gave her a beating.

"You don't want to give the bottle to the baby that way," he told her.

Papa required strict obedience. The children had to mind on the dot.

Sometimes he merely looked with eyes full of meaning. And when Papa gave them his "firm eye," they didn't dare disobey. They knew the consequences.

One day Papa promised the children a picnic. They were all excited about it, and talked of nothing else the night before and all that morning.

When the food was packed into the wagon, the children climbed on excitedly. Susie climbed up the wagon wheel, which was strictly against orders.

Her father saw her do it, and reprimanded her.

"Get down off the wagon!" he ordered. "I've told you many times not to climb the wheel. What if the horses should start up suddenly? Go into the house."

That was a real blow. Tears streaming down her face, Susie marched slowly inside and upstairs to her room. She didn't look out of the window, but she heard the wagon drive off.

No one else had any fun that day, either. The picnic was spoiled.

Mamma disciplined the children, too. But she wasn't as strict or strong as Papa. She used a measuring stick to slap their hands, but she didn't have enough strength to make it hurt.

Papa was good about taking the children to town with him, and on other short trips. He thoroughly enjoyed them, and relished teaching them to observe the things of nature.

As they rode along, he pointed out the trees and birds and rocks and flowers--by name--or, at night, the stars and sky. The children became well-founded in nature study and astronomy.

Or he would tell them stories of battles of the Civil War.

And he often quoted passages in Greek or Latin, or from poetry or drama.

Papa had a story to tell whenever he returned from going somewhere, about something interesting he saw on the way. It might be an unusual stone or rock formation, or tree.

One time he and George came back and told the little girls about a tree they saw that had branches that separated and then, higher up, grew together again. It was so unusual, Papa took them all to see it.

Papa often said, "Train a child to see, and you don't have to teach him to learn."

For both him and Mamma, education was important. He was anxious for his children to do well in school, and was displeased if they got poor marks.

On the other hand, he could make education seem very interesting as he helped teach his children about the world around them.

Mamma also was a good teacher and took an interest in her family's education. She often read aloud while the others ate, or read to the children during playtime after she was crippled with arthritis. It was a good way to keep them quiet and at the same time teach them something educational.

Among the books she read were, "The Last of the Mohicans" and "David Copperfield." She said she was afraid if she didn't read to her children, they would never read the classics after she was gone.

While reading to them, Mamma had the children look up in the Atlas new and strange places, or in the dictionary new words.

Papa had a cherished library, and stressed the importance of books to his children. He let them look through his books on special occasions.

Both Papa and Mamma themselves were well educated. Papa particularly had a great breadth of general knowledge. The children went to Papa about everything--he was like an encyclopedia.

The family had a flare for writing poetry--especially little jingles.

Papa's poetry was flowery. For example:

TO A DEAD BIRD

Thy course, my pretty bird, is run!
    Thy happy day is past!
Thou'll never greet tomorrow's dawn.
    Today hast been thy last!

Other times it was sentimental, such as:

MY LOVE AND I
(Written for his wife)

Hand in hand we walk thru life,
    My love and I,
To join as "one" in coming strife,
    My love and I.

I am her husband, she my wife,
    As blade and handle make a knife.
So we are joined for coming life,
    My love and I.

We oft have pledged our vow to vow,
    My love and I,
And softly breathe those pledges now,
    My love and I.

She is the bow and I the dart,
    I am the seal and she the heart,
And we are useless, quite, apart.
    My love and I.

George's poetry was more jingly and down to earth:

EDITH
(His baby sister)
(For her first birthday)

Her hair is white and her teeth number six.
She just pulls your wool which makes your head itch.
She pulls the cat's hair and paper does tear,
Besides playing in victuals when sitting with Clare,

    Little Edie has got blue eyes,
    And tho she is pretty, she seldom looks wise.
    She is learning to walk tho she cannot creep yet.
    She's a dear little girl, and brother's own pet.

Shortly before Thanksgiving Papa was riding his horse through a field when he noticed a small wild goose alight in some weeds.

Keeping his eye on the exact spot where it was, he cast out his whip and caught the goose around the neck. It had an injured wing and couldn't fly.

The goose, gray with some white on its head, was put in a large coop made for a hen with chicks. It seemed contented, and got fat as Thanksgiving approached.

One day John and Margaret were playing around the coop. Papa had told them not to touch it, but John thought doing so "wouldn't hurt." He opened the door and, swish, the goose escaped. It crawled under the woodpile which had been made of wreckage from the barn after the tornado.

John and Margaret were really scared. They would really get punished when Papa found out. But George caught it again.

It was killed for Thanksgiving. As the family sat down to a table of steaming good things, with the roasted goose in the center, Papa announced:

"Everyone must compose a poem about the goose before we eat."

"Oh, that will be fun!" exclaimed Angie.   And Clara asked, "How shall we start?"

But the younger children looked downcast, and Johnie complained: "I'm hungry!"

Nonetheless, Papa got out a pencil and paper, and brows were wrinkled in thought. This was the result:

> Papa: This goose came to us out of time
>   Was fed and fattened for a rhyme.
>
> Mamma: Behold the vain and vagrant goose,
>   Now civilized and made of use.
>
> Angie: He was fed and starved and fed,
>   But grew not one whit thinner,
>   'Til at last he slept in a gravy bed
>   And graces our Thanksgiving dinner.
>
> Clara: Oh! goose, by what did you come,
>   Wind, water or air?
>   I advise you to fly away home,
>   And send me word when you're there.

And this was George's:
> An old gray goose got his head in a noose,
> And that was done by my father.
> He was kept in a pen that was made for a hen,
> And John said he was a great bother.

15.

George was walking along a road near his home, whistling a tune. It was a beautiful day, sunny and bright. The flowers were blooming. Birds were chirping in the trees or flitting from place to place.

George picked up a stone and threw it at a bird resting on a fence. The bird dropped to the ground, dead.

Alarmed, George picked up the poor little creature. It lay in his hand, its eyes closed, its life gone.

A pang of remorse stabbed through his chest. He didn't expect to hit the bird. He didn't want to kill it.

He never forgot that incident. He swore he never again would purposely kill any creature except for good cause.

His pang of conscience was in line with his moral outlook on life.

He was born into a religious family. His mother was a sincere Christian, anxious to bring up her children in the way of Jesus. Her ancestors had been God-respecting people. Thankful Williams Chesebro--her grandmother--took Mamma to the highest part of the house when just born, as a symbol of the hope that she would live a high-minded life.

George's father, too, was very religious in his youth, and influenced his son's life to the good.

This Golden Thread of Godliness was a treasure handed down to George by his forebearers.

Their religion was earnest and sincere. They believed that a person should do what he believed.

Papa never worked on Sunday. Even though it looked like rain, and grain or hay was out, it made no difference. He rested and his horses rested.

Religion was a natural part of their family life. Every morning either Papa or Mamma lead morning prayers, and read from the Bible.

On Sunday morning, they usually gathered around the organ after breakfast, and sang while Mamma played.

Grace was said before meals.

Every Sunday they went to church. If they were sick or Mamma had to stay with the babies, they had Sunday school at home.

Smoking and drinking of alcoholic beverages were strictly avoided.

Mamma tried conscientiously to teach her children to be good Christians.

She stressed gentleness and consideration for others, which, she said, would mean more in the final account than show and sound in this world. She often said a ruffled temper is no more desirable than a ruffled collar.

She tried to teach her children not to lie or cheat or steal-- not by preaching but by example and by words of encouragement and understanding at the proper time.

If her children said things that seemed to be untrue, she was reluctant to associate them with liars unless it became certain that they had lied. Then she told them what she thought, that it was wrong to lie and that she hoped they would not form this dreadful habit, which would make trouble and regrets for themselves and friends.

A confessed fault she seldom punished even by a word or by laying blame. A wrong to another had to be atoned if only by expressing regret or by giving a kiss where a hurt had been inflicted.

In all ways she tried to help her children feel close to God. She appealed to the Bible as authority when a question of duty arose. And in times of special joy or need she spoke of God as of a human friend.

One time her training almost backfired. Grandpa and Grandma Amanda were away. Mamma, Lucy and John went over to their house to check on things. Mamma picked a bouquet of pinks in the garden.

"Should you pick Grandma's flowers without asking her?" asked Lucy, questioningly.

"I'm sure it will be all right," replied Mamma, almost guiltily. "Grandma wouldn't mind. I'll make things right with her when she comes back. I don't think they'll last, anyway."

As George started his teens, he began to take serious interest in religion. One day he came home from Sunday school, quite excited.

"Mamma," he said, earnestly. "I want to join the church."

Mamma didn't hesitate.

"If you love Jesus, then you may," she said. That apparently was the criterion in her mind.

A few days later, George came home, puzzled and confused.

"The preacher said I should feel like a sinner and be converted," he said. "Won't I be able to join the church?"

"A person doesn't have to be converted all at once to be a Christian," Mamma replied. "I'll go talk to Mr. Sturdivant."

Mamma was ushered into the pastor's office.

"My son said he told you he has been a Christian all his life," she began, sitting tensely on the edge of her chair.

"I realize his spiritual state may seem shocking and heathenish to a regular theologian such as you.

"But I don't think a boy like George needs to feel he is a sinner and be converted. George always tries to do what is right. He's conscientious, and he always has been that way.

"He has become a Christian already, gradually.

"He seems to think he would be nearer Jesus by entering the church, and I can't forbid him even though others might think he has been neglected.

"The Christian's experience of conversion, I think, is repeated with some people many times in one life. It occurs often in early Christian life, many times at a later day, sometimes in the hour of death, and some people never are conscious of it. Yet they are faithful Christians, known to all men by their fruits as such.

"I don't think joining the church makes any more direct relationship between God and the soul than the performance or neglect of any other duty.

"I fear George might be misunderstood by an examining committee or rejected because of his lack of verbal knowledge.

"Since this would grieve and discourage him, I have ventured to come and see you."

She hesitated, wondering what Mr. Sturdivant would say.

He smiled and leaned forward on his desk.

"Don't you worry," he reassured her. "I think you're right. I'll talk to the examining committee."

And George was one of 30 young people, along with Clara, who joined the church that year.

16.

A strange emptiness greeted Papa as he opened the door.

Dishes, curtains and chairs were missing. The house was strangely quiet.

"Where is everyone?" he called.

There was no answer.

Going into the sitting room, he found books and papers missing.

"What's this?" he asked. "Where is everything? You don't suppose that wife of mine has moved already! The house isn't done yet."

Out the door he marched, and two blocks down the street, to where workmen were putting the final touches on the family's new house.

"Why, the plaster isn't even dry," he thought to himself. "We've had the stove going for a week just to dry it out."

Into the new house he strode. And there, among personal effects, miscellaneous articles and boxes, worked Mamma.

"What's the big idea?" demanded Papa.

"I just got tired of waiting," replied his wife, quietly. "I'm moving in today. We're going to stay here tonight."

"But the walls still need painting . . "

"We can paint them while we're here," Mamma said.

"We can't get all the furniture moved by tonight," Papa objected. "The snow's a foot deep outside."

"Angie, Clara and George can sleep at the old house." Mamma had it all figured out. "The little children can sleep on the floor . . Besides, this is my house. We built it with the $2,000 Grandpa left me in his will."

Papa hemmed and hawed a little more, but he started moving.

Most of the downstairs things had been transferred by nightfall. Things were progressing so well, Mamma sent word to the older children to bring bedding on a sled and come, too.

The children slept on makeshift beds on the sitting room floor. Angie told fantastic fairy stories before they went to sleep.

All were recovering from whooping cough. Clara got to whooping during the night so badly she feared she would never get her breath again.

Papa seemed to have the same fear, because he hovered around her with a nail keg in his hand.

In order to get the property they wanted, Mamma and Papa had to buy a small house already there. A friend, Mr. Will Mullens, bought the house on credit, and moved it away. Papa had the children help figure the principal and interest, as a practical lesson in partial payments.

The Tallmons' new house was located on the outskirts of town. Papa built barns and other farm buildings. And he bought a 120-acre farm about half a mile away.

So the family had a farm atmosphere, even though they actually lived in town.

George spent most of his out-of-school hours helping his father with the farm work.

He was called "Sleepy-Eye" at school, because he had a hard time staying awake during class. His head would bob. "Sleepy-Eye" was the brand name of a flour popular at the time.

"What's the matter with your brother?" one of a group of girls asked Clara on the schoolgrounds one day. "Doesn't he go to bed at night?"

"He gets up early and plows until time for school," Clara explained. "After school he plows until dark. Then he milks the cows and does the chores. He doesn't get to bed until about 11 p.m."

After that, he was called "Sleepy-Eye" no more.

George was timid in school--afraid to speak up. The teacher would ask him a question and he would whisper the right answer--and then say he did not know.

But outside of class he was a match for any of the boys. Short and stocky, with muscles made strong by hard work, he was hard to beat in a wrestling match.

And there was always competition of some kind during recess. The boys would leave the school building bumping and pushing at each other.

A rooster fight was a game in which opponents folded arms, and then bumped each other. Goal was to push the other fellow out of line.

Square wrestling also was popular. Two boys placed hands on each other's shoulders, and then went to it. The match would last until one boy had been thrown on his back. Clothes had to be strong because they were grabbed, pulled and yanked.

During winter, the coach set up a boxing ring in the basement. No one could defeat George. He'd just walk right into his opponent, with fists flying, never caring if he got hit. It was all offense with him.

One time, though, he received the short end. As a school custom, whenever a boy came to school with new shoes, two boys would hold him erect and the others would spit on the new possessions. It was not considered proper for anyone to wear anything but old clothes.

One day George went to school with brand new boots. They had soft leather tops, and looked very nice. It didn't take long for them to be spotted.

"Look at G.A.'s new boots!" someone yelled. And before George knew what was happening, he was off the ground and getting the treatment. He kicked and squirmed, but it was no use. His boots were never new again.

George suffered from a stomachache for months. He rushed off to school in the morning after chores, rushed home at noon for lunch, hurried back to school, and then rushed home after school to begin the chores again.

One day he was out in the fields cultivating corn with a team of horses when a dark cloud appeared in the sky. Soon big drops of rain began to fall.

It wasn't a bad shower. George knew he should have kept on working. But, being a boy, and since he was getting tired of working, he used the shower as an excuse for a rest and climbed under the wagon at the edge of the field.

As he sat there, a bolt of lightning suddenly struck in the corn where he would have been if he had kept on working.

He was glad then that he had stopped.

John, his brother, helped with the work some, but he was not so conscientious as George. He was more apt to play around.

One day, George was plowing with John. They uncovered a snake. John started playing with the wriggly thing.

"Get back to work," George ordered. "If you're not back at work next time around, I'll wrap that snake around your neck."

Next time around, John was still playing with it, so George wrapped the snake around his neck.

Ever after that, John had an aversion to snakes. He killed them whenever he saw one.

George felt to blame, and was very sorry for what he had done.

George loved animals. Especially horses. He knew a horse's every whim and wiggle.

"If you want to know what a horse is going to do," he told his little sisters one time, "just keep your eye on his ears or his tail.

"If he tries to touch the ends of his ears and puts his head down, you may be sure he is going to buck. If he keeps his ears pointed at the side of the road, he is looking for something at which to be scared.

"If he waves his ears around in all directions, he is planning mischief. If they lean slightly backward, wagging with every step, he feels purely lazy. Should he put his ears decidedly back and shake his tail nervously, he is likely to kick."

George normally was kind to animals.

Maybe a tiny lamb would lose its mother on a stormy night. He would bring it into the kitchen and he and the girls would nurse it back to health.

If the weather was cold, he made a coat out of a grainsack for his young calf to wear.

He was patient with animals. One time he was having trouble getting some piglets onto the scales. He had built a framework and made an approach, but they refused to go on. Finally, he backed them on.

One year Papa gave him a colt to break. George gentled it, fed it and played with it until it was very tame.

Then, when it was old enough to ride, he taught it to carry him by first putting a blanket on its back with a belly-cinch; then, a saddle, and finally, pulling the colt to a pole and climbing on himself.

The horse just walked off, carrying him.

Cats were a little different. They multiplied by the dozens around the farm, and it was his unpleasant job to drown the little ones. He put them in a tub and placed bricks on them to hold them down.

One time he left them on the back porch, and the little girls sorrowfully took the dead kittens and buried them, with flowers on their graves.

Sometimes the execution was carried out with vengeance. One cat was drowned because it had been eating chickens. Another--an old tomcat--was hung for killing young kittens by chewing their necks.

George used the kittens' box to lure the tomcat to his doom. He fixed the box so it would fall down onto the animal, after the tomcat was under it. Then he carefully slipped a rope around the cat's neck.

The younger children were not allowed to witness the execution. But they watched from the upper story windows, and could see the lantern light and the older children down below.

Another time George beat a dog to death--for a good reason. He thought the dog was rabid.

In general, though, he was good to all animals, including cats and dogs.

Lucy came running into the house one day.

"Mamma, come out and see George," she cried. "He's feeding all the cats at once!"

Mamma and the other girls went out to see.

There was George, milking the cow. And around him was a semicircle of cats--black, white and spotted--all standing on their hind legs. George was directing a stream of milk from the udder into the open mouth of each one in turn.

Mamma laughed. It did look cute.

"I've heard of cowboys," she remarked. "But this is the first time I have ever heard of a cat-boy!"

After that, George was widely known as the "cat-boy." And every night for years, the cats lined up, some the Tallmons' cats, some belonging to neighbors, waiting for their warm, fresh dole.

George hurt some roosters one time, unintentionally.

He was having trouble getting them to roost. Every night he would catch them one by one and place them on the roosts in the chicken house.

One night a couple of roosters were giving him an especially bad time. They just wouldn't roost, and insisted on staying outside.

Provoked, he stepped on each of their heads as he was carrying them heads down, back to the chicken coop. They sat on the roost very well that time, and he thought he had solved the problem.

Next morning they were dead.

George, with many responsibilities, seldom had time to play with his sisters. But once in a while, he had fun with them.

He enjoyed turning cartwheels from level to level in the haymow, for their benefit.

He also liked to tease his sisters--in a joking way.

One year he fed out a litter of pigs. He gave each a name. When he called them to dinner, he went down the list in regular order:

"Come Gallagher, Murphy, Clare, Angie, Sue, Lucy, de Sausage, Van Tulia, Ham, Pork!!"

He'd sing out so all the neighbors could hear. The girls were rather insulted and a little embarrassed.

He teased Margaret by feeding her turnips to her cat-- Margaret loathed turnips and took it for granted her cat did, too.

And he grabbed Lucy and tickled her. She squealed beautifully--and that added to the fun.

Lucy wore her hair in pigtails. One day, she was teasing George. She nagged at him, and followed him around. It was time for him to change his clothes and do the chores.

He started upstairs to his room, and she followed. He couldn't get rid of her. So he grabbed her pigtails, drew them through the door, and closed the door on them.

Then he changed his clothes and went out the window to start the milking.

It wasn't long before she made enough noise so that someone came and freed her.

It was late in the year and the grass was getting short in the pasture. Papa rented 10 acres to guarantee an adequate supply of feed.

George was busy mending harness when some neighbor children came running into the yard.

"The gate's broken in your rented pasture," they shouted. "Your cows are getting out."

George turned to Margaret and Hester, who were playing house in the corn crib.

"Bring a board to fix the gate," he called. Then off he ran to herd up the fugitive cattle.

The little girls dutifully brought a board. It was as long as they were tall. They carried it between them, one on each end.

George called again.

"Take the board back," he shouted. "The gate was just unlatched."

So they headed for home. It seemed a long way and the board was getting heavy. They climbed through a gate to take a shortcut across the barnyard.

Margaret was on the back end. As they reached the corn crib, she dropped her end, and the board went bump, bump, bump along the ground.

Old Ned, the horse, was eating in the corner of the corn crib. Frightened by the unusual noise, he whirled and kicked--his hoof striking Hester squarely on the right side of her head. She doubled up and fell to the ground.

Margaret screamed. George came on the run and carried the unconscious Hester into the house.

The other children were engrossed in a story Mamma was reading at the time--"The Last of the Mohicans."

"Hester's hurt," George announced.

No one paid any attention.

"Hester's hurt."

Still no reply.

"I guess she's dead!" he exclaimed.

He got lots of attention then.

"What happened to her?" cried Mamma, as she rushed to her side.

"Old Ned kicked her," George explained, laying her down on the couch.

Mamma loosened Hester's clothes and the girls brought warm water. Mamma tenderly washed her and put her to bed. Hester just lay there, limp. They didn't know whether she'd live or die.

The other children went outside and sat in a row on the cellar door.

"If she would only come to!" Margaret exclaimed.

Hester was still unconscious when bedtime came, and Mamma was up with her most of the night.

Next morning Mamma and Papa went out to the porch.

There was Hester, swinging in the hammock, apparently all right (but maybe not).

17.

While in town one day, Mamma reached over the counter of a friend's millinery store to shake hands with her.

"How are you feeling?" the friend asked.

"I am feeling comfortable when I have nothing to do," Mamma replied, "but I can't pretend to do anything."

Said an energetic, fine looking woman who was trying on a new bonnet by the mirror: "There could be no worse illness, to my mind, than that. I would much rather be very sick for a short time, and then be well and able to work."

"Oh, no!" Mamma replied, "I have been calling myself highly favored. I am relieved from responsibility, in mind as well as in fact. I have time to enjoy my home like a good grandmother (if I were a grandmother). My advice is respected, my commands obeyed (if I insist upon them) and if not so useful as others, I feel I am not without some value to the household."

But Mamma wasn't always so philosophical about her condition. Sometimes she was depressed.

"I may as well give up," she wrote in her journal. "I am of no use. Can't order the food, can't mend the clothes, can't read the papers, can't feed myself, can't sleep nor think nor talk--just feel aches and worries and fears and the blues."

But sometimes she was complacent.

"I am having a very comfortable time, truly," she wrote. "Plenty to eat, drink and wear; company, comfort and leisure such as I seldom have known. Yet as strength increases my work seems to increase, too. Plenty of work, care and worry--these should go with the list of my blessings. My husband is pleasant, kind to me and careful of the children. How very lost and lonely I would be without his company and care."

Little did she know what lay ahead.

Papa felt hot, then cold, then strangely weak as he worked late at the Houghton country school one icy winter day.

The pupils had long since been dismissed, and he was correcting papers before trudging home through the cold for supper.

He put more wood on the fire, then felt too hot, and took off his coat. He pulled out his handkerchief and blew his nose again--it had been running all day.

He felt too ill to work any longer. So he turned down the lamp on his desk, put on his coat, and made his way outside.

That strange weakness swept over him again. His legs felt like lead. The distance home seemed unbearable. He slipped and fell into a snowdrift. Struggling to his feet, he went on a little further, then slipped again. He felt like he was climbing a giant mountain. Would he never get there?

Finally he saw the light ahead. He reached the house and pushed open the door.

The family was sitting around the stove--all studying with the one kerosene lamp.

"I don't feel good," he muttered.

"Don't you want some supper?" Mamma asked.

"I'm going to bed."

Papa went into the bedroom, struggled with his clothes, and climbed into bed. Soon the family heard strange words coming from his room through the open door.

Papa was talking funny--silly. Mamma went to see what was the matter. Papa had a high fever and was tossing and turning.

And that was the beginning of a hard siege with pneumonia.

The children went to friends, neighbors and relatives. Papa was very ill.

Mamma nursed him, and the big girls helped by doing the housework. The entire burden of the farm work fell on George's shoulders.

Papa was given quantities of quinine. Care was also taken to maintain exactly the same temperature in the house at all times.

Three stoves were kept going--one in the bedroom, one in the kitchen and one in the living room.

A male nurse was hired to care for Papa.

A neighbor, Mr. Wood, had had pneumonia a short time earlier. His family had tried to get him to go to bed, but he insisted on sitting by the stove. He said, "If I lie down, I'll die." He died anyway, sitting up. So the family was worried about Papa.

Sometimes Papa was rational, sometimes delirious. Nothing suited him. And he was determined to sell the old house.

"Young Fred Card wants to buy it," Mamma said. "But he doesn't want to pay what it's worth."

"But I must sell it," Papa insisted. "I must get it off my hands, cleaned up. I'm going to die, anyway."

So Mamma sold it for the lower price.

Margaret went to stay with Aunt Squire while Papa was sick. She was lonesome and homesick. Then her doll accidentally fell out of the window and Aunt Squire bawled her out.

So Margaret just packed up her things and went to another home where the other children were staying. She probably gave that woman an even greater load than she was handling, but she was allowed to stay.

Papa repeated often his belief he was going to die.

"I must see my children before I pass on across the great divide," he told Mamma.

"Oh, you're going to be all right," Mamma reassured him, although she had her own misgivings.

"No. The time is short. I must see them."

So Mamma brought the children home. She stood to one side of the door and let them in, one at a time.

"Careful! There's a ghoul behind the door post," Papa told Clara as she came in. "You didn't know I was rich, did you?"

Later that evening, Mamma and Clara were relaxing in the sitting room for a few moments after a long and weary day.

"Papa isn't well," Clara ventured.

"No, and I am very much concerned," Mamma replied. "I'm worried about you children."

"Why us?" Clara asked.

"I have only about two more years to live," Mamma replied, her voice calm and serious. "It would be better if Papa lived to take care of you rather than me."

"But you're not going to die," Clara insisted.

"Papa would be in a better position to take care of you," Mamma continued. "I am an invalid and can't work like he can."

"But Angie's already teaching school, and I can get one next fall," Clara said. "George can take care of the farm. . "

"Yes, I know," Mamma went on. "But look at what a hard time we're having now. Very little is coming in. Papa's not working. Doctor and nursing expenses are increasing. And the regular bills must be paid."

"Papa's going to be all right," Clara insisted.

"I hope so," Mamma replied. "I've been praying to God every night to take me, rather than him."

Next day, when the doctor came, Mamma mentioned again that she was praying that Papa would get well.

"Do you think it will do any good?" the doctor asked, dubiously.

"I'm confident it will," Mamma replied. "I have known of other cases where people were saved from death by prayer."

And her prayer was answered. Papa began to get better. It was still a long process, but progress was steady.

Finally, one day, the doctor said he had good news.

"George can get out of bed and sit in a chair a little each day," the doctor advised. "But he must be very careful. He still is a sick man. The illness has left adhesions in his lungs.

"And," he turned to Papa, "you'd better move to a warmer climate. You won't live through another winter in Iowa."

From then on, Papa steadily improved. By May he was up and around, and by summer he was able to do some of the farm work.

One of the children's jobs while living in Grinnell was to pick potato bugs off the potato plants.

They used a pail of water and kerosene, and a stick, and knocked the bugs into a can, which they dumped into a bucket. It was an all-day job.

Sometimes the Jones boys would pass by on their way to town. They lived out in the country, and the boys, Burt and Lynds, were students at Papa's school before he became sick.

The boys always took a shortcut cross-lots, and came close to the potato patch. And they always walked with one following the other.

"Here come the Joneses, walking Jones-file," the girls would say. Then they would chuckle.

The Jones boys were among Papa's brightest students at Houghton School, and were intensely interested in nature study, especially birds. A neighbor who was a drunk and a carouser, but also an ornithologist, had opened a whole new world of interest to them. He taught them the names of birds and how to kill and stuff them. He also taught them how to collect and preserve bird eggs.

So fascinated did the boys become in natural science that Lynds became the official local bird watcher and later dedicated his life to the study of nature--as a professor of zoology and ornithology at Oberlin College.

Burt's interest in biology was more along other lines, such as snakes. He picked them up by the tail, and tied two of them together to see which would get free first.

The two boys started a nature study club, and Papa was able to help them during his convalescence. He suggested that they join the Agassiz Society, a nation-wide natural history club organized by Louis Agassiz, a Harvard professor and leading naturalist of the time.

They did, and George, Clara and Angie, as well as several other young people in the community, became members.

The club met once a month to hear reports and study shells, rocks, birds, astronomy, bugs and plants. The young folks had many good times together.

Mamma started a junior chapter for the younger children. Both groups published journals, in which they printed essays by members of interesting little episodes observed in nature.

An example was:

Experience With a Heron

A Mr. (George) Washington (Tallmon), living on a prairie farm in Iowa, one day caught a slim dark bird which had become entangled in the reeds.

He took it home and, holding it to the light, examined it. "Greenish slate-colored plumage, a long greenish bill, long green legs soiled with standing in the stagnant water; kind of heron, no doubt."

Being suddenly called to the barn, Mr. W. shut the bird up in his bedroom. Returning an hour later, he took a lamp and entered the room, peering about for his guest.

He found it, but not until his foot had fallen on something cool and moist on the floor: which proved, like the things found on his bed, to be part of the heron's supper, being a generous supply of frogs and snakes.

The unwilling prisoner became at once the unwelcome guest and was vigorously cast out into the rain-soaked night.

As winter approached, Papa remembered what the doctor had said about going to a warmer climate. One day he announced that they were moving to California.

"No, we're not," Mamma replied.

"The doctor says I must for my health."

"You can go, but we're going to stay here."

"But how can you get along?"

"We'll get along fine."

"But how about the debts from my sickness?"

"We'll manage."

"Well, I'm going west," Papa said. "I've been wanting to go for a long time. I'm going to sell out here, and start anew, where land is cheap. I can get a good price for my farms, and we can buy many good acres out there."

"I don't want to move," Mamma replied, firmly. "We're settled here. I'm tired of pioneering. We're not going to move any more! . . You'd never let me put my money in another house in my own name, anyway. I know that!"

"Apparently you think I don't handle our money properly." Papa was tiffed. "I suppose you could do a better job yourself!"

"I believe I could," Mamma retorted. "Anyway, my health would not permit me to face the rigors of pioneer life."

Papa went anyway, and when his letters came telling about his trip, Mamma refused to answer them..

Finally, he wrote to George, instead.

My Dear Boy,

Would you like a letter from Papa? I trust you would; and because I think YOU would enjoy a line from one who has always loved you, worked with you and for you; and whom you have always known better, perhaps, than any one else, and who has great hopes for your future--that I gladly spend a little time in writing, tho with pain.

I have written several times to your mother at her request--without getting any reply to even one of my communications.

If she thought I would continue to write under such circumstances, she will meet with disappointment, I greatly fear--but some people never perform any duty faithfully and well, and I presume she has concluded that some things she has in view and letter writing don't go together . .

I thought of you all at home (am I allowed to say home?) I hope you did not suffer loss or harm, tho you had no hard coal--tho the animals, I fear, did not fare so well.

I think of you now as doing all the chores alone, without help or sympathy from those who might aid you, if they would.

Clara should milk--or Sue could learn, but I fear you will get no help from that source. Johnie can help some--but he is delicate and slow, and you must not expect too much from him--you must not scold him.

Keep up your good spirits, my boy, and do your best, and tho you are not appreciated now, you shall not fail of your reward--you may perhaps ask yourself what reward I have today for all my toil and self-denial during the past 20 odd years.

I say to you that I have it in my own self-respect and consciousness of having done my best, and in the assurance that you and the other children, as you grow older and form a more just and larger judgement of things, will not at length condemn me, because I could not complacently accept the entire conditions of my environment.

Well, I have escaped, I have broken away, I have snatched my honor from thraldom and disgrace. I have bought the right to be at peace, but I am not happy . . "

Mamma's attitude softened later, and finally she mailed this letter to Papa:

Dear Papa:

It is about 6 p.m. Yesterday we received quite a long letter from you telling more than before of the life about you . . Georgie and Johnie are out at the barn at work. Sometimes they wish like children that they could shirk a little and when they come indoors dread starting out to the cold and dirt that calls them.

The care of so many animals is surely rather hard upon Georgie. I believe his part is harder than anyone's but Angie's . .

Wonder whether you heard how Mrs. Miller and Briggs sued--me? for your bill for nursing. I paid it . . We have hard coal now . . Mr. Mullens has paid $12 since you left. Sent to him this a.m. and got $1. Don't think from this that we want the money you have been earning. We surely do not. We want you to keep it for yourself. In some way we are going to manage . .

I have had but one nervous chill since you went away. .

Responsibility for the farm work at home fell heavily upon George. He worked early and late, and missed a lot of school.

In class, he was lackadaisical and sleepy. When the superintendent asked him a question, he would look at the superintendent half awake, then say he didn't know.

One day, the superintendent called George into his office.

"You haven't been doing well in school, George," Mr. Hart said. "I think we won't be able to let you graduate this year."

The blow struck George hard. He couldn't graduate? What would his father think? Mr. Hart left him, and as he sat there in the superintendent's office, the tears began to trickle quietly down his face.

One of the other boys, Ed Sanders, happened by and saw George. He didn't say anything.

Papa's letters kept coming. They told about the wonders of California, and smelled fascinatingly of the orange and lemon blossoms they contained.

He wrote about the mild weather, the berries and fruits-- and about an eagle he saw in the mountains.

"I wish I could send you some of the nice fruit," Papa enthused in a letter to Margie. "Would you like an orange, or a handful of almonds, or soft shelled walnuts, or some figs or strawberries? As I cannot send these things, I will eat a few for you!"

He loved it there--and suggested that Mamma sell and move out--as there was "lots of demand for hired girls."

This was probably to plague Mamma, and she was properly indignant.

Papa slept in a tent, as the doctor wanted him to, and worked for a man who owned bees. When Papa was ready to leave for home, late in March, he wanted to give the man something.

The man wouldn't take anything. But, he said, if Papa wanted to buy some honey, that would be nice.

Papa bought 12 four-gallon cans and sent them home to Iowa. The honey lasted for years. It sugared, but still made wonderful honey when melted.

Papa took many other souvenirs with him to Iowa. It was a big moment when he arrived. The children, all excited, had a veritable museum.

He brought a dark sponge that opened out, a double ebony horn (seaweed), and a citron--like a big lemon--dried and not spoiled.

Each article had a story which he would tell to the delight of the children.

He also brought a trap door spider's hole picked up on the desert . . a geoid formed of crystals made by water dripping in the mud . . shells from the Pacific Ocean . . a piece of tile from an old church roof . . salt crystals from the Great Salt Lake . . pine nuts . . edible acorns . . yucca root baskets . . sagebrush flowers . . an Indian stone mortar and pestle . . and five sewing work boxes made from Joshua trees, lined with red silk. All of the articles were special treats.

But perhaps the most special treasure was a real live horned toad!

"It's not a real toad," Papa explained, "but a kind of fat-bodied lizard."

The children didn't care. They were fascinated by the little round creature with horns on his head.

"It seems stiff and sleepy," remarked Clara.

"It hasn't had anything to eat for a week," Papa explained.

Later, the toad warmed up, and ran around the house. Someone accidentally rocked a chair over it and pinched off the end of its tail.

It seemed to like music, and liked to lie on the window sash in the sunshine.

The family fed it egg yolks; it did not like flies.

When the weather was warmer, Papa put the toad in a can of dirt and placed it outside. It got away, and weeks later was found in Susie's garden.

It was placed in a box with a pane of glass on top, but escaped again.

Then one summer day, Mr. Hurd, a bachelor who lived across the road, came over all excited. He had a tin can in his hand, capped with a board.

"Mr. Tallmon! Mr. Tallmon!" he shouted. "Look at the monster I found. It was sitting under the boards of my walk. Oh, my body and soul, man!"

Papa calmly took the can from Mr. Hurd. He was pretty sure what it was.

"Be careful!" Mr. Hurd warned, excitedly. "It's a big huge monster! I've never seen anything like it in these parts before. Oh, my body and soul, man!"

Papa removed the board and emptied the can into his hand.

There it was--the horned toad--much larger than before, and black and fat.

18.

"Is that you, son?" Mamma asked as George came trooping into the house and dropped his books on the table.

"Yes, it is," George replied. He came bounding into the room where she was reading, and planted a kiss on her forehead.

"Can I get you something, Mamma?" he asked.

"No, thanks, George."

"Maybe some milk or an apple?"

"No. That's all right. Thanks for offering. Did you go some place after school? Aren't you a little late?"

"No," George replied, a little surprised. "I came right home."

"But the clock says nearly 5 o'clock," Mamma said.

"It must be wrong. I left school right at 4."

"Maybe Papa set it ahead," Mamma mused. "He often set my clock too fast, before he was sick. He carries a good watch, but it hasn't had the correct time, save by accident, within the last five years. To tell people that he keeps it ahead of time is one way in which he thinks he airs his superiority."

"Papa says early rising is a habit to be admired," ventured her 16-year-old son, plunking himself into a chair.

"I never saw a person except one crazy man who could do two days' work in one," Mamma vowed. "If nervous people can't sleep, it is no gain to their home circle. It just makes them a porcupiny inmate of the house after noon--if not before noon, also."

"But doesn't Papa work hard--when he is able?"

"He likes to make people think he does. He likes to show off what a big man he is around town. He likes to make people think he's smart. But I've suffered so much from the smartness of others that it is a 'sore subject' with me."

Mamma softened, sighed, and added, "I have always tried to be a good and understanding wife. No woman I am sure could in my place have been more patient or self forgetful, and naturally the reward I get is a chance to be more patient and self denying still."

"I think Papa appreciates all you do for him," George offered.

"He doesn't appreciate anything but his personal comfort, convenience and food for vanity," Mamma insisted. "That's why he wanted me to turn this house over to him. He wanted that power, control and pride of possession . . "

"What was that?" asked Papa, coming into the room unexpectedly. "What power and pride of possession?"

"Oh, nothing," said Mamma.

"You were saying something," Papa insisted. "You were talking about me, weren't you?"

Mamma couldn't deny it.

"I was just saying you wanted the deed to this house because you liked that power, control and pride of possession," she admitted.

"Well, the man of the house should control the finances, shouldn't he?" Papa shot back, defensively.

"Not when he goes to speculating all the time," Mamma retorted. "Not when the family never knows when the roof may be sold over their heads. I'm going to keep the deed to this house so that when all else is gone I will still have shelter for my babies."

"You've always thought you could manage better than I or any other person on earth," Papa declared, testily. "All right, then, let's see what you can do!"

Grabbing a paper from the desk and making broad strokes with a pen, he scrolled out the following:

"I, G.W.T., a man in middle age, having had a wife, S.C.T., for more than 20 years, who takes the liberty of criticizing me in business matters--I having a farm of one hundred and twenty acres, near Grinnell, free from debt, and a farm in Franklin Co. of 320 a. mortgaged for $3000, hereby agree that the said S.C.T. may, if she will today sign a mortgage of $800 on the farm near Grinnell, have the entire management of the farm, stock and farm tools for the support of herself and family and the payment of the mortgage."

Then, crossing the room, he threw the paper down in Mamma's lap and stalked to the bedroom.

They could hear bureau drawers opened angrily, and clothes ripped from the closet.

Then Papa came briskly through the sitting room.

"Where's my good shirt?" he demanded. "And my spects?"

Mamma said nothing.

"The remembrance of what I have endured this summer is a shuddering nightmare to me!" Papa snorted. "No living man ever submitted to such treatment, and maintained his manhood and self-respect."

Mamma said nothing.

"I hope you'll make a very fine farmer," Papa continued, as he crossed through the room going the other direction. "There must be some ability among so much pretention."

Mamma kept on reading.

"I suppose the summer climate will do me lots of good," Papa added, carrying a trunk and some shoes to the front door. "I'm taking Johnie with me."

"Johnie?" asked Mamma, almost unbelievingly. Then, gritting her teeth, she said no more.

Soon Papa went to the barn. George was already starting the evening chores.

"I'm doing the most unwise thing of my life," Papa announced, as he began hitching up the team. "There are ample resources for all our wants if I remain at home. But if I go away, as your mother wishes, it is doubtful if both ends are made to meet. I would gladly stay, but for your mother's stubborn and ungoverned temper, and jealous inordinate selfishness. May you never feel their irritating and grinding power!"

Before long, the wagon was packed tight with clothing, provisions and a few tools. Father and son mounted the seat. And the team and wagon disappeared in a cloud of dust, heading south.

Soon their letters began returning to Grinnell, datemarked from Iowa, Missouri--and then Kansas. Then, Papa wrote that he had rented a farm at Fort Scott. Would the family please send a plow, and some books, and other supplies?

Mamma refused to write, so it was left to George to keep up the correspondence. The letters were addressed to him, not Mamma.

George wrote back that he would send the equipment.

Mamma and George managed as best they could. But times were hard. Not only was making a living difficult, but they had to face an added burden of many debts still unpaid.

George worked long, long hours, caring for the farm, doing the field work and squeezing in the chores. He didn't even have John to help him.

Burt Jones came to board for a while, and Mamma hired a Mr. Johnson.

Clara and Angie both were teaching school, which helped with the family income. Nevertheless, that winter was one of the hardest the Tallmons ever had to face.

George planned to sell a fine-looking herd of hogs, which were getting fat, to pay the mortgage. But they became sick and all died. That was a big blow.

It was decided to butcher the old cow--old Nigra--for the winter's meat.

She was so skinny and rawboned the family tried to fatten her up first. But in spite of all the feed they gave her, she didn't look a bit fatter.

Finally, Mamma said they should wait no longer. George didn't want to do the butchering. So Burt said he would do it.

He knocked old Nigra in the head, cut the jugular vein, and let her bleed to death.

George helped take the innards out and cut her up. The meat was very fat--like they had never seen before! They hadn't realized how fat she had gotten. Since she was a dairy cow, it hadn't shown. They dried out gallons of tallow.

Some of the meat was corned but most of it was buried in snow in a big box back of the house.

Angie said she wouldn't touch a mouthful.

"I'd as soon eat my own grandmother!" she vowed.

She wouldn't use even the milk gravy made with the fat.

Clara protested: "But, Angie, it isn't Nige any more. It's just meat." But Angie couldn't see it that way.

The family lived on a shoestring. They ate middling mush, and used salted tallow for butter. However, they did have lots of vegetables stored from the summer's crop, which was a help.

One day a man came to see Mamma. It was just a business conference, but George didn't know it. He was disturbed.

Filling a pail, he threw water against the window, to register his complaint and to tell the man it was time to leave.

After chores, George went to the desk, took out a pen and a sheet of paper, and addressed a letter. He wrote that the family missed Papa, needed his help with the family income, and would he and Johnie drive the team home again?

But the words fell on unresponsive ears. Papa wrote back that he could not come home. Papa scoffed:

> I am sure you underrate your ability and your mother's. Her attitude toward myself was the principal cause of my leaving home--one word of regret at my going, or request that I remain at home, would have kept me there--and only a change of that attitude can make it worthwhile for me to return.
>
> (You know with what reluctance I left last fall. I have spent all I had of money, and obligated myself, for much more--the most of which would have been saved, had I stayed at home. And I doubt if I have been any better, for being hence.)
>
> What you say about my coming home by team, is not practicable. The mud would impede, and the exposure ruin me. No, when I come, it must be in good weather and on good roads, or I must sell everything, and come by rail.
>
> I do not despair of coming home sometime-- notwithstanding the talk you mention, which talk is no emination of mine. The only impediment to my speedy return is your mother's stubborn and ungoverned temper.
>
> Last summer is a nightmare to me. Her persistant disapproval of my best efforts, her sleeping on the floor, on lounges, or with the children to annoy and prevoke me, her letters of ridicule and censure to our friends, etc.- -all constitute such an aggravation as I can not bring myself to volunteer to again endure, however much I love my children and home.
>
> I will do my best, and help all I can, but we will all be happier for my staying away for a season at least.

The next day, another letter came, addressed to Mamma:

> Dear Wife,

Georgie writes me that you forbid his sending me the few books I ordered. As I ordered no books, that are not mine, I cannot understand why you should refuse to let me have them!

It would seem to be only for spite work, which is hardly becoming a person who makes so many claims to wholesome virtues as yourself. For very shame, allow him to send me the few things I request!

Since you have a large library of your own--and I do not interfere with that--have you so little sense of the eternal fitness of things, as to also covet mine?

As there are two unabridged dictionaries, send me one, as there are two sets of 'English Literature,' let me have one set. I also want one Bible, one geography, one physiology, one botany (if it can be spared), one arithmetic, one grammar, one U.S. history . . . my pictures of the children you sent to Cal., the first picture of you I ever had (and any other you choose to send me), my spects . . . "Sanford & Myrton" to read to Johnie (I will return it by mail as soon as I have done with it, as it is yours) . . . and some books of a general nature to read when I am lonely . .

Now, my dear wife, deal kindly by me, and you will never regret it. I need these books, you do not, and if you did, they are mine, and the first instinct of a generous mind is that each one should have his own! Send them at my expense.

You must not feel mortified or humiliated, because I did not jump at your offer for my return. I could not accept it, with any hope of harmony or happiness.

You doubtlessly thought, that I wanted to come home so much, that I would accept any conditions. I did want to come home, and do want to come now, but what gain would it be to me or you, for me to come and rent somebody's farm, no one knows where, or work around by the day or month--knowing nothing as to how you were getting along, or if knowing, still unable--because not permitted--to do or say ought to set you right--or lift your burden!

If I am entirely out of reach, you will not be subject to scrutiny, or hampered by divided councils--nor can you charge me with your mistakes, or get rid of responsibilities that, of right, go with the assumptions of ownership and authority you have made.

. . . Hoping to hear from you soon, and that you will prove to be a good farmer, etc., I remain your loving husband, G.W. Tallmon.

George put down the letter, went to his room, and knelt by the bed.

"Dear God," he said, "please do away with this strife. Please give us a happy home."

His prayer was answered--but not immediately.

19.

A fire was blazing in the kitchen stove and eggs were frying in the frying pan. Water was boiling in a kettle, ready to receive a portion of middlings.

It was dawn, and George and Burt Jones were the only ones up.

Burt was staying at the Tallmon house, helping George with the farm work on a cooperative basis. He brought his team over and helped George, and then George went to the Jones' farm and helped Burt. Burt was doing most of the work on his father's farm by then.

"We must feed the pigs, the calves, water the horses, and get down some hay," George was telling Burt. "And then we can start shucking corn north of the barn."

"You won't beat me today," Burt replied.

"Oh, yes, I will!"

Their voices were getting louder and louder.

Suddenly there was a bang! bang!

Mamma had thrown a couple of shoes against the door. She was too crippled to get up and remind them to be quiet, as others were still asleep. She had called to them, but received no answer.

George just shrugged his shoulders and grinned. "I guess we'd better eat and get out of here," he said. He knew what she meant.

Soon they were out in the field picking corn, husking the ears as they went. George took one wagon, and Burt another, and they raced to see who could fill a wagon the first.

The wagons had a buckboard to catch any ears not slung just right. Each took two rows at a time. Burt let George start first, and then tried to catch up.

Across the field they raced. Burt began edging up on George.

"Look out behind you!" Burt joshed.

George put on a spurt toward the end, but Burt kept coming strong, and forged ahead just before the finish line.

"You couldn't beat a tortoise!" Burt jibed, throwing himself, panting, onto the grass.

"You were just lucky!" replied George, laughing.

Burt picked himself up and leaned over to check his hitch. His back was toward George. George procured a small pumpkin growing in the corn field. He heaved it. It caught Burt squarely in the back and broke to pieces.

Burt turned around, a surprised look on his face. It kind of hurt. Then both he and George burst into spells of laughter.

Burt won the admiration of the girls, too--even the little ones. He was laying a herringbone brick walk that Papa had not completed.

Little Clover had an impediment that made her lisp. She had a sore throat, but was watching Burt that day as he worked. When anyone came along and made any objection to the way Burt was laying the bricks, she jumped on them. She'd say:

"Burt, he'th all right! I like him!"

Burt and the older girls helped George pick sprouts off the potatoes down in the cellar. It was a time-consuming job, and took two full days.

It gave Burt a chance to become even better acquainted with his former teacher--Angie--who was only six months older than he.

In his odd moments, George broke the three young mules, Tom, Dick and Harry, to harness by driving and working them with Old Belle.

He also carefully gentled a young Jersey bull, and gradually worked a harness onto him. Then he hitched the bull to the cutter. It was quite a sight to see a Jersey bull pull a cutter across the field.

With more training, George was able to climb onto Nemo, and actually ride him down the road. It was fine fun, although Nemo ran away one time and George had his hands full regaining control. George was pleased with his accomplishment.

Then, one evening, George came in for supper. Mamma said she wanted to talk to him.

"I know you enjoyed breaking Nemo," she said, "and you did a good job. But the neighbors are complaining. A bull is undependable. You might have an accident. Some of the children might get hurt."

The slightest look of anger filled George's eyes.

"I've just gotten the bull trained right," he objected. "I can handle him all right."

"I don't think you'd better hitch up Nemo any more," Mamma insisted.

George said no more. But his usual smile was gone. He whanged the bathroom door with his fist as he left the room.

Clara looked after him in surprise. That was unusually strong action for George, who seldom became angry.

But he didn't ride the bull any more.

Papa's letters told of the crops he and John were raising-- corn, sorghum, sugarcane, hay, watermelons, and other farm products.

Crops weren't good, he reported, and expenses, including board, were eating up profits. He asked George to send patches from a pair of pants he left at home so he could mend a coat-- much as he hated sewing.

He complained of being sick most of the time. One letter told of being down to 120 pounds. He was starting his second ounce-bottle of quinine to offset a burning fever.

"If I die here, you must come for J. and take what little I am worth--have left--for yourself and him, according to my will," Papa wrote.

Johnie, he said, was "fat and well."

"He works very diligently at most things," Papa added. "He prides himself on his knowledge and ability to work and thinks himself quite your equal at most things. I let him have his good opinion of himself--only hoping that as he grows older he may approach yourself in cheerful willingness if not in effectiveness."

George began attending a YMCA group in Grinnell, along with his friends Ed Sanders and Alvin Barker.

The Y was located over one of the stores on Main Street. There was a game room and auditorium; an organ, library and reading room.

In the game room boys played checkers and other games. A high school teacher was physical education instructor and ran the boys through dumbbells, etc. There was also a class in handwriting--the Spencerian literary style of writing--and other principles of penmanship.

Jesse (Jig) Masey, professor at the college, gave lectures on his trip to Europe.

The Sunday afternoon service was much like a church. There were songs and someone gave a talk. The pre-ministerial college students jumped at the chance to give such a talk.

In the fall, George, along with Susie, entered college. Papa was not sure his son would have time for school.

"I don't see how you can do all the work you have on hand, cut all the corn and plow 40 acres--and go to college, too-- besides digging potatoes, etc.," Papa wrote. "How I wish I was with you to help--I cannot do much--but I venture to say that I would accomplish more in a week than almost any other man she could get around her."

George dropped out of school, deciding to take a home study course instead. But Papa was skeptical.

"Your Chautauqua course will not amount to much, I fear--as far as mental discipline and pure education are concerned," Papa advised. "But go ahead--it will be better than nothing--though fitting you for nothing!"

George wrote back that things were going better at home.

Papa began to talk of coming home. At first he mentioned the possibility, but said he didn't think he would.

Then he asked: "Does your boss intend to hire any more men to help carry on the farm? Will she rent the place next year? On what terms will she rent? Would she rent it to me and Johnie? Please find out and write us."

Next he began asking questions about home: "What debts, that Mamma thinks I ought to pay, are still unpaid? What will the income of the farm probably be this year? Have you made any debts this season, that you must meet this fall?"

Then: "If I cannot see my way clear to come home, I want you to know that it is through no unwillingness on my part."

Before long, Papa wrote that he and Johnie were coming home.

It was a joyous time when they arrived. There was lots to catch up on and much talking to do. Papa made it clear that he would start anew his responsibilities as father and husband.

He returned to Kansas temporarily to finish up business there. While he was gone, Mamma wrote him a conciliatory letter.

"Dear husband," she said. "Thus I reply to the 'Dear Wife' with which you began your letter to me.

"If you can truly love me and I can trust that you do, then you will be dear to me always . . .

"I think if you had seen the children marching this evening you would have forgotten your lame hands as I did my feet . .

"George was drillmaster. They enjoyed it so well they were loath to stop--all but John, who is not used to floating with the current, I suppose.

"It will be more hard for you than for him, I think, to become one of a family instead of being the only person under consideration, though perhaps I ought not to say so after evidence you are giving that you intend to do the right thing (and please me).

But, ever since I first knew you, you have shown you could make yourself do what you pleased when it pleased you to. And now you can come and work for us like a man and a father, and a Christian, also.

"Do you suppose you can be a husband also in feeling? I wonder sometimes how wifely I shall about to be . .

"Last night Clara gave Mr. Proctor $5, saying you sent it to him. She left $5 also at Walter Little's and took a receipt for it, for you . . . She next went to Dr. Harris' (and) . . left $15 for him as you desired . .

"There is no sense, my dear, in your saying you cannot regain your good name. Everyone will gladly appreciate your trying to pay up the old debts, that is, unless you say to them as to me that your good name was lied away, when they might not believe you.

"I have got a bill from the Grange for over $50--to be settled by the end of the year . . "

The winter was cold, but Papa seemed to get along all right, although he complained of not feeling well.

Mamma was becoming more and more of an invalid. Most of the time she spent in a chair. She could walk across the room very slowly, very painfully. She was in terrible pain day and night.

Nice days she was able to spend in the garden. She loved beautiful flowers. With the help of the children she was able to keep them growing.

George dug up the ground for her. Each of the little children were given something to plant. Then they felt the plants were partly theirs.

Usually Mamma didn't try to go to church. The damp stone floor kept people with rheumatism away. But, on one occasion she did. The girls helped her get ready.

"How pretty you look!" Lucy told her, and she blushed like a young girl.

One day Mamma sat in her chair, sewing. She held the needle in her hand as best she could, and clumsily pushed the needle in and out of the cloth.

Hester was carefully brushing and combing her long hair. Clover brought a cup of hot chocolate, and Edith ran to get a footstool for her feet.

Edith accidentally bumped Mamma as she passed by.

"Don't do that!" Mamma scolded her, sharply. Then her tone softened. "I'm sorry," she said, "but when you bump me, it hurts awfully."

"I didn't mean to," said little Edith, her eyes down, an anxious look crossing her face.

"I know you didn't," soothed Mamma, touched by Edith's cute way. "Come here, let me hug you."

"Read us a story!" Edith begged.

"All right," said Mamma. So she read a fairy tale, and sang some songs she knew as a girl.

Then she started telling them about when she was in Louisiana, and asked Clara to get out the big banana leaf and the palm leaf she brought back with her.

When the story was over, the younger children ran outside to play.

"That was a happy time," remarked Clara. "It's always fun to hear you tell stories."

"I wish I felt more like it," Mamma replied.

"I keep hoping you will get better," Clara said. "It seems you improve for a while, and then you suffer a relapse."

"I don't want to leave you children half grown," Mamma said, sadly. Then she lay her head back against the wall, and added, "I feel tired. I think I'll go back to bed for a while."

That winter, a siege of grippe hit the family. Edith had it first, and then Margaret got it, and had to stay home from school for awhile.

In March, Mamma caught it, too. She got up too soon, had a setback, and had to return to bed. She was quite sick.

Then, one day, when Clara and Margaret were the only ones home, they heard strange noises from her bedroom.

"What was that?" Margaret asked.

"Sounds like Mamma!" exclaimed Clara.

They rushed to her room and found she had had a stroke. She could not talk, and was unable to use one of her arms and one leg.

She kept trying to tell them something, but they just couldn't figure out what it was. Later they decided she wanted her hair combed. It hadn't been combed that day.

"A bit of lime, deposited in one of her joints, was carried to her brain, stopping a blood vessel," the doctor explained.

Mamma was paralyzed three weeks.

She couldn't talk. The family could understand when she tried to say, "Yes," or "No." She would nod or shake her head. But that was all.

She tried to tell the girls something one day, but they couldn't understand. They made suggestions, but they were so far from what she wanted, it was funny. They all laughed about it. She made a joke out of it; she let it be funny.

She indicated she wanted a paper and pencil. They were brought to her. She tried so hard to write, but she couldn't control her hand. The girls couldn't make out what she was trying to say.

Once she managed to murmur, "Johnie." That was all.

Most of the time, she lay quietly in her bed. The family spent as much time as possible in her room, talking to her.

The strain was perhaps hardest on Papa. Worried and concerned, he often went in to speak to Mamma, and sit by her bed.

Lucy was ill with pneumonia. Her bed was in the same room as Mamma's. Clara and the older girls were busy caring for both of them. Angie was teaching in Dakota.

Neighbors stopped by to see how Mamma was getting along.

One of them remarked, "And she's only 47!"

"Is Mamma going to die?" little Edith asked at the supper table one evening.

"She's very, very ill," Papa replied, gravely.

"Does she want to die?" Edith asked again.

"I don't suppose anyone wants to die."

"She told me she didn't want to leave her family half grown," Clara offered.

"But I heard her say just before her stroke: 'I'm so tired! I want to go home,'" Lucy reported.

"Maybe she's ready to go, then," Papa said, his voice breaking just a bit.

Clara quickly changed the subject.

Papa moped around the house. He spent all the time he could, talking, consoling, being with her. He didn't feel equal to doing the chores; many essential things were left undone.

"Don't leave me, Mamma!" he implored. "Don't leave me! I love you. I need you!"

But, gradually, Mamma became worse. She weakened, and her illness became more and more debilitating.

The family gathered about her bedside, taking turns trying to speak to her, assuring her of their love. Papa was there constantly. He watched griefstricken as each day she seemed to get weaker and weaker.

Then, one night, Papa awakened the children to tell them she was going. It was March 1, 1890.

The family gathered around her bed. She was breathing heavily--a sign that death was close.

George was out doing the morning chores. He didn't want to be there.

Mamma took Papa's hand. She shook and shook and shook it.

No one said a word. But, by the light in her eyes, they could tell she forgave Papa for all the unhappiness he may have caused her.

Then her eyes closed. Her hand shook no more.

She tried to breathe; she fought for a final breath.

Then the breaths came no more. Her head fell to one side. She lay there quietly, at peace.

Tears ran down the children's faces. Papa was like a ghost.

She was gone now; she was with Jesus.

20.

Word was sent to Dakota, and Angie came home for the funeral.

Neighbors and friends were wonderful. Someone brought food, and others helped prepare dinner. The house was decorated with pink carnations.

A coffin was set up in Mamma's bedroom, and guests gathered in the living room.

The service was simple but beautiful. The minister spoke of the wonderful woman and mother Mamma had been.

Then the coffin was carefully loaded onto a wagon and the procession to the cemetery began.

Lucy, still recovering from pneumonia, wasn't able to go, and she was too bashful to go to the kitchen where the women were working.

So she hid in a closet--a cold closet where she should not have been, with her pneumonia. But she was found, and a kindly woman made her come to the kitchen, where it was warm.

After the funeral was over, and the guests were gone, Papa sat down to write a poem to express his grief:

My love is dead. Deep in the ground
I buried her from out my sight.
I raised me up to see the light
And wondered, for 'twas black as night.

My soul is dead. Its light went out
Mid strife for life too hard to bear
The crosses of this earthly care
And crushing burdens of despair.

The family entered an era of happiness and peace after Mamma's death.

Not that she wasn't sorely missed. But the old strains were gone. And Papa was a different person.

He did his best to serve as both mother and father--and did well. He was more kindly than before.

If the girls' cooking didn't turn out the way it should, he would say:

"That was mighty nice. If you try a time or two more, you'll have it just like you want it."

He always encouraged his daughters. "You're the best cooks I've got," he'd say.

He seldom lost his temper any more.

One day he surprised the little girls with a red bicycle. They had done a good job with something--had made the effort. He wanted to reward them. They were thrilled.

Shortly after Mamma died, one of the children came down with scarlet fever and diptheria. The others were banished to homes of friends. When they were finally reunited, Papa was obviously pleased.

"I found it lonely with just one sick child," he said.

Little Edith came home from school nearly every day, crying with an earache. Papa usually was sitting in his big chair in front of the stove.

He would comfort her, put some warm oil in her ear, and then take her onto his lap and hold her.

It would be cozy and warm in his arms, and he'd tell her how his father, when he was a boy, fixed his ear when he had an earache.

"My father," he said, "took a hickory stick. One end he put in the fire, and the other in a bowl. The sap ran into the bowl. Then he poured the warm sap into my ear. It felt so good!"

Papa really missed his wife. One day the girls were sitting around the room when he came in.

"Pretty nice bunch of girls," he told them, "but you can't hold a candle to your mother!"

Papa got up early in the morning--2 or 3 a.m. Later, about 5 a.m., when it was time for the girls to get up, he tapped on the ceiling.

Clover was best about responding. She rapped on the floor with her shoe to show she was awake and getting up.

First child dressed and downstairs in the morning won so many pennies. Margaret was slow and seldom got the prize. Once in a long time she did.

Papa, up early, got a head start on breakfast, before he started the chores. He put cornbread or biscuits in the oven and then called the girls, who were supposed to supervise taking the hotbread out.

"Come, girls! Come girls!" he would call, and then go out to do the chores.

The hotbread was baked in a big black pan. Breakfast was a real meal--with biscuits, eggs, potatoes, and ham or bacon.

Although Papa went to bed early, he didn't make it possible for his family to do so.

He stayed outside until the chores were done--often until 8 o'clock at night. Then the family ate, and the girls had to do the dishes and their studying. This made it hard and late for the girls. But that was the routine: they were used to it.

Clara was so sleepy one night she just couldn't do the supper dishes. She lay down and went to sleep on the steps, leaving the lamp lit. Papa came along and blew out the light and sent her to bed, leaving the dishes until morning.

The housework was divided among the girls.

Susie--after Clara left home--posted a list of assignments inside the cupboard door. The schedule changed every week. If one of the girls didn't like a particular job, she knew next week she would have something else to do.

The girls were pretty good about cooperating. And, of course, Papa was a court of last appeal.

While doing the dishes, the sisters sang, told stories, or practiced things learned in school. Susie made up games to help dishwashing go faster.

For example, two special dishes were designated as a king and queen, and others as attendants. The washer was given a head start, and the wiper had to wipe attendants before wiping the king or queen.

The wiper tried to catch up, and the washer attempted to wash fast enough so that the wiper didn't get her king and queen. She might get some of the attendants, but the washer tried to get more attendants in line before the wiper was down to less than two dishes.

Generally the wiper won in the long run--by the time the washer reached the pots and pans, washing was too slow to stay ahead.

When the little girls did the dishes, the dishpan was put down on a chair. Or they stood on a chair or stool.

The girls had other chores to do--such as putting up fruit for the winter. One year Clara canned 365 quarts of blackberries.

The girls decided one year to celebrate Thanksgiving as the Pilgrims did. There were great plans and whisperings and much activity around the kitchen.

When the family came to the table, a few kernels of corn were laying in front of each plate. That was all.

"What's this?" thundered Papa.

"The Pilgrims were thankful for small blessings," Susie explained, fearfully.

"Well, bring on the Thanksiving dinner," Papa insisted. "We are not Pilgrims."

"We wanted you to say grace over the corn kernels, and then bring on the rest of the food," Susie said, almost in tears.

But Papa wouldn't do it. He insisted that they put on the whole dinner before saying grace.

The girls didn't drink coffee when they were young--their mother didn't, either--and they tried to persuade their father not to, either.

He was sympathetic, and agreed with their plan. But later they discovered he was getting up early and fixing his own coffee.

So after that, he had his coffee brewed for him regularly.

Papa went to Chicago every fall to lay in supplies and clothing for the winter. He brought back underwear, groceries, crackers by the barrel, sugar by the 100 pounds, shoes, maybe a new coat for everyone.

Some years, last winter's clothes were brought out from the "Sunday trunk" and apportioned to whichever child they would fit.

All of the children stood in a row to be measured. Hester always objected to wearing a coat someone wore the previous year.

The clothes were rather plain, and not too appealing to young girls. Papa made them wear high-top, heavy shoes. They had to polish them with men's polish which you spit into and brushed on.

Margaret hated to go to church. She wouldn't have minded if the family had sat in the back. But Papa insisted on walking clear to the front, and then standing by the aisle and letting all the little girls file into the pew, one at a time.

A visible smile swept over the entire congregation. Margaret could have sunk through the floor.

The girls had their chores to do outside, too. Such as herding the cows to pasture, driving the horses when Papa and George were shucking corn, or pumping water for the calves.

They had their fun times, though. Picnics at Jones' Grove were a special treat. The grove was full of plum, crab apple, hickory and other trees, and people from town came out to gather the fruit and nuts.

George always asked permission from the Jones family, which owned the grove. Most of the people just helped themselves, even though they had to pass between the Jones' house and barn to reach the grove.

Part of the fun was singing as the wagon made its way into the country and through the woods, or unpacking the baskets and dinner pails, or picking violets and bloodroots and bluebells.

By this time, Angie and Clara were old enough to have boy friends. The two Jones boys were getting rather sweet on them; Burt liked Angie and Lynds was enamored of Clara.

Whenever the sisters' beaux came to call, George and the other children seized the golden opportunity to heckle them.

One of the tricks--George at the helm--was to throw pails of water on the windows, to make the lovers think it was raining.

The younger children had to go upstairs to bed. But they made a lot of noise, and let the slats fall out of the bed in the room exactly above the library, where the young couple was sitting close together.

Often when Lynds, after visiting Clara, was ready to go home, he found the legs of his horse lashed together with a trace chain, or a wash boiler tied to its tail.

One night Lynds tied his pony by the hay barn. While he was in the house, George transferred the pony's saddle to a Jersey cow, put the pony in the barn, and the cow in its place.

Then George and the others hid in the granary to see what would happen.

At 10 o'clock, Lynds came out. He realized it was a joke, and he was pretty sure George was behind it.

So he jumped on the cow and rode off anyway. The cow balked a little, but he got it out the driveway and down the road, running.

George sprang up and yelled, "Stop, horse thief!"

Lynds kept going.

George gave chase on foot, yelling, "Whoa!" But the cow didn't pay any attention.

George tried to crawl under a barbed wire fence that separated him from the road and catch the reins. But he couldn't keep up with the cow.

Finally Lynds stopped the mount and got off himself.

That was the last of the tricks George played on Lynds while Lynds was courting Clara.

21.

The family was gathered around the big, round table, eating supper. The men were still dressed in their dusty farm clothes, but their faces and hands were well scrubbed.

"Pass the meat, please," asked John, "--and the carrots." He was starting to shoot up, and it seemed he was always hungry.

Lucy passed the pork chops and Margaret the carrots. Everyone ate for a while in silence.

"Guess what day next Sunday is, Papa!" Hester's eyes shown.

Papa knew, but he made a wild guess. "Fourth of July's passed. It can't be Christmas yet. Is it Thanksgiving?"

"No," exclaimed Hester. "It's Aug. 31. It's my birthday. I'll be nine years old!"

"Will you really?" asked Papa. "Why, it doesn't seem that long since you were born. Let's see, we were living in town by that time, weren't we?"

"Yes," replied Hester. "I was born in the saloon house."

"So was I," chimed in Margaret. "None of us younger children got to live on the farm."

"The older children were lucky," complained Clover.

George advised, "There are advantages to living in town."

"But we've never even seen Wild Rose Farm," said Hester. "We feel cheated."

"Well, you're not going to be cheated any more," declared George. "I'll take you out there for Hester's birthday."

The children were so excited they could hardly finish their supper.

"We're going to the farm! We're going to the farm!" they exclaimed, clapping their hands and jumping up and down.

"You settle down and finish eating, or you won't go," Papa warned.

Eagerly the children leaped out of bed when the day arrived. George hitched up Old Ned and the girls fixed a picnic lunch. Soon they were off, headed for the country.

George pointed out the farms and hills, flowers and crops, and wild lilies growing alongside the road.

They turned a corner, drove under a train track, and George said: "Right here is where the property starts." He pointed, "There is the grove of trees Papa planted. And, down the road, you can see the farm buildings."

They drove nearly half a mile along the dirt road, and then turned into the driveway. They passed the big barn with stone foundation, and drew up in front of the little white farm house.

Mose Robbins--the man who bought the farm from Papa-- came out to greet them.

"The little girls have never seen the farm," George explained. "I promised to bring them out to see it."

"Look around all you want," Mr. Robbins replied.

George took his sisters on a tour of everything--the big barn where Jennie the mule was hurt; the horse barn; the pen where Peggy, the big spotted sow, stood with her front feet on the fence; the barn lot where Bill William the mule chased Angie; the pasture where Snowball, the white cow, hid her twin calves, and all the other places they had heard so much about.

When the little girls reached home, tired and happy after a long day, George helped tuck them into bed.

"Thank you, George," each of them said. "We don't feel cheated any more."

George was someone special to his little sisters. They admired him, talked to him, and had fun playing with him.

Edith took hold of his hands, and then walked right up the front of him, like up the side of a wall. Often he would swing her, toss her into the air, or do other athletic stunts with her.

During the winter, George took the girls for rides in a bob sled over the snow.

He was a big brother who was dependable, kindly and nice to have around.

He was also known around Grinnell as a boy with high ideals, and very conscientious--a serious-minded, quiet, unassuming young man. He was known best as one of the Tallmons, and a brother to the Tallmon girls.

He spent most of his time helping his father. He got up in the morning, got dressed, did his chores, got his meals, and went through the day's routine, quietly and without a fuss. He did little talking, except around the table.

He liked social times once in a while, such as the Agassiz meetings. He didn't talk to girls much. He had a girl friend, but worshiped her from afar. She wouldn't give him a tumble.

George's faith was earnest and practical. He believed a person should do the things he knew were right. And he tried to practice his beliefs.

He never uttered a profane word. He wouldn't tell, or even listen, to dirty stories. And he refrained from smoking or drinking as a matter of principle.

Although a short, stocky, muscular fellow, he was never a person to engage in a fight. He was more apt to laugh troubles off.

He had a compelling desire to do something to help make the world a better place. That was one reason why he joined the YMCA. He served as a sort of leader for younger boys.

One night as George was walking home, some boys were throwing stones at a scared little yellow kitten clinging to the top of a telephone pole.

George asked what they were doing.

"Oh, having some fun," they said.

"Why don't you take on someone nearer your own size?" George asked. "I'll stand here by the pole and you can throw stones at me instead."

Strangely enough, the boys did not throw a single stone. They slipped away one by one. Then the kitten's protector called and coaxed until the little animal backed cautiously down the pole and into his big, kind hands.

"Poor little kitty cat!" he soothed. "There! Go on into your poor little mistress' house, and don't run off again. This is a big, bad world!"

Another night, George arrived home late from the YMCA. All the lights were out, and the family had gone to bed. George thought it would be fun to climb up the trellis and in through the window.

Maybe he was feeling extra gay because a family of girls from across the street was staying temporarily with the Tallmons, as their mother had died.

Quietly, he climbed to the roof in the moonlight, then slipped in through an upstairs window, and went to bed.

He thought no one knew what he had done, but he found out differently when he went downstairs to breakfast the next morning.

He was greeted by a chorus of feminine voices, singing to the tune of, "She sat on the veranda and played her guitar," only with different words.

Their song started out like this: "Little Georgie went down to the YMCA, YMCA, YMCA."

And it went on to say he had been to the bad circus grounds (only he hadn't--the girls were just teasing), had come home late, and climbed through the window so no one would hear him.

The girls sang the song to him every chance they got.

Another night, George noticed a wagon full of corn parked across the street. A scoop shovel had been left on the load. A wicked idea flashed through his mind, and he soon was in the wagon, pushing the corn up against the sides, leaving a great hole in the middle.

He didn't take an ear, but it looked as if half the load had been removed. Then he went to bed.

Next morning, when he went downstairs, Papa seemed upset.

"Did you see anyone on the street last night?" he asked George. "Someone stole half a load of corn from the neighbor's."

George laughed and laughed and laughed.

"No one stole any corn," George gasped. "I just scooped the corn to the sides to make it look as if some was gone."

Papa wasn't amused.

"Our neighbor was very angry," he said. "Don't you know better than to do something like that? You go right over and apologize."

"It was only a joke . . " George sputtered.

"I don't care," Papa ordered. "You go explain to him."

So George unwillingly crossed the street.

No one stole your corn," he nervously explained to the neighbor. "When I came home last night, I thought I would have some fun. So I pushed the corn around the sides, to make it look like some was missing."

"Someone stole my corn," the man insisted. "Sure you didn't do it?"

"Not an ear is missing," George assured him. "It just looks that way."

But he couldn't persuade the neighbor until he jumped into the wagon and shoveled the corn into the middle, as it was originally.

22.

George, downtown on a Saturday evening, was attracted by the sound of a band playing on a street corner.

Drawing nearer, he saw a middle-aged man dressed in a blue soldier's suit with blue and red cap, blowing a horn. Beside him was a woman wearing a dark blue dress and a blue silk bonnet with a red ribbon across the front. She was pounding on a tambourine.

Three or four other men, also in uniform, were strumming or tooting various instruments. One was beating a drum.

A crowd had gathered and was listening to the song they sang. George recognized the tune as a popular song of the day. But the words were different.

As he drew close, he realized they were singing a Christian song. And on each of the men's caps and the woman's bonnet were the words, "Salvation Army."

The group carried two flags, one an American flag and the other a yellow, red and black banner with the slogan, "Blood and Fire." The words, "Salvation Army," were also written across the face of the big drum.

The song was lively. And the crowd that gathered listened attentively. Some were townspeople doing their Saturday night shopping. Some were young folks like himself. One was the town drunkard--that night fairly sober.

The song came to an end. Then the captain spoke to the crowd.

"Salvation is available to all who repent," he told them. "No matter how deep your sins, God will forgive you if you only give yourself to Him. Tonight we are holding services in Salvation Hall. Come with us and hear the wonderful message of Jesus."

And, with that, the band broke into a new song and began marching down the street. Many of the people turned away. But some followed--including the town drunkard.

Something about the earnest little band of soldiers intrigued George, and he followed, too.

Soon they reached an old store building in the poor section of town. The band turned abruptly from the street and, playing loudly and fearlessly, marched into the well-lighted hall.

George followed along with the others, and took a seat in one of the plain wooden chairs.

The captain, his wife and the soldiers climbed the two or three steps to the platform and sat down. Then the service began.

There were more songs--stirring, lively ones. There was prayer. There were testimonies by the soldiers. Then the captain preached a ringing message on repentance. "You have to be consecrated," he said.

At the end, the captain invited those who wanted to give their lives to Jesus--to come to the pentiform, and show publicly that they repented of their sins and were converted.

George did not go. But he watched as the town drunkard and two or three others went forward and knelt at the altar.

As he walked home, George could not forget the Christian group that was so earnest, and whose teachings were not so different from the faith he had learned all his life.

He started attending meetings more often. Soon he was consecrated as a soldier himself.

Every night he played a cornet in the band, and helped with the services. He even got up and talked when he had to, although he was backward about doing so.

At the close of each service, he helped mingle with the congregation and talk individually with the people about repentance.

Some of the Salvation Army people were surprised that George, from such a socially prominent family, would enter Salvation Army work--and after attending only a few meetings.

His family was surprised and somewhat upset, too. Especially Papa.

And when George approached his father and told him, "I'm going to become a Salvation Army officer," Papa was mortified.

"I'll pay your way through the finest theological school in the country if you want to be a minister," Papa promised. "But, don't you join that radical outfit!"

"What's wrong with the Salvation Army?" asked George.

"I can't see how a boy like you from a high-class college community can go into an organization which caters to people who drink, play cards and dance," Papa objected. "You live in a town where there is a college atmosphere and people are respectable and interested in intellectual development. The only people who ever go to those meetings are from Sleepy Hollow. They're just drunkards, morally careless and diseased people."

"But they are the very people who need help," George insisted. "The Salvation Army reaches a lot of folks who would not know of Jesus otherwise."

"Natually I'm pleased with any help given to anyone," Papa allowed. "But the Salvation Army is made up mostly of people who have backslid, and some backslide again. Some of its people don't have the stamina to live up to its teachings. Their private lives aren't always lived to the best advantage."

"I think they're very earnest," George insisted. "Maybe a few have backslid. But look how much worse they would be if they had never joined the Salvation Army."

"I don't agree with their method of 'winning souls,'" Papa scoffed. "Loud music on the streets, preaching on the corner, shouting, 'Halleluiah.' How dignified is that?"

He looked at his son, and pressed home his point.

"George, you are college material. I'll pay your way through Harvard, or any other seminary in the country. You could do so much more as a trained minister. You could reach the respectable people, who would appreciate your message. Of course, there is also my pride. I want my son to go as far as he can."

"But, it's the down-and-outers who need help," George insisted. "It's the immoral people who need the message. Maybe services are held on street corners. Maybe they are loud. But that's the way to reach these people."

Papa had seldom seen his son so adamant.

"The Salvation Army is low, rude and unrefined!" he snapped, growing impatient. "To think that my son would lower himself to that level! The Salvation Army shouldn't even call itself an army. It's just a bunch of peculiar radicals, full of the riffraff of the community."

"Winebibbers, murderers--" replied George, quietly. "Jesus fraternized with the riffraff of his age."

Papa saw that he was getting nowhere. His son, normally so obedient and willing, was determined and unshakable.

"I'll tell you what," Papa finally said. "You go to South Dakota and talk to Uncle Albert. He's a Methodist minister. You talk to him, and see what he has to say. He can give you good advice."

George agreed to go, and within a few days was discussing his problem with the Rev. Albert Carhart. His uncle was sympathetic.

"I'm not sure I have made the best use of my life in the ministry," he confided to George. "If that's the way you feel called, perhaps that's the way you should go."

George returned home determined more than ever to become a Salvation Army officer.

"I feel that is the thing for me to do," he told Papa, simply. "I must do what I am called to do. I must do what I feel is right."

Papa was bitterly disappointed.

The girls, too, were shocked and humiliated. Margaret was embarrassed and very much ashamed. It was as if her brother couldn't afford an education to become a minister!

"George could make a lot more of himself in the ministry," she told Lucy. "The Salvation Army seems so uncouth."

"George isn't being very thoughtful," Lucy agreed. "The full care of the farm will fall on Papa's shoulders."

When the time came for George to leave for Omaha to enter cadet training, Lucy helped him get ready.

As she packed his bag, she included a note for him to find later, in which she quoted Longfellow: "Do your duty and leave the rest to God."

She meant to imply that George should stay home and do his duty to his father, and that God would see to it that he got a chance to serve Him.

But George took it to mean that he should do his duty to God and his conscience, and leave the consequences to the Lord.

"Are you sure you're doing the right thing?" Clara asked as George gathered his things together.

"I believe the Salvation Army is a way for me to do some good," he told his sister.

Reluctantly, Papa took George to the train station to see him off.

The train pulled into the station and George mounted the steps. He turned back to his father.

"I'm sorry to be leaving you, Papa."

"Well," Papa retorted, "it sure looks like it!"

23.

George found Salvation Army training rigorous. Part of the instruction was actual field work among the slums of Omaha. It was tough--and dangerous. He was mauled once or twice by hoodlums.

The down-and-outers didn't want to be helped.

Trainees were kept busy selling War Cries, the Salvation Army paper. The recruits also took food and clothing to people in the slums, held meetings, and prayed with the ones who showed interest.

They didn't have much to eat, and only watered-out milk to drink.

Once while George was playing in the band on a street corner, someone threw an apple and hit him in the face, cutting his lip.

But George wouldn't give up. This is what he had decided to do, and this is what he was going to do.

He looked at the note Lucy had packed in his bag. "Do your duty and leave the rest to God."

He was doing his duty, he thought to himself, and God would take care of his father's displeasure and other problems.

Next chance he had, he must thank Lucy for her note. It was a wonderful consolation.

Life in the training garrison was under rigorous military discipline. Every act and every move was under strict orders.

George's instructor was a grizzled old colonel who had been with the Salvation Army since its start. He kept a stern but kindly hold on the class of young recruits who filled the plain, high-ceiling room.

He told them how the Army was organized in England by William Booth, a Methodist minister who decided to devote his life to working with "people everyone else had forgotten."

"Worldly pleasures and elaborateness must not interfere with the work," the old colonel reminded them. "That is a cardinal rule.

"All wealth should go toward helping the poor and unfortunate. That is why Salvation Army officers cannot wear gold or other jewelry. Jewelry is evidence of personal wealth and stress on material things."

George glanced at his watch. He had traded his gold case to his father for a silver one--because of this rule.

"When you are conducting a salvation meeting," the colonel continued, "conduct it vigorously, with holiness and concern for the unsaved souls.

"Speak as a dying man to dying men. How would you speak if you were sure that in 60 minutes you with 19 others in that hall would be in eternity, and at present you alone are saved?

"In such a case, how you would entreat and warn and implore and weep! Do as much like that as you can every time you stand with God's message of mercy among the poor sin-smitten, dying souls.

"Stick to your Bible, be much on your knees, sacrifice self, follow Jesus. Thus get power that will make stronghearted sinners bend. Be a soul saver."

George lived for weeks without doing anything wrong or deliberately sinning. He didn't have a chance to do differently. He lived in an atmosphere of almost continuous prayer, praise and service, and didn't have time for wrongdoing.

He decided he would never get married, but just work for God and souls.

But alas for noble resolutions! Within three months he found out that a certain little Danish girl was setting her cap for him.

Promptly turning himself around, he devoted himself to booming War Cries. Only to find that every pretty face he saw and every nice girl he met had an attraction for his poor lonesome heart.

He kept his mind on his work, though, and at the end of the training period, he was commissioned a lieutenant. His first assignment was Ottumwa, Iowa.

Captain Shaddock was waiting for him when his train pulled into the station.

"Well, hello there, Lieutenant Tallmon," the captain greeted him. "Welcome to Ottumwa. You don't know how glad I am to see you! I've been without an assistant for three months."

They walked on down the street, passing the business houses, and climbed the stairs to the two-room apartment over the Salvation Army hall. The rooms were plain, and the only furniture consisted of an old-fashioned double bed, a couple of chairs, a desk and a table.

"Set your bags in here," Captain Shaddock said. "I'll show you the hall downstairs."

Captain placed a key in the lock and pushed open the door.

The hall was plain, too--just one large, square room with a platform at one end, and several rows of chairs.

"We have an active corps, but numbers are small," the captain said. "See that broken window up in front? Some toughs tried to break up a meeting last week. Ottumwa is a hard old shop."

Then, glancing at his watch, he said quickly: "We must eat supper. Street meetings start in an hour."

They returned to the apartment, and, as Captain was setting a meager amount of bread and cheese on the table, George wondered what Ottumwa would be like.

He soon discovered that life there was even more strenuous than the training garrison. He and the captain had little food or money. They were busy from morning until late at night holding services, visiting homes, praying with the sick, selling War Cries.

Often they went for days on almost nothing to eat, or very little. The corps bills had to be paid first before they could take any money for themselves.

But George was not disheartened. Zealously he went about his work.

One day he was selling War Cries, stopping at every business establishment down the street. He came to a saloon and plunged right in.

The place was crowded with men at the bar. George started down the line.

"Would you like to buy a War Cry?" he asked the first beer drinker.

"Get out of here with those," the bartender ordered. "We don't want any of you salvationists around here."

Then he grabbed George by the arm and threw him out the door--right between two policemen. George walked on down the street.

Next week George was selling War Cries in the same neighborhood, and went into the same saloon again. The reception was entirely different. The bartender made everyone in the place buy War Cries, and purchased one himself.

George never knew what caused the change of attitude, unless it was the policemen who had been standing at the door the week before.

Another day George was soliciting house to house in the residential area. The activity served not only as a source of revenue, but also as a means of bringing the work of the Army to the attention of the residents.

George prayed with the people if they asked him in.

He went to every house, regardless, by custom. When he came to the Catholic Church rectory, he knocked on the door.

A priest, with black suit and turned-back collar, answered. Before him stood a young, sincere-looking young man dressed in the blue uniform of the Salvation Army.

"I am collecting funds for the Army of the Lord," George explained. "We carry the Word of Jesus to the unfortunate and lost. We help them gain the salvation of their souls."

The priest, somewhat amused, somewhat impressed, invited George inside.

Another priest was standing in the hallway and accompanied the two into the living room.

"Let us kneel in prayer," George said, and they all knelt down together.

"Oh, Lord," George prayed, "be with this house, and these people. May they make an important contribution to Thy Kingdom, and may they be blessed in every undertaking. Amen."

"What is your work?" asked the second priest as they rose from their knees.

"I am a soldier of the Salvation Army," George replied. "We hold services regularly every night except Monday and four times on Sunday at the hall in town. We also work with the unfortunate and the troubled, and maintain relief homes for the oppressed."

"Let me give you something for your work," the first priest said, pulling a large wallet from his pocket.

"I would like to, also," added the second priest.

They pressed coins into George's hand, and George thanked them and headed out the door.

"The Lord be with you," George said, tipping his hat as he walked down the street.

In other ways, George tried to do his job as conscientiously as possible. He played in the band on the street corner each evening, and helped Captain Shaddock with the services.

He gave testimonies, mingled with the congregation, and conducted youth classes on Saturdays.

Down underneath, he was bashful and timid. But he pushed himself forward because he felt called to that work.

Sometimes he found his Salvation Army uniform was a door to helpfulness. People came to him who wouldn't come otherwise--people with problems, those with sickness in their families, those in need, those who wanted help. George always did whatever he could.

Sometimes the requests were of major importance, sometimes they were merely on a friendly basis.

Like the Negro barber who operated a shop next door to the Salvation Army hall in Ottumwa. One day the barber stopped the lieutenant as he came home.

"Massah!" the black man said. "You all help me, please. Ah mus' be haunted--or jinxed, or somethin'!"

"I'll be glad to do what I can," George replied. "What's the trouble?"

"Well--" The barber hesitated. "Ev'y mornin' when ah tries to clean this heah keahosene lamp, the chim-nay breaks. Ah's just mus' be jinxed!"

"Let me try it," George offered. He took the chimney, cleaned it carefully with a cloth, and then replaced it. Everything worked fine.

"See!" the barber exclaimed. "You all don't haf a bit o'trouble."

"You try it again," George suggested, handing the lamp back to the Negro man.

As the barber started to slip a piece of cloth down the inside of the chimney, a flash of light drew George's attention to the man's hand.

"I think I know what's wrong!" George exclaimed. "That diamond ring on your finger is probably cutting the glass. No wonder the chimneys were breaking!"

The barber took off his ring and cleaned the chimney. It worked fine.

24.

Ella Shaffer came bursting into the old, run-down, poorly-furnished house in Keokuk, Iowa, where her family lived.

"Emmie! Emmie!" she shouted. "The new lieutenant has arrived!"

"How do you know?" her younger sister asked, without much concern. She continued to iron a dress, using rapid, quick strokes.

"I took some berries down to the captain," Ellie explained. "And HE was there! He's 22--and is he handsome! Wait 'til you see him!"

Fourteen-year-old Emmie showed a little more interest.

"How tall is he?" she ventured. "Is he married?"

Ella looked at her sister suspiciously.

"Why do you want to know?" she asked. "Are you going to marry him? He isn't so very tall, but he's sure good looking. And very nice! You'll never guess his name!"

"It's probably a common one like Jones or Smith or Peterson . . "

"No, it isn't that common. But it's easy. Just think of a man's height."

Emmie thought for a moment. "I don't know what you mean. . "

"You know, something that is high up . . . "

That didn't help much, either, and additional prodding and hints did no good.

Finally, Ellie gave a clue. "It ends in '-man.' And how tall is he?"

"You . . mean . . . 'Tall . . man,'" Emmie finally guessed.

"That's right," Ella replied. "Lieutenant Tallmon. And when you marry him, your name will be, 'Mrs. Tallmon.'"

"Don't be silly," Emmie said. "I don't care about boys. And he's too old."

But when sister Lillie and her fiance, Dave Alexander, said they were going downtown, Emmie asked for a ride-- supposedly to visit a girl friend of hers, but actually in hopes she might see the new lieutenant.

It worked out perfectly. As the buggy started to cross Blondeau Street, Captain Jordan and a young man dressed in Salvation Army uniform came stolling down the sidewalk from the left.

They were talking earnestly together. Almost mechanically, they stopped at the street corner to wait for the buggy to pass. Emmie got a good look at the dark-haired young man.

She wasn't the least bit impressed. Why, the lieutenant wasn't nearly as handsome as Ellie had indicated. She thought him rather ugly, with his small mustache and round face.

The men took no special note of the buggy, nor of the little, shy, brown-haired girl sitting in the back seat. She turned and watched as they continued on across the street after the buggy had passed.

Emmie knew that she should get out at that place, as her girl friend, Annie Blixt, lived down Blondeau Street. But she waited for another block before asking Dave to stop.

That night, the new lieutenant was busy greeting people and getting the hall ready when Emmie and Ellie arrived for evening meeting.

He didn't pay too much attention to the young girls, although he spoke to them and asked their names. He seemed pleasant enough, Emmie thought--in fact, very nice, quiet and kindly.

As time went on, Emmie and Ellie grew to know the new lieutenant better. They were members of the Young Soldiers' Society, which he conducted, and they saw him at other meetings and services at the Salvation Army hall.

Then, one day, he announced that the Young Soldiers' Society was going on a picnic to the park. The lieutenant made it sound exciting. He asked if anyone could furnish a buggy.

"I think I can," Emma offered. "I'll have to ask permission."

Her father wasn't home, but her mother, reluctantly, said she could drive if Lieutenant Tallmon would hitch up the horse.

"Can I go? I want to go," begged Emma's nine-year-old sister, Sadie.

"Emma doesn't want to take you," Mrs. Shaffer told her.

"You can't go," added Ella.

But Sadie insisted that she wanted to go. And, unknown to her sisters or mother, she slipped into the buggy anyway.

Lieutenant Tallmon led the horse from the barn. He hitched it to the buggy. Then he walked down the street to take care of other details for the picnic, leaving the horse and buggy facing at right angles to the barn.

Emma started to get into the buggy from the side opposite the driver, away from the reins. The horse thought it was time to move and started up.

Before she could yell, "Whoa," the wheel of the buggy caught the corner of the barn. It shuddered, tipped and fell onto its side with a thud.

Fortunately, the horse didn't try to run. It just stood there looking back. Sadie crawled out through the curtains, and Emmie jumped off.

Lieutenant Tallmon, hearing noise of the accident, turned back. Not one word of reproach to Emmie; he was not that way. Instead, he quietly and patiently tipped the buggy up again, found a shaft had been broken, and put the horse back in the barn and the harness away.

Mrs. Shaffer was much concerned.

"I should never have let you use it," she moaned to Emmie. "What will Father say? And Sadie, you're staying home."

Other arrangements were made, and before long the young people were at the park. Lieutenant Tallmon erected the swing he had brought along--no play apparatus was available otherwise. Emma noticed how agily he worked.

Just then came a scream. It was from a girl preparing the lunch.

"Snake! Snake!" she cried.

Lieutenant Tallmon walked calmly over to where she stood, petrified by the sight.

"It's only a garter snake!"

He leaned down and picked up the wriggling reptile by the neck. Quietly he carried it into the bushes.

"Oh, lieutenant, you're so brave!" the young girl cooed.

When the swing was fixed, Lieutenant Tallmon gave each of the girls a turn. He made sure that they all had a swing, and, in a quiet, patient way, was fair to all.

But he took a special interest in a certain pretty little blue-eyed girl, who shyly stood back while the others had their turns first.

"I'm sorry about the buggy," he whispered to Emmie, as he prepared to swing her. "Can your big brother fix it?"

"I don't have a big brother," Emmie replied. "My only brother, George, is too little."

"That's too bad," the lieutenant said.

"My father will fix it, when he returns from his trip. He's handy with tools."

After a pause, she added, "I've always wanted a big brother."

The lieutenant gave her an extra hard push.

And he swung her more than any of the other girls that afternoon.

All that summer and fall, Lieutenant Tallmon was kept busy assisting with the work of the corps. There were meetings every night and all day Sunday, starting with knee drill at 7 a.m.

One evening, before the meeting started, several rough-appearing youths in workmen's clothes came striding down the sidewalk and into the Salvation Army hall.

"What's going on here?" one asked, in a loud and boisterous voice.

"What kind of a hangout is this?" queried another, fingering the low curtains that decorated the front windows.

"Hallelujah!" shouted a third.

Lieutenant Tallmon realized they were a bunch of young toughs looking for something to do. A sense of irritation swept over him as he stepped to the door. They were there for no good.

"Would you fellows mind leaving?" he asked.

One of the toughs, his long black hair plastered closely to his head, stepped forward.

"Who's going to make us?" he challenged.

The lieutenant grappled with him, and was doing well until some of the other toughs joined in. They picked him up, gave him a shove, and tossed him through the glass door. It broke with a crash, the pieces tinkling to the ground.

George sat there, a little dazed, his head protruding through the window. Captain Jordan heard the noise and came to his rescue. Captain told the hoodlums to leave, or come in and sit down. That discouraged them and they walked on down the street.

Emmie arrived about that time.

"What happened?" she asked. When George explained, she said, "What did you do that for?" rather disgustedly. "Don't you know better than that?"

"It was rather foolish," George admitted.

Toughs weren't the only problem the corps faced. Like most other Salvation Army stations of its day, it faced a continual battle to keep going financially.

Many evenings, Captain Jordan and Lieutenant Tallmon came home after a long day's work, short on funds and not knowing where their next meal was coming from.

Often, on an evening like that, there would be a knock on the door. It was Emmie.

"I've brought you some food and other things from Sister Cadwell's," she would announce. And on the table she set a basket of provisions.

"That's very kind of you," Captain Jordan told her.

"Tell Sister Cadwell this is certainly wonderful," the lieutenant added.

And Emmie would hurry off home.

One night George dreamed about the little blue-eyed, brown-haired girl. He told Jordan about it the next day.

"Oh," replied Jordan, amusedly. "We have a romance going here?"

"No," George said. "Emma's just a little girl."

"But she is very sweet . . She'd make you a nice lieutenant . . . "

"She's just a little girl," George said. "And I'm not ready to fall in love. I am just working for God and souls."

"But you do kind of like her . . "

George hesistated a moment.

"I guess the Lord wants me to have someone in my heart to keep me steady . . " he said, thoughtfully.

One evening after meeting, when the first snow had fallen, Emmie was helping the lieutenant put away the song books.

"Captain Jordan and I are farewelling next week," he told her.

Emmie was surprised. "Oh, yes?" she exclaimed, "you are?" Then, when she had time to regain her composure, she asked, quietly, "Where are you going?"

"To Centerville," the lieutenant said. "I'm going to miss Keokuk. And I'm going to miss a certain little girl I know."

"I'm sorry to hear you're leaving," Emmie replied.

"I'd like to ask you a favor," the lieutenant went on. "Something very special. Do you remember that day at the park when I was swinging you? Do you remember that you said you always wanted a big brother?"

"Yes."

"Well, I'd like to be your brother. May I?"

"Yes, if you want to."

"And may I write to you?"

"Yes, that would be nice."

"I'll write to you as soon as I reach Centerville," the lieutenant promised.

When the letter came, it was addressed, "Little sister." And it was signed: "Your big brother."

25.

One evening when Emma came home, a letter was waiting for her on the table.

It was from George. He was home on furlough, and was going to St. Louis with the Grinnell band. The band would stop over for an evening in Keokuk.

Emma spread the word, and she and Ella were waiting when the train pulled into the station. The band got off and marched proudly up the street, playing a snappy tune.

Emma looked for George.

"There he is!" she exclaimed to Ella. He seemed to notice them, too. He couldn't wave, but there was a twinkle in his eyes.

The band marched to a downtown corner where a street meeting was in progress. Then it marched with the Keokuk corps to the hall for the "Big Go" service.

The hall was packed with people. Emma and Ella found seats where they could see the Grinnell band well.

After the meeting, people were talking. George came over and spoke to Emma: "I can't visit with you now, but I want to walk home with you."

Later, the two sisters and the lieutenant walked along the tree-lined streets, brisk in the cool spring night air. George walked beside Emma. It was the first time they had seen each other since he had been transferred away from Keokuk more than a year before.

There was lots to talk about--what he was doing now, what had become of old friends, what her life had been. The mile went quickly.

At the Shaffer home, he said goodbye, and disappeared up the dark street. The band was catching the late train, and he must get back.

"He certainly is nice," Emma exclaimed, as she and her sister climbed the steps and went into the house.

Emma and George corresponded more regularly after that. His letters were brotherly letters--always nice. They helped her in her faith, and told of his doings.

In her Christian life, Emma had no help from her folks. In fact, her mother would have been just as pleased for her to be a little more wild; run around to dances, for example.

George and Emma saw each other again that summer, when Emma went with the Keokuk corps to the camp meetings in St. Louis.

She waited on tables. General Booth, the founder of the Salvation Army, was there, and it was a big affair. People came in droves, even though the meetings were held in Forest Park on the outskirts of the city. Every night the hall was packed.

Both Emma and George played in the band--he the slide trombone and she second cornet. But they didn't see much of each other. He was an officer and she a soldier, and Army rules forbid them from being too intimate.

Their letters continued regularly that fall and winter, as big brother to little sister. George's letters were beautiful, and every line glowed with kindness, gentleness, benevolence--and modesty.

Then, one day, as he sealed a letter, his captain remarked: "I guess here is one of your love letters."

George flushed slightly, quickly slipped the letter into his coat pocket, and hurried out to mail it.

But that night he wrote another:

St. Jo. Mo.
Feb. 26 95

My dear little sister--

Captain looked at a letter I addressed to you and said I guess here is one of your love letters. Now really I never thought before that I was making love to you all this time but I suppose that is the proper word if I didn't want to admit it even to myself.

I knew I felt like saying more than I ever have but I have been stupid enough to imagine that all this time I was keeping my little secret and that you wouldn't know the difference.

You see my father and mother were engaged when they were young. She was only 15 and they were so good that they agreed together to deal with everyone they met about their souls.

I made up my mind years ago that I wouldn't make their mistake and well I will just tell all my experience.

When I started to school I took a shine to a little girl and "worshipped her afar off" for 16 years. I never had much to say to her in fact I just wouldn't give her up and she wouldn't let me get very intimate. When God called me into the S.A. I gave up the girl and thought I never would get married but just work for God and souls.

Alas for noble resolutions . . (I found) that every pretty face I saw and every nice girl I met had an attraction . .

I left Omaha and went to Ottumwa . . and since I had found out that girls were dangerous I got off the track on the other side and fell head over heels in love with an old married woman (47 yrs) who was very kind to us and in fact did her best to make me like her.

Then I came to Keokuk and I hardly knew what to think of myself only that I was a poor weak soft silly boy and I resolved to profit by the past and lose my heart no more.

But on that fateful picnic when I thought I was devoting myself alike to all the children I found that I enjoyed swinging one of the little girls more than any of the rest and I gave up right there and said I guess the Lord wants me to have someone in my heart to keep me steady.

Emma is just a little girl and I will not say anything to her or anyone else . . .

When I left Keokuk my heart failed me for fear you wouldn't write me and I had no right then to ask you to. But you did write and such an unselfish good sensible letter that I was completely captured if there had been any doubt before.

My sisters (other sisters) told me that I ought not to write to all you girls because you were all most young ladies and I would be breaking hearts if I was not careful. So I just let the others go.

Then, in pencil, around the edge of the letter:

And I won't say any more about these things for a long time if I may be just
Your brother

He carefully addressed the letter:

Miss Emma Shaffer
1213 1/2 Main Street
Keokuk, Iowa

Then he put the letter away in a drawer and didn't mail it. A week later he wrote, on a very special occasion:

St. Jo. Mo.
Mar. 1st 95

My dear little sister,

I hesitate about calling you little any longer for this is the day you are "sweet sixteen."

May you be truly sweet in your soul and may your feet be shod with the preparation of the gospel of peace. Eph. 6:15. And may you in preparing for the Golden Streets have the perfect trust which David expresses in the 23rd Psalm. God bless you.

You see I am almost a preacher for I have started a sermon with a Negro love song for a text. I wish I was better so that I wouldn't be writing and saying so many things that are well not very solid and helpful.

I have just been reading the life of Mrs. Booth. I didn't know Our General and his wife were so good and successful people. Such earnest holy hard working Christians deserve continued victory and my prayer to God is "make me good and keep me close to Thee."

It is late tonight and I must go to bed. I thought the least I could do for you on your birthday was to write and tell you I am sorry I can't send you a present of some sort. But keep believing next year things may be different . .

Mar. 2nd

Your letter came today. My how blue you are. Since when did you discover that you were not smart enough to be an officer? Don't be discouraged child (underlined) but just press forward and the Lord will make you a power in his hands to win souls.

Please excuse the expression child. I imagine I am gray headed. You know I was disappointed because you had to leave school but knowledge is not salvation and I never had much to say about it.

But you can do lots of good anyway. I wouldn't have you go into the field to please me or anyone else but just think of the wonderful privilege of giving all your time and talent to God.

God bless you don't feel blue but just go ahead.

I am glad if I ever was a help to you. If I hadn't hoped to be, I never would have written to you at all. But I will say that since I commenced lots of times I wrote just because I enjoyed it.

Of course I always do and always have desired your highest good and every God bless you I ever spoke came from the heart.

What I started out to say was that tho I started to help you I had got lots of help and pleasure for myself from the very first and to tell you the truth have been kept steady by thinking about my little sister.

You see there are such a lot of chances for an officer to get stuck on somebody all the time and I have been no exception till I met you.

After meeting--

Had a common kind of time tonight. Rough crowds, small collection, few soldiers and no souls. But just believe and keep on praying better times will come. O Lord keep me good. Did I put that prayer down somewhere else in this letter? I guess I did and then went to meeting and hurt the Captain's feelings.

You see I think I know what is best sometimes and I was so cranky and saucy tonight without making any explanation to him that he was very much hurt. Would you have thought that of your "brother"? I hardly should. And I didn't intend (underlined) to be bad.

I just looked over the sheet I wrote before supper. It gets very suggestive of a love letter toward the last. I suppose now that you are a young lady I have a right to write a love-letter to you once in a while. (May I?) I always felt it would be wrong when you were little. But I am seven years oldest yet. O well never mind.

I believe the Lord wants me to be your brother just now and I will be the very best brother I know how (underlined) and try to avoid any remarks on thoughts that don't suit Him.

I know that the Devil is and will bother you about going into the work but don't let faltze views of your abilities or magnified difficulties in the shape of home duties hinder you in the least.

I believe you and Ella will both be officers soon God bless you to be true. And may He bless Keokuk in every way.

I am still your loving brother.

George.

Keep praying for us here.

He mailed that one.

Another week passed. That other letter in his desk drawer kept burning in his mind. Several times he took it out and read it, then returned it to the drawer.

But he didn't mail it.

That night he sat down and wrote again:

St. Jo. Mo.
Mar. 18 1895

Dear little sister--

I wrote to you this morning and according to my pencilled promise on the edge of my other letter said almost nothing about what I filled my other letter with, "My love for you."

But I have been thinking today and I don't believe it was right for me to say as much to you as I did without saying a little more and asking you if we can't be more than brother and sister sometime.

I have nothing to offer you but a place to fight and work for God beside me. Or rather I feel like asking the privilege of fighting beside you for instead of feeling as a young man ought who is trying to persuade a fair lady to give herself to him I feel so weak and unworthy that it seems as if I am asking you to throw yourself away to even think of giving up a useful life of a single officer that is ahead of you to be the wife of a one horse captain. By the way I am not a Capt. yet.

I don't know how old you would have to be before H.Q. would let us marry and of course all our plans would have to be made subject to their consent.

I have thought that we would give too much time to writing and thinking about one another if we were engaged but I don't believe I will ever get any more nervous than I have been today and I know I would wait a week or even two for a letter if it was necessary.

If any good sense carries the day you won't see this letter. Tonight I will call myself

Your lover.

He mailed that one.

Then, after it was gone, he got to worrying about it. Maybe he had said too much. Maybe he had been too bold. Perhaps he had spoiled everything.

He quickly wrote a note, apologizing and asking her to overlook the letters and forgive him. Then he waited painfully until an answer came--if it would come at all.

It seemed like ages until Thursday. A letter came from Emma! Quickly he tore it open . . .

She had "forgiven" him. But what was there to forgive him for? What nice letters he had sent! She enjoyed every one of them!

That gave him encouragement. The next day, he mailed several pictures of his family at home.

Two or three days later he wrote:

St. Jo. Mo.
Mar. 24 1895

Dear little sister--

I sent the pictures (all I have) last Friday and I expect you have received them all right.

After I sent them I was afraid that there was not enough postage. You can return them the same way and so make it even.

I didn't have any picture of Angie or her husband nor Hester. And Clover's picture don't do her justice. Susie and Lucy are three years older than when their pictures were taken.

That is a very good picture of Clara and Lynds. The child in the picture with Margie is Angie's little girl. My father is a little older than that picture but still looks very much like it. Don't think that my brother's picture is mine and don't think that my picture (taken 13 yrs ago) is my brother.

That picture of my mother was taken 13 years ago. I spoiled it keeping it in the sunshine.

I was feeling rather blue when I got your letter last Thursday but when I found you had forgiven me I felt just as good as ever. Not but what the work is very hard but you know I wouldn't be happy in the finest corps in the country if I felt as if I had hurt your feelings.

The mail-man just brought me a lot of letters, one from home, one from Capt. Bernard, one from the R.R. company with a permit and last but not least a letter from Brigadier to come to St. Louis at once to practice in the band for Mrs. Booth's meetings. He added that I was not farewelling so you see if I can get enough car fare I will see Mrs. Booth and take in the big meetings.

I wish you might be there to enjoy them too. If I could see you as well but then I shouldn't know what to do. If I did see you I would be more embarrassed than I was last time.

Since you asked if I cared I better tell you some of my recent doings. Last night I took an old lady home after meeting and the night before I escorted two little girls. It was all done from a sense of duty.

I am so nervous on account of the mail I just told you about that I can't think. So I must stop writing. God bless you. Keep happy and fully trusting the Lord . .

Your loving brother

Capt. is addressing the envelope but he didn't see this.

A few days later George received orders to go home to Grinnell on furlough and await assignment to a new station.

It wasn't too far out of his way, so on the way to Grinnell he stopped over in Keokuk.

Emma was nearly speechless to see him. Her mother invited him in and asked if he could stay for supper and overnight.

The whole family sat and visited with him during the evening, except for Father Shaffer, who was traveling. Then they went off to bed, and George and Emma were left to talk alone.

George told about his own work and other things. He always talked nicely, Emma thought.

Then the conversation turned to more personal matters.

They talked of when he was stationed in Keokuk, and of how they met.

"I was just a little girl," Emma recalled. "I wasn't ready to fall in love then."

"Neither was I," George replied. "You were the little girl I picked out to center my attentions on so I wouldn't get married."

"But I'm glad you did," Emma replied, her eyes smiling up at him. "I'm glad it all worked out as it did."

"I wouldn't have it any other way now," George agreed. "Not for anything!"

As they retired for the night, he going to his room and Emma to hers, they hesitated for a moment in the hallway.

He turned to her, gave her a sweet little good night kiss (on the lips) and whispered:

"God bless my sweet little girl."

26.

Emma awoke the next morning, still aglow with the memories of the evening before.

She dressed and went to the kitchen to help prepare breakfast. Her mother and Ella were already there.

"He kissed you last night, didn't he?" Mother asked, slyly.

"You like him, don't you?" added Ella.

Emma felt badly about their teasing. It almost spoiled the kiss, which had been such a holy thing to her.

Then George came and, after breakfast, she apologized: "I have to go to work early clerking at the store, and won't be able to go with you to the station."

"That's all right," George replied. "I wish you could, but I have a few old friends downtown to see, and then I'll catch my train."

He stopped by the store for a few moments to wish her farewell, and then was gone.

George stopped over in Ottumwa, and while there attended a Salvation Army meeting. He was surprised to meet an old friend from Keokuk, John Haynie, father of a girl who knew Emma.

Haynie was a barber who had moved to Ottumwa. He had been an active soldier at Keokuk when George was stationed there.

Toward close of the meeting, a gang of toughs came by and tried to break it up. George stood in the doorway and refused to let them in.

"We'll get you later," one of the thugs shouted, as they disappeared down the street.

George thought no more of it, until he and John were on their way back to George's hotel room.

Suddenly, as they strolled through a dark stretch of sidewalk, George caught the sound of footsteps pounding on the roadway behind him. He turned to see three young hoodlums rushing at him.

One, dressed in dirty pants, gray cap and with a two-day beard, had a knife in his hand. The other two, similarly attired, carried rocks.

George stepped aside, then grabbed one fellow. They went down in a huddle, and rolled and struggled in the dirt. First George was underneath, then on top--and then he pinned the tough with a leg grip.

He released him, stood up--and the tough came at him again, with head down. He grabbed the fellow at the neck, lifted him off his feet, and dropped him to the rear.

He turned, ready to receive the tough again. But the youth struggled to his feet, looked at George for a moment, and then turned and walked off down the street.

Looking around, George saw the other two getting the best of Haynie. John was bleeding from a knife scratch on the face, and had been cut on the head with a rock.

George rushed to his aid, and pulled one of the fellows off his back. A sister from the Salvation Army corps joined in, and she and George threw the man over a fence and down into a cellar where a building had been burned. He didn't get out until the fight was over.

The toughs--including some of the rest of the gang--threw a few rocks after that, but the main battle was over. Haynie stormed off to the police station and signed a complaint.

George stayed two days in Ottumwa, waiting to help testify at Haynie's trial. But the police didn't arrest the boys. To George, the time there seemed like laying in jail. He was ready to go on home to Grinnell, without waiting any longer.

He wrote to Emma:

> Time hangs heavy on my hands and I must write you a little. I don't want to do like some people I know and write every other day, for that would take some of the Lord's time but we haven't done that yet and I don't believe we ever will.

Writing letters is not a very satisfactory way of making love and I am so glad I had a chance to see and talk even a few hours with you. Do you know I never saw you alone but once before in my life? I feel better acquainted and if possible I like you better than ever.

I had a notion to come back and say a better goodbye but I am very bashful the same as you . . .

You have changed my ideal of a girl. I used to think I would fancy a large black-eyed black-haired girl. Now I like a little blue-eyed brown-haired girl and if I hadn't made a solemn resolution not to ask her any more than I did when I was in Keokuk I might--I won't let you off so easy next time God bless my little girl (underlined).

You needn't answer this part of the letter unless you feel like it. It wouldn't take many words from you to make my heart rejoice but I won't say any more to you about it just now only please don't go back on me right away . . .

Why were you going to stop writing to me; or won't you tell! Does anyone tease you because I came to see you? . . Don't forget to send me Bradley's letter. I am not jealous of him but I just want to know what he said.

You see "dearest" I don't care (in theory) (underlined) if you do write to anyone and if you should find someone else that suited you better than I do I would step out of the way.

I don't feel this way but it is the way I have justified myself in writing to you all the time when I felt as if you were a little girl and I was too old to make advances to you.

You don't seem so little now and I trust that our further correspondence and acquaintanceship will serve to increase our regard for one another and in His own time the Lord may smile upon my suit.

If you will just let me write for two or three years more we can see about the rest . . .

But things did not work out that way. Soon after George reached Grinnell, he received a letter from the Brigadier.

Such an important letter! He opened it at once. What did the Brigadier want?

Then his heart sank. The Brigadier had learned he was writing regularly to a soldier of the Keokuk corps, and had stopped to see her.

Was it wise for an officer to be devoting so much of his time to a soldier? Was he doing justice to his work? Please send a full report.

And then, at the end of the letter, the information that Lieutenant Tallmon was now promoted to Captain Tallmon!

George felt partly worried, partly angry. He wrote to Emma--and received the immediate reply: they would stop their correspondence. She didn't want to interfere, or be a burden in his work.

Her letter was short and once again reserved--he sensed a feeling of hurt, although Emma did not say so.

George sat down and wrote a firm, bold letter to the brigadier. He liked the Keokuk soldier--she was the sweetest, most wonderful girl he had ever known. Someday she, too, would be a Salvation Army officer. But, they would stop their correspondence or do whatever else the brigadier saw was right, if he wanted them to.

The brigadier's reply was fatherly. The captain had gone into Salvation Army work to serve the Lord. That should be his one main concern. Anything that detracted was wrong.

He wouldn't say that the captain should stop the correspondence, but on the other hand, he couldn't believe that the Lord would be leading the captain if he said go on. There might be some justification for the correspondence if there were an engagement. And the engagement, of course, must be approved by headquarters.

The next step was obvious. The letter went thusly:

Grinnell, Ia.
Apr. 25th, 1895

Dearest little Emma--

I am enclosing the Brig. letters to me and as I can't act on his advice without writing to you I take it as his permission.

I am ever so sorry I wrote to you anything about his writing to me for I might have known I could get an answer from him before you would worry about hearing from me and then it would have saved you all the pain I feel sure you have suffered.

My poor dear little girl. I have shed a few (very few) tears myself about this thing. It was carelessness or thoughtlessness on my part that got us into this trouble. I am so sorry I hurt you so . .

I have hinted at my feelings and even told you I liked you better than anyone I knew. I thought I wouldn't ask you anything definite until we were still better acquainted for it means a great deal to promise to love and live for someone for life.

And besides that I feel as if I had the advantage of you for I know you and your folks not only as I saw them but I have heard about you through others and really have a good chance to know you pretty well and I love you with all my heart as I never cared for anyone else in my life.

On the other hand you haven't had such a good chance to know me and I have written as anyone good or bad might but if you are not afraid and will (H.Q. willing) be my little wife I will have something to write to Commander about. Can you answer this when you answer last week's letter?

May God bless you my dearest. Amen.

I have nothing to offer you but myself and a chance to fight with me in God's Salvation Army. I believe you have often thought about this. You needn't wait on ceremony to answer. The sooner the better.

Don't mind what the Brigadier says to me concerning health for I guess he is thinking of Ella.

I might tell you how I attended an outpost meeting or some other happening but I don't feel like it this time.

I received your congratulations you poor dear little sister you don't need to call me Capt. I wonder if your heart came into your throat when you wrote that like mine did when I read it.

God bless you and keep you.

Your big lover (underlined).

Please answer soon.

And he also sent another letter that day to Keokuk:

Grinnell, Iowa
Apr. 25, 1895

Bro. & Sis. Shaffer--

My dear comrades I wrote a letter to Emma today that had something more in it than mere friendship. From the time I can first remember until now I have always had a great deal of contempt for a man who would make love to a little girl.

When I commenced writing to Emma I did not admit even to myself that I was guilty of anything of the sort and still as I look back now I don't know what else to call my actions but love making.

I ought to have written fully to you before I said what I have to her but as a Salvation Army officer I have been looking at my course of action as H.Q. would look at it and almost overlooked the fact that Emma is only a little girl and has her parents to advise and control her movements and decisions.

As I have let my heart run away with my head and fallen in love with your daughter my superior officers advise (command) me to write to the Commander for his consent.

This advice was given with the hope I have reason to believe that our affection for each other would prove to be nothing but a fancy and would die a natural death during the customary year of engagement.

I don't know how you feel about this for I haven't anything to offer a wife except a life of privations and hardships as the world looks at it but one of many privileges and blessings to a person who desires the salvation of souls.

As to my character you have as good an idea as if I should try to describe myself. My family connections are very good. I have just cause to be proud of some of the ministers and teachers who are near relatives and among all my known ancestors and a wide acquaintance of uncles and cousins I never heard of one who was given to drink or was a criminal of any kind.

My father is worth about $10,000 but this don't amount to much as there are 10 children of us. And we older ones advise him to use up what money is necessary to keep and educate the others.

My own chances for learning were good. I graduated high school but being a poor scholar I am not very thorough.

To change the subject and come to the point I want your consent to an engagement with your little girl. I wouldn't say anything to you or her at this time but HQ seems to require either this or that we should stop our correspondence.

I believe a long or short engagement would amount to the same thing for I don't believe we could go any farther till she is of age.

I am your respectfully and prayerfully,

Lieut. G.A. Tallmon

(Above the letter, written upside down:)

I address the envelope Mrs. so someone will be sure to get it at once.

Emma wrote back a happy, shy letter of "Yes," and her parents gave their consent--as long as the sweethearts waited until Emma was older to be married.

By this time, George had been assigned to a corps of his own--the little town of Maquoketa, Iowa.

He wrote the necessary letter to National Headquarters, and awaited a reply.

Emma lived those days in the clouds. She could hardly wait for each letter from George. She couldn't eat--she had no appetite. Her every other word was "George" this or "George" that.

Then one day she came home from a Salvation Army meeting to tell Mother the thrilling news--she had a chance to go to an Army council in Burlington. And George would probably be there.

"May I go?" she asked eagerly.

"Yes," Mother replied. And as Emma went dashing out of the room, Mother remarked to little sister Sadie: "She's going to marry him or else!"

Emma accompanied Captain Deering on the trip. Captain Deering was Emma's Salvation Army corps officer, and he was like a pastor to her. He was very tall and had light-colored hair and bushy eyebrows.

They rode the train, and arrived in Burlington in time for the first meeting.

Emma, as a soldier, couldn't sit with George, an officer. He sat up front.

But she could hear him speak. And she thought how wonderful it was when he prayed.

She was sure no one had ever known any love like hers before. All these people--they didn't know what love was really like!

Emma had little chance to see much of George until the final night. Officers were not allowed to mingle with soldiers.

But that night he stopped at her hotel, and they went for a walk. It was thrilling to be together.

As they walked, he was humming a tune.

"What are you singing?" she asked.

"Oh, just a song I know."

She listened a little more closely. It was "Clementine," only he was singing it, "O, my darling, Emmaline."

Emma began telling of an experience of a few days before.

"It just scared the daylights out of me!" she exclaimed.

George stopped.

"Oh, don't say that!" he objected. "Don't ever say that!" Apparently he didn't feel it was proper to speak so lightly of death.

Emma took it to heart. She never used the saying again.

They walked in silence, and then Emma remarked:

"I don't know why you didn't fall for Ella. She is a good conversationist. She's friendly, she's a good speaker. She's pretty and more your age. I'm tongue-tied and shy."

"But you are the one I love," George replied.

They walked some more, and then George asked, "How did you and Ella happen to join the Salvation Army? Your folks are not soldiers."

"It was by chance," Emma said. "It must have been God's will."

She went on.

"Mother and a neighbor lady went to a Salvation Army meeting one time just for a laugh--just for something to do. Like many other people, they looked down upon the Salvation Army as a group of misguided people.

"When they came home, they told Ella and I that we should go, that it was really a kick. Next time, we went along.

"Well, we were very much taken with the service and the sermon. We had never thought much about such things before.

"When we were told we had been sinning and must repent, we were very much impressed.

"When the call for penitent-form came, we went forward with tears streaming down our faces. We knelt and prayed and promised to do right the rest of our lives.

"It was a marvelous and new experience. I had a new outlook and a new life.

"Mother was very much provoked and she and the neighbor lady got up and left. She was sorry she had ever taken us."

"You must have been quite young," George said.

"I was 13 and Ella was 15," Emma replied. "I was converted by an English sailor, tough and rough. He had been converted and had given his life to Christian service.

"He almost raved as he preached, but he was sincere. Some people would have turned away a little girl of 13 as being too young to bother with."

"I'm certainly glad he didn't," George said. "You never know what good, Christian work can do. Often seeds are sowed and the person who sowed them never knows of the good he has done. And yet he has changed lives completely and his influence goes on and on."

"I was told I must give up cards and coffee, and that gambling, smoking and drinking were wrong," Emma continued. "I hated to give up cards, because I enjoyed playing them. But I was told they were one thing Christians didn't do.

"I started saying grace at home. I asked my folks if I could pray before meals. They kind of laughed at the idea, but said I could if I wanted to--it didn't do any harm.

"Then I decided to try praying after meals, too, like they do in the Army. But it didn't go over very well. It was hard for one little girl to buck the family."

They walked along the dimly-lighted streets, unaware of time, completely absorbed in each other's company.

Emma told of how her father, whose name was John Wesley Shaffer, was a good Methodist when he was a young man. He was even superintendent of the Sunday school for a while.

But then he fell away from the church, got to drinking "for business reasons," and backslid badly. He probably wouldn't have fallen if Mother had backed him up, but she wasn't much interested in religion.

Some of Emma's earliest remembrances were seeing her father and his friends sitting around smoking, drinking and playing cards.

Because of his heavy drinking, Father was always in debt and the family poor. He would run up debts and then would move.

He would go on to some other town, make arrangements and then send for his wife and the children. Emma had memories of being told to "scrootch down" in the train, so that she and her sister would look younger and Mother wouldn't have to pay a fare for them.

Sometimes, before the family followed Father to a new home, men would come to take away the organ or a table or something else, to settle debts.

Emma worried continuously about how the family would get along, how they would pay the rent, where they would get enough food.

Her education also was neglected.

She didn't start school until she was 7, and she went only two full years. Her father kept moving around, and often her mother would say, "It's too late to start a new school this year. We'll just wait until next fall."

When Emma was in sixth grade, her younger brother needed books, so she had to give hers to him and leave school. She never went back. Her father believed girls would grow up to be mothers and didn't need an education.

Her life was not all unhappiness. She had many happy memories. For instance, her family was very musical.

Her father had a wonderful bass voice and loved to sing, and her mother could both sing and play well, by ear. Emma and Ella were musical, and Emma had an especially sweet voice. They had many happy hours together.

George told of his family's trials and times of happiness, and before they knew it, it was nearly 1 o'clock.

"I must get you home," George exclaimed. They hurried back to the hotel along deserted streets. At the door, George took her hand, held it tight, and said, "This has certainly been a wonderful evening."

"Yes, it has," she replied.

He kissed her, and they said goodbye. She slipped inside, and he walked down the street humming a merry tune.

They saw each other the next day just briefly, and soon were riding trains taking them in opposite directions.

Back home in Maquoketa, a letter from general headquarters was waiting. George snatched it up, ripped it open and found this message:

> Chief Secretary's Office
> 120, 122, 124 West 14th Street
> New York City
>
> May 13, 1895
>
> Captain Tallmon,
> Maquoketa, Ia.
>
> My dear Captain:-
>
> I am instructed by the chief secretary to acknowledge the receipt of your communication of the 8th last, referring to your proposed engagement and to inform you that the same has been referred to the Engagement Dept., and after due consideration you may expect to hear from us again.
>
> Yours sincerely,
>
> Harry Woight
> Captain.

George couldn't wait until he had heard from Emma. So he forwarded the letter on to her immediately. He also enclosed the love letter he had written several months before, and wrote:

> I have lots of work ahead of me today so I will hurry this off and write more when I have more time. My soldiers held meetings every night in real good shape and I believe in perfect harmony . .
> I will never forget Burlington. What a blessed time I have had, a spiritual feast to my soul and a

beautiful visit with you. What a thrill of pleasure it gave me just to take your hand in mine.

I didn't even try to tell you how happy I was and I won't try now. This is a bright pleasant looking world this morning.

May the Lord help me to be worthy of all his goodness in me (and I must say it) of the love of the dearest little girl I know. God bless you.

With all the love I know how to express.

I am your Capt. (underlined twice)
(all yours)"

Then, penciled around the edge:

P.S. You may answer this when you wish. I believe I will write next week just a day earlier so you will be sure to get the letter on Saturday and we can have a little more method in our correspondence . . . "

A few days later George received another encouraging message from national headquarters.

New York City
May 18, 1895

My dear captain:

I am desired by the chief secretary to adknowledge receipt of your letter to the commander asking for permission to become engaged to a soldier of the Keokuk corps and to say that the matter is having consideration and you will hear from us at soon as possible.

Will you please let us have the name of the girl immediately who you desire to become engaged to.

Believe me, faithfully yours,

Peter Glen
Staff-Capt."

Next came word in two weeks:

Midland Chief Division

St. Louis, May 30, 1895

My dear Capt.:--

The brigadier instructs me to say that he has received your letter regarding the insurance, would say, that you had better get it insured in the Phoenix Insurance Co., for $500. Trust that you will be able to collect money for same before you leave. After the policy is made out and signed, kindly forward the same on to us.

After you farewell you will kindly go at once, and not stop off in Keokuk. Regarding Springfield. We have no objections to your stopping there for one night on your way to Joplin.

Trusting that your last days in your present station may be your very best, I remain,

Yours faithfully,

L. Glassey
General Secretary
Dictated.

George did as he was told. He terminated his affairs in Maquoketa, and left for Joplin. He did as he was told. He did not stop in Keokuk.

When he reached Joplin, he was as far from Keokuk as he had ever been--down in the lower western corner of Missouri.

He felt dejected and hopeless. All the plans and dreams seemed a long, long ways off.

Among the first letters he received was one from Captain Deering, who had just been transferred from Keokuk to Muscatine, Iowa:

I left Emma well, and I suppose disappointed that you did not come through Keokuk, although she did not say much.

She took me down to the depot Tuesday morning in the buggy. I told her I did not think Brig. would let you come that way. She is a thorough Salvationist and I think lots of her. She is very young yet. I tried to help her all I could so that (if it comes to pass) she might some day make you a good lieut. . .

George was given a furlough that summer, and arrived in Grinnell just in time to accompany the family on its annual camping trip to the Iowa River.

It was 20 miles from the Tallmon ranch to the river--a full day's journey with a carriage and a lumber wagon filled with children and supplies.

As they rode along, the children played games, such as choosing the houses they passed.

"The next one is my house," one would say, "the next one is yours." And then they would wait to see if they got a "good" house or a run-down one.

At the river, they had fun. They went boating; they fished, swam and waded.

On this particular occasion, George's sister Clara and husband, Lynds, went along.

George and the others skipped stones across the water. Then they ate lunch.

As they finished the sandwiches, fried chicken and salad, George asked his youngest sister, Edith, "Will you eat an orange if I give you one?"

That was a real treat, and Edith replied, "Sure!"

So George went to a thorny hedge nearby and picked a large, round, green and definitely unappetizing fruit. It was from the osage orange, as the hedge is called.

"All right," he said, offering it to her. "Let's see you eat it. You said you would." Then he grinned.

Of course, she didn't.

Shortly after dinner George went for a swim.

The river at that point was in a treacherous place. Its bottom was sandy, and shifted from day to day. One day there would be a bar, and the next day a deep hole in the same place.

George had little experience swimming. He was far from an expert.

He swam for a while, then tried to stand up. He couldn't. The water was way over his head.

Alarmed, he took a few more strokes, then put his feet down again. He still couldn't touch bottom.

Frightened, he swam a few more strokes. He still couldn't reach security.

Now he nearly panicked. He already was tired from swimming, and couldn't take another stroke. It was a long way to shore.

He was frightened, really frightened. What was going to happen to him? Was this the end? He thought of dear little Emma. Would he ever see her again? Would she be devastated if something happened to him?

He floundered around, trying to keep his head out of the water.

Most of all, he concentrated on trying to save himself.

But, what could he do? Flounder some more?

He felt himself sinking; he felt the cold water about his face.

Suddenly there was a cry for help. Those on shore could hear the first of the word, "Help," but the last was drowned out as his head went under.

The girls were petrified. Lynds grabbed a boat, and tried to push out from shore. It caught on a sand bar.

"Hurry! Hurry!" the girls cried.

"Hel--! He---!"

Lynds pulled the boat back, got past the sand bar, and headed for George. The girls held their breaths. They watched as Lynds paddled desperately toward the stricken swimmer.

Lynds knew if he wasn't careful, George, as any drowning person is apt to do, might pull the boat over. So, when he reached George, Lynds grabbed him by the hair, pulled him up, and managed to get his arms over the side of the boat.

Then he pulled George in and rowed him to shore.

George climbed out of the boat and lay on the grass, catching his breath.

"He's all right," Lynds assured the others. "He doesn't need any artificial respiration."

Everyone breathed easier.

In time, George was back to normal--his sisters and brother-in-law thankful that he had been saved.

Later on, whenever George told the story of how he nearly drowned, he'd say:

"That was one time I was glad someone pulled my hair!"

27.

The miles couldn't keep George and Emma apart. They saw each other again during the summer at the annual camp meeting at Forest Park in St. Louis.

George was busy operating the ice cream concession.

But he could lean on the old counter and get an occasional glimpse of her. It meant a lot just knowing she was there.

Emma thought maybe he might treat her to some ice cream, at least once, but he never did. She knew he was low on money.

The last night, they went for a walk together. There was a rule against it, but they went anyway.

"It's the last night, and camp is being broken," George rationalized.

They sat on a park bench and talked and talked--about the future, their families, their hopes and dreams.

"It would be serious if an officer was caught with a soldier out here," George said. "But I don't want to go back."

"If we went back now, we might get caught," Emma replied.

George noticed the auditorium in the distance.

"Let's walk over there," he suggested. He took her hand, and they walked through the dark shadows of the trees and across the green lawns.

They slipped into the old tabernacle.

George turned and drew Emma into his arms.

"I love you," he whispered. Then he drew her still closer.

The hours passed swiftly as they stayed close together in the quiet auditorium. They talked as they had never talked before. About intimate little things, the minutest history of their lives. It was like Heaven just to be there.

When the first dim light of dawn slipped through the trees, George said, "I must take you back to your quarters. We can't stay out all night."

So, quietly and quickly, they made their way out of the auditorium and back through the park. And when George whispered, "Good night!" and left her, his watch pointed to 4 a.m.

Next day the camp broke up, and George returned to Joplin. But his thoughts returned often to a shy little girl and the happiness they had shared in St. Louis. His lieutenant complained that George kept hugging him in his sleep.

For the next three months, George waited impatiently for a letter from headquarters. None came. No mention was made of his engagement.

His spirits dropped, and he became "gloriously blue."

Matters were made worse one Saturday night when some drunks attended the meeting. They were very disruptive, and tried him to the uttermost.

When the meeting was over, all the soldiers went home angry or discouraged. George felt useless.

He had been asking the Lord to give him more feeling, and the Lord did.

At knee drill, he couldn't even pray for crying. There were only two present, including himself. George felt all broken up and nearly worthless. Then he put in the time until holiness meeting with the Lord and felt a little better.

Not many attended this meeting; in fact, George sat alone in the hall until fifteen minutes past eleven. Then a few people came in, including a young recruit George had been discipling.

She had left the platform and then repented and came to the penitent-form in a public meeting. But she hadn't come in the proper frame of mind, so George made her stay off the march and platform until she did.

It almost broke her heart, and now here she was, coming with earnestness and sincerity. That cheered George immensely.

("When we get married it won't be such a delicate job for me to deal with young ladies or better you can do it," he wrote to Emma.)

In the afternoon, two new people gave their souls to Jesus, and this raised George's spirits even more. Then some food was sent in between meetings, which made matters even better.

That night George received another soul. He felt happy and contented as he went to bed. And next morning, he received a letter from Captain Hawk with a dollar in it, and, best of all, a letter from Emma.

"I don't feel blue anymore and though I still see my shortcomings I won't let them discourage me," he wrote back to Emma. "I will trust God, not only for victory over sin, but victory over every trouble.

"Your good loving letter has done me lots of good," he continued. "I haven't enjoyed a letter so much since the one when you consented to be my wife and everything was so uncertain then that I hardly dared to be happy.

"It seems as if I will be so happy I won't know what to do when we are permitted to be together . . . "

His joy was short-lived.

He received a communique from headquarters.

Farewell and leave for Boulder, Colo., his next assignment.

He was being sent even farther away from Keokuk.

George's train took him west, farther than he had ever been before.

Slowly, the train crossed the barren cornfields of Nebraska and made its way through the lower plains of Colorado. Then it began climbing the long slopes of the Rocky Mountains.

George arrived at the little mountain town, north of Denver, and soon became acquainted with the people there. He found himself in charge of a small and hard-pressed corps.

The crowds were small, due to the wintry weather. Once again he lived on a meager diet and fared poorly.

Often he and his lieutenant had nothing more to eat than an apple and some crackers, a bunch of soft bananas someone gave them, or a bag of flour and a peck of apples bought for 15 cents.

Then one night George went out into the weather when it was snowing and cold, and his lieutenant was sick. Next morning he awoke with an attack of the grippe.

He lay in bed, his ankles aching, sicker than he had ever been in his whole life, he was sure.

Fortunately, his father's niece operated a boarding house in town, and took him in. His appetite was enormous, and he ate and ate and ate. She nursed him back to health, but it was a long process.

When he was finally able to return to work, he was assigned to Canon City, south of Denver, where conditions were much better. The corps included 20 active soldiers, and income was regular. The captain's quarters contained five nicely-furnished rooms.

"Plenty of room for you, only I am afraid it would be lots of work to keep them all clean," he wrote to Emma.

His ministry was more rewarding, too.

Among those he helped was a young father named Davis, who lived in a nearby small town.

The town didn't have a church of its own, and ministers from Canon City took turns conducting services there each week.

Captain Tallmon always walked the five miles--even during the heat of summer.

"I don't think I'd of walked today if I were you," one of the young girls told him as he arrived, sweating and hot, one Sunday morning.

"Well, you know," he replied, "I have a mission to fill."

One time, a poorly-dressed young man, his wife and four children walked into the hall and sat down. The father appeared a little bored with the whole service, until the captain started to speak. Then he listened intently.

The family disappeared before George had a chance to speak to them after the service, but the father was back again for the evening meeting. He attended quite regularly during the next few weeks.

Then, one day, when the captain invited those giving their souls to Jesus to come forward, the young man hesitantly approached the penitent-form.

He knelt there, his head bowed, his eyes down, his body shaking as if in silent sobs.

George turned the service over to his lieutenant, and knelt beside the young man.

"I've been a sinful man," the young father said. "I've neglected my wonderful wife and my four children. I've been spending all my time and every cent I can get in saloons."

George talked with him, and prayed with him, and the young man seemed to understand.

"Just lay your burdens at Jesus' feet," George assured him. "Ask the Lord to forgive you, and He will."

"Lord, help me," the young man prayed. "Lord, forgive me my sins. I want to be a follower of Jesus. I want to do Thy will."

Suddenly, the man jumped to his feet.

"God does!" he exclaimed. "God does forgive me! I know He does, in my heart!"

"And do you acknowledge Jesus as your Lord and Savior?" George asked him. "And do you promise to live a new and clean life?"

"I do," he promised.

And townsfolk found that Davis was, indeed, a changed man. Captain Tallmon helped him find a job in the railroad--not a high class job, but a dependable one.

He became a good, steady breadwinner for his family, a faithful soldier in the Salvation Army corps, a conscientious father, and a respected member of his community.

Although George was busy, his thoughts often strayed to a young brown-haired, blue-eyed girl in Iowa.

He dreamed of the time when they would be married and she would serve as his lieutenant.

Was he loving her too much, and neglecting his other duties in his devotion to her? Was the Lord giving him a little taste of fear and apprehension because she had almost taken the Lord's place in his heart?

He prayed for forgiveness and asked the Lord to make him good. And he thought: If God will let me have Emma as my own, my only one, we will always serve Him.

He sat down at the table and wrote to her.

"O! Emma," he said, "if I could only see you tonight. But then I can't. Is it wrong for me to allow myself to become so desperately passionately in love as I feel tonight?

"I once told you that I supposed I would be a better Christian if my heart was broken. But if I knew that you felt as bad or worse than I did I am afraid I couldn't stand it. . "

Time passed as he carefully penned the message, and he closed by expressing "more love than I can tell or show except by a long life with you. Your own George."

Then he folded up the letter, slipped it into the envelope, licked the flap, and addressed the front.

As the summer wore on, Emma was constantly in his thoughts. Letters were a poor way for sweethearts to communicate, but they were better than nothing at all.

In her letter, she told of being on tour with the Flying Squadron, a chorus of girls that went from town to town singing at Salvation Army affairs.

At each town, the girls were "billeted out" with friendly families.

At St. Louis, she stayed with a Mississippi River steamboat captain and his family, prominent in the community. The captain's wife liked Emma very much. The wife was upset when she learned that Emma had not been baptized. So she made arrangements to have it done.

Emma excitedly wrote that she sang before a thousand people at St. Louis--by accident and with no prior notice.

On this particular occasion, Ballington Booth, son of the founder of the Salvation Army, was to be speaker. But he didn't show up.

So the officers in charge called on the Flying Squadron to sing. Emma sang the solo, and her voice was heard by the vast audience that filled Exhibition Hall, the largest meeting place in St. Louis.

Ballington Booth never did arrive.

Later it was learned that he had split with his father. He was ordered back to England, but he and his wife refused to go. They wanted to stay in America.

As a result, Ballington Booth started his own movement-- the Volunteers of America--which resembled the Salvation Army and was active for many, many years.

Following the tour, Emma returned home. But she was not happy. She didn't like her father's drinking and carousing. And he was opposed to her plans to enter the Salvation Army.

Her father became interested in the new Volunteers group and took his two daughters on a tour, partly to offset Emma's interest in the Salvation Army.

Then he assumed command of a station in a little town north of Keokuk, taking his daughters with him and leaving his wife and young son home alone.

Emma didn't like it, and finally refused to stay with her father any more. She returned home, and worked in a canning factory, canning tomatoes, at $3 per week.

Her father was furious.

George, reading her letters, was worried. He decided something must be done. Before long, Emma received some very special news.

George had persuaded his superior officers to allow her to become an officer! She would be stationed immediately in Colorado, without customary cadet training!

As soon as she earned the money for the fare, he would come for her, take her to Grinnell to visit his family, and then on to Denver.

Emma was bursting with excitement. Her mother was willing. But her father, who by this time had given up the Volunteers work, wasn't.

He told his wife she would be sorry, and threatened not to work in order to punish her if she let Emma go.

Nevertheless, Emma and her mother went ahead with plans.

"I'm as tired as I can be tonight," Emma wrote. "I worked all day (10 hours) at the factory and only made 65 cents. But I'm very thankful I am able to work and I'm not going to complain. Every cent I make is only helping me to get nearer to you and more happiness than I have had in the last few months, I hope.

"Father is in better spirits although he doesn't speak to me a half dozen times. He says if I stay home he will try to do better, and although I hate to say it, I don't believe he will for he doesn't try now nor will he then. He told Mother he expects Ella and I to work all winter and I really can't do it.

"Lillie is quite pleased to think I can go to Colorado with you; she thinks it is the best thing I can do and so does Mother. Lillie likes you better than all of my folks . .

"I haven't heard from your sisters yet and I won't go to Grinnell unless I hear from them. I expect they are busy and I'm afraid if I go there I'll be in the way, but they were very anxious to have me or wrote that way . . "

The sisters did write, and arrangements were made for Emma to meet George in Oskaloosa. He was waiting for her when her train pulled into the station.

His eyes shown as he took her by the arm and escorted her to the waiting room.

"It's been 14 long months since I've seen you," he exclaimed. "It's so good to see you! . . How's your folks?"

"They're fine, but Father was so angry, he would not talk to me when I left."

"Don't you worry about that," George replied. "Everything's fine now. I can hardly wait to introduce you to my family!"

"Do you think they'll like me?" Emma ventured.

"Of course they'll like you!"

Soon they were speeding across the Iowa countryside, fields golden brown in the September sun.

As the train neared Grinnell, Emma's heart pounded and her hands felt clammy in her lap. Would they really like her?

Two of George's sisters were waiting at the Grinnell station to meet them. Emma recognized them from their pictures.

They greeted Emma warmly, and escorted Emma and George to the big house on Eighth Avenue. The rest of the family, including Papa, was just as friendly.

"Make yourself right at home," Papa smiled. "How was the trip? John, you take Emma's coat and suitcase. Come on in. Dinner's all ready."

Soon all were seated around the big, round table. Emma still felt a little inferior and out of place in such a well-educated family. But she knew she was welcome.

George was proud of his little fiancee, and enjoyed showing her off the week they stayed in Grinnell.

They attended the Congregrational Church on Sunday. Then George's sisters took her on a tour of the college grounds.

"Now I've been through college," Emma laughed.

One day she and George drove by horse and buggy to Chester, a little town north of Grinnell, for a Salvation Army service.

They stopped by the Jasper County farm where George was born. An old bachelor was living there then. He let them look around. Emma was excited to see just where George had lived as a baby, and to hear George repeat some of the old stories--such as Clara throwing rocks at the rattlesnake.

As they rode on, Emma thought how special it was to be with her sweetheart, out here on the Iowa prairie--or, for that matter, any place! The fun of being together was wonderful.

During the service, Emma sang a new song she had learned, with a catchy tune. The words went like this: "I love Him best of all. He is my dearest friend."

The song was strictly religious and referred to Jesus. But everyone knew that she and George were engaged, and it sounded as if she were singing to him.

Several times after that, she sang the same song while George was with her. She never realized the significance until years later, when George pointed it out to her. He said he didn't like the song she sang, not at all. It embarrassed him.

One evening after supper, George and Emma strolled into the living room. It was dark, and he sat down on the organ stool.

"We'll have to catch the train first thing in the morning," he said, reaching up to pull her down onto his lap.

She stepped aside.

"What's the matter?" he asked. "Don't you want to sit on my lap?"

"I don't think it's proper," she replied, "even if we are engaged."

"You're right," he said. "You're right."

But later she wondered if she really was right.

The sisters fixed a lunch for George and Emma to take, and saw them off at the station.

They rode all day and all night, sitting up in a chair car. During the night, Emma slept intermittently. When she awoke the next morning, as they rode along, his hand was on hers.

She was shocked. Showing affection in public! She quickly removed her hand.

George pointed out the window.

"Now you can see the outline of the mountains," he said.

Emma was fascinated. It was the first time she had ever seen any real mountains. She watched absorbed as the outlines gradually grew larger and changed into purple ridges.

28.

Emma's first officers in Denver were a married couple-- Ensign and Mrs. Stuyvasent.

The husband gave her good training. He insisted on making her do things that were hard for her to do.

The Stuyvasents were very nice people, but Emma was homesick. Everytime she sat down to eat she cried. She was as homesick as anyone ever gets. And this in spite of the fact that she had left an unhappy home.

George, stationed at Greeley, 50 miles away, felt concern and worry when he received her letter telling of her grief. If only they could be married! He needed her to care for him, and he could be a comfort to her. But, Army regulations forbade marriage for a year after formal engagement. It was impossible.

George slowly returned Emma's letter to its envelope. And he kept wondering what to do. Perhaps she would become adjusted . .

Emma didn't stay there long. The Stuyvasents moved. She was transferred to the Old Bay Market Mission, which served as Salvation Army headquarters in Denver and living quarters for the officers and staff.

Emma stayed with a group of single girls. The gates of the mission were locked at night, and no one could get in. The accommodations were fine. Denver was a well-to-do corps, as Salvation Army corps went.

She sang for special meetings. Among them was a big meeting for Booth Tucker, a member of the fine aristocracy of England. He had married Emma Booth, daughter of the founder of the Salvation Army.

Tucker liked her singing. He told her so. It was a great compliment.

In October, Emma was assigned to a corps at Central City, a little town in the gold mining country.

The town was prosperous, and the corps did well. They had good meetings and good collections. Emma was able to send special things home and, for the first time in her life, was able to dress well.

Her family was having a very hard time. Her father refused to work all winter, making good his threat to punish Emma's mother for letting her go. It wasn't until spring that he found a good job selling windmills.

A woman officer was in charge of Emma's corps.

"I don't like to sing, so you can lead the singing," Captain Martin told Emma when she arrived.

That was all right with Emma. She didn't like to talk. It took about all the courage she could muster, anyway, to take part in the Salvation Army meetings, let alone be leader.

It was especially hard to sell War Cries or go to people's houses to talk to them about being a Christian. Sometimes someone would shut a door in her face, and Emma could hardly stand that.

It took courage and nerve to do these things, but Emma did them because the Army stressed and taught that it was necessary to do your Christian duty if you ever expected to go to Heaven.

Part of her job was to go into taverns and pray with people right there, or invite them to the Salvation Army hall.

It was easier for women to do this. The bartenders and patrons were usually polite to girls. But they weren't so gracious with Salvation Army men. Instead they would ask: "Haven't you a better way to make a living?"

Emma always went with a group, never alone. Even so, her Salvation Army uniform was a protection. Salvation Army girls were respected.

One night after meeting, a group of women from Emma's corps visited a saloon and prayed with a drunk man. When they left, he followed, and asked them to pray with him some more.

So they took him to the hall and prayed, and he supposedly was converted that night. Whether it lasted or not they never knew.

Emma, fresh and pretty, was well liked. All the boys were attracted to her, and several would have liked to have asked for a date. But none did, knowing she was engaged.

It was an Army rule that officers could collect their salary only after they paid their bills. If they wanted more money for themselves, they had to go out and solicit for it by selling War Cries.

Emma went to the city clerk of the town, just as the soldiers went to all the businessmen, and asked for a donation.

The city clerk always bought a War Cry.

This time, however, he also handed Emma a note. She didn't pay any attention to what it said until she got outside. Then she read it: "I love you."

She never went back, not until just before she left Central City. When she went back, the captain was with her, and she told the man she was leaving soon. He gave her $5 for her car fare.

Emma sent the note to George.

George, meanwhile, was having his own problems in Greeley. He opened the Salvation Army hall one Sunday morning and found it ransacked. The rear door was ajar and his cornet and banjo were gone.

George immediately notified the town marshal. A search located someone who reported seeing the thieves headed south from town.

At 10 o'clock, George found himself at La Salle, five miles south of Greeley. The roads were so sandy he couldn't follow the marshal, so George decided to go to church while the marshal chased burglars.

George later recovered the banjo from a man who had bought it. But the cornet was still lost and the thieves never were located. George felt very badly about it.

As the winter season approached, Emma became ill. She had to go to bed for a while, and she could not sing well because of trouble with her throat.

When George heard she was sick, he decided to ride to Central City on his bicycle, a distance of 80 miles.

It was a long and tedious trip, requiring two days. He followed the winding mountain roads, which were sometimes little more than a couple of ruts where horses and wagons passed.

The weather was cold, the country was rocky and hilly and the roads were steep and hard to climb.

He had no brakes, and it was all he could do to keep the bike under control going downhill.

On one particularly steep hill, he tied brush onto the back of the bicycle as a brake. But the bicycle got out of control and ran into a canyon. He fell off, sliding down the bank on the seat of his pants.

He picked himself up, and put his hand on the bottom of his pants. The gravel had ground a hole, not only through the pants but through his drawers as well.

He was on his way to see his girl, with a hole in his pants!

He continued on, and when he arrived in Central City, he found the Salvation Army hall and knocked on the door.

Captain Martin appeared.

"I'm Captain Tallmon," George told her. "Is Miss Shaffer home?"

"She's in bed," the older woman replied. "But I know she'll be happy to see you. I'll tell her you are here."

George waited, cap in hand. Soon the captain was back.

"Come into her room," she said.

Emma was surprised and pleased to see him.

"But how did you get here?" she asked.

"I rode my bicycle."

"All the way from Greeley?"

"Yes. And I can only stay a couple of hours. I had trouble getting here. The roads were steep and I took a tumble."

And then, with a twinkle in his eye:

"I'll never do it again. You're going to have to marry me if you want to see me any more."

He asked if there were someplace where he could borrow a pair of pants while he mended his own. Emma suggested the hotel next door.

Soon he was back, and mended his pants while they talked. Then he left on the homeward journey.

Major Bell, when he heard of Captain Tallmon's long and arduous trip for such a short visit, remarked: "Oh, what devotion!"

Major Bell thought a lower climate would do Emma some good. So he asked her to come to Denver for a visit.

She met with nothing but kindness. Four or five Salvation Army people met her at the train. And she had a nice talk with the major before meeting.

Emma stayed a week, and then returned to Central City. Within another week, good news came. It was a letter from headquarters.

She had been named lieutenant!

It meant that she had become an officer without going to cadet training school, as was customary. There was no school in Colorado, and Major Bell was afraid if he sent her to officers' school some other place, she might be sent to some other part of the United States, and he would lose her. So he was instrumental in persuading headquarters to name her an officer direct.

Now she was an officer like George, and the way was cleared for their marriage. Quickly, she wrote George the wonderful news.

Major Bell happened to be in Greeley the day the letter arrived. He had left Denver before his mail came, and hadn't heard about the promotion yet.

George told him that Emma had been named a lieutenant, and how happy they were. Major Bell was dumbfounded. He was surprised that George knew so much. He asked to see the letter and read it very carefully.

"She deserves it," the major exclaimed. "She's a wonderful girl!"

After Major Bell left, George had many other things to do--calls to make, soliciting to do--and he didn't have time to answer the letter right away.

When he arrived home, he was very tired. Fortunately, he had a very small meeting that night, so he was somewhat rested when the meeting was over.

Then, just as he thought he would have time to write, he had to stop to talk with a fellow in the hall until quite late. When he reached his room, his landlady was working nearby, and he talked quite a while with her, when he wanted to be writing the letter to Emma.

Finally, he began:

Dearest

Your loving letter was waiting for me when I got home tonight. What a dear good girl you are. I couldn't ask for a more faithful little lover. My heart almost aches with love like your cheeks did with smiling the time we went to Chester (1/4 of a year ago).

It don't seem possible that the husbands and wives in some of the unhappy homes I see could have ever been lovers like we are. Our prospects are bright compared with other young people.

If they are happy we will be so much more so, I am sure . .

If H.Q. dates our engagement Dec. 19th it may be they will want us to wait that long but if they will allow it I like your thought about the camp meeting, but we can tell all about this later on.

You did receive quite a number of nice Christmas presents. I am glad you have so many friends . . I will try to forget that I couldn't send you anything since you are so kind in excusing me . .

I am ever so sorry about your throat but you know more about taking care of it than I can tell you. If you have to stop singing for a while to save your voice it is better than keeping on till your voice is really gone.

My poor little girl it is a real severe affliction isn't it but don't look on the dark side of it. If on the one side there is danger of your throat getting worse on the other side it is possible and probable that it will get absolutely well some day . .

No I hardly expected my Lieut. so soon and I have made as great a reconsecration as you have, I presume. For if you feel unworthy I feel too that we have been very kindly dealt with. And as if I have received countless blessings more than I deserved.

Any little bother you may have caused me has been more than repaid long ago. I never expect to get over praising the Lord for letting me have you. If the past few years have been blessed the future will surely be better . . .

But bright hopes soon dimmed. George and Emma waited in vain for some word on their wedding. And Emma's health continued to be poor.

She consulted Dr. T. S. Ashbaugh, a local physician. He couldn't find anything specifically wrong. Maybe it was the rheumatic fever, maybe mountain fever, maybe just weakness from insufficient diet.

George finally decided to write to Major Bell, asking if their wedding date could be hurried up. Back came the discouraging reply:

I regret to say that I can give you no definite answer upon the subject at the present moment and seeing that the Commander will be in Colorado in the course of a few weeks I think it will be wise to postpone the taking of any steps in the matter until he arrives.

The question of the lieutenant's health however is a very serious one and I cannot help thinking that if she were well the case would wear a more hopeful aspect.

In any event I am sure you will do your best to be patient.

Yours affectionately,
H. Bell

Major

By this time, George had been transferred to the little town of Cripple Creek, 30 miles west of Colorado Springs and about 120 miles south of where Emma was stationed in Central City.

Because of Emma's illness, she was tranferred to Pueblo. Major Bell thought the lower altitude and better climate might help.

Emma was made assistant to a 40-year-old woman, Captain McIndoe, who had tuberculosis, although no one realized it at the time. Emma slept with her for six weeks, but was careful always to lie with her face the other way because she knew the captain was sick.

Emma, just 18, was young enough to be the captain's daughter. Emma had to do all the open air work, including holding meetings on the icy street corners and taking care of the corps.

The work was hard. Emma was homesick. Her mother kept writing and urging her to return to Keokuk. Emma still wasn't well. She didn't know what to do. She wrote to Dr. Ashbaugh. He advised her to go home.

"The high altitude is against you," he said.

Emma gave in, and decided to return home. Before she left she attended a council at Colorado Springs, because she knew George would be there.

As usual, they didn't have much time to be together. She was soloist for the evening service on the last day of the meet. Her throat was better now.

George made arrangements for her train tickets home. And he sadly bid her goodbye as the train pulled into the station. It was so hard to have her go!

"Goodbye, my sweet little girl!" he told her, grasping her hand as the train ground to a stop. "I'll be thinking of you and praying for you!"

"I'll miss you, too," she replied, demurely.

He helped lift her baggage onto the train. She climbed aboard, and, as the engine started up, puffing and chugging, she waved goodbye from the window.

George waved back, then stood there sadly, watching the train pull out from the station and grow smaller and smaller down the track. Then he remembered!

He had forgotten to tell her she would have to change trains at St. Joseph!

Back home in Cripple Creek, he wrote her an apologetic and sad letter:

My darling girl--

I expect you are somewhere out in Kansas by this time. I forgot to tell you that your ticket read St. Joseph instead of Kansas City. It was a very thoughtless thing for me to do but I hope you won't be bothered by it.

I do hope and pray that you will get along without any accident and that you will not be too sick to enjoy yourself at least a little.

O why haven't I got more faith! I really feel quite cheerful about our future. It makes me lighthearted to think that perhaps we can remain and work in the Army all our lives after all our worry of the past few weeks.

I know you will do your best to have a real rest and you can trust me to take care of myself and we can both trust the Lord yes and our superior officers too.

Don't forget to give my love to your folks . . . God bless you. We are not so very far apart for love knows nothing about distance. (I found your picture.)

I will write as soon as I hear from you perhaps sooner.

With lots of love and a kiss
Your George

Emma made train connections all right, and arrived in Keokuk early in the morning--about 4 o'clock. She used the last bit of the $5 the city clerk of Central City had given her to hire a hack for the ride to her house.

The next few weeks dragged as George anxiously waited for some word from headquarters on their marriage.

He felt responsible. He knew Emma would have a hard time with her folks. He knew she was sick and lonesome in Colorado. He felt it was his responsibility to care for her.

If they could only be married! That would solve everything. They could be together and help each other.

But they couldn't be married without permission from headquarters. And that permission wasn't forthcoming. What could he do? He couldn't go against headquarters--not without being kicked out of the Army.

But Emma needed him. They wanted to be married. There seemed no hope.

He wrote often--more often than he should. When he didn't get an immediate reply, he addressed his letters to Emma's sister Lillie. Maybe Emma was staying out there.

He haunted the mail box. He could think of little else.

Letters didn't come. He waited desperately. Oh, what could be the matter? Her letters had never been misdirected nor lost. Had she become discouraged and decided to stop writing?

Was she sick, very, very sick? But, if she were, someone would let him know. What could be the matter?

He couldn't rest. He lay awake nights. He walked along the street, kicking tin cans. He wanted to hurt something alive, but he couldn't because he was saved.

He tried to forget his anxieties by hard work and lots of climbing. But he couldn't forget.

And then he wrote to the Commander.

29.

It was a warm, pleasant Monday in June. The trees were green, and the children, out of school for summer vacation, were playing in the streets.

Mother Shaffer was sewing and Emma was talking to her. There was a knock on the door.

Emma went to see who it was. She was shocked. Standing in the open doorway was--George!

"I've come to marry you," he said.

"But, but, I'm not ready," Emma replied. "I haven't got any wedding clothes. The decorations . . . I wouldn't have time to clean things up."

"I'll give you three days," he replied. "Marry me now, or you must come to me next time. I won't come back."

"But what about the Army?"

"I wrote to the major and told him I must take care of you. I said you were having a hard time, and my first duty was to you. I said I would go back into the Army later, if they wanted me to."

Emma realized how hard the decision must have been. George had vowed to be true to the Army. He had broken his promise--first by leaving without permission, second to marry without permission. She knew the consequences--dismissal from the Army.

"Don't you want to marry me?" he asked, noting her hesitation.

"Of course I do, George," she said. "I received your letter saying you were going to do something about it. But I never expected this. Come on in. I must talk it over with Mother."

They walked into the dining room, where Mother Shaffer was sewing a petticoat for Emma.

"George has come to marry me, and he wants to marry me in three days," Emma explained, dubiously.

She didn't expect her mother's reaction. Mother Shaffer didn't even hesitate.

"That's fine," she replied, matter-of-factly.

"But, but--" Emma stammered. "How can I get ready that soon?"

"I think we can do it," her mother said. "I'll hurry and finish this. I just have to finish crocheting the lace and sew it on. You can wear your Salvation Army uniform without your bonnet . ."

"That will be something new," suggested Ella, who overheard the conversation and came running in from the other room. "The dress is blue--and old, too. Let's see, something borrowed . . I'll lend you some hairpins!"

Emma was still hesitant.

"I was hoping I'd have a new dress," she said.

"If you don't come with me now, I'll see that you get a wedding dress when you do," George promised.

But Emma had made up her mind.

"No, it will be all right. It will be a simple wedding. But that's all right."

"Fine," said Mother. Turning to her 15-year-old son, she said, "George, you go out to Lillie's farm and see if you can get a ham or something."

And to the prospective bridegroom:

"You get out of here. We have work to do. Go see some of your friends downtown. Come back in time for supper."

The house was abustle for two days. There was fitting to do, and cleaning, and decorating. George stayed out of the way. Father Shaffer went with him to apply for the marriage license downtown.

When it came time to choose a minister, Emma suggested the Methodist preacher.

"The only Sunday school I ever attended was Methodist," she said. "And Lillie was married by him."

"Isn't there a minister who lives two or three houses from here?" George asked.

"Yes, Reverend Hannemann."

"Let's ask him."

"But he's a German Evangelical pastor."

"What difference does it make, as long as we are married?" George asked.

Emma said no more, although she thought George was a little stubborn. But he didn't want to make an issue of denomination, as long as they couldn't be married within the Salvation Army.

Wednesday night, the eve of the wedding, an electric storm blew in. Emma had never seen such a storm before in her life. The lightning flashed and clapped; the thunder roared, and the wind howled through the trees.

The next day, the weather cleared. That night, after the wedding, the night was calm and beautiful. It seemed an omen, foretelling the future.

The wedding was at 8 o'clock, June 24, 1897. Only Emma's family was present--Mother, Father, Ella, George and Sadie. Emma and George stood before the pastor and recited the solemn vows, repeating the words given to them in German-flavored English by Reverend Hannemann.

Then the pastor lifted his hands. "I now pronounce you husband and wife. What God has joined together let no man put asunder."

The family rushed forward to offer congratulations. Father Shaffer beat George to the punch and kissed Emma first. Then George kissed his new bride sweetly.

Young George slipped out of the house and went to find some of his friends. They came back with pans and drumsticks to shivaree the newlyweds, by making noise outside the front window.

Emma and George stayed there that night, and next day left on the train for Grinnell.

As they rode along, across the fields of growing corn, they were extremely happy.

"Now we are man and wife!" George exclaimed. "Our dreams have come true!"

"If only we were going to have our own little home," Emma sighed. "Any poor little home would do. I wouldn't care what it was. Maybe we could rent a little farm. Then everything would be perfect!"

"We will have our own room at Papa's," George replied. "He said he had a big house--so why not stay there?"

Soon after they arrived, George wrote to his Army superiors and said he was married. They replied promptly--he was suspended indefinitely, as a disciplinary measure.

George obtained a job with John Houghton, and also helped his father on the farm. Emma was welcomed by the sisters, and treated royally.

Tiny, pretty, quite blonde and very sweet--they fell in love with her. She could crochet and do so many lovely things. She could sing, and was sweet and generous about doing it whenever they asked.

The sisters were amazed how George could put his fingers clear around Emma's little waist. And they were full of compliments when she put on her Salvation Army uniform to go to church.

"There's something about that bonnet--that fringes the face so sweetly," Clover said.

George fell into the old routine of chores and farm work.

One day he mentioned he had a colt to break, and was going out to the barn to hitch up Autumn for the first time.

"I want to go," said Emma.

"No, you'd better not," George replied. "That colt has never been hitched to a wagon before. I have to use the old cart and old harness because Papa is using the good ones on the other horse. No telling how frisky Autumn might be."

But, Emma, flushed with young love, insisted:

"I want to go. If you are killed, I want to be, too."

So she went along.

Susie and George were chums while in their teens. Often they would go together to meetings and other affairs. Now she was taking a pre-med course at the college.

One evening Susie asked: "George, will you go over to the college with me tonight? There's a special lecture on fastidium botulitis."

Her sisters quickly answered:

"Susie, you should know better than that. George is a married man now. If you want him to go, you must ask his wife to go, too."

"That's all right," Emma replied. "I don't have anything to wear, anyway. Go on and go, George."

But, of course, George didn't.

Later, when they were alone, he asked her why she didn't want to go places with him more often.

"I want to show you off," he explained.

"I don't have any proper clothes to wear," she said.

"But, can't you wear your Salvation Army uniform?"

"It's a woolen dress," she said. "It's too hot to wear in the summertime."

"I wish I could buy you a dress," he replied. "But Papa hasn't given me any wages, yet. And all the money I earn from John Houghton I feel I should pay off those debts from the Salvation Army. Maybe we'll be able to get you something nice pretty soon."

Next time Papa was downtown buying clothes for his girls, he bought a "waist" for Emma. But it didn't fit, and she was disappointed.

It was haying time. All available manpower was working in the fields. Even the girls were helping.

Edith was driving a team hitched to the hay wagon. She had just come in from the field with a load. George stood behind her, ready to hook the hay wagon onto the loader.

"All right, back up, Edith," he called to her.

She backed the team--and backed and backed until she caught George between the wagon and the loader.

"Oh, giddie up," he managed to yell, and the horses started forward.

Edith looked back, and there he was, rolling and writhing on the ground.

"George! George!" she exclaimed. "Are you hurt?"

He struggled to his feet and laughed.

"Don't worry, Edith," he replied. "It could have been worse. Just hurt my chest some."

The other men helped him into the house, and he sat down in a chair.

Emma rushed over to comfort him. "Are you all right?" she cried. "Are you all right?" She was a little provoked by Edith's actions.

"I'm fine," George assured her.

"Shouldn't you go to the doctor?" Emma urged him.

"I'll be fine," he insisted.

He laid off work for a couple of days, and his chest bothered him for several weeks. Otherwise he had no apparent ill effects. Later he learned that he had suffered a broken rib.

One evening at suppertime Emma decided to fix some coleslaw as a surprise for George--just like her mother used to make it.

She got it all finished, and set it on the table. The family began to eat, and she watched expectantly as he first tasted it.

"Oh!" he cried, wincing. "This is SOUR!"

Emma ran crying from the table. George followed, and caught up with her as she reached their room.

"I didn't realize what I was saying," he said. "I didn't know you fixed it. I have always had coleslaw sweet, and I was surprised when I found it sour."

But Emma never made him sour dishes again.

Mealtime was one time when all of the family was together. Usually one person read aloud while the rest ate. The story was some classic, which helped their knowledge of literature.

Other times their conversation turned to scholarly subjects--astronomy, biology, history. The Tallmon girls knew every tree, every flower, every star by name.

George's father suggested one evening that maybe Emma would like to go to college while she lived as a bride in Grinnell.

"But I didn't even finish grammar school," Emma replied, a tinge of bitterness in her voice. "I can't go to college."

"You could take a music course, perhaps," Papa suggested, but Emma was already running from the table in tears.

"What did I say that was wrong?" Papa asked.

George caught up with Emma as they reached their room.

"Oh, you're such a little girl," he whispered as he drew her into his arms. "I've married a little girl."

"Oh, George, can't we have a little home of our own?" Emma begged, as she laid her tear-streaked cheek against his shoulder. "If we only had a small farm. I am willing to work hard. I could take care of the chickens and the garden . . "

"What's the matter here?" George asked. "Isn't the family treating you right?"

"They are all very nice," Emma replied. "But they are different than me. They are well educated, and I am not. They talk about scholarly subjects I know nothing about. They speak such perfect English, and I sometimes make mistakes. And Papa --he don't understand that I can't go to college because I never finished more than the sixth grade."

"My sisters may be well educated in school, but school learning isn't everything," George reassured her. "They know their town, school and farm. But in the ways of life, they haven't knocked around like you have. In some ways, they are more ignorant than you. You have travelled, and they never have. Your experience helps make up for any lack of schooling."

They sat down together on the bed.

"And the house isn't as neat and clean as I am used to," Emma continued. "The same, dirty stiff towel hangs in the washroom. The dish towels are black and smelly, and hang over the back of the stove. The house is untidy. But they insist that I am a guest and shouldn't help!"

"Are you sorry you married me?" George asked.

"Of course not!" Emma managed to smile through her tears. "But I don't feel well, I guess. I keep having weak feelings, and my stomach feels upset in the mornings."

George sprang to his feet, excitedly.

"Do you think--maybe?"

"I think maybe so," Emma replied.

"Oh, that would be wonderful!" George exclaimed. "You just lie down here and rest . . "

"No," Emma replied. "I'm all right now."

"I'll get you something else to eat . . "

"Thanks, but I've had enough."

"Maybe a drink of water then . . " And before she could object, he rushed off downstairs.

After that, the sisters were even more insistent that Emma take life easy and not help with the work.

"You must not overexert yourself in your condition," they would say.

Emma led a leisurely life. All she did was lie out on the hammock, eat apples under the apple tree, and read books. She caught up on many books children read when they are 13 and 14 and earlier--like the Louisa May Alcott series and others--ones she had never had a chance to read before.

"Can't I have at least one job?" she asked.

But the sisters wouldn't hear of it.

As autumn turned to winter, Emma and George talked often about the new little baby that would come to gladden their lives.

Emma didn't want to have her baby at Grinnell. And George wanted to go back into the Salvation Army. So they decided to write to headquarters and ask if he could be reinstated.

He had broken the rules by leaving Colorado. He had broken them again by getting married. But his request for reinstatement was accepted, and he and Emma were assigned to the little town of Atlantic, Iowa.

Emma decided to go home to Keokuk to visit her folks over Christmas, before going to Atlantic. She wanted to see her new little brother.

She wrote that he was a "very beautiful baby."

"I'm sure he is," George wrote back, "but just wait until you see ours!"

30.

Iowa can be bitterly cold in January, and this Saturday night in the small town of Atlantic was no exception.

Townsfolk and farmers' families from miles around were in town to do their week's shopping. People hurried from store to store, huddled tightly inside heavy coats, scarfs and caps.

Occasionally they stopped on the sidewalk long enough for a customary chat with friends and neighbors.

Hard-packed, dirty snow lay in the gutters, and the sidewalks and streets were icy.

On the street corner, a Salvation army brass band played a merry tune. A drum pounded and a trumpet led the chorus. There was singing and the sound of a tambourine.

Captain Tallmon, dressed in his blue serge uniform, led the song. His flat blue cap carried the words, "Salvation Army," written in red across it.

> Only trust Him, only trust Him,
> Only trust Him now.
> He will save you. He will save you.
> He will save you now.

And then the verse:

> Yes, Jesus is the Truth, the Way . . .

A crowd was gathered, listening. Most were grown-ups. But there were a few young folks among them.

A policeman walked up, motioned Captain Tallmon to one side. The band continued playing. The police officer spoke into the captain's ear.

"We've had some complaints," he said. "I don't want to have to put you in jail for causing a disturbance. Would you try to keep the music a little quieter?"

"We are almost ready to go to the hall," George replied. "Yes, we'll be more careful. Thanks for telling us."

The officer walked on, and the band swung into:

> Bring them in, bring them in,
> Bring them in from the fields of sin . .

Captain lowered his cornet, and, as the rest of the band played softly, he invited the crowd to join them at the Army hall.

"Come now. Come tonight," he urged them. "This could be the most important night in your life. The hall is only a short distance away. Come and join our fellowship."

And, with that, he motioned to the band, and, as he led the way, it marched off, playing as it went, proudly displaying the United States flag and the Salvation Army flag—red for Jesus' blood, yellow for fire of the Holy Spirit and blue for purity.

Some of the onlookers turned away, prepared to continue their shopping and then go home.

But many others followed the marching band as it disappeared down the street--shoppers, hangers-on, genuinely-interested people, people who wanted to keep warm.

There was no other form of entertainment in town, and people would go if for no other reason than to have something to do. There was no competition except the saloons--and socials at the church, which were never held on Saturday evenings.

At the hall, the small band marched proudly into the barren room, down the center aisle between the plain wooden chairs, and onto the platform.

The flags were placed in their standards.

The officers, soldiers and converts took seats on the raised platform, and the handful of visitors sat in the rough chairs below.

The band continued playing. Captain walked back and forth on the platform, playing his trumpet, and Emma, standing nearby, pounded the tambourine. When the music stopped, the captain announced:

"We are most happy to welcome you folks to our service tonight. With your help, we will have the victory. Jesus is so good!"

"Amen! Amen!" shouted the soldiers in unison on the platform.

"Amen!" Captain replied. "And, now, let's sing, 'There is Power, Power, Wonder-Working Power.'"

The band struck up the chord, and the congregation sang with gusto:

There is power, power, power, power, wonder-working power
In the blood of the Lamb.

There is power, power, power, power, wonder-working power
In the precious blood of the Lamb!

The soldiers shouted, "Amen! Amen!"

Captain Tallmon, a smile on his face, an air of quiet sincerity and warmth about him, added:

"Jesus is waiting. He wants to come into your life. Just give Him a chance!"

Then the band swung into another song, as the congregation sang the words:

> Lord Jesus, I long
> To be perfectly whole.
> I want Thee forever
> To live in my soul.
> Break down every idol,
> Cast out every foe,
> Now wash me, and I
> Shall be whiter than snow.

Then the verse:

> Whiter than snow, yes, whiter than snow.
> Now wash me, and I shall be whiter than snow.

Captain Tallmon liked that song especially, and sang it with feeling. He was a dedicated young man, dark-haired, round-faced, mustached and handsome.

The song was followed by more stirring music coupled with lively "Amens."

Then Captain Tallmon called upon the soldiers to give testimonies.

Sister Jones told how she had been a sinner until one day she attended a Salvation Army meeting and was converted.

She wept as she recalled how she had come forward, knelt at the penitent-form, and gave her soul to Jesus.

And she added:

"I'm glad I'm saved and trusting in Jesus. I'm going on to make Heaven my home!"

As the other soldiers shouted, "Amen! Amen!" the band moved into the strains of "There Is a Fountain Filled With Blood." And the congregation sang the words:

> There is a fountain filled with blood
> Drawn from Emmanuel's veins;

And sinners, plunged beneath that flood,
Lose all their guilty stains.

The dying thief rejoiced to see
That fountain in his day;
And there may I, though sinful, too,
Wash all my sins away.

Then Brother Henry told of how he had "broken every commandment." He had no regard for anyone but himself. What he wanted to do, he did, even though it was wrong in the sight of the Lord.

Then, he found the Light--and dedicated his life to Jesus. Jesus, he learned, was the glorious salvation for lost souls.

"Amen!" Amen!" came the reply. And the band played and the congregation sang:

The whole world was lost in the darkness of sin.
The light of the world is Jesus.
Like sunshine at noonday His glory shone in.
The light of the world is Jesus.

Captain Tallmon walked back and forth across the platform, swinging his arms and beating and waving the tambourine to keep things lively.

He wasn't the best singer in the world, but he could follow the tune, and his smile was contagious. The loose metal disks, in pairs on the edge of his tambourine, jingled and jangled as he pounded the shallow, one-headed drum against his fist, in time with the music.

As the tune died away, Captain Tallmon asked his assistants to pass the tambourine among the audience for the collection. One or two people got up and left.

Then he asked his wife, who had been sitting with the soldiers, "Lieutenant Tallmon, will you sing us a solo?"

Strumming her guitar, Emma played a popular tune of the day, and sang words composed to fit the occasion. She had a beautiful, high soprano voice, and people always enjoyed her singing. People said she sang "like a bird."

Her long, wavy light brown hair was combed back, and tied into a bun so she could keep it under her bonnet. She had lovely skin. Her face glowed with the radiance of young love. Her uniform, along with a wrap-around, were, as always, neat and immaculate.

The song told of how a young father had spent his evenings in a tavern, while his starving wife and children wept in their cold, cold home alone.

His daughter, at the request of the mother, went to find him. But he was busy drinking and carousing, and pushed her rudely away.

Distraught, she wandered about, strayed down by the river, fell in and was drowned. When the father learned of the tragedy, he was remorseful and sorry about his evil ways.

He wandered into a Salvation Army meeting, learned of God's saving grace, was converted, and lived a good, Christian life the rest of his days.

"Thank you, Lieutenant Tallmon," the captain said, his eyes shining with pride.

Then he turned to the Scripture reading, taking his lesson from I Peter 2:1-3: "Put away all malice and all guile and insincerity and envy and all slander. Like newborn babes, long for the pure spiritual milk, that by it you may grow up in your salvation; for you have tasted the kindness of the Lord."

Closing the Bible, he began:

"As a boy, I lived on a farm near Grinnell. My father and sisters live in Grinnell still. One year it was pigging time. The first to have pigs was an old sow.

"She bore two little scrawny ones, and then, she died. That left those poor little pigs without a mother.

"We tried to give them warm milk from the cow on a stick--but they kept crying and searching for their mama."

George told the story in a homespun, gentle way. His concern for the little piglets was apparent.

"The next day another sow had her litter. She produced 10 little fat ones. We added two more 'guests'--the little scrawny orphans.

"How they did push and shove to get their supper! And, as they drank of the life-giving milk, they became fat and healthy like their 'brothers.'

"These little pigs, seeking the milk they needed, are like mourners who long for the pure spiritual milk of the Word. And, when they find the nourishment they need, they grow in Christian stature.

"For Jesus said: 'Blessed are those who hunger and thirst for righteousness, for they shall be satisfied' (Matt. 5:6).

George walked back and forth on the platform, stressing his points in a sincere but quiet way, not at all boisterous.

"It is not easy to be a Christian. It means giving up worldly things. But it is very worthwhile and important--and necessary if the world is to become a better place to live.

"A rich young ruler who came to Jesus asked, 'What must I do to inherit eternal life?' (Luke 18:18-23).

"Jesus advised him to keep the commandments--not steal, not commit adultery, honor your father and mother, not lie, not cheat.

"'All these I have kept since my youth,' the man replied.

"Jesus listened and then said: 'One thing you still lack. Sell all that you have and distribute to the poor--and you will have treasure in Heaven--and come, follow me.'

"And the man turned away sorrowful, for he was very rich.

"But Jesus said: 'If any man would come after me, let him deny himself and take up his cross and follow me' (Matt. 16:24).

"We don't have to be perfect, in order to be Christians. All we must do is believe, have faith, and try to do our best.

"We must be sorry for our sins and ask God's forgiveness. Even the worst of sinners can be forgiven if they are truly sorry.

"Jesus made this plain: 'I came not to call the righteous, but sinners' to repentance (Matt. 9:13b).

"Jesus died for our sins. He was hung from a cross with nails through his hands and feet"--and George pointed to his own hands and feet--"and He did this so that we might be saved. Through him, our sins are forgiven.

"But we must believe in Him. We must dedicate our lives to His service. Then we will go to Heaven.

"This week," Captain continued, "I was visiting Sister Edwards. She is just recovering from a very serious illness. She was cheery and rested, and looking 'fit as a fiddle.'

"'You had quite a siege, didn't you?' I asked.

"'Yes,' she replied. 'The doctor had given me up for lost. But I was not afraid to die. Once I was. But now that I am saved and believe in Jesus, I am looking forward to going to Heaven.'

"What she says is in line with Jesus' promise: 'Truly, truly, I say to you, he who believes has eternal life' (John 6:47).

"In order to believe, you must have faith. You must know in your own heart that Jesus is the way of salvation. You must dedicate yourself to His service.

"A woman who had been ill for 20 years had heard reports about Jesus' ministry. He was coming to town. She thought, 'If I touch even the hem of His garment, I will get well.' So, while He was surrounded by a crowd, she slipped up behind Him and touched His garment, and immediately became well.

"Jesus, in spite of the crowd, asked, 'Who touched me?'

"The woman, in fear and trembling, admitted that she was the one.

"And He told her: 'Daughter, your faith has made you well. Go in peace' (Mark 5:25-34).

Captain stabbed the air with his finger.

"Jesus wants you. He is calling you. Regardless of your sins, He will forgive you, if you are truly sorry.

"He is like the shepherd with 100 sheep. When one goes astray, He leaves the 99 on the hill and goes in search of the one that is lost.

"And when He finds that one, He rejoices more over it than over the other 99 (Matt. 18:12,13).

Then George stopped, turned to the congregation, and quietly implored, "Is there anyone here tonight who is a sinner and who is not saved? Won't you come forward, kneel before the penitent-form, and ask God to forgive your sins?

"Come forward, and let Jesus come into your life. Tell Him you repent of your sins. Tell Him you want to be a follower of His. Tell Him you will sin no more.

"Won't you come forward?"

A young girl--perhaps 17--rose from her seat and, with tears rolling down her cheeks, walked down the aisle with hands folded. She knelt before the mercy seat.

Captain Tallmon motioned to a young lady soldier on the platform, and she went to the young girl's side. They knelt together and prayed together.

Other soldiers from the platform mingled among the visitors. They asked the people one by one, "Are you a Christian?" And if the reply was negative, they were invited to come forward and give themselves to Jesus.

Most of the people answered politely, "Yes, I am," or "I'm not sure."

One clean-cut, well-shaven man--his brown hair just starting to get bald--was incensed.

"I'm as good as a lot of you people who call yourselves Christians!" he insisted.

"That's undoubtedly true," the soldier replied. "None of us is perfect. But Jesus wants us to give ourselves to Him, and be good for His sake."

The man said no more. He just sat in his seat in a huff, his arms folded.

The band, meanwhile, was playing a song of salvation.

> Come all who would to glory go,
> And leave this world of sin and woe;
> Forsake your sins without delay,
> Believe, and you shall win the day . .

And then, another:

> Who will be the next to follow Jesus?
> Who will be the next His cross to bear?
> Someone is ready, someone is waiting.
> Who'll be the next a crown to wear? . .

Just then a group of soldiers drew back from the penitent-form. One spoke to Captain Tallmon. Captain stopped the song, and announced:

"I am happy to say that this young lady has had the victory. She is now a Christian. We are very pleased, and we welcome her as a soldier in the Army of the Lord."

Then, turning to her, he asked:

"Would you like to say a few words?"

"Yes," the young girl replied, shyly, the tears still rolling down her cheeks. She began a halting testimony:

"I am so happy . . God has forgiven me . . for my sins. I will go forward now . . and try to live . . a good Christian life . . "

Then she and her sponsor took seats on the penitent-form bench, along with the other soldiers, facing the audience. She was now a full-fledged soldier of the Lord!

"Will anyone else come forward and give themselves to Jesus tonight?" Captain asked. "Jesus wants you to come."

He motioned toward the new convert.

"Just as this young woman has made a complete change in her life this very night, you, too, may come forward and do the same. Won't you come?"

The man who insisted he was as "good as a lot of you people who call yourself Christians" rose from his seat and stepped forward.

He knelt before the mercy seat. Captain Tallmon turned the meeting over to his wife, and went to kneel by the man's side.

While Emma exhorted others to come forward, the captain prayed quietly with the man, encouraging him to confess his sins and repent.

Then, speaking so all could hear, Captain Tallmon prayed for the soul of the man.

"God, help this man to be willing to give up his sins. Help him feel that You have already forgiven his sins. Help him promise to sin no more. This man needs You. Help him realize that the time has come for him to live a Christian life and grow in grace. He will be happier then, and he will be a different man."

The congregation then sang, "Just as I am, without one plea . . " and the captain spoke quietly with the man again. He explained how he, George, believed in Jesus, and said the man could, too.

Suddenly, the man stood up.

"It's no use," he said, and returned to his seat.

"If not tonight, then perhaps later," the captain suggested. "We will pray for you. Come again!"

31.

Atlantic was a pretty little town surrounded by farmlands and located in the western part of Iowa.

They liked it there. But soon they found that life, even there, was little different than other Salvation Army assignments.

Following months of plenty on the farm, they began to feel once again the rigors of Army life.

George's father gave him $50 for his entire six months' work when he left. In time it was gone.

After that, they had to depend once again on the kindness of Army contributors and the War Cries George was able to sell.

At first, Emma helped as much as she could with the Army work, including assisting with the meetings and singing. But, as she began to show the effects of her pregnancy, she stayed home. Women didn't appear in public when it became evident they were expecting.

On the other hand, she enjoyed "keeping house" for George, making their simple home as neat and clean and comfortable as she could, within the restrictions of her approaching motherhood.

The two-room apartment they shared--their first home-- was located in front of the Salvation Army hall, over a store building. The rooms were bare and plainly furnished. Emma made them livable and home-like.

George and Emma prayed together before and after meals, at noon and before going to bed. They thanked the Lord for allowing them to be together, and so happy!

George was busy night and day. There were meetings every night except Monday--that was soldiers' meeting. Saturday was a big service, and there were three big meetings on Sunday.

During the day, George covered the town and surrounding areas on his bicycle, selling War Cries, or visiting parishioners.

Emma began making preparations for her baby.

An important consideration was what to name the new little offspring.

"If it's a girl, let's name her 'Susan,'" George suggested one night at the supper table, "--for my sister and mother."

"But I don't like that name," Emma objected. "It makes me think of a dirty little girl named Susan I once knew."

"What if it's a boy?" George asked.

"We should name him 'George,' for you, Emma replied quickly--then hesitated. "But I don't like the middle name, 'Albert.'"

They talked of other names as the weeks passed and the time of birth approached. But none seemed to suit.

"Why don't we name her 'Susan Elizabeth' in honor of both grandmothers?" George offered. But Emma insisted she did not care for the name Susan.

"Let's name her 'Edith,'" Emma suggested. "That's my sister Ella's middle name. And if we call her 'Edith Grace,' that will honor your oldest and youngest sisters."

There wasn't much the new papa could say to that. And so that was the name chosen.

When time came for the baby to be born, Emma went to stay with a old English woman and her husband. They were old Salvationists, and Mother Hardy took Emma under her wing.

The Hardys slept upstairs, and gave their nice downstairs bedroom to Emma and George. They were a sweet old couple, and didn't charge the Tallmons anything for staying there.

One evening, Father Hardy and Emma were home alone. George was at the hall, and Mother Hardy also was attending the service.

Emma felt sleepy all evening, and slept most of the time on the couch.

At 9:30, George and Mother Hardy came home and the Hardys went to bed.

"I think something's about to happen," Mr. Hardy told his wife, as they climbed the stairs. "Emma slept most of the evening."

Emma and George soon knew it, too. About midnight Emma awoke and said, "My baby's starting to come."

Her labor pains were still infrequent, and they slept off and on until 6 a.m. Then they got up, and George went for the doctor at 7. Emma had never seen the doctor before, although George had told the physician he'd be calling on him.

Things progressed slowly, and by noon the doctor, George, the Hardys and Emma were still waiting.

It wasn't until almost 2 o'clock that the birth seemed imminent.

The baby wasn't anxious to come. George held Emma's hand. The doctor worked and sweated. Emma pushed and shoved and cried out as the pains came and then subsided. George tried to comfort her.

Then the doctor got out his instruments . . .

When the baby was born it was a girl! And a beautiful, round-faced, very red baby, too. She seemed healthy, except for two cuts on her little head where the doctor's instruments had pressed.

A surge of joy enveloped Emma as the new little baby was laid in her arms. It was May 6, 1898.

She held little Edith Grace close, and moved back the blanket so George could see. "Isn't she beautiful?" she asked, excitedly.

"She certainly is!" George smiled, his eyes shining and his face beaming with new father pride.

Just a little red face and a little red fist was all that could be seen inside the folds of the blanket. But what a precious bundle!

But the doctor was pessimistic.

"You should be thankful she is here and not out in the cemetery," he said, while visiting several days later. "You had a very hard time with her, Mrs. Tallmon. You must never have another baby again."

Emma laughed. "When George and I were married we said we were going to have a dozen children--and I still think so."

When little Edith was three days old, a severe storm came up while George was out in the country selling War Cries.

George saw the dark clouds forming in the west, but didn't think much of it at first. Soon the sky grew dark and lightning flashed. And then the rain began to fall--in big, heavy drops.

George found refuge under a tree, thinking the storm would soon blow by. But the rain kept coming, and it was evident that a severe storm was on hand.

It was getting late--almost dark--and Emma would be worried.

George decided to make a dash for home, and take his chances on getting wet. So he pushed off on his bicycle.

When he came to the railroad tracks, he decided to take a short cut. He started across the trestle--bump, bump, bump.

By that time the rain was coming in torrents, and the last stages of daylight were fast disappearing.

George looked ahead and through the dusk saw that a train was coming. But he thought, oh, well, he had room enough to pass alongside the track.

But when the train came up on the trestle, he realized he didn't have as much room as he thought.

Frightened, he put his foot down for support, and moved over to the edge as far as he dared.

He could hear the staccato of the raindrops striking the river water down below.

The headlight of the engine grew larger and larger, as the train came rumbling toward him. The next instant, the engine rushed by him. Then he felt the swish of the cars and the pounding of the wheels.

He was nearly jarred off the side, but managed to hang on.

As the train disappeared into the darkness, George tried to regain his composure and quiet his pounding heart.

He pulled his bicycle back into the center of the tracks, and slowly rode the rest of the way along the trestle--bump, bump, bump.

Just as he reached the end of the trestle, he heard a snap and his bicycle collapsed beneath him. The jarring of the trestle had broken a bar on the frame. He would have to walk home.

Back at the Hardys, Emma became increasingly concerned. She kept peering out the window as the daylight disappeared and the rain poured down.

"I know George wouldn't stay where he was," she insisted, as Mother Hardy brought supper on a tray to her bedside. "He knows I would be upset. But, what has happened to him? Why doesn't he come?"

"Now, he's all right," the dear old lady reassured her. "He probably was a long ways out of town, and he can't travel fast in this weather. Now don't you worry."

But Emma did worry. And she was nearly desperate when the door finally opened and George came in, dripping wet.

He kissed her, and began to remove his wet jacket.

"Didn't you worry about the storm?" Emma asked him, anxiously.

"Yes, I worried," he acknowledged. "And things were just as bad with me as you dreamed they were."

"If you hadn't come pretty soon, I don't think I could have kept her in bed much longer," Mother Hardy said.

32.

After six months in Atlantic, George and Emma returned to Grinnell for a family reunion.

Susan was graduating from college, and her little nephew, Lester Jones, was quite impressed.

"You going to be a doctor?" he asked.

"Yes, I am," Susan replied.

"You going to be a doctor?" he was quite unbelieving.

"Yes, that's right."

He puzzled for a moment, and then asked again, in a solemn voice: "Then you wear pants?"

Little Edith Grace was three months old when she was "dedicated to God" at a ceremony at a camp meeting in Des Moines.

It was a hot August day, and she was fussy. So her papa took her into the back room of the Army headquarters to quiet her.

He sat down on a window ledge and just then the window came down, hitting her on the head.

She cried and cried. Her mama was called, and was very upset.

Edith was not hurt. After crying for half an hour, she quieted down and was pretty good during the dedication. But her mama's song during the meeting was not quite up to par.

George's next station was Oskaloosa. There was a typhoid outbreak in town, and the Tallmons were warned not to drink from the well by the house.

Carrying their water from across the street was a lot of trouble. And the well water looked so clear and sparkling.

Finally, George said: "It's all right to use it."

Soon Emma was sick, awfully sick. The doctor said she was on the verge of typhoid, and advised them to leave town immediately. They did, and Emma recovered.

Later, through a friend, the doctor inquired whether Emma had died. They didn't realize that she was in that serious of danger!

Decorah, their next station, was a Scandinavian town. They reached there in the dead of winter, 25 below zero, and crowds were slow. They were desperately poor.

They were walking down the street one day, pushing Edith in her buggy, wrapped up as best they could with what few blankets they had.

An old man stopped and said: "Here. Here's $1. Go buy a blanket for that baby." Mama bought a large brown shawl, and it was still in the family 100 years later.

Next stop was Lansing. George won a stereopticon--or "magic lantern"--for selling more War Cries than any other officer in the United States.

The stereopticon proved to be more valuable than they realized at first.

Fort Dodge, their next assignment, was a large corps but one in heavy debt. George felt responsible for paying off the debt--but how?

He decided to use the stereopticon to show pictures of the Salvation Army and its work at meetings in Fort Dodge and surrounding towns.

George threw pictures onto the side of store buildings while Emma sang songs about Army projects such as relief work among unwed mothers.

One of the songs told about a woman "poorly dressed," who stood on a "cold and dreary pavement" with "a child upon her breast."

She was "someone's darling" who had been "sacrificed" upon the lust of the world. But, Jesus stood beside her, and "wiped away the falling tears." And though her sins "be as scarlet," "they shall be as white as snow."

The meetings made a big impression on the crowds.

When headquarters heard that George had paid off the corps debt, officers were enthusiastic. Soon he had a new assignment:

To travel all over Iowa and Nebraska, raising funds for Army work. No longer would he be in charge of an individual corps.

George wasn't too happy with the new program.

"I don't like collecting money," he said. "But if I can be more useful that way, I'm glad to do it."

"At least we'll receive a regular salary," his wife replied-- $11 per week plus house, furnishings and expenses.

Emma returned to Grinnell to live in the vacant Army barracks, and to await the birth of her second child.

As the date approached, Emma became wore and more uneasy. She remembered what the doctor had said about no more children. Would everything be all right?

They discussed names for the baby, and had trouble deciding, once again.

If it were a boy, Emma wanted to name him George, after his father. But she still didn't like the middle name, "Albert."

"I know," she decided, "let's name him, 'George Allison' after Flora Allison, the girl who is rooming at your sister's house. I think she's a very nice person."

"I'd rather you named him, 'Peter,' George replied. "But, you're having the babies. You name them."

As the date approached, Emma became more and more uneasy. She was still concerned about what the doctor had said. Would everything really be all right?

The due date came and went--Oct. 18. Still the baby did not come. Each day's waiting proved difficult, and Emma became increasingly anxious.

Finally she exclaimed to her sister, Ella, who had come to stay with her:

"I don't care what happens, as long as I get through."

Then, on Nov. 18--one whole month after the baby was due--the time came. When Emma realized the birth was imminent, it was the middle of the morning, and George had already gone to work. He had came home to stay as the birth time drew near.

Ella walked a mile to the Tallmon house to tell the family George was needed. Edith rode her bicycle out to the cornfield where George was husking corn to tell him.

He dropped everything, took Edith's bicycle, leaving her to walk back to the house, and headed for town. He summoned the doctor. Two hours later, at 1 p.m., the baby was born.

It was a fat, roly-poly, healthy baby boy. And Mama had hardly a bit of trouble. They were a happy family.

Little Edith loved baby George to pieces, talked by his bed, was proud of him.

When George's sisters came to call, little Edith insisted that they come with her to see "baby brudder."

"He looks like you, Emma," the sisters said.

But they were shocked to see Mama sitting up in bed three days after the birth.

"You'll die. Something awful will happen," Lucy warned.

"The doctor told me to," Emma replied. "I'm enjoying it. I'm looking forward to bathing the baby within a few days."

When baby George was a week or so ,old, he began crying constantly, and wouldn't nurse. He cried and cried and cried all the time. Nothing his mama or Ella could do seemed to help.

Finally Emma sent for a doctor. Her own doctor was out of town, so another one, a young one, came. He gave the baby some medicine, and the baby never cried again.

When the regular doctor came back and saw what medicine had been prescribed, he said with concern: "Throw that stuff away; it's not fit for babies or anyone."

Little George grew progressively worse. Within a few days, a general paralysis began spreading over his body. His father came home from traveling to stand by.

Emma sat up with her baby night and day--doing everything she could to comfort him.

One night, she had been up all night. George, who had been sleeping, said, "You go to bed now, and I'll sit up with him."

Emma had a fear the baby was going to die, but she agreed to trade places with George. Soon she drifted off into troubled sleep.

Before long she woke up. George was lying on the bed beside her, fully clothed.

"How's the baby?" she asked.

"He's well," George replied, softly.

She knew what he meant.

Emma cried and cried. She told herself she should have known the baby would die, but she had hoped so much he would not. Quietly and softly, the tears came. She wept and wept.

Next morning was Sunday, and George stopped by at his folks' house as they were eating breakfast.

"Well, he's gone," George informed them, and then went out to help with the chores. Just that blunt and matter-of-fact. The family was surprised.

But George kept the emotion inside. He used his faith and thoughts--and reasoned about death. He believed in accepting God's will, and had faith that a person, if he lived a good life, would go to Heaven.

They decided to bury little George that day, and not wait longer. It started to snow. There was a simple service at George and Emma's house. The Congregational minister gave a short talk.

Lucy, Flora Allison, Clover and Ella were there. Grandpa didn't come. George put the little white coffin in the buggy.

"You must not go in your condition, Emma," the others said. "It's too cold."

So Emma stayed at the house with baby Edith.

When the party returned, everyone gathered around the organ to sing hymns.

It was too much for Emma. She broke down, and ran crying to the bedroom. George didn't follow. He couldn't help her--he couldn't change things.

For days, Emma grieved. George tried to comfort her. He bought her a $6 watch for Christmas. It was one of several little things he and others did to console her.

But Emma blamed herself.

"Losing little George was probably my punishment for fretting over having another baby so soon," she insisted.

She prayed:

"God, give me another chance. My children will always be welcome. Give me another baby and I will never fret again."

33.

Following little baby George's death, George and Emma went back to stay with his folks, giving up the vacant Grinnell barracks. George continued his travels.

Then, one Saturday, he came home and said:

"We're moving to Des Moines. I've made arrangements to live in an apartment next to the Stanleys. They are the officers in charge of the Des Moines corps. They can keep an eye on you, and it will be easier for me to get home on weekends. Travel accommodations are better to and from a large city."

He added, "You remember the Stanleys, don't you?"

"I think I do," Emma replied. "Isn't she the up-and-coming captain who made a fine record as a corps officer?"

"Yes," George said. "Even as a girl soldier, she was a wonderful and fiery speaker. Her husband was a well-educated man who, nevertheless, worked as a postal clerk on a train. He got to drinking. Then he was converted. In the Salvation Army he met Mrs. Stanley. They got married and became Army officers."

"How many children do they have?"

"Two little girls. I think you'll like them."

The apartment was upstairs, over a store. The Tallmons lived across the hall from the Stanleys. They shared the same bath.

Mrs. Stanley was gone most of the time, doing corps work or holding meetings. Her husband stayed home and did the housework and looked after the children.

One morning Emma met Mr. Stanley in the hall.

He asked, "Aren't you going out today selling War Cries?"

"No, I wasn't planning to."

"The corps is behind in its debts," Stanley said. "You only sit home here, anyway. You should be out there helping Mrs. Stanley."

Emma ran back into her apartment in tears.

When her husband came home, he saw her red eyes and red cheeks and asked, "What's the matter?"

"Nothing serious," Emma replied.

"Tell me," George insisted. "I want to know. What's wrong?"

"Well, it was Mr. Stanley. He thinks I'm lazy. He said I ought to be out helping his wife. But I can't go out and leave Edith alone. Anyway, I don't like outside work."

"That's all right." George took her into his arms. "You don't have to do corps work."

"I take care of his two girls when he's away," Emma continued, looking up into his soft eyes. "That's helping, isn't it? Actually, I think he's the one who is lazy. He could go whenever he wants to, because I am always available to care for his children."

"That's true." George leaned over and gave Emma a kiss. Then he stepped back. Emma went on.

"He doesn't do anything but stay home most of the time. His children are spoiled. And his apartment isn't even tidy. It's upset and dirty, and the little girls' dresses are never clean."

She stopped. "But maybe I shouldn't criticize him."

"It helps to see other people's faults sometimes," George replied, sitting down in one of the chairs. "Then we can improve ourselves."

Just then Edith came running in from where she had been playing. She climbed up on her papa's lap, put her arms around his neck and exclaimed, "I woves 'oo."

Papa hugged her, and then slid her down onto his knee, to give her a horsey-back ride.

"Giddie-up, giddie-up," he recited, as he galloped her up and down on his leg.

"You must be hungry," Mama said, as she rushed to the kitchen. "Supper will be ready in a few minutes."

It was an extra-special weekend. And when Papa left once again, Mama said to him, "Jesus is so near, so precious. He has given me so much to be thankful for. The very best, dearest, kindest husband, one I should be willing to lay down my life for if necessary. Then my sweet little Edith, dear baby girl. I am such a blessed woman!"

"I am also very blessed--to have such a sweet and wonderful wife, and such a darling baby girl," George replied. "Jesus has been very good to us."

In his work, George journeyed from town to town all over Nebraska and Iowa. He usually traveled by train, but if the schedule did not suit him, he walked or caught a ride to the next place.

When he entered a town, he went up and down the business street, asking for contributions from the merchants. He stayed in cheap hotels and ate sparingly at restaurants. Some days he barely made expenses.

Late that fall, George and Emma rented a little house on the edge of Des Moines. Mama's baby was due late in December or early January. Ella came to stay as the time drew near.

Once again Mama and Papa couldn't agree on a name. So Papa suggested:

"Let's alternate. You name this baby, and I'll name the next."

Mama chose "Emma Elizabeth," in honor of the baby's mother and grandmother.

"All right," Papa agreed, but a little reluctantly. Mama knew why: he didn't really care for the name "Emma," even though it was his wife's name.

A decision on a boy's name was not so definite.

There was a chance the infant would be a New Century baby--born on Jan. 1, 1901. All day passed, followed by a night of dark and stormy weather.

Mama had left some plants in the window, between the window and shades. Outside, snow was falling and making pretty designs against the panes.

They went to bed. Toward midnight Emma called George and said the time had come. He pulled on his coat and plunged out into the cold and hard-driven snow to notify the doctor.

Little Emma Elizabeth wasn't a New Century baby. She was born at 2 a.m.--two hours too late. Papa stayed with his wife throughout the ordeal, holding her hand and comforting her. He was most solicitous in his gentleness.

The doctor went home, the family went back to bed, and in the morning the world outside was a beautiful white. The plants in the window had frozen.

That day, Papa sat down to write announcement letters to the relatives.

As he penned the first note, he wrote: "Emma is fine," and then started to say, "Emma is a beautiful little baby."

But that was confusion. So he wrote: "Bessie is a beautiful baby. She weighed 9 1/4 pounds and measured 20 1/2 inches."

When he showed the announcements to Mama, she was somewhat indignant. She wondered if he hadn't planned all along to call her Bessie. He had a sweetheart as a boy named Bessie, and he always liked the name.

But she said no more, and from then on the new addition was Bessie.

Little Edith wanted to go outside and play that day in the new-fallen snow. But it was too cold.

"I'll tell you what," Papa offered. "You watch from the window and I'll show you a surprise."

So Edith watched with her little nose pressed against the pane as Papa, dressed in overcoat, scarf and earmuffs, built a snowman--to her delight.

"Oh, Papa!" she exclaimed, clapping her hands. "Oh, Mama, see the 'no-man! See the 'no-man!"

Mama couldn't come to the window because she was confined to bed. But she knew what it was like.

"Yes," she said, "and the snowman even has a little coat, and hat, and rocks for eyes and a carrot for a nose!"

Bessie was a fat and pretty baby--very healthy--but Mama worried about every little thing, because she had lost George.

She made no complaint when the baby was restless or fussy during the night--because it was such happiness to have her.

Papa, too, was happy and proud to have a little girl.

"The Salvation Army is not a good place to raise a boy," he said.

The family moved to Omaha a short time later. Bessie was dedicated to God while they were there.

The Army always made a great to-do over the event. Sometimes the occasion was sensationalized. A story was put in the paper, and the public invited.

The headlines in the daily Omaha paper read: "BABY TO BE GIVEN AWAY BY SALVATION ARMY." Down farther in the article it added, "To Be Dedicated to God this Afternoon."

Many people came and had to be told that a baby wasn't really going to be given away.

That summer Emma was put in charge of a "fresh air camp" for 25 poor children from the city's slums.

It was one of the first such summer camps ever held in the United States, a forerunner of the later YMCA, Boy Scout and Girl Scout outings.

The camp was held at Fort Omaha, not far from where Boys Town was later located.

It was not a difficult assignment. Emma could stay in the buildings with her babies. And she had little do except to supervise the camp.

In August, after the camp was over, Mama left with her two children for Indianapolis. She planned a six weeks' visit with her family before Ella's wedding. Her sister, Ella, was to be married in September.

Papa came in time for the wedding. The Buffalo exposition was in progress, and the newspapers were full of stories about the attempted assassination of President McKinley. He lay gravely ill in a coma from a gunshot wound in the stomach.

After the wedding, Papa and Mama and their two girls left for home. Just before they reached Chicago, newsboys boarded the train, shouting, "Extra! Extra! Extra!"

The big black headlines told the story: President McKinley had succumbed from his wounds. The impact on the train passengers was devastating. Old men cried like babies.

"This is a sad day for our country!" Papa said, gravely. "What a shame! What a tragedy! McKinley was a good President. He did much good for our country. And, now, he has made the supreme sacrifice for all of us!"

At Chicago, the family left the train and were walking through the big Union Station when suddenly they bumped into--

Papa's father!

"Why, we didn't know you were here!" George exclaimed.

"I know. I was at the fair in Buffalo," Grandpa explained. "I just decided to go at the last minute. Wasn't it a tragedy about the President?"

"A terrible tragedy," George agreed. "But, tell me, were you there when he was shot?"

"I didn't see him get shot," his father replied, solemnly. "But I was in the crowd."

They traveled the rest of the way to Grinnell together, and Grandpa told more of what he had seen at the time of the shooting.

34.

George's younger brother John was not a bad person down deep. But, at the same time, he had a mean disposition, and was hard to get along with. He didn't pull with the family somehow.

When George and Emma were living in Des Moines, he was just out of the army, and stopped by often to see Emma and to play with little Edith.

Often he took trips away from home. The family wouldn't hear from him for weeks. Then perhaps they would get a postcard saying, "I'm all right," but nothing further about where he was or what he was doing.

He had been gone for two years, and they only knew that he was somewhere in California.

Then, in November, 1901, he was sitting in a barber shop in Dallas, Tex., waiting to get a haircut.

Suddenly there was a commotion outside. He rushed out. A large crowd had gathered. He pushed his way through and saw two men making their dogs fight by cutting them with a knife.

It was never clear just what happened. The crowd was pushing and shoving.

Perhaps John was jostled and he jostled back. Perhaps someone didn't like it and told him so, curtly. Perhaps John came back with a fast reply, as he was wont to do.

Or perhaps one of the men with the knives reared back into the crowd to make more room.

At any rate, John felt a sharp pain. He was stabbed in the groin--deeply. He was bleeding.

"Better get some dry earth on that to stop the bleeding," someone suggested. John went down to the river and coated the wound with mud. In a few days, it was bloated and infected.

Reluctantly, he went to a nearby Catholic hospital. He was put to bed immediately. The nuns were obviously concerned.

He refused to tell them who he was or where he lived. They tried to persuade him to write home, without success.

He grew worse. Lockjaw set in. Finally, when he realized how seriously ill he was, he wrote a short letter home:

"Dear father. I am in Sisters hospital at Ft. Worth Texas. Have been stabed an getting seriously ill. Come down. John C. Tallmon."

The nuns took his father's address from the envelope and sent an immediate telegram.

"Your son is dangerously ill, come at once. Sister St. Dennis."

The telegram arrived in Grinnell first--on a Monday morning--and Grandpa left immediately by train. He didn't reach Fort Worth until Tuesday evening.

By that time, John was gone.

There was nothing he could do but make arrangements to ship the body back to Grinnell for burial.

He had difficulty locating John's papers. Insurance papers, for one thing. The nuns found a bank book tucked down behind the bed, showing John had saved his money. But nothing else.

Grandpa searched and searched--and finally, on a bonfire in the back yard of the apartment where John lived, ready to be burned, he found the insurance papers. Someone, in cleaning out John's room, had thrown them out.

With a sigh of relief, Grandpa picked up the papers and returned to his hotel. Then he made arrangements to return to Iowa.

The funeral was simple but impressive. Many friends and neighbors came. Emma and the girls traveled alone from Omaha, and George followed as soon as he could. He arrived while the services were going on. Then George and Emma and their children returned home.

Emma and George hadn't lived in Omaha long before Emma received a special assignment.

George came home one day and said: "Brigadier wants you to take over the Council Bluffs corps." Council Bluffs was right across the river from Omaha.

Emma was flabbergasted.

"Me?" she gasped. "How can I? I'm not very good at that kind of work, and besides I have the babies to care for."

"Well, the brigadier explained that the Council Bluffs corps is in heavy debt. We are already receiving a salary. And we can live in the officers' quarters and pay rent there. That will give the corps an income, and any money from collections can go to pay off the debt. Brigadier said there are young girls among the soldiers who can care for the children while you are away. And I'll be glad to help you on weekends when I am home."

Emma, when she saw that George would be happy for her to try it, said she would.

Emma went to the owner of the hall formerly used by the Salvation Army.

"Can we use the hall again?" she asked.

He declined.

"I know we are in debt to you. Will you let us use it if every cent we take in goes to pay off the back rent?"

"In that case, yes," the owner replied.

Emma had small crowds. But among them were people she could talk to. Every week she had a good collection to take to the landlord.

For Thanksgiving, the corps put on a dinner for poor people at the hall. The soldiers served turkeys donated by local merchants and roasted free by a bakery. Emma did the other cooking.

More than 100 people, men, women and children, crowded the hall.

Edith was four at the time. When all the poor children and people were eating, Mama brought Edith to the hall and let her watch, as she had promised.

Emma had a successful ministry there. Several people were converted during the services. One fellow came regularly after his conversion. Every night he prayed for Emma first, before anything or anyone else.

Several times Emma was called to visit sick people.

A little baby, member of a poor and needy family, was very ill with pneumonia. She took care of the baby every night, all night, for six or eight weeks. The baby recovered--but later one of its brothers or sisters knocked over its high chair, and the baby was killed.

Another time Emma was called to visit a sick young lady, a soldier in the corps. She talked and prayed with her for an hour, and then learned that the girl, one of a group of such soldiers who lived together, had just been quarantined for small pox.

On a third occasion, Emma stayed overnight with a woman ill with typhoid fever. But she didn't contract either disease herself.

She left Council Bluffs with an active corps of soldiers and everything paid up to date.

That Christmas, Emma and George were visiting the family in Grinnell.

"We're going to move to California," George's father told him.

"Oh, really?" asked George, only a little surprised.

"Yes," Grandpa replied. "You know, since long before Susan died, I have dreamed of moving out there."

"Yes, I know," George said.

He remembered how Grandpa had traveled to California the year after he was so ill with pneumonia. The wonders of the Golden State had captured his heart.

Later Grandpa made another excursion--along with a group of well-to-do men. They were given a tour to interest them in California.

"After John died," Grandpa went on, "I made up my mind I was going. So, I took another trip out there and visited all the major college towns. I'd like to be close as possible to a college where the girls can attend school."

"What did you decide?"

"Well, I chose the University of California at Berkeley. It seems like a very good college, and Berkeley is a nice college town."

"Sounds fine," said his son. "When are you leaving?"

"As soon as I can sell my property and make the arrangements."

George was soliciting in the area, and, when moving time came, Emma returned to Grinnell to help. George was there on weekends.

George and his father were sitting, talking, one night after dinner.

"Why don't you leave the Salvation Army and come west, too?" Grandpa asked. "We can buy a farm and you can settle down there. We can work it together. You are the only son I have left, and I need you."

George noticed how old his father was becoming. But he shook his head.

"No," George said. "My work is with the Salvation Army. That's where I belong."

Emma made the same suggestion the next morning, as George was preparing to leave.

"I get so tired of you being away from home all the time," she sighed. "We could settle down on our own little place and make a new start."

"I don't like to be away so much, either," George replied. "But this is our work, and I must be away."

Emma stopped combing her hair and turned to her husband.

"If you dealt with people, I could see that we might be accomplishing something. But you are only collecting money. I don't see where you are doing any outstanding work."

George looked at her, then laid his hand on her shoulder and gave her a squeeze and a pat.

"The money is needed, and is being used for worthwhile purposes," he explained. "Don't you remember how hard a time we had while I was in charge of a corps? There are many programs sponsored by the Army that need financial help."

"I know that, of course." Emma felt a little impatient. "Money is the big problem in the Salvation Army. But that's the thing I don't look forward to--a life of poverty like when I was a girl."

"There are more important things in life than material things, Mama," George reminded her. "We are officers in the Salvation Army. We are dedicated to Jesus' work. Everything else is of less importance. Sometimes it is necessary to sacrifice a little."

"I know," she said. "But I would so much like to just have our own little home, our own little family, and just be together!"

"And I would like that, too. But, at least our life is better than when you were a girl. You lived in a less desirable family, and some of the things that happened weren't good. Some of the things you said weren't the best . . . "

He paused a moment, then asked, quietly: "Are you sorry you chose a life of service beside me?"

Then, in a moment of despair, he added, "You act sometimes like you no longer care for me."

Emma flushed.

"You act like you no longer care for me!" she replied, coldly.

"I'm sorry," George said, concerned when he saw she was upset. "I didn't mean to hurt your feelings."

But Emma turned away. She was deeply disturbed by his comment.

George looked at his watch and saw that he must hurry to catch the train. He started to kiss her goodbye.

She turned her cheek, not her lips.

Dismayed, he picked up his suitcase and walked out of the house, downhearted and disillusioned.

The train came puffing into the station, and he climbed aboard.

As it pulled away, a poor fellow with two satchels came rushing onto the station platform. The look of entreaty and hopelessness on his face was enough to stop anything with a heart.

But the train went off without him.

George wished he was off, and the fellow was on, in his place.

As the train left the houses and streets of Grinnell far behind, a single thought kept churning through George's mind: She never, never gave me her cheek before. She never, never, ever did that before.

The train rolled on toward George's destination--the town of West Branch. George penned a letter to his wife:

> Dearest Emma--
>
> I didn't miss my train this morning though I really wanted to see it go off without me . .
> I am real sorry I said what I did this morning. I know you feel worse than I ever did over any of your failings. And I didn't tell you in a loving way but I do love you mama.
> It was a sad little face that I kissed. You acted like you thought I had wronged you but you know love I didn't mean to be so unkind in what I said.
> It is not my business to find fault with you. I told you this morning that I was sorry. We better both be good darling for broken hearts are hard to heal.
> I hope you feel better now. God bless you.
>
> Your own loving
> George

Next day he wrote again:

> I am waiting waiting for a freight train. I like to wait. I feel just like it. I didn't want to see anybody today. I tried to miss my train but couldn't.
> I have got $4.70 here today; that is $3.12 above my expenses and I would gladly give twice that for a kiss from you but you gave me your cheek mama. That was all.
> You never did that before sweetheart and I had told you I was sorry. But then "Boys flying kites draw in their white-winged birds. You can't do that when you are flying words."
> Mama darling what made you send me off this way. How could I be happy, how can I work. What if I shouldn't get home.

The night train on the Iowa Central that I would probably have been on last Saturday if I hadn't been sick was wrecked and four people killed.

But don't be afraid dear. I am coming home all right. I will be there Saturday night.

I am a day late now and won't get your letters in Cedar R. till Friday but I hope you will be well.

God bless you,
Your George

The next one was written from Tipton the next day:

Dearest Emma,

Here I am pulling into Tipton $5.71 better off than I would have been if I had stayed home but feeling kind of blue.

I refused to go and help a minister in his meetings last night because I didn't feel just like it but I am going to cheer up and be more sensible today.

How foolish I am to feel bad after nearly five years of married life when you said I acted like I didn't care for you. I used the words first myself but not the way you took them.

I have cared for you and planned for your comfort and happiness ever since you promised to be my wife and you have been just as faithful in your devotion to me, and I would not have allowed this to stay in my mind only that it was my fault anything was said.

I spoke first from the best of motives, and as I have a perfect right to speak to you or you to me. But I did wrong to bring up the subject again especially in the way I did (regarding a number of things she had said as a girl that he thought were improper).

I know you have forgiven me in the generousness of your loving heart and probably would have forgotten long before this if I had kept still so I will say no more unless you wish to mention it.

It is cold this morning. The thermometer stands at zero. I had a poor room and no breakfast at my hotel. I will get a lunch at Tipton but don't know what I ought to eat. Fried stuff, eggs and potatoes are not good for me neither are cookies or doughnuts. If I go without any breakfast I will be in danger of eating too much dinner . .

I hope you and the babies are well and that my father is around as usual. How nice it would be if I could help in this moving etc. and yet do my work in the Army.

God bless you love. I am sorry I won't get any word from you till Friday.

Your loving
George

When the week was finally past, and George's train pulled into Grinnell, the streets and houses were covered with a February blanket of white.

George wrapped his scarf around his throat, pulled his overcoat around him, and, leaving his seat, walked to the exit doors.

When the train stopped, he climbed down the steps--and there before him, waving to draw his attention, were his father; Emma; two of the younger sisters, and a bundle of blankets--all seated on a horse-drawn sleigh.

George walked briskly to where they were, returned their cordial greetings, and saw Emma with her face radiant and her eyes smiling.

He climbed in beside her, squeezed her close, and was interrupted by the bundle on the other side, which said:

"Papa! Papa! Grandpa said I could come if I kept warm inside the blanket. Aren't you glad?"

He squeeze Edith, too, and said:

"I certainly am glad!"

And Grandpa drove home.

35.

It had been a hot, sticky June day in Omaha. When night came it was not any cooler.

Mama closed and locked the doors, but kept open the upstairs windows, hoping to let what little breeze there was inside.

Edith and Bessie were already in bed, sleeping fitfully because of the heat. Mama noticed how wet they were--and the bed was--from the dripping perspiration.

Once again Mama went to the window and peered toward the west. The sky was black and ominous, as much of it as she could see in the darkness. Not a star could be seen.

The wind was stirring the trees now, and an uneasy feeling swept through her as the branches swayed and the wind howled.

She got undressed and slipped into bed, not even tolerating a sheet over her. But she couldn't go to sleep. Loneliness swept over her, and she felt a concern deep within her.

Then it came--far off in the distance--a low, rumbling sound. Soon there was another, a little closer. A light flashed across the dark room, followed by a roll of thunder.

She had known thunder storms all her life. But she never liked them. And it was even worse when she was alone like this.

Papa was somewhere out on the road, visiting some far-off small town. She wondered what kind of a hotel he was staying in tonight.

Suddenly there was a bright light. It lit up the room like day. Then it flickered, grew bright, flickered, and died out. One, two, three, four, five seconds. Then came the low, rumbling, booming thunder--loud and ominous.

She lay there tense. Another flash. Another boom. More, more. She wished that the storm were over.

Then came a wailing sound. It was the sound of a woman crying.

Mama cringed, and lay there rigid. It was the woman who lived next door.

Mama remembered how the woman's husband had explained when they moved in a month before. Their little boy had died when his wife was away at a church convention. She carried on like this nearly every night.

Now the woman was singing. Some missionary song. The husband had given up his job as a hardware department manager for a big Omaha store and stayed with her constantly.

The woman was calling now for her lost son. Her voice grew angry--scolding, scolding. There she was singing again.

There was only a narrow passageway between the houses. Mama wouldn't let her girls run through, because she was afraid the woman might throw something down on them.

The wailing grew intense. There was a sharp flash of light. Every article in the room could be seen in clear detail. Then came a shattering, booming, rumbling roar. The rain outside came pelting down in sheets, pounding against the windows.

Emma turned her head and buried her face into the pillow, trying to be calm, trying to forget, trying to have courage.

Then the storm passed, the woman was quiet, and Emma finally dozed off into fitful sleep.

It was Saturday afternoon, late--almost suppertime.

"If you watch down the sidewalk, Papa should be coming," Mama told four-year-old Edith.

Edith watched and soon, not far off, she saw her father--dressed smartly in his blue uniform and flat, red-trimmed hat.

She ran to meet him.

"Papa, papa!" she exclaimed, as he caught her up in his arms.

"How's my little girl?" Papa asked. She threw her arms around his neck, and gave him a hug and a kiss. Then he set her down, and they walked, hand in hand, back to the house.

Papa kissed his wife, and then said:

"Wasn't that a bad storm we had last night? Were you frightened? I was thinking about you."

"I was scared," Emma admitted. "I don't like to be here alone when it storms like that."

"I don't like to leave you alone, either, dear," Papa replied.

Mama looked at him with pleading eyes.

"Oh, Papa," she begged, "can't we move away from here or do something so you can be home more?"

Papa said nothing.

"There's a letter there from your folks," Mama told him, as he laid away his coat.

Papa opened the letter. Sale of the home place and farm at Grinnell had gone through, and Grandpa had received his money.

Mr. Fuller, son-in-law of Tom Foster, had bought the house and five acres in town. And Grandpa's 10-acre farm brought $10,000! That meant more than $1,000 for each of Grandpa's children--"a good down payment on a farm for George in California."

Papa folded the letter and returned it to its envelope.

He did some tall thinking during the next few days. He thought about his father--getting old, only one son left, needing some help. He thought about Mama--scared at night, lonesome, tired of his being away from home so much.

And now, since Mama was going to have another baby, a new factor had arisen.

"It would be better if we didn't have to raise any boys in the Salvation Army," Papa had told his wife. "Living in slums and the poor parts of town is not the best environment for a growing family."

But he also remembered that he was a member of the Salvation Army--he had devoted his life to that work--and it was his Christian duty to do the tasks assigned to him. An officer was considered a backslider--a lost soul--if he ever quit.

While George was contemplating all these things, a bank official gave him a check one day while he was out soliciting.

"This is for the Salvation Army Rescue Home," the donor told him.

"Fine," George replied. "That's what it will be used for."

When he looked at the amount, he was amazed to see it was $25!

"Thank you, sir!" George exclaimed.

He turned in the contribution in the usual way on Monday, noting that the money was designated for the rescue home.

Sometime later he was talking to the woman who headed the rescue work and asked what she thought of the donation.

What donation? She knew nothing about it; she had never received it.

George was very much disturbed. He went straight to headquarters.

"It's all Salvation Army work," the brigadier explained. "What difference does it make?"

"It makes a lot of difference," George replied. "If that is what the money is given for, it should be used for that purpose."

George was bitterly hurt. He had promised the donor the money would be used for rescue work only. How could he solicit and make promises if the promises weren't honored? How could he stay in the Army if that was the way things were done?

He went home and talked it over with Mama.

"My father is getting old," he said. "Perhaps he needs me out there. He can spend his time on the farm and be a help to us. A farm is a much better place for growing children. I can go back into the Army later on."

"Then we're going to California?" Mama asked happily. "Oh, Papa, do you think we can?"

"I think maybe we will," Papa replied.

36.

Papa began to make arrangements to leave for California. He notified headquarters, and wrote to Grandpa.

Grandpa wrote back, pleased as anything. He would look for a ranch for George to buy as soon as he had the chance.

New officers were assigned to Papa's job. They came to see the house and agreed to buy Mama and Papa's furniture.

Mama felt a little bad about giving up her sewing machine and organ.

"I wish we could take them with us," she said.

"It would be too expensive to ship them."

"Then we must buy new ones when we get to California," Mama insisted.

And Papa promised.

Papa checked on the fare. With his Salvation Army card, he and his family could travel half fare on the train. That was $25 each for Papa and Mama, plus $5 for the berth. The children rode free.

Just as everything was set, their plans were shattered. The little girls came down with the whooping cough. They coughed, they vomited--they were sick little children.

There was nothing to do but stay in Omaha. Papa rented a furnished room and continued soliciting for the Salvation Army. Mama took care of the girls.

At the end of a month, the girls were still coughing. But the doctor said they were past the contagious stage, and it was all right to start the journey.

They took the train to Smith Center, Kansas, where Burt, Angie and family lived and where Burt was minister of the Congregational Church.

They spent a month there. George solicited in nearby small towns during the week, and spoke at church on Sunday.

Evenings, he relaxed, read, or talked with his brother-in-law. One evening, while they were chatting, the children began turning somersaults on the grass.

"Can you do handsprings and walk on your hands?" George asked them.

"No," they replied.

"I could when I was a boy."

"Oh, could you, Uncle George?" The children were all eagerness. "Will you do it for us now?"

George was game. "All right," he said. "I guess I can still do it."

He took the things out of his pockets, and turned a handspring right there. And then he walked on his hands.

The children were delighted. From then on, it was their goal to learn to turn handsprings and walk on their hands like Uncle George.

Grandpa wrote from California and said he had found a nice ranch for George. It was at Morgan Hill, a little community in the southern part of the Santa Clara Valley, south of San Jose.

The ranch consisted of 16 acres--five acres in fruit and the rest in hay. And the price was $2,750. George could use the $1,000 he inherited from his mother's estate, and his father would furnish the rest. George could pay off the balance at $100 per year.

George wrote back and told Grandpa to go ahead.

When it came time to leave, Papa wired to Chicago to reserve a lower berth. Then Papa, Mama, Edith and Bessie packed up and prepared to leave.

The Joneses went down to the station to see them off. It was 10 o'clock at night. The Tallmons climbed aboard, and the train pulled away.

They asked about their reservations. The conductor could not help.

"I wired to Chicago to reserve a lower berth," Papa said. "It's difficult for my wife to use an upper berth."

"I'm sorry," the conductor said. "All we have left is an upper berth."

So they had to take it.

All four slept in the same berth--Bessie between Mama and Papa, and Edith at the foot.

They were used to sleeping that way, and often did while away from home in the Salvation Army.

But the upper berth was most uncomfortable. And they had no warm food--only the lunch they brought, and nothing hot to drink.

For a woman half through her pregnancy, it was not good, and Mama got sick at her stomach--obviously--at night.

Finally the man in the berth below took pity on them, and on the third night changed places with them.

Crossing the country, nevertheless, was a new experience. Papa pointed out to Edith places in Colorado where he and Mama had been. The tall mountains and vast deserts were strange new sights--altogether different from the farmlands of Iowa and Nebraska where they had lived.

Papa drew pictures of sights they saw to amuse Edith as the train puffed slowly across Utah and Nevada.

Then came the high and beautiful Sierras of California, the Central Valley, and finally the expanse of San Francisco Bay.

This was California--their new home!

Grandpa and the girls were waiting at the Berkeley station to greet them.

Soon they were seated inside the tall, two-story residence on a hill within sight of the Golden Gate across the bay, telling of their experiences and hearing of the wonders of California.

The date was Sept. 8, 1902.

"You'll like the ranch in Morgan Hill," Grandpa promised. "But the place is leased for another month. In the meantime, you must stay with us, and George can help me add a third story to this house."

A few days later, Grandpa took Papa to Morgan Hill to see the new ranch. Papa was favorably impressed.

Then, when time came to move, Papa and Mama went by ferry to San Francisco to shop for furniture.

With $100 saved from Salvation Army work, they furnished the entire house. Everything they bought was brand new except an organ purchased at the Emporium for $10.

Mama could hardly wait.

Finally, the big day came. Everyone got up early and helped with breakfast. Mama packed the last minute things. The little family said happy goodbyes and climbed into the buggy. Grandpa drove them down to the ferry building.

Papa bought tickets and they walked to the pier. As they watched, a wide, flat-bottomed boat grew near and slipped between the rows of closely-placed pilings shaped like a "V."

The men on the dock lowered a ramp onto the boat deck, and passengers and freight began streaming ashore.

Then Mama, Papa and the two girls climbed aboard.

Soon they were gliding across the waters of San Francisco Bay. The engines of the white ferry boat thundered and roared, and the paddle wheels churned beneath them.

Grayish-white seagulls followed the boat--their keen eyes glued on the water as it came together behind the ferry. Every so often a gull suddenly dove straight for the water--and usually came up with a tiny fish in its beak.

The little family watched from the deck as the shores of the East Bay receded behind them. Then they walked to the front of the boat and saw Yerba Buena Island approaching.

Soon Yerba Buena Island was passed--and then the shores of the city of San Francisco drew near.

Off to the right, somewhat straight ahead, they could see the famous Golden Gate--an opening through the hills to the ocean. To the left, the bay extended out of sight--to the south and toward their new home.

Soon the ferry was sliding into its dock, and the ramp was lowered. They were in San Francisco!

They found their way out of the ferry building and into the bustle of the city. Before them, stretching away to the hills, was Market Street, the backbone of the city.

Catching a streetcar, they clanged and clattered on the side streets until they reached the Southern Pacific depot at Third and Townsend Streets.

They had to wait for train time in the expansive station lobby. Finally, the call came, "All aboard!" and they found their places on a train which had backed into a stall along one of the concourses outside the lobby.

The train chugged through the residential sections of San Francisco, then into the outskirts and out into the country.

Southward it moved--but only slowly, stopping at every little hamlet. Cows were grazing, and a woman--a farmer's wife-- was trudging along a dirt road.

They passed through the towns of Burlingame, of San Mateo, and of Redwood City. Then, as they approached the new town of Palo Alto, Papa said:

"This is the home of Stanford University. Watch along the track here on the left."

Mama watched, and as the train thundered across a bridge, she saw two tall, giant trees, with upswing branches and dark-green needles. The red-colored trunks were so big it would take two people with arms outstretched to reach clear around them.

"Those are redwood trees," Papa said. "They're really big, aren't they?"

"I've never seen any like that before!" Mama exclaimed. "They are beautiful, too."

"Palo Alto is named for those trees," Papa explained. "Palo Alto means 'tall tree' in Spanish."

After awhile, they passed through San Jose, a thriving, bustling little city, then once again into the country, through orchards and ranches.

When they came to a little hamlet, Papa pronounced the name: "Coy-o-tee."

"What a strange sounding name," Mama noted. Papa said a coyote was a strange little animal something like a dog.

Every place the train stopped, Edith jumped from her seat. She thought she had reached their destination.

"No, not yet," Papa had to tell her.

Finally, Papa said, "The next station is ours."

The train puffed into the station marked, "Morgan Hill," and ground to a stop. As the engine bubbled and hissed, the family climbed off.

"This is Morgan Hill, our new home," Papa announced.

"It sure is good to be here!" Mama said, excitedly.

Papa picked up their luggage and, as the train pulled away, they walked to the main street of town, one block away.

"We'll stop and get some groceries," Papa said.

"And I need a broom."

They spotted a store, "Mason & Son, General Merchandise," and went in.

"We are Mr. and Mrs. George Tallmon," Papa told Mr. Mason. "We just bought the old Story ranch on Dunne Avenue."

The storekeeper was cordial.

"Welcome to Morgan Hill," he said. "Did you folks just get in?"

"Yes," Papa replied. "And would you mind taking us out to the ranch when you deliver our groceries?"

The old man said he would be glad to.

It was a hot, dusty day, and Dunne Avenue, just a wagon road, was a sea of dust. But Mama didn't mind. She was on her way to her own little home, just for them.

Mr. Mason drove an open spring wagon. Mama sat in front, next to Mr. Mason, along with Bessie and Edith. Papa stood on the wagon bed and leaned over the seat.

They drove for a mile, and then Mr. Mason slowed down and turned into a driveway.

There, behind a tall cypress hedge, stood a little, square white house, about six or seven years old.

Across the driveway was a large red barn. And to the rear was a tall tankhouse topped by a windmill.

"Do you like it?" Papa asked.

"Yes, I do," Mama replied. "It's just wonderful! Just like I had dreamed. But--isn't someone still living here?"

Sure enough, the renters hadn't left yet. When Papa knocked, Mrs. Gregg came to the door.

"Oh!" she exclaimed. "We weren't expecting you until tomorrow."

"This is Oct. first," Mama said, "the day we were supposed to come."

"There must be some mistake," Mrs. Gregg replied. "But, come on in. You can stay overnight, anyway."

"That would be nice," said Papa. And so they brought their suitcases in.

"Would you like to look around?" Mrs. Gregg asked. Mama said she would, and Mrs. Gregg showed her through the house.

There was the kitchen, the front room and three bedrooms, joined by a hall.

A long porch ran along the outside of the house, across the kitchen and then down the side. A summer kitchen--a shed lean-to--was located close to the porch just outside the kitchen door. It contained a big old- fashioned cook stove for use during hot weather.

And just beyond the kitchen was a wonderful luxury--running water! The faucet tapped the supply in the tankhouse just beyond.

The far end of the porch, next to the summer kitchen, was enclosed. It contained the bathroom, with zinc tub. It was not a finished room, and water for the tub had to be carried from the kitchen.

The water, though, ran out of the tub afterward--just drained onto the ground outside.

Mr. Gregg, a carpenter and a cripple, showed Papa around outside. They looked at the barn, the adjoining tool shed, and at Mr. Gregg's chickens.

He offered to sell Papa some young hens--"because it would upset the pullets to move them." Papa agreed to the bargain.

The Greggs also had saved a pail of peaches from the year's crop for them. Mama canned them later--the first canning she had done in her life.

Mr. Gregg showed Papa the place in the front yard where the first Mrs. Story had been buried shortly after the house was built.

"She was supposed to have been the first person to die in Morgan Hill," Gregg related. "Later, after a cemetery was established, her body was transferred there."

Just then the men were called in to supper. They sat down to the table and, after Mr. Gregg said grace, began to eat. There were eggs, from chickens on the ranch. But Mama noticed they served no butter.

"You know, this house was tied up in court proceedings before your father purchased it," Mr. Gregg said. "It was built by Seymour C. Story while his first wife was alive. After she died, he married again.

"But Mr. Story had trouble with his second wife. She married him for his money. He deeded the property over to his daughter, Mrs. Rochelle. Your father bought the property from her, although it was actually owned by Story."

Mama and Papa slept that night in the front bedroom, along with Edith and Bessie.

Next day, their furniture came. So, while the Greggs moved out, piece by piece, the Tallmons moved in. Mama and Papa unloaded the packing box and the trunk they brought from Omaha.

They distributed the furniture among the five rooms. The little range was placed before the kitchen chimney. The kitchen work table, with rounded bins of various widths underneath, was set close by the door leading to the back bedroom.

The black walnut dining table, just large enough for the family of four, stood before a window with view of the red barn and ranch outside.

Papa crossed the road and gathered fuel for the range from among the heavy Dunne woods.

When everything was in order and everyone gone, Mama threw her arms around Papa, exclaiming, "This is our house! This is our house! We finally have a house all of our own!"

37.

The first Sunday in Morgan Hill, Mama wasn't able to go to church because Bessie couldn't walk through the thick dust.

Instead, she stayed home and played hymns and Salvation Army songs on the organ.

Edith and Papa got ready and went. They made their way along Dunne Avenue to the Presbyterian Church, located at the edge of town.

The church was closed. A sign read, "No services today. Pastor on vacation."

So Papa and Edith continued on into town and attended the Methodist services. There was no Salvation Army corps in Morgan Hill.

By next week, Papa had bought a horse and buggy, and the whole family was able to go.

They set out in best bib and tucker--Mama dressed smartly in her Salvation Army suit, the girls spotless and neat, and Papa in his Army uniform.

As they approached the Presbyterian church, Papa started to slow down.

Edith immediately objected.

"Papa!" she exclaimed. "Aren't we going to OUR church?"

Papa smiled.

"It's not good to shop around," Papa said. So they drove on to the Methodist church.

A crucial juncture in family history had been passed.

Because of that simple decision that Sunday morning, the Tallmons' lives were vastly altered and forever changed.

The family was welcomed warmly by the Methodists. The women at the door introduced themselves as Mrs. Catharine Stone and her mother, Mrs. Walrath. Others spoke to them. Then Mama and Papa continued on into the church.

Papa, cap in hand and carrying Bessie on his arm, followed Mama and Edith to a pew.

He sat down, placed the cap on the floor in the aisle, and put Bessie on his knee. He smiled at the little girl in the row in front of them, who had turned around to see the new family.

The girl noticed his thick mustache, the twinkle in his eye, and the way the corners of his eyes wrinkled like crows' feet when he smiled.

And her mother was impressed by his tender, understanding glances at his wife; his loving looks at the baby, and the air of peaceful serenity about him.

After the services, other people introduced themselves and welcomed them to Morgan Hill.

The minister shook hands with them at the door. Noticing Papa's Salvation Army uniform, he asked where he was stationed.

Papa explained that he had left active duty and had bought a ranch at Morgan Hill, where he planned to make his home.

"Say," Reverend Van Anda said, "I wonder if you will do me a favor. I have to lead services tonight at the Amada church at Coyote. Would you mind conducting services here?"

"I'd be glad to," Papa replied. And so he did.

Mama brought her guitar and, laying Bessie on the hard front pew, sang the solo. Papa led the service and gave the sermon.

Next week, the whole story was in the Morgan Hill Times. And the editor said Mama had "a sweet voice."

After that, Mama and Papa helped out with the evening service on several occasions, and Papa began taking an active part in the life of the Methodist Church.

He taught an adult Bible class, and Mama attended. The class met in the back rows of the pews, in a corner of the rough-hewn, wooden, plain-built church.

Edith happily went to Sunday school class--and took a leading part in the lesson. But Bessie was frightened, and wouldn't go to nursery class.

She wanted to go, but was too bashful. So Papa took her with him to the adults' class.

Papa, even though he now was attending the Methodist church, didn't forget his Salvation Army connections. But the nearest corps was in San Jose, 20 miles away. That was half a day's journey by horse and buggy.

A group of Salvation Army officers came to Morgan Hill on one or two occasions, and Papa helped them with street meetings. He also solicited in the Morgan Hill area when he had time.

The response was limited. The Salvation Army was virtually unknown in the West. People were curious and came to the street meetings, but that was as far as it went.

On one occasion, a small boy was acting up while the outdoor meeting was going on.

Papa, dressed in his Army uniform, was talking to the crowd.

"Be careful, Carl," the boy's mother warned him, pointing to Papa. "He's a policeman."

The boy settled right down.

Papa's first job was fixing a pump at a ranch near the foothills, west of town.

A man came to the house and asked if Papa could mend a pump. Papa said yes--he had fixed lots of them--and went and fixed it. He received a day's wages--$1.50.

Papa learned later that Mr. Gregg, who had rented Papa's house, had recommended him.

In those days, the countryside was wooded--mostly with oak trees--except for small openings or vistas here and there. Often the vistas led from one to another.

A person could stand in one green meadow, with birds singing and the wildflowers in bloom, and look through the trees into another meadow, and from there into another meadow beyond.

In the fall, the grass was dry and the wildflowers were gone. But the moss-covered trees and underbrush were picturesque in their colors and shapes. And the ground was covered with leaves, acorns, low bushes and berry plants.

This natural beauty was falling victim to the onset of fruit ranches. The land was being subdivided. And the big, old, rugged, spreading oak trees, with their low-hanging branches, had to go.

Papa found a job with Mr. Barrett, pulling stumps from the Dunne Woods as part of a crew.

His pay was $2.50 a day for a 10-hour day. And he had to furnish his own horse.

Since he didn't have one, he went to San Jose and bought a horse--a big, dark-colored stallion. The man said it was a fine horse--it could pull good.

Papa used it one day and found it was not as represented. The horse had heaves--horse asthma. It couldn't work. So he took it back.

The horse trader was angry.

"That's a good horse," he insisted.

But Papa knew it wasn't.

He asked for his money back. The man refused. So Papa, rather than arguing, stopped payment on the Omaha check he had given the man, bought another horse somewhere else, and went back to work.

A few days later the town constable, Lucas Petrone, showed up at the field where the men were working.

"I'll have to place you under arrest," he told Papa. "I have a warrant out of San Jose, charging you with issuing a fictitious check."

Mr. Barrett went with Papa down to the station. He put up the $1,000 bail necessary for Papa's release.

"What will people think of us?" Mama worried when Papa told her about the episode that night.

"I'm not going to worry," Papa replied. "Because I know I haven't done anything wrong."

Papa hired a lawyer. On the appointed day, he went to San Jose to face trial.

His lawyer stated the facts. Papa had bought a horse, it wasn't as represented . .

"Case dismissed," the judge declared.

So Papa was exonerated.

Pulling down huge live oak trees was a job that required know-how and proper equipment.

The stump pulling crew used a windlass--a large pulley with a bar through it and a cable wrapped around it. The cable was tied to the tree, fairly high up, and to the base of a nearby tree or stump--down low for maximum pull.

It was sort of a block and tackle in a horizontal position.

A team of horses was harnessed to the bar, and walked slowly around and around, winding the cable upon the drum. The horses had to go in a wide circle, and step over the cable each time around.

Slowly, slowly, the tree would start to come over, and then, it would fall.

A thousand head of Angora goats, owned by a French family, lived in the woods. The goats were beautiful with their long, flowing hair.

As each tree fell, they rushed up the trunks and ate moss from the branches as high as they could reach. It was quite a goat delicacy, and they cleaned it right off.

Papa's job was to drive the horses as they plodded round and round the capstan.

Sometimes the anchor tree, rather than the one that was being pulled, would start to come. Then the men would have to stop, move the cable to another anchor tree, and try again. It was Papa's job to watch the anchor tree.

Three times one morning the anchor tree started to come. The other men were cussing and swearing, but Papa said not a word.

"How can you keep so calm?" asked one of the men at noontime, as they sat in a circle in the shade of an oak tree eating their lunches.

"Oh, I guess it's my Salvation Army training," Papa laughed.

"Were you in the Salvation Army?" the man asked.

"Yes," Papa replied. "I was a captain in Iowa and Nebraska before I moved out here."

"Good," said the man. "Now we can keep you straight. We call the other George 'Swedish George,' and we can call you, 'Salvation George.'"

And so they did.

Most of the men in the stump pulling crew were Italians, Mexicans or Portuguese. There were Tony Rosa, Johnnie Gallardo, Milt Molarno, Jack Casella, August Casella, Carlo de la Razio, among others.

Johnnie Gallardo was a big, husky Mexican--a callow, self-assured young fellow who boasted he could out-wrestle anyone in the world.

Papa mentioned that "as a boy, I was a good wrestler."

Johnnie wanted to take him on.

"I can lick you with one hand behind my back," he boasted.

Papa accepted the challenge, even though he was short and lightweight--145 to 150 pounds--and Johnnie weighed 180 to 190 pounds and stood 6 feet, 2 inches tall. Also, Gallardo was 21 or 22, almost 10 years younger than Papa.

The other men watched with anticipation, expecting to see Papa get soundly defeated.

They grappled, Papa was too quick, got a good hold, and threw his opponent to the ground.

Johnnie, the picture of astonishment, picked himself up, brushed the dust off his clothes, and never bragged about his fighting ability around the stump crew again.

One day the crew was pulling an extra big, heavy tree in a field on the southwest corner of Tennant and Murphy Avenues.

Papa, as usual, was driving the team around and around the sweep.

The cable bit into the red sap of the giant oak tree. The cable was taunt with tension. The tree wouldn't budge.

Suddenly, a hook on the double tree broke. Papa was only eight or ten inches away. He was hit in the stomach.

The impact doubled him and rolled him, head over heels, 50 to 100 feet across the field.

The other men, horrified by what they saw, ran to his aid.

He lay there, white as a sheet.

"He musta be dead--broken inside." Jack Casella was sure.

The men carefully picked George up and laid him under a tree. They used denim jackets as a pillow under his head, and poured water over him to revive him.

He lay there for a long time--it seemed like an hour or more--and then began to stir.

The Italians ran for their wine jug--they had some left from lunch. One man lifted George's head, while another raised a cup of wine to his lips.

But George, who was regaining consciousness, turned his head away and closed his lips.

"Itsa good for you," they insisted. "Helpa make you well."

"Thanks," Papa replied, sitting up. "I know you are being thoughtful, and it's nothing against you. But I don't drink liquor, even as a medicine. Anyway, I'm not hurt. What happened?"

"The double tree broke," Mr. Barrett replied. "You had quite a wallop. You'd better lie here for a while until you feel better."

Papa rested a little longer, but soon was able to get up and go back to work.

"And he not drink da vino when he'sa hurt," Jack Casella said, as the men returned to their jobs. "He'sa quite da man."

Another time, Papa came mighty close to blowing himself up.

The boss asked, "George, will you go to town and pick up a box of dynamite caps?"

George mounted his horse and rode to town. He picked up the box of caps, placed it in his vest pocket, and rode back at a fast pace, the brush slapping across his chest as he rode along.

When he arrived at the spot where he had been working, the boss was shocked.

"You're a lucky man, George," Mr. Barrett exclaimed. "The way you were riding that horse through the brush could have easily set off one of the caps."

But Papa didn't know any better. He was inexperienced.

Mr. Barrett later placed Papa in charge of blazing the best trees. So many per acre were to be saved.

Many of the big, beautiful old oak trees left standing for years afterward, among the Morgan Hill ranches, were those picked out by Papa.

Later Papa became crew foreman.

Papa was driving a horse and wagon near town one day when he spotted a young, husky black man walking along, carrying a roll of blankets.

"Say, mister," the man called as Papa approached. "Do you know where I can get a job?"

"There ought to be one, some place around here," Papa said as he stopped. "Maybe I can get you a job with the stump crew. Climb aboard. I was headed there now."

So the young fellow climbed up on the wagon and they started off. Papa noticed his companion was powerfully built, with big hands and feet, and bulging muscles.

"Where are you from?" Papa asked.

"I'm from Baltimore," the black man replied. "I heard so much about California I hopped a freight and came out. But I can't find any work."

"Well, maybe something will happen here," Papa said, optimistically. "We're short on help."

When they arrived at the clearing, Papa took the stranger over to Mr. Barrett and asked if the boss could use him.

"Well," Barrett said. "I could use another man. But I don't know what the owners would say about hiring a Negro."

"Suppose he works for me, then," Papa offered. "And I'll use him to work for you. Then you can pay me the salary he would get, and I can pay him."

"All right," Barrett replied. "I wouldn't do this, if help wasn't so hard to find. But as long as he's working for you, it will be all right."

Nigger John--as the men called him--proved to be a good, strong and faithful worker. The boss made arrangements for him to care for the owners' horses, and live in a one-room cabin near the livery barn, close to town.

Big John worked on the stump pulling crew for several years. He was an upstanding, honest fellow, but a gruff one.

One day, the grocer's boy, Floyd Stone, stopped to watch the men work. He got to fooling around the stumps.

Big John went over and told him, harshly, to get away.

"I don't want to see any little boys killed," he thundered.

Floyd continued playing about the stumps.

Then Papa went over and explained to the boy:

"That cable is likely to snap, and could cut a man right in two."

Papa spoke quietly, patiently, and Floyd listened.

The boy didn't stay any longer, and left the area.

38.

Autumn leaves were turning brown in the Dunne Woods and the sun was setting in the west as Mama, Papa and the two girls headed toward their little home.

They had been to town to buy a few groceries for the weekend.

Papa was driving, Mama was holding Bessie, and Edith sat on a seat on the floor facing Mama. They were riding in the new buggy Papa had bought soon after their arrival in Morgan Hill.

Papa spoke quietly to Betty, the little brown mare. She was a nice, gentle horse--the family pet. Papa had "given" her to Mama.

Papa began singing a little jingle he made up:

> Peggetty-Peg. Peggetty-Peg.
> Travel along on your little brown leg.
> Peggetty-Peg. Peggetty-Peg.
> Travel along on your little brown leg.

It was a special time, and Mama was filled with joy and happiness.

"Oh, it's so wonderful, wonderful!" she sighed. "To have a home of our own! And to think I can have you with me all the time. It's wonderful!"

Papa put his arm around her and drew her a little closer.

"It IS wonderful, love," he said. "And this is such a nice community and such a beautiful place to settle down!"

Ahead of them, across the narrow valley to the east, rose the brown hills of Pine Ridge. To the rear, just below the setting sun, was Murphy's Peak, its sharp, pointed top ascending into the sky.

Alongside the dusty road, the ground was covered with dry grass and fallen leaves. Birds were twittering in the trees beyond, settling down for the night. A squirrel ran up a nearby oak tree, acorns in its pouch.

Mama and Papa began to sing:

> My sweet little home in the valley -- yodel --
> I live there so happy and free.
> There winds with the bright flowers dally -- yodel
> And birds sing as they cling to a tree.

"I have to work harder here," Papa said. "But the wages are good and I am with my family."

Then he sang:

> Don't you know, don't you know
> What a feller has to do,

When he has a little family
Depending on him so?

He should try to be a man,
And do the best he can
For Molly and the baby,
Don't you know?

Soon they reached the tall cypress hedge and the little white house. Papa slowed down, turned into the driveway, and came to a halt. Everyone got out, and Papa drove on to the barn to put Betty in her stall.

Mama walked back down the driveway to see if there were any mail.

"My sweet little home in the valley," she hummed. "I live there so happy and free . . . "

Living on a ranch was a new and exciting experience for Mama. She loved the scenery, the rolling hills, the brown and yellow trees just losing their leaves. And she enjoyed the animals and pets and chores.

Every living thing on the place had a special personality. Even the hens were named.

Of special interest was the incubator left in the summer kitchen by the former occupants. The incubator was table-height, flat, and stood on legs of its own. A hood protected the top, and a little flue carried away the fumes.

"Let's try it out," Papa suggested one day.

So they put in two or three dozen eggs for a starter, and set the little kerosene lamp going.

The only difficulty was that they turned off the lamp when they were away from home. They didn't know the eggs had to be kept warm--the same temperature--continuously.

"I don't want my pretty little house to burn down," Mama said.

Three weeks passed, and no chickens appeared. So they kept the incubator going longer. At four weeks, a few hatched, and lived for a few days.

One chick finally grew to maturity.

They set their hens after that, using the natural way.

When Mama and Papa moved to Morgan Hill, they were warned to keep the chicken house locked at night. But one time they forgot and left the door open.

That night, after everyone had gone to bed and everything was dark, Mama awoke with a start. She could hear a rumpus outside, a great amount of cackling and commotion.

"Papa! Papa!" she cried. "Something's in the chicken house!"

Papa sleepily climbed out of bed and pulled on some clothes. He rushed outside, Mama right behind him.

The chickens were out of their pen, and scattered about the yard, hiding under the hedge or other places they could find, cackling loudly.

Papa gave a shout. There was rustling in the bushes and the sound of something running away. It disappeared into the darkness.

"Coyotes, no doubt," Papa said. "We scared them away just in time!"

After that, they were extra careful about keeping the chicken house locked up.

Major was an old black dog that was very gentle. He was a stray that had made himself at home at the Tallmons', and they kept him.

He carried the cats around by the back of the neck--they liked it. He was a nice dog, a family pet.

But he had the bad habit of chasing chickens, and sometimes broke eggs and ate them.

One morning, Mama went to the chicken coop and found Major lapping up a raw egg. Several other empty egg shells lay nearby.

She was furious.

"I hope you take that dog away and never bring him back," she exclaimed, crossly, to Papa. "He's nothing but a nuisance!"

Papa drove off to work, Major following along behind, as he usually did.

At the field, Mr. Barrett, the boss, was busy getting things ready to start the day. Papa drove his horse around the capstan, hitched it up, and then helped Mr. Barrett move the cable to a new tree.

Major loped along with them.

"That dog's in disgrace," Papa mentioned, in his usual quick way. "He's been eating eggs and my wife doesn't like it. I'll have to get rid of him."

Nothing more was said, but a short time later, Mr. Barrett called Major over, picked up an axe, and hit him over the head.

Mr. Barrett, a rough, gruff man, hated dogs, anyway. He kept a rifle on the seat of his buggy all the time, prepared for any eventuality.

He threw Major into a stump-hole.

Papa, when he realized what had happened, was shocked. He felt terrible.

"I didn't mean to kill the dog," he exclaimed. "I only meant to give him away or something."

But the dog wasn't dead.

Just then, Major came dragging out of the hole, badly hurt and one eye hanging out. Papa had to finish killing him.

That night, Mama noticed that Major wasn't with Papa. She asked why.

"Did you give him away?"

Then Papa told her the whole story--how he had only said, "I'll have to get rid of that dog," and Mr. Barrett took it upon himself to kill him, and how Major came climbing out of the hole.

A feeling of despair swept over Mama. She broke into tears.

"That poor little dog," she cried. "And to think a few fussy words from me caused his death!"

She also felt Mr. Barrett's actions were unjustified.

"I can't get over how a man could be so cruel! And the fact that Major did not die right away makes it so much worse!"

She woke up crying for nights afterward, and for weeks she couldn't speak of Major.

But an ever greater tragedy was in the offing.

Betty, the pretty little brown mare, was the family's pride and joy.

Whenever she got loose, she ran downtown. Invariably, she could be found standing at the church, with her nose up to the tree where she was tied every Sunday.

Papa and Mama used her to buy groceries, too, but she never went to the store by herself.

There was no corral at the Tallmon ranch, and Papa tethered the stock in the grass. That's probably how she got away so often.

Polly was Papa's work horse. She was the one he bought when he took back the horse with asthma.

Polly was gaunt, sway-back, big and old, not at all like Betty. But she could sure pull.

One of Papa's jobs was to load wood onto freight cars at the Tennant Avenue station.

By taking advantage of a slight grade, it was possible to use a horse to move the cars. The full car could be started downhill by releasing the brakes. Then the horse was harnessed to the empty car, and by pulling from the side of the tracks, the car was towed to the place where the down-grade began.

On this particular morning, Polly was sick or unavailable, so Papa took Betty instead. He hitched the little brown mare to the step of the car.

Betty pulled, and the car moved forward. It went too far, started down the incline, got going too fast, and before anyone could stop it, Betty caught her foot in the track and was hit by the car.

Papa ran to see how badly she was hurt. Her leg was broken. She was whining and thrashing.

"That's all right, Betty," he patted her gently, trying to soothe her. "That's all right, girl!"

But he was worried. He knew what had to be done. He knew the tragedy that had occurred, and he was sick about it.

"We'd better shoot her," one of the other men said. They went to get Mr. Barrett's gun.

Papa hated to go home that night. He hated to face Mama and the girls. Betty was such a favorite!

He went in.

"I have something terrible to tell you," he said. "Betty was hit by a freight car, and we had to shoot her . . ."

"Not Betty!" Mama exclaimed.   Then she broke into tears.

That evening Mama sat by the lamp and cried a long, long time. The children cried, too, because Mama was crying. Papa sat in a corner, feeling blue. It was a black, black day.

After awhile, they got another horse--a gentle white mare named Dolly. She was a nice horse, too, and soon found a place in their hearts.

But she never really could take Betty's special place.

Papa always liked animals. He never shouted or yelled at them, and was always kind.

One day he noticed some animals pastured near where the stump-pulling crew was working. It came Sunday, and Papa knew the animals would need water that day. If he didn't haul it for them, no one would.

It wasn't his responsibility. They weren't his. But he hitched up his horse and spent part of his Sunday carrying water to the thirsty animals.

Victoria was an intelligent little fox terrier. She, too, followed Papa wherever he went.

One day, while Papa was helping to dynamite some stumps, she got ahold of some poison. Papa didn't realized it until that evening, when he was milking and noticed Vic having spasms. He gave her some warm milk, and it helped. After awhile she seemed to be all right.

A week later, they were working in the same field again, and Vic found some more poison. When Papa noticed her, she was violently ill and vomiting. In only a few minutes, she was dead.

Papa laid her in the wagon and carried her home that night. He had a sad tale to tell the children. Then he went out and buried little Vic.

The children cried and cried. After they went to bed, Edith kept sobbing and hooping it up. It wasn't that she really felt all that bad about Vic's death. But she loved a little bit of the dramatic, and she wanted to show how sorry she felt.

Finally Papa went to her door.

"All right, Edith," he told her. "That's enough. You've had a real good cry. It's time you were stopping and going to sleep."

That was all; he did no preaching. But right then and there Edith learned a lesson she never forgot.

You can feel sorry without making a big show about it.

39.

It seemed as if Mama's baby would never come. The last two or three weeks were especially trying.

"All things come to those who wait," wrote Grandpa from Berkeley. And Mama waited.

Her doctor was a fine man, an efficient doctor, of higher calibre than could be expected in such a small town.

And it was good. For when the baby was born, on Feb. 18, 1903, the cord was wrapped around its neck. There was a moment of suspense--and then all was well.

It was a boy--a big, fat, 9 1/2-pound baby with brown hair and blue eyes--and a dimple in his chin. Papa was proud, and Mama never tired of holding him and looking into the dear little baby's face.

It was Papa's turn to name the baby, and he picked out "Raymond Albert," in honor of a cousin and an uncle. Albert was his own middle name, also.

Mama didn't especially care for the part Albert, although it was "all right."

Papa's sister, Lucy, came from Berkeley to care for Mama and the family. While she was there, her boy friend, Harry Miler, came to see her several times. Later they were married.

Bessie didn't know what to make of a little brother. And when Papa said, "Your name is Bessie now," she objected.

"I 'Baby,'" she insisted in an injured tone.

"All right," laughed Papa. "You're Papa's baby."

After that, she made it clear to everyone: "I Papa's baby."

Bessie, as a tiny girl, talked stylish.

"Oh, deah," she would say. "My haih." She'd drop her "r's."

Edith would say she was going to do something. Bessie would chirp in, "Me, too!"

Often Papa and Edith went to church alone. In fact, someone, noticing that Papa always came to church with Edith, asked, "Are you a widower?"

"No, I have a wife at home," he replied, amusedly.

Mama had to stay home with the little ones. But she sat down at the organ and sang Salvation Army songs and hymns during church time. Often Bessie climbed up on the organ bench beside her, and "played" and "sang" too.

One day Mama discovered Bessie at the organ, thumping away and singing at the top of her voice, "'Appy 'ome! 'Appy day!" just like she had heard her mama do.

Spring came, and the bare trees returned to life. They produced buds and then the most beautiful blossoms Mama and Papa had ever seen.

The hills around the valley were green with new grass. The wildflowers burst forth, and the ground under the trees was a carpet of pink and green. Poppies, violets, buttercups and many other flowers were in bloom.

Then, suddenly, the calendar turned backwards. Papa awoke one morning to find trees and roofs covered with a thin blanket of white.

He didn't realize the significance at first, but soon learned that a very late, unusual frost had severely damaged his fruit crop.

His peaches were almost a complete loss. So were the cherries and almonds. His prunes were damaged, but not as seriously. Most of the small trees were almost fruitless.

The rest of the ranch was disappointing, too. When he harvested the hay crop early in June, he found the yield very limited. His vegetable garden, also, was not very encouraging to an Iowa farmer.

Grandpa often visited from Berkeley and helped Papa around the ranch. He got up early--as early as 4 a.m.--and chopped wood for an hour before breakfast. That was his daily ritual.

And he set traps all over the orchard to catch gophers.

"It's too bad you have to work on the outside so much," he told his son one morning as Papa was hitching up to leave for a day's work with the stump pulling crew.

"I have to, in order to make ends meet," replied Papa with a laugh. "This ranch doesn't produce much. The income will not be 5 per cent on the investment, even when I count the rent of the home equal to the work done on the place. I heard one of the men at work say that this is the poorest land in Santa Clara County. It's so rocky.

"It wasn't as good a ranch as I thought," Grandpa admitted.

"But one thing is certain," Papa added, as he climbed onto the wagon. "We have a lovely home in a community which will bear comparison with any. And we received a welcome which could have not been much more cordial if we had been sent here in charge of some church."

"At least you have work to do," replied Grandpa. "And don't worry about the payments on the ranch. I'll be glad if you just pay the interest."

As Papa drove away, Grandpa got busy doing some odd chores around the place, before going into the house to work on his Spanish lesson.

And when he returned to Berkeley, he sent down some groceries "to help Georgie out."

Papa took a job at the Cunningham's dry yard. The Cunninghams had the largest dry yard of any in the southern part of Santa Clara County, and employed dozens of cutters and field hands.

The women sat at long tables and sliced open apricots with paring knives. They become adept at laying open the fruit with one hand, removing the seed with a deft twist, and placing the two apricot halves on a large tray--all with one smooth movement.

Papa's job was to keep the women and girls supplied with boxes of fruit to cut. Cutters were paid by the number of boxes they did. So he tried to be extremely fair about distributing the boxes and keeping everyone supplied. He didn't want to favor anyone, nor discriminate against anyone.

There was one exception, though. The Simpson girl, a poor little orphan living with relatives in Morgan Hill--he may have favored her a little bit more than the others.

Papa was always jolly and even-tempered, and the cutters liked him. He wasn't like some of the men they'd had.

"We're glad you came to supervise the fruit cutting," a woman told him one morning, "because we know we won't get a cross word."

One day, shortly after Papa started working for the Cunninghams, a well-dressed young man of about 30 knocked on Mama's door.

"My name is John Crumm," he told her. "I'm from Pittsburgh, Pennsylvania. I came out to California for my health. I just got a job working for Mr. Cunningham, and I need a place to stay for my board and room. Your husband said maybe I could stay here."

"Why, I'm sure something can be worked out," Mama replied. "Come on in. Put your suitcase in the front bedroom, and make yourself comfortable. It's almost time for dinner, and I'll talk it over with Mr. Tallmon when he arrives."

Mr. Crumm was delighted.

"If I can gain and go back home well, my sister will rise up and call you blessed," he vowed. He was convalescing from typhoid fever.

Papa had no objection. But Grandpa, when he heard Mama was going to have a boarder, advised against it.

"You can't afford it," he warned. "You'll have to buy meat, and you'll eat meat, too. You'll spend all you make on extra food."

Down deep, Mama realized that Grandpa may be right. But she was determined to show him. She would keep Mr. Crumm at all costs.

As it turned out, she did hitch up the horse and buggy each day and go to town for meat. She didn't make much money, but she saw to it that her boarder was well fed.

Every morning, Mr. Crumm went off with Papa through the orchards to the dry yard. Every night, just at sundown, they came home.

Pretty young wife, Emma Shaffer Tallmon, followed her husband into the Salvation Army, then mothered 12 children.

(Below): Young Salvation Army couple, George and Emma, with babies, Bessie and Edith.

The George Washington Tallmon family, Grinnell, Iowa, 1891. (Standing):
Lynds, Clara, John Arthur, Clover, Lucy, George Albert. (Seated): Angie, Su;
Margaret, Edith, George Washington, Burt, Hester. Mother died 1890.

(Below): The George A. Tallmon family, Morgan Hill Ca., 1926. Edith, Bess
Raymond, John, Willard, Susan, Donald, Alice, Dorothy, Evelyn, Melvin.

...ge W. Tallmon home in
...nell, Iowa.
...ow): Susan and George
...Tallmon. (Right): George
...allmon in Salvation
...y, inset as he looked in
...). (Bottom): Angelina
...John Carhartt, his
...dparents.

(Above): Edith, Bessie, Raymond (left), John, Willard. (Left): Edith with baby Bessie. (Below): Grandpa Tallmon with baby Willard.

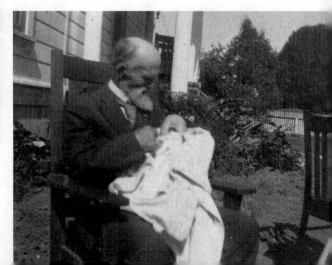

The little girls often went to meet them. As they approached, Mr. Crumm would lie down on the ground and say: "Pick me up."

Edith looked at the big, husky man.

"I can't. You're too big!"

"Sure you can," Mr. Crumm replied. "After all, I'm only a crumb." And then he would laugh.

Mr. Crumm didn't need the money he made. He brought his checks home and threw them into his suitcase, never cashing them until he left town.

But Mama's therapy and the golden California sunshine were good for him, and he went home healthy and brown.

While working at the dry yard, Papa sometimes went to town on errands. He was more than willing to bring anything the workers asked--until one day when George Schilling asked a favor.

Schilling was an old bachelor who lived not far from the Tallmons. He used "are" in more ways than one, and always chewed tobacco. The tobacco chewing was repulsive--he was continually spitting all over the floor and ground.

"Get me a couple'a chaws of tobaccy," Schilling asked, as Papa was preparing to leave for town. He started to pull out his big purse.

"I'm sorry," Papa replied, quietly. "I can't do it."

"Why not?" Schilling asked. "Ya be goin' t' the store, anyway, aren't ye?"

"Yes," Papa conceded. "But I'm afraid I can't get it for you. Anything else, I'd be glad to. But I can't buy tobacco for anyone. It's against my principles. It's nothing against you, understand. You're my friend. It's just that I don't believe in helping someone obtain tobacco."

When he had left, young Tom Rootes, Mr. Cunningham's step-son, told Schilling:

"Aw you don't know what you're chewing, anyway."

"Oh, yes, Ah do," Schilling insisted.

Tom said no more. But when he got a chance, he picked up some dry horse manure, crumbled it up, and mixed it with Schilling's cigar cuttings. Schilling kept the cuttings in a small paper bag, too large for his pocket. He parked the bag on a ledge or other convenient place.

The other dry yard employes, who saw what was going on, watched with amusement as Schilling pulled out his "tobaccy" for next chew.

As he placed it in his mouth, they wondered if he would guess.

But he chewed and chewed the mixture, and never knew it was anything but tobacco. He was unaware of the trick until Tom informed him the next day.

When prune harvest time came, Papa helped on the dipper. He supervised speed of the dipper when the foreman, Ted Dassell, was gone.

The job required judgment. Some men would dump in a box of prunes, talk awhile, and then dump in another, not paying attention to what they were doing. The result would be either overloading the dipper with too many prunes, or underloading it at less than capacity. But Papa always did a good job.

The prunes were dipped into hot lye water, in order to crack the skins and help the fruit dry better when laid out in the sun.

Other times, Papa controlled the output at the end of the grader where the fruit rolled onto drying trays. This required judgment, too, in order to fill the trays to just the right capacity.

Papa was liked by the Cunninghams, and he worked in the dry yard for several years. He later was made foreman, and worked directly under Mr. and Mrs. Cunningham.

He was in charge when they were both gone.

Mrs. Cunningham had the highest praise for Papa.

"Mr. Tallmon is as dependable as a clock," she told one of the workers one day. "If he tells you he'll do something, you can rest assured it will be done. I can go away and leave the dry yard in his charge, and I know the job will be done just as good as if I had been here myself--if not better."

"Yes," replied the worker. "He's a wonderful man. And he's always here on time, ready to start, when the day begins."

"He never gets angry nor upset," another woman said.

"And I've never heard him cuss," added a man who was passing by. "I don't know if he knows how. He's a good foreman."

40.

Grandpa took a great interest in the Morgan Hill ranch. Often he came to visit, and helped Papa with the chores, the haying, or chopping wood.

He and Mama became closer friends. Often she would fix him a cup of coffee, sit down and talk with him, and listen to his troubles.

He always considered her a city girl, and seemed surprised she did such a good job keeping her house neat and caring for her family.

He loved the little children, too. He talked with them, told them stories, and sent poems he wrote himself from Berkeley on special occasions.

One of them was sent to Raymond on his first birthday:

> My love is just a little chap,
>   And Raymond is his name,
> With feet upon the lower stair
>   That leads to life and fame!
>
> For he is one year old today,
>   Can walk--and run as well--
> Sometimes runs into mischief,
>   But that I'm not to tell!
>
> May Heaven bless you, little man,
>   And make your burdens light,
> Or better give you grace
>   To always bear them right.

Another he sent to Edith on her sixth birthday:

> Grandpa knows a little girl
> Who loves birthdays so well
> She would not give her sister one,
> Not e'en a little "spell."
>
> . . For birthdays are her very own,
> Just like her eyes and nose,
> She couldn't give an hour away,
> Not even if she chose!
>
> . . If Grandpa made the birthdays
> For little girls and boys,
> He'd have one come each month or two
> Filled up with brightest joys!
>
> But then he might do this instead--
> What grieving if he should--
> Stop giving out of birthdays,
> To any but the good!

Grandpa felt badly about the poor output of Papa's ranch, and often sent down clothes or groceries "to help out." Some of the groceries, purchased in cut-rate stores in San Francisco, were of low grade and poor quality, and Mama had to spend hours sorting out the good from the bad.

Grandpa also sent dresses and underwear for the girls and a new little suit for Raymond.

The girls' clothes usually weren't suitable, but Mama made them do. Grandpa would have done better sending the money and letting Mama pick them out.

Raymond's little suit happened to fit just right. It was his first, and he was very proud of himself.

It was nice of Grandpa to send those things. It showed his generous nature. But he also was very possessive.

For example, Polly, Papa's work horse, dropped a female colt. It was born on June 17, 1904.

"We'll call her Grinnell," Papa said, "because she was born on the anniversary of the Grinnell cyclone."

Grandpa shrugged his shoulders and said only, "She's a very beautiful colt. I would like to have her."

And he insisted on paying for her feed and pasture.

Ranch production continued poor. Papa's orchard consisted of nearly six acres of young prune trees which produced very little fruit. The other 10 acres was hay land, and the soil was poor and rocky--the bed of an old stream. Income was scarcely enough to pay the $100 due Grandpa each year.

"Maybe you'd better sell out, Georgie," Grandpa suggested.

But Papa had a better idea. Grandpa was buying a 10-acre ranch next door to Papa's place, with a big mortgage on it. It was a better place than Papa's. It already was in fully-bearing prune and peach trees, although the house was much poorer.

And the price was only $900--a third of what Grandpa had paid for Papa's place.

Papa decided that if he could sell off the rear portion of his own ranch--the part facing on Diane Avenue--he might be able to raise enough money to buy his father's place. Grandpa was going to give up his mortgage, anyway.

Papa had little trouble finding buyers for his land. A widow lady from Petaluma, Margaret Elizabeth Wiers, took 3.86 acres. And Luther Cunningham, the owner of the dry yard, agreed to buy two more acres. The total proceeds was $500.

Papa went to his father.

"I would like to borrow $400," Papa said, telling Grandpa his plan. "Then I should have enough land to produce an adequate living for my family."

"Fine," Grandpa said. "You sell your property, and I will be glad to loan you the money."

Papa sold the land and received his $500. Grandpa offered to take care of the necessary papers. He was going through San Jose, the county seat, on his way to Berkeley, anyway.

"That will be fine," Papa said, and gave the funds to his father.

A couple of weeks later, Mama came rushing out to where Papa was working in the barn. She was very much upset.

"What's the matter mama?" her husband asked.

"Here, read this letter," she said. "It's from Grandpa."

Papa opened the letter and it said:

Berkeley, Cal.
Apr. 26 05

I almost feel as tho. I had committed a crime, in as much as I find the deed to the Fuller place in my name-- not in yours. I had only thot of it as yours--and yours it shall be, but perhaps I will have more interest in it if I keep it for a time, and fix it up. I am getting short of means, and will needs go away pretty soon, but before I go, I will give you a deed to all of it. It, with what you have, may sometime furnish you a living.

We will go on and work the place just as usual-- unless you choose otherwise--and I will try and fix up the house sufficient to be inhabited by humans--tho. I will have to be as economical as possible. --When this street work is paid for, there will not be much money left for my disposal.

The money you gave me, I will endorse on your note, and you can feel that you have returned cash to me according to agreement! I think I will be up on Sat. as I have some papers to fix up at San Jose, and must use my man Friday on Sat.

Affly. Papa.

"What are we going to do?" Mama cried, almost in tears.

"Nothing."

"Nothing?"

"No, there's nothing much we can do." Papa folded up the letter. "It means that we have given up six acres of our land and have nothing to show for it. But Papa does say he will deed it over to us later. And I'm sure his intentions are of the best."

Papa continued to work and rent his father's place just as before, and Grandpa continued to visit Morgan Hill and stay with George and Emma while fixing up the little two-room house next door.

One morning after breakfast Mama noticed a group of men and extra horses out in the yard.

"What are they here for?" she asked when Papa came in to get something.

"Oh, they are going to help me move the summer kitchen over to the Valchesters'," Papa replied.

"The summer kitchen!" Mama was dismayed.

"Yes," Papa explained. "The Valchesters just bought some land across the road beyond the Fuller place. They have three children and no place to live but an old one-room shack. I gave them the summer kitchen so they would have some place to cook besides the bedroom."

"But I use the summer kitchen when I do the laundry," Mama objected. "And I like to cook out there on hot days."

"I knew you probably wouldn't like giving it up," Papa replied, quietly. "But it is something we can do for the Valchesters. They need it more than we do. When I finish adding onto the house, I'll fix a place to do the laundry. Is it all right if we give it to them?"

Mama grew silent.

"It's all right," she said, although she didn't really feel that way. And the men placed the summer kitchen on skids and dragged it over to the Valchester place.

The Valchesters were one of several families that bought cleared land across the road, planted trees and lived in shacks, until they could get started.

Mr. Valchester planted a commercial vegetable garden, and he and Mrs. Valchester worked at the grammer school as janitors.

One morning Mama awoke with a start. It was still dark, but she could hear the thump-thump of the noisy old gasoline pump going outside.

Papa was still asleep beside her. She shook him, and whispered, "Someone's running our pump."

Papa roused up.

"That's all right," he said, sleepily. "It's Valchester. I let him use water from our well to water his vegetables."

"Water his vegetables?" Mama exclaimed.

"Yes. He needs to water his commmercial garden, and has no well of his own."

"Are we going to be awakened every morning with that noisy old pump?" Mama asked.

"Not on Sundays. He wanted to pump water on Sundays. He said it was his best day, because he didn't have to work at the school that day. But I said I couldn't let him use the water on Sundays. Any other day would be fine."

"You're charging him for the water, aren't you?" Mama was concerned.

"No," Papa replied. "Except that he is to pay for the gasoline and keep our water tank full. They are having such a hard time, it's something we can do for them."

Mama rolled over. Nothing much she could do about it.

And she knew Papa usually was a little evasive on matters like this, because he was afraid she would not entirely approve. She was glad to help people, but she thought sometimes Papa was a little more generous than necessary.

Mama and Papa's children grew like little weeds in the warm California sunshine.

Edith was in first grade and was learning to read and write--slowly and painstakingly. Fair-haired Bessie was old enough to carry wood for Mama.

Raymond was Papa's boy. He looked just like Papa, with his handsome round face and dark brown hair.

"My a boy!" Raymond said proudly. And sometimes he had a masculine way of asserting himself.

One time he was sitting in his high chair, and became impatient for a drink of water. Everyone was busy and paid no attention to him. Finally he shouted:

"I wanna a dink a dink a dink of watah watah watah in my g'ass g'ass g'ass RIGHT NOW!" And he banged his glass on the table.

One evening Mama was away, attending a lyceum concert put on by a traveling company. Papa let the children make a house under the dining room table. They pulled the tablecloth sideways and made the nicest playhouse.

Before Mama got back, they all pitched in and cleaned things up. Papa didn't mind the children playing house, but he knew it would worry Mama if her house were upside down when she arrived home.

Another day, Mama had to drive to town for something. The girls were supposed to look after Raymond.

On the way home, Mama looked down the dusty old road and could see a tiny child. She thought: that must be Raymond.

It was.

He had reached almost to the railroad tracks, trudging along. It was almost a mile. She picked up the tired little guy, placed him on the buggy seat beside her, and took him home.

Toward dusk one day, Papa went across the road into the Dunne Woods to get some cows. Unknown to Papa, Raymond followed. Papa came back another way, and Raymond got lost.

Mama came to where Papa was milking. "I can't find Raymond. Have you seen him?"

"No," Papa replied. "Do you suppose he followed me over into the woods?"

"Oh, Papa!" Mama exclaimed.

A hurried look around the ranch failed to locate him. Papa and Mama and Edith and Bessie went searching in the woods. It was getting dark.

They hadn't gone far when they heard a little boy crying, down beyond some trees. They went and found him. Tears were streaming down his little face, and he was frightened and dirty.

"Poor little Raymond!" Mama exclaimed, picking him up. "Poor little baby! Everything's all right, now! Poor baby!"

He snuggled close, and stopped crying.

They took him home, washed him up and fed him some warm supper.

Next day Papa built a gate and a fence across the front of the house, to supplement the big cypress hedge which grew along the road. He fastened chicken wire at the bottom, to make sure the fence was both boy-proof and chicken-proof.

After that, they had no more trouble.

By that time, the family had outgrown the little single-seat buggy Papa purchased when they moved to Morgan Hill. Papa and Mama decided to buy something larger.

Papa mentioned their plans to Grandpa.

"Mama wants a surrey with a fringe on the top."

"I see," said Grandpa.

That's all he said.

But a few days later, a crate arrived from San Francisco. Grandpa was there, supervising the operation. The men pried off the outer boards, and the family waited expectedly.

It wasn't a surrey. It was a spring wagon.

A look of deep disappointment crossed Mama's face. "We were planning to get a surrey," she said.

"Yes," added Papa, "something that would protect us from the sun and dust as we ride along."

"But a spring wagon is much more practical," replied Grandpa, with a shrug. "Look, the seats are removable. You can use it both as a buggy and as a wagon."

Mama and Papa were very disappointed--especially Mama. A light pleasure carriage, such as a surrey, would have been much more sporty. But once Grandpa had bought the wagon, they had to take it. And what most of the relatives didn't know, they had to pay for it. It wasn't the gift it seemed to be.

It was another case of Grandpa deciding what they should have and getting it for them, rather than letting them decide for themselves.

Mama's sister Ella came from the East to stay with her while her fifth child was coming. Ella's husband followed a few months later.

Aunt Ella was a good cook and an efficient housekeeper. She had been tall and thin as a girl, but now was getting quite dumpish.

She was like Hazel in the magazine comics in the way she did things. The children, when they came to the table for meals, were spotless--down to the neck and up to the shirt sleeves.

Grandpa wanted Doctor Susan to be with Mama when the baby was born. Mama was afraid Susan might have to remain

several days in Morgan Hill, and was worried about it, because Susie was just building a new practice in Berkeley and it wasn't good for her to be away.

But everything worked out all right. Papa called in the morning--May 18, 1905. The baby came that night.

It was a boy!

Papa beamed with pride and joy as he came out to tell Ella's husband and the others the happy news.

"His name is John Carhart," Papa said. "It's a family name. John was the name of Mama's father and my brother. Carhartt was my mother's maiden name."

Papa wrote and jokingly told John Crumm, the young man who had boarded with Mama and Papa the year before, that he had named his new son John, for him.

Mr. Crumm wrote back and said he knew Papa didn't, because there were others in Papa's family named John. He knew Papa was only kidding.

Ella's husband, Cal, was ironing diapers for Mama one day when the doctor arrived to examine her. (Mama used the local doctor after Susie returned to Berkeley.)

"You don't have to iron those diapers," the doctor said. "Just fold them up."

Mama had always ironed the diapers, to be sure they were dry and so they would look neat.

A family that was increasing meant a bigger house was needed. So Papa, with Grandpa's help, got busy and added a new kitchen, pantry and bathroom in the area where the summer kitchen had been. The old kitchen was turned into a dining room.

Grandpa came over one day and asked Mama if she wanted a new front porch. She said she would, so he built one for her.

John grew fast and was a healthy little baby. A few weeks after he was born, Mama experienced her first reaction to a "large family."

The Tallmons were attending a church picnic, and Mama was talking about her latest offspring.

"Don't you have any more children," the minister's wife told her. "You have four now and that's a nice family. That's enough."

Mama was embarrassed and humiliated, and hated to go out in public after that. But it didn't bother Papa.

41.

Grandpa fixed up the little house next door for Papa's sister Angie and her family, who moved to California from Kansas.

Angie's husband, Burt, wanted to make a new start in the West. The family had already spent a year in Rocklin, California, and Burt wanted to go to Oregon to look for a place to settle permanently.

The first day in town, the Jones family stopped at Mr. Stone's grocery store to buy provisions.

Mr. Stone greeted them cordially, and asked the young boys, Lester and Arthur, if they were coming to Sunday school.

"Oh, yes," they replied. "If there's a Sunday school, we'll find it. We'll be there."

When Sunday came, all the little cousins got ready for Sunday school. The Valchester children went, too.

There were Margaret, Lester, Arthur, Howard and Dorothy Jones; Vera, Ivan and Ollie Valchester, and Edith, Bessie and Raymond Tallmon. Papa helped each find his class.

After Sunday school, the children went to church with their parents. As they sat down, they saw Mr. Stone, the grocery man, sitting in the row just in front of them. He smiled to them.

During the long service, some of the little ones became somewhat fidgety and restless. Mr. Stone reached into his pocket and brought out a handful of peppermints. He gave them to the children to pass around. He was the man to sit behind, as far as they were concerned!

The children had fun playing together, too. Howard and Arthur, Edith and Bessie were cronies.

"You never saw a bunch of cousins get along better together!" remarked Aunt Angie.

The boys even condescended to play dolls and play house, and the girls agreed, in turn, to go out and climb fences.

Lester and Margaret, who were older, had chores to do. So the four younger ones would strike out together.

They often played in the dirt--or mud--of Dunne Avenue. They dreamed of how the road someday would be surfaced, and how much fun it would be if it were paved with rubber, because then they would bounce!

Arthur was the eldest, almost 9. Edith was just 8. Howard was 7, and Bessie, quiet and chubby, was 4.

The children were fascinated by the Valchesters' old horse, Blind Bart, who hauled water by the barrel on skids from Grandpa's place.

He got his name because he was "blind in one eye and couldn't see out of the other," according to Papa.

During the long summer evenings, the adults sat and talked on the porch after the work of the day was done.

The children played in the yard nearby or sat and listened to the adults.

The hot summer day was just turning into the cool of the evening, and crickets could be heard chirping in the distance.

The windmill squeaked nearby. Sometimes the water would overflow, and Papa would have to run and stop the windmill.

During the day, he usually kept track of the water level pretty well. But, in the evenings, sometimes he would forget.

First warning was a drip, drip, drip of the water as it overflowed the elevated tank. The warning was followed by a full outpouring of the water, falling into the coal bin below.

One evening, Papa pulled a piece of stone out of his pocket and showed it to his sister Angie. It was a dull, emerald shade of green, with a natural polish.

"Do you know what this is?" he asked.

"Jasper!" Angie replied.

"Just like the name of the county in Iowa where we were born," Papa noted. "I found this stone along a creek today and brought it home for Emma."

"Can you find jasper around here?" asked Angie, eagerly.

"Oh, yes," Papa said. "It's rather scarce. This is the first I've seen. But I've heard others say they have noticed it. I found an Indian arrowhead the other day, too."

"An Indian arrowhead?" Angie was instantly fascinated.

"Yes," said Papa. "There used to be lots of Indians living in this valley."

"We have several Indian mortar rocks around the place here," added Emma. "They are rocks hollowed out by the Indians and used to grind acorns from the oak trees."

"They used long, thin stones as the pestle, and rolled them around and around in the hole in the larger stones, to crush the acorns," explained Papa.

"That's so very interesting," Angie declared. "What did they use the acorns for?"

"They ate them," Mama replied. "Acorn mush was an important item in their diet."

Just then a bird flew down among the rambling vines which encircled the porch. It paused a minute and then flew away.

"Oh, there must be a linnet's nest in there," Angie exclaimed, excitedly.

"Yes, there are lots of nests in there," Mama related. "The birds seem to love those vines. People say we should tear them down, because the birds eat the fruit. But they also eat insects, and probably deserve a little fruit as a reward."

Angie looked a little closer.

"Those are passion vines, aren't they?" she asked. "See the little blue flowers? Every part of the flower represents something about Jesus and His crucifixion."

She picked a flower and pointed to it.

"The number of petals corresponds to the apostolic succession," she said. "The pistil is shaped like a cross. Other parts represent the Trinity and the disciples."

Mama admired the beauty of the flower Angie held. "It's very lovely," she said.

"You have poison oak out here in California, too, don't you?" asked Angie, as she set the passion flower aside.

"Yes, it grows all around here," Papa said. "We have to tear it out when we clear the woods."

"Don't you get poison oak when you work with it so closely?" Angie asked.

"I get it a little, not bad," Papa said. "Mama caught it on her feet, sleeping with me. Some men on the stump crew got it so bad they were almost blinded--their faces were so swollen. When you get it that way, it's bad."

"Is there anything you can do to protect yourself?"

"I've heard people say if you eat some of the poison oak, you immunize yourself against it," Papa said. "I've never tried it."

The grownups went on talking.

The older children got to discussing what they had heard.

"Uncle George said if we eat some, we won't get poison oak," Margaret noted, as they huddled in the yard.

"I don't want to have my face all swollen up," added Arthur, seriously.

"Let's see if it works," suggested Margaret. So they ran across the road and hunted among the woods for a poison oak plant.

The plants were easy to find. The children broke off some small twigs and leaves--not too much--and chewed them up.

Triumphantly, they went back and told the grownups what they had done.

Their mother was alarmed.

"Spit that stuff out in a hurry!" she exclaimed.

"But Uncle George said it would keep us from having poison oak . . " Margaret insisted.

"I said it might work," Papa replied. "No one ever told me it would."

"And you could have taken too much!" Angie worried.

The children spit out the poison oak, and their mother hustled them into the house to wash out their mouths as best she could.

The experiment was inconclusive. Margaret and Arthur didn't show any ill effects.   But they never caught poison oak anyway, even though it was plentiful and the children often went into the woods to pick violets and other wildflowers.

One day, when all the children were over at Aunt Angie's house, she got to telling them about when Papa was a boy.

"Did you know that your father used to have pigs that knew their own names?" she asked Edith and Bessie.

"No!" the girls said, all excited.

"Yes," Angie replied. "He used to call, 'Come, Gallagher, Murphy, Claire, Angie, De Sausage, Van Tulli, H-a-m, P--o--r--k!' and they would all come running to get their supper."

"Say," Margaret exclaimed. "Why don't we surprise Uncle George?" And then she told them her idea.

That evening, just as dusk, Margaret gathered all the children together in the front yard. It had been a warm day, and the front door was open.

Lester stood by, and began calling, "Come, Gallagher, Murphy, Claire, Angie, De Sausage, Van Tulli, H-a-m, P--o--r--k!"

Across the yard came the rest of the children, squealing and grunting and making sucking noises. They were his pigs.

Papa laughed and laughed--in his quiet way. He laughed until he almost fell out of the chair, and until the tears rolled down his cheeks.

"You remember, don't you?" Angie asked.

"I certainly do," Papa replied. "Many's the time I called the pigs to supper that way.

"And they always came--even Claire and Angie," he added with a twinkle.

Papa enjoyed another stunt, also.

The Valchesters owned a phonograph with big, curving horn, and a horizontal handle that you turned around and around to wind up the device and make the record play.

Phonographs were strictly luxuries, and for the Valchesters to have one was much like a family just off relief rolls buying a computer. Nice but not necessary.

One of the Valchester boys owned a little, junior-sized phonograph, with a little tin horn and handle. He earned it by selling subscriptions, then sent away by mail.

It could play the same records as the big phonograph, only even more squeaky and scratchy. All the children of the neighborhood listened and listened to the records, and learned to sing the songs.

Arthur, especially, learned to mimick the records, and sing the songs with all the scratches and flourishes. He'd put in the announcement at the beginning, and sing with the same squeaky, scratchy voice.

Papa got a kick out of standing beside Arthur, pretending to wind him up. Then Arthur would start off on that crazy take-off of the record:

"Squeak! Cr-r-r-r-r--r!" Then, in a squeaky, high-pitched, unnatural voice: "The song, 'Blue Bell,' sung by Helen McCullough. Cr-r-r-r-r." (That was the static on the record.) "Columbia Records." "Cr-r-r-r r-r-r-r-r-r-r!"

Then came the squeaky, flat music by the orchestra, and then the song, sung in squeaky, odd voice, imitated exactly by Arthur:

"Goodbye, my Blue Bell. Farewell to you. One last fond look into your eyes so blue . . . . "

Papa enjoyed Arthur's version greatly, and so did the others in the family.

The children sometimes went over to the Dunne Woods and watched the tree-pulling operations. The mothers were wary about their going, because they were afraid they would get hurt.

But Papa was good about saying he would keep an eye on them. He didn't seem to mind their being there. And the children were good about staying where they were told to.

They knew if they didn't, they'd be sent home.

The children were impressed with Big John, the husky Negro man who worked with the crew. It made no difference to Papa that Big John was black--he would just as soon work with a colored man as anyone. There was not a bit of racial animosity in his bones.

The children were amazed by Big John's size--he wore Size 12 shoes. When he shut his fists up tight, there was room enough for Arthur and Howard to sit, one on each clenched fist.

Then Big John would slowly lift them, up over his head, sitting on his fists, and then down again.

Lester, who was 11, was old enough to help Papa. He got up early in the morning and went with Papa to pick up Big John at his shack near town. Then they drove to the field where they were pulling stumps.

Lester drove the horses, and John cut up the wood. When they had a load, they hauled it to the Tennant Avenue station. It was hard work lifting it into the box cars.

At noon, Lester, Papa and John sat down in a box car to eat lunch. It was a thrill for Lester to be able to eat there with the men.

Papa opened a nice, orderly lunch. Lester's was fairly neat. But John had a dinner pail, and into it he had poured bean soup, bread and a conglamoration of other things. It looked like something scraped off the dishes.

Lester looked at it in amazement.

"John! John!" he exclaimed. "What messes you do make!"

Papa threw back his head and practically rolled out of the box car with merriment. He laughed and laughed and laughed. He thought that was the biggest joke, and told everyone about it when they got home.

That was when Mama started making a lunch for Big John.

One night, the livery barn caught fire and burned to the ground. Big John, who took care of the horses, was away at the time, and didn't know of the tragedy until he returned.

Margaret and Papa drove by the place several days later. They saw the old darkie, anxiously combing through the ashes.

Papa turned to Margaret with a concerned look on his face.

"Why didn't we think of that before?" he exclaimed. "We should have buried the horses before he came back. If we had only thought of it!"

Big John was searching for bones and remains of the animals to bury them "properly."

When peach season arrived, Papa was kept busy harvesting the fruit on Grandpa's place and his own. Part of the job was hauling fruit from the orchard to Cunningham's drier.

The boys enjoyed going along.

Papa, with Lester's help, would leave the fruit, get the empty boxes loaded, and then they would start home. The order of the day was for Arthur, Lester and Howard to crawl up on the seat next to Papa and say, "Tell us a story about when you were a boy." And Papa always would.

Papa told stories with lots of embroidery, and made you feel as if you were really there. His whole family was gifted that way--in being able to tell stories vividly.

One day Papa was taking a load of fruit with a skittish team to Cunningham's dry yard, located back of Grandpa's place, facing on Diana Avenue. In order to get there, it was necessary to drive the team along some fences and through some gates.

Papa stopped to take the boxes off the wagon. The horses were headed north. Just as he took the last box off, the horses bolted, running north along the fence.

Lester was surprised to see his uncle high-tailing it, not north, after the horses, but west, through the fence and across the field. He soon saw why.

Papa had figured, and rightly so, that the horses would follow the fence, which made a left turn after going north for a while.

He timed things just right and got there just as the wagon went by, crawled up, and grabbed the reins. Lester had extra respect for Papa's ability with horses after that.

Papa and Grandpa offered the boys 1 cent each for the tails of any pocket gophers they could catch. The gophers were quite a pest.

The boys got some box-traps and caught a lot of gophers, especially at Papa's. Lester was better at it than Arthur.

Then they turned in the gopher tails and collected their 1 cent each.

Lester was anxious to earn some more money, too. Papa encouraged him to ask for a job at Cunningham's drier. So Lester did, and got a job cutting peaches.

There was work to be done at home, too. Papa acted as overseer for both his place and Grandpa's. The children picked prunes.

The summer of 1905 was so hot the prunes were cooked on the trees by the hot wind. They smelled cooked. But they had to be harvested anyway, for what they were worth.

42.

Papa, although a Methodist, was indirectly responsible for starting a Catholic church in Morgan Hill.

It all began when Papa organized a Junior Epworth League for young people at the Methodist Church.

Every Sunday afternoon, Papa rounded up a group of youngsters--his own, the Joneses, the Valchesters, neighbors and others--and transported them to the church in his spring wagon.

At first the group was small. But as word got around, and those who came invited others, the Junior League grew. Papa always had a wagonful, and others came on their own.

Papa conducted the get-togethers like a smaller version of a Salvation Army meeting. His idea was to get the children to thinking on the right path, rather than to commit themselves to Christ in a public meeting right there.

Some of the children who came were Catholic. There was no Catholic church in town then.

Among the children who attended was Geraldine Fay, a little Catholic girl who lived across the street from the Methodist Church.

She was invited by Maxine Boutell, the plumber's daughter, who lived next door. Geraldine was all excited when she asked her mother if she could go.

"Well," her mother decided, after giving the matter some thought, "I guess it won't do any harm."

Geraldine and Maxine, hand in hand, crossed the highway and the foot bridge leading to the church. Papa was just arriving with a load of children.

As the children were climbing off the wagon, Maxine ran up and announced, proudly:

"Mr. Tallmon, this is my friend Geraldine!"

"Why, hello, Geraldine," Papa replied, with a big smile. "We're happy you are here."

Just then another child ran over to him and asked a question. He bent down and talked to the child, then patted him on the head. Other children crowded around and held his hand or pressed close, talking with him, as they walked toward the door of the church.

Mr. Tallmon began the meeting with a stirring song. The room was filled with the voices of little children.

They sang, "There's No One Like the Lowly Jesus," "Trust and Obey," and many other tunes from a little red songbook. One of the children's favorites was, "My Sins Were as High as the Mountain."

The children lifted their hands high over their heads as they sang the first line, " . . as high as the mountain."

They dropped their hands for the second line, "They all disappeared in the fountain."

They "wrote" in the palm of their hand as they sang, "He wrote my name down," and they pointed to the sky as they continued, "For a palace and crown."

"Oh, bless His dear name, I am free . . . "

They also sang:

> I washed my hands this morning,
> So very, very white.
> And lent them both to Jesus
> To work for Him til night.
>
> Little feet be careful
> Where they take me to;
> Anything for Jesus
> Only let me do.

Mr. Tallmon led them in a little prayer, and recited Bible verses, including his favorite, John 3:16:

For God so loved the world that he gave His only begotten Son; that whosoever believeth in Him, shall not perish, but have eternal life.

A hush came over the children, and Mr. Tallmon began telling the story of Daniel in the lion's den. With lots of flourish and detail, he described how Daniel worshipped God, in spite of a law to worship only the king, Darius.

The king ordered Daniel thrown into the den of lions, but God saved Daniel, shutting up the lions' mouths. In the morning Daniel was still alive. From then on, the king ordered everyone in his kingdom to worship God only.

The children sat in hushed silence, drinking in every word. They clapped when Daniel won the king's favor. And they listened carefully when Mr. Tallmon stressed that God will stand behind those who love Him.

At the end of the league meeting, following the benediction, Mr. Tallmon asked, "And who would like to go on a picnic?"

A multitude of hands went up. A chorus of voices said excitedly, "I would!"

"Fine," Mr. Tallmon said. "We'll go next Saturday. Meet here at the church at 9 a.m. If anyone needs a ride to the church, let me know. We'll have lots of fun, so don't miss it!"

A host of children were waiting eagerly when the Tallmon wagon pulled into the churchyard on the day of the picnic.

They all climbed aboard, including some mothers who didn't want their children to go alone. Some fathers brought their own wagons. Off they started--a happy, noisy and eager crowd.

They drove to a nice spot, near a creek, and all climbed off. Papa organized foot races and other games.

At noontime, Mr. Tallmon announced that lunch was ready, and the children crowded around the big table.

It was piled high with the most wonderful food. There was lemonade in big boilers, salad, chicken, vegetables, sandwiches--everything to make a picnic just right. Children came back for seconds, and some even for thirds and fourths.

When evening drew near and the shadows began to get long, a weary group climbed onto the wagons and headed for home.

Word spread about the wonderful times the Junior League was having. More and more children of all faiths, including Catholics, began attending.

When the Catholic authorities heard of it, they decided something must be done. So plans were started to build a Catholic church in Morgan Hill--all because of Papa's Junior League program!

Although Papa was active in the Methodist Church, he occasionally had a yen to attend a Salvation Army meeting, which he did sometimes in San Jose.

All the family climbed onto the spring wagon and drove to San Jose. Then they went out on the street corner to help save souls with the Salvation Army corps.

The Salvation Army unit at San Jose kept a cornet especially for Papa, when he came. He could go out, with no "lip" at all, and play very well.

Mama wore her Salvation Army uniform and went. Everyone went, including the Joneses when they were living in Morgan Hill. All stayed for the service, and arrived home late at night.

In addition to the San Jose meetings, Mama, Angie and the children spent one week attending a Salvation Army camp meeting at Pacific Grove, near the ocean, during the summer.

They rented a tent, cooked their own meals, and slept on the ground. All had a grand time. Every morning, boys came around with drums and horns, playing, "You Can't Get Them Up in the Morning," to wake everyone up.

They had big meetings in a circus tent erected for the occasion. There was preaching. There was exhorting. There were lessons on living the Christian life.

Included were slides picturing a life of sin, of drunkenness, and of destruction of families, as compared to living a good life, of happiness, and of families going to church together.

One of the slides showed a baby at his mother's knee, and the audience sang appropriate parts of the song, "Once He Was Somebody's Darling."

The slides went on, showing the boy a little older and going to Sunday school, as the audience continued with the song. Then, as a young man, he went to the city (always the lure), entered business, and got to drinking and associating with bad companions.

Finally, the slides and song ended with, "And now he's only a tramp found dead on the street." That was the climax. That was where the message "hit home."

The children's meeting, which was separate, included a sermonette, a sort-of Sunday School lesson, and devotions. The lady in charge was very sincere but, in Arthur's opinion, misguided.

She told the children they were sinners, and urged them to "come to Jesus, come to the mercy seat" (which was located down in front), kneel, and repent of their sins.

Edith, with tears in her eyes, went forward, but Arthur sat back in his seat, becoming more and more stubborn.

Edith came back, sniffling and wiping her nose, and with her eyes red.

"What did you do that for?" Arthur whispered to her. "You're a good girl. You haven't sinned."

"Yes I have," Edith insisted. "I've been terribly naughty. I've disobeyed my mother."

"No, you have not," Arthur insisted. "And neither have I."

During the time the families were at the camp, the children sometimes walked down to the beach and went wading in the ocean. They didn't wear bathing suits, but merely took off their shoes and let the waves break about their feet.

The day before they were scheduled to leave, Margaret, who often ran errands for her mother, walked downtown to buy something. On her way back, she passed by the beach and stopped and took off her shoes. Her mother's pocket book was in her clothes.

As she was wading in the water, she suddenly felt the pocket book slip from her jacket pocket and fall into the surf. She grabbed for it, but it disappeared into the waves.

She was frantic, bewildered, confused. What should she do?

A friendly man, seeing her trouble, fished for the pocket book, and finally found it.

What a relief!

The money was still there, and everything else--except--except--one thing.

The train tickets were missing.

Margaret's heart dropped. The tickets home. They had no tickets home!

The man searched some more, but to no avail. The situation seemed hopeless.

"What are we going to do?" Margaret cried when she got back to camp. "What can we do?"

"There's nothing to do," Mama replied, "except to get ready and go down to the train station."

They explained their predicament to the station master. He smiled and said he would telegraph to Morgan Hill and verify they had purchased return tickets. Then, he said, he could give them new ones.

So that's what they did, and that's how they got home, although they missed the morning train and had to wait for the afternoon one.

Angie gave Margaret the purse as a reminder to be more careful in the future. Margaret kept the purse for years afterward.

One Sunday shortly after the trip to Pacific Grove, Papa was driving a wagonload of youngsters to a Junior League meeting.

As they approached the railroad, they saw a tramp walking along. The children started singing, "He's Somebody's Darling."

Papa shushed them up for fear the tramp might hear.

In September, Mama and Papa set out in the spring wagon on a camping trip to the coast. They left the two older girls with Aunt Angie, and took Raymond and baby John along.

The weather was beautiful, and the ride was pleasant. Raymond, 2 1/2, sat between Mama and Papa, and John, four months old, lay in Mama's lap. He was perfectly content during the entire trip.

After they went over the Mt. Madonna grade, they stopped the first night near Watsonville. Mama and the children slept in the wagon on the hay Papa had brought along for the horse to eat. Papa slept under the wagon.

It was pleasant and reassuring to lie there at night and hear Dolly chewing and snorting and stomping her feet.

The next day, they continued on. They were climbing into hills, near the ocean, when suddenly they came face to face with an ox team pulling a load of red-colored logs.

Papa had to crowd over to one side of the road to let the team lumber by, their chains clanking as they rounded the corner.

It wasn't long before Mama and Papa spotted green forests in the distance. Then, as they drove up over a hill and rounded a corner, they found themselves within an awe-inspiring redwood grove.

The tall redwood trees and the still, coolness of the woods were unforgettable. Papa stopped before one of the largest of the big trees, and looked up into its tall branches, its top disappearing into the heights above them.

They admired its rugged, beautiful form, and the way it stood so straight and tall and graceful.

Papa jumped off the wagon and stretched his arms across the base of the tree.

"Why, it would take three or four men to completely encircle it!" he exclaimed.

The next day, as they drove along an eucalytus-lined road, Mama and Papa decided it would be nice to take a baby eucalyptus tree home in memory of their first camping trip in the big state of California.

Papa dug up a nice looking little eucalyptus tree and put it in the wagon. It was not more than 12 to 15 inches in height. He planted it out near the barn when they got home, and it became a landmark for the ranch, visible for miles.

When the tree was about six feet tall, a horse broke off the top, and after that it was crooked. It served as a post for a gate and the corner of the corral. It was still there after the gate, the corral and the barn were gone.

Children and grandchildren and greatgrandchildren climbed in its branches, played in its shade, gathered its seed pods and enjoyed its flowers. It was a special favorite for years.

43.

Angie and Emma were two entirely different personalities.

Angie must have been much like her mother. She was deeply religious, high-minded, a fine person, and sweet. But she seldom got much done.

Emma, on the other hand, was an efficient housekeeper. She prided herself on keeping a neat house and with getting all of her work done. She always had meals ready on time. Her children were well-clothed, well-fed and tidy.

Angie spent more time mothering her children. She loved them, did things with them, played with them, read to them. She was wonderful about putting on little programs and theatricals with the children.

She would write poetry, compose music and spend hours upon hours on costumes.

Emma didn't have time. She was too busy cooking and sewing and ironing.

The Jones children were gathered around the table one evening, and their mother was reading to them. Just as the story was reaching its climax, and everyone, including Angie, was sniffling with the pathos, Emma came to the door. She was obviously put out.

The table was still uncleared. Dirty dishes were stacked in the sink, and the stove was covered with empty pots and pans.

Emma quipped, "Maybe I'd have time to read to my children, too, if I didn't have so much to do."

She laid the meat pie she had brought on the table, and left.

Angie was in tears. She lay awake all night, tossing and turning. Next day Emma came over and said she was sorry. She shouldn't have been so hasty. She didn't mean what she had said.

"I only wish I was artistic and clever, and could write like you!" she exclaimed.

"That's all right," Angie replied. She thought to herself: that's just like Emma--forgive and forget so easily. For Angie it was not so easy.

Later that morning, one of the Jones children brought this poem over to Aunt Emma:

Too bad you can not write, you say?
That I do not concede--
For what, my dear, is the empty word
Without the deed?

You make your daily poetry--
Your home so fresh and neat,
Your table to the eyes a poem
And all good things to eat.

And every wash-day morning
 (It is a pretty sight)
I see so fair on every line
"Symphonies in white."

You give all due consideration
To measure and to feet
Of four, bright, sparkling ballads
 (You call them children sweet).

And so you write your poems
The dear home-hearts to bless
There is no doubt about it,
They are a great success!

Actually, the two women complimented each other, although it wasn't done deliberately.

Mama, worried about the Joneses' health, invited them over for dinner ever so often. Papa gave them fresh milk every day. And Mama sometimes did their washing.

When Aunt Angie had company, likely as not Mama would end up having them over to her house. Angie just couldn't get around to it, it seemed.

On the other hand, Angie included the Tallmon children in the little programs and parties and special things. They got in on some fun and attention and experiences they might not have had otherwise.

One of the best-remembered programs was given at Christmas time at the Tallmon house, with the Stone family invited.

Angie rigged a make-shift "stage" across one end of the living room, with a curtain across the bedroom door to hide the actors before they came out to perform. The adults looked on from seats about the room. The children sang songs, acted in skits, and recited poetry.

The children enjoyed the performance immensely. Edith was especially delighted with one song they sang. It was about waves on the ocean going to bed: "Night cap, white cap, night cap on." Edith sang and sang, putting her whole heart and soul into it.

In another act, the children came onto the stage in long white nighties and white caps, carrying lighted candles. They sang a song about "little maidens with curly heads." Then, one by one, they blew out their candles and went off to bed, until no more candles (children) were left on the stage.

Bessie said a piece in her little, sweet, cute way about the Golden Rule. She came out onto the stage all by herself, very bashful-like, and hardly dared look at the audience.

She hesitated, and Aunt Angie had to prompt her. Then she began, talking quite rapidly:

> 'Tismas now is he'e a'ain,
> And, oh, my dolly dea',
> I'm eve' and eve' so much olde'
> 'An I was last yea'.

I t'ied to be a bette' gi'l,
For I lea'ned the Golden Ule,
And Mama says 'at bye and bye
Maybe I'll go to school!

And 'ou must t'y and lea'n it, too,
And t'y and 'membe' it, too:
Do . . unto othe's . . as you would . .
Dat dey . . should do . . to 'ou!

She received a big applause, and there were tears in Papa's eyes.

At Easter time, the children had a chance to perform before an even bigger audience. They were asked to participate in the Easter program at Sunday school.

They all lined up in stair-steps--according to ages--and marched onto the stage. There they sang a song about the Easter lillies.

Little Raymond, not yet three, was on the end of the row. He was the last one to go up, but the first one to come down. When it was time to leave the platform, he became embarrassed, and didn't know what to do.

The children behind him nudged him, but he wouldn't budge. Finally, the rest just went around him, and, as each went by, Raymond, in his embarrassment, gave them a slap.

Mama was terribly embarrassed.

Bessie did have her chance to go to school that year--but only as a visitor.

All of the children--Valchesters, Joneses and Tallmons-- walked to school together. It was a mile-long hike down Dunne Avenue to the school.

Margaret--the eldest--was in charge of the younger children. She was called "Chicky" at school because she was like a hen, with a bunch of children around her most of the time.

Often she was seen high-tailing it across the school yard, headed for home, a flock of children following after her.

Margaret took Bessie to school one day. During class, Bessie sat on Margaret's lap, and finally went to sleep.

When it came time for Margaret to recite, she motioned to the teacher that Bessie was asleep, and she couldn't rise. The teacher motioned back that she could recite sitting down.

Margaret rode a bicyle loaned to her by the Berkeley aunties. She didn't ride it to school because she had to see that the younger children got there. But she did ride around home and went to town on errands.

One day she had a flat tire. She asked Papa to help her.

"Don't you know how to fix it?" he asked, good-naturedly. "I'll show you."

And he got a piece of string, tied it to the inner tube, and pulled the tube around and out. Then he helped her fix it.

In March, Mama's sister's family, her parents and her brother, George, all moved to California from Iowa.

Mama's sister's husband, Dave Alexander, sold their home in Iowa before moving west. They stayed with Mama and Papa for a few days, and then bought a fruit ranch about half a mile farther out Dunne Avenue, opposite the end of Murphy Avenue. George Shaffer, Mama's brother, remained with Papa and Mama.

The Alexanders and the Shaffers liked California, but they didn't care for the earthquakes that came every so often. They were a little worried about them.

Angie, on the other hand, thought they were fascinating. They came occasionally, rattled a few dishes, jarred the house a little, and then were gone.

Often they came at night, and Angie's children always seemed to miss them.

"We wish WE could feel an earthquake," they said.

Angie promised to call them next time.

On April 18, 1906, Papa awoke before dawn, just as the first rays of light were peeping through the window. Mama was still asleep beside him. He leaned over, looked at the clock, and lay back down again. It was 5 o'clock, all right. He'd better get up.

While he was lying there, still not quite awake, hating to get up, he felt a slight tremor.

"An earthquake!" he thought to himself. Then he smiled. "I wonder how Mama will take it."

Mama was still asleep. Usually an earthquake came and went in a few seconds. But this one kept on. Mama awoke with a start.

"Papa!" she cried. "Oh, Papa, the lamp!"

Papa, too, remembered the kerosene lamp on the dining room table, left burning because Bessie was afraid of the dark. If the lamp tipped over, it would set the house on fire!

Meanwhile, at the Joneses' house, Angie felt the first tremors.

"Children, children!" she called, happily. "Wake up! It's an earthquake! It's an earthquake!"

She was all excited. This was a natural phenomenon--the children should experience it.

But, by that time, they didn't need to be told. It was very obvious.

The house shook, and then shook again. It twisted, and turned, and rumbled.

Papa managed to struggle out of bed and head for the door. The house was rolling like a ship in heavy seas. Although he was staggering like a drunk man, he somehow made it out of the room.

In the half-light of the early day he could see the lighted lamp on the table. He lunged toward it, and blew across the top of the glass.

Just as the flame flickered out, he heard a rumbling noise behind him. Frightened, he turned to see what it was. Just then he felt a sharp blow on his shoulder and another on his head.

He staggered from the blows and nearly lost his balance. He almost collapsed to the floor.

Dazed, he barely realized that the chimney above him had collapsed and fallen into a rubble of bricks two feet high beside him. The air was full of dust from the pile.

He had been hit by falling bricks. It was just fortunate he was not a few inches closer to the chimney; he could have been killed by a shower of heavy missiles.

Mama got up, and, carrying baby John in her arms, started through the hallway into the girls' bedroom. By the time she reached the hallway, the house was twisting and turning so badly she couldn't walk any farther.

She could only stay there in the narrow, dark hallway, rocking with the house, trying to stand up and hanging onto her baby.

She could hear things falling, and the house was creaking and groaning.

Desperation and horror swept over her.

"This is the end," she thought. "This is the end. We'll never live through it."

Lester and Arthur were sleeping together when the earthquake struck. Lester, still nine-tenths asleep, thought Arthur was rocking the bed to wake him up, as Arthur sometimes did.

But Lester didn't want to wake up. It was too early. So he reached over and socked Arthur one, and yelled, "Quit it!"

"No, no, Lester," Arthur cried. "It's an earthquake!" Lester finally awoke and realized what was happening. The whole room was rocking and pitching.

The bottom of their bed rose right up to the ceiling, it seemed, and then dropped down to the floor. The furniture kept dancing out into the middle of the room and back to the wall again.

Margaret tried to get out of her room, but a big writing desk in the living room kept rolling across the doorway. Every time she got it pushed out of the way and started through the doorway, it rolled back into the way again.

Howard was sleeping in the kitchen under a three-cornered shelf. A big, round alarm clock fell and hit him on the head.

He staggered into the living room, carrying the clock in his hands.

"Look, Mama!" he exclaimed. "It didn't hurt the clock a bit! It didn't hurt the clock a bit!"

Just then there was a knock at the door. Howard went to see who was there. It was Mr. Valchester from across the road.

"What's going on?" he asked.

Arthur and Lester reached the window just in time to see the oak trees slash down and kick up the dirt with their branches, and the ground rolling and pitching like swells on the ocean.

Full grown fruit trees dipped from side to side until their branches touched the ground.

Then, as they watched, the earth grew silent and the trembling stopped. The earthquake was over.

Over at the Tallmons, a little boy climbed out of his crib, and headed for the dining room door. It was Raymond. Everyone had forgotten him. He looked up, and through the open ceiling where the chimney had been, he could see the stars.

Papa, still somewhat dazed, staggered back into the bedroom.

"Are you all right?" he called to Mama.

"Yes," she replied, still shaken by the experience. "The girls are all right, too."

"I'm going back to bed," said Papa. He was still groggy from being hit by the bricks.

"I'm staying up," Mama replied. She wasn't sleepy any more.

The house was a mess. There was plaster all over everything. The dining room floor was a rubble of bricks, plaster and other debris. Plaster on the table was so thick the tablecloth was completely covered.

Dishes from a cupboard in a corner of the kitchen had fallen into a pile on the floor, and most of them were broken.

In the living room, a vase of flowers sitting on the top of the book case had fallen down, spilling water over the books. Some of them were ruined. Chairs were overturned.

Mama walked into the kitchen to inspect the damage.

"Oh, Papa!" she exclaimed. "My basket of freshly ironed clothes!"

Papa, who by this time was feeling a little better, went to see. A pail of milk, left sitting on the table for the Joneses, had upset into the basket on the floor.

"Oh, Mama, what a shame!" he sympathized.

He went outside on the porch.

"Oh, look," he called. "The water spilled over the sides of the tankhouse!" Mama came outside, too. Sure enough, the sides of the tank were still wet and dripping.

Mama decided to take some food from the screened cupboard back into the house for breakfast. When she opened the cupboard, a strange sight greeted her eyes. The cream from the milk was smeared all over the top of the shelves.

Papa said: "I'd better go over to Angie's house and see if they are all right."

But just then they heard a little girl crying inside the house. They rushed inside. It was Bessie. She was standing beside the living room sofa, weeping as if her heart would break.

"Bessie, Bessie, what is the matter?" Papa asked, his voice concerned.

"My doll! My p'etty tina doll!" Bessie sobbed. "She's--she's--killed!"

Papa looked down on the sofa. Bessie's china doll, with real blonde hair and blue eyes, was smashed to smithereens. Something had fallen on it when the earthquake came.

"Oh, what a terrible shame!" Papa exclaimed. And Mama took Bessie into her arms and tried to comfort her.

"It's our earthquake casualty," Papa said.

When Bessie felt better, Papa said, "I'll go over to Angie's, then," and left, walking down the road to the Joneses' house.

As he drew near, he noticed their chimney had fallen, too, but--he noted--to the outside. He knocked on the door and walked in.

"Are you all right?" he asked Angie, who came to greet him.

"Oh, yes," said Angie. "It was quite an experience. But we are fine. Howard was hit on the head by the clock, but it didn't hurt him."

They felt a rumble just then and the floor shook under their feet.

"Another earthquake," Papa exclaimed. "Maybe you'd better come over to our house for a while. There may be some more."

Angie and the children went over. Other neighbors gathered, too. They sat outside under the trees, comparing notes. They were afraid to go inside for fear something more might happen.

But Mama went ahead with breakfast. The little earthquakes didn't bother her.

"I lived through the big one," she insisted, "and I can live through the little ones."

The children went to school as usual. When they arrived, the chimney was perched precariously at a crazy angle.

But the principal was home sick in bed, and the teacher didn't dare take the initiative to dismiss school.

A little Portuguese girl sat in front of Lester in school. Lester didn't like her because, he said, she came to school smelling of garlic. On this day of crisis, he saw a way to "get even" with her, and also have some fun.

He figured out the aftershocks came at regular intervals.

As the pupils lined up to enter the school building, Lester tapped the little girl on the shoulder and said, "We're going to have another earthquake at 10 o'clock."

The girl was jittery already, and it scared her to death. As they went inside, he tapped her on the shoulder again.

"You just watch," he said. "We'll have an earthquake at 10 o'clock." She was petrified.

Word got around, and soon all the boys were telling the girls in front of them, "There's going to be another earthquake at 10."

The boys started keeping time.

"Twenty more minutes!" they whispered. "Ten more minutes!"

By the time five minutes were left, the girls were hysterical, the teacher had found out, and had scolded the boys. But she, herself, wasn't entirely calm.

Square on the dot of 10 o'clock, there was a rumble. The building started shaking and the plaster falling. The girls began to scream.

"Get up and get out!" the teacher shouted.

She threw open the door, and all headed for the outside in a rush.

Soon the school trustees came and said school was dismissed until the building and chimneys could be checked to see if they were sound.

School never met again that year.

44.

On the way home from school that day, the children noticed a large cloud of smoke to the north.

The adults had seen it, too, and wondered what it was. It continued all day, and by evening, had become even larger. After dark, they could see the glow of flames red against the sky.

"It's some kind of a major conflagration," Papa said. But there was no way to find out. The trains weren't running, and all communications were down.

Within a day or two, however, they knew. Parts of newspapers and refugee stragglers began filtering through to Morgan Hill, and they learned the cause of the smoke and flames 70 miles away.

San Francisco was on fire! A third of the city was in ruins. Hundreds of people had been killed. Thousands more were homeless.

And that wasn't all. San Jose was badly damaged. Stanford University at Palo Alto was hard-hit (among other things, the new Italian-built mosaic facade at Memorial Church had crumbled and was a pile of debris). Part of the state hospital at Agnew was shaken down, and scores of mental patients were killed or injured.

"By comparison, we were very fortunate," said Papa. The people of Morgan Hill began gathering clothing and supplies for the earthquake victims.

Then came word that the military was passing through Morgan Hill on its way to San Francisco to guard against pilferage.

Lester, Arthur, Bessie and Edith were allowed to walk down to the highway to watch the soldiers as they passed. There were men on foot, the calvary riding its horses, and the baggage wagons pulled by big horses.

It was all very fascinating. But the children were concerned about the "poor people in San Francisco," who were homeless and hungry.

Hearing about San Francisco made Mama and Papa worried about the folks in Berkeley. For all they knew, they might have been killed. There was no way to find out.

Then, their worries were over. Grandpa appeared at the ranch.

"We were concerned about you, too," he said, "so I decided to come down and see how you were. I had quite a time getting here."

He told them how he crossed the bay on a ferry boat, and found San Francisco in ruins. He joined the people streaming out of the city by whatever transportation was available.

The trains were jammed, but he managed to fetch a ride. At San Jose, he was considered a refugee and was put up overnight in the Catholic church. It wasn't until the next morning that he was able to explain that he was going to his son's house in Morgan Hill, and wasn't a refugee at all.

Not long after that, another worried relative arrived in Morgan Hill. It was Burt Jones. He, too, had come to see how his family was.

"In Oregon, we heard that Santa Clara Valley had sunk and was inundated by the bay," he said. "I was nearly frantic. I couldn't telephone, or telegraph. So I caught the first train I could and came to see if you were all right."

He hugged everybody, and was assured everyone was fine. Then his excited children said to him: "Oh, Papa! You MUST come and see where the bricks fell through the roof."

So Burt, Papa and all the children--everybody--went on an inspection tour.

"My!" exclaimed Burt, looking up through the broken ceiling into the sky above, "that chimney really did collapse!"

"Come, Papa," Margaret urged him. "You must go up to the attic for a better look. And everyone has to take a brick."

The rule was, her uncle George explained to Burt, no one could climb to the attic without carrying a brick. This was just a little friendly rule to soften the job of carrying bricks up later, when the chimney was replaced.

The children eagerly climbed the ladder--each one toting his brick. All except Raymond. He was just too little, and his brick was just too big.

Ivan Valchester came to his rescue. He lifted Raymond into his arms, and carried both Raymond and his brick up the ladder so that Raymond could see the sights.

The Joneses began making plans to move away. Burt had been selling books in the Portland, Ore., area, and decided that that would be a good place to settle. He left Morgan Hill for Oregon after staying a week. The family was to follow.

Before they left, Papa and Mama invited the Joneses to go on a picnic to Mt. Madonna, over towards the coast. It was an all-day trip, up a narrow, winding, dirt road to the top of the mountain.

It was a pleasant, sunny day, and everyone was in high spirits. Papa helped the children compose a poem, which included the line, "1906--the day of falling bricks."

They drove through the Llagas Valley to Watsonville Road via the Adams School, and then turned toward the mountains.

They drove and drove, the horses pulling hard as they climbed the steep grades. Soon the Santa Clara Valley, with its orchards and ranch buildings, was left far behind. The picnickers were driving through wooded glens, green with grass and colored with May wildflowers.

As they neared the top of the mountain, they noticed the road, in some spots, had slipped out.

They had to drive around the slippages.

"Those were caused by the earthquake," Papa said.

They continued farther, and, as they rounded a turn, they noticed a boundary fence which had shifted so that the two ends no longer met. Then, as they came upon farm buildings in an open area, they were surprised to see a barn split apart and each half moved away from the other.

Papa stopped the horses to look at the amazing sight. Boards and timbers were splintered by a giant force which had ripped the barn in two.

"Did the earthquake cause that, too?" Edith asked her papa.

"Yes," he said.

"How could it?"

"Well," Papa started to explain, "the barn happens to be located right on the main San Andreas fault, which runs through this area. When the earthquake came, the ground on each side of the fault moved in opposite directions, causing the shift. Half of the barn was moved one way, and half the other."

"That's truly amazing," commented Angie. "Just think of the great forces brought to play at a time like that!"

"Yes," agreed Papa. "It's almost unbelievable."

They continued on. Suddenly, around a bend in the road, the horses came to a quick stop. The road was blocked by a vertical bank of dirt.

The road had shifted. Part of the road had sunk and part lifted so that Arthur, standing on the lower part, had to lift himself to his tip-toes to see over the upper part.

They could go no farther. The children and adults climbed down from the wagon, and walked the rest of the way to the place where they planned to eat. It wasn't far.

On the homeward journey, Lester wondered how Papa would ever make the steep grades downhill. He soon found out.

Papa stopped, tied a chain to each of the front wheels, and the other end of both chains to the front of the wagon. Then neither of the front wheels would turn.

Then they started down the hill, the locked wheels acting as brakes.

A few days later, the Joneses were preparing to leave. Papa and the boys were loading shipping boxes onto the wagon, while Angie was gathering last minute things.

Someone discovered baby John, hardly big enough to walk, trotting off with a gold-lined silver cup in his hands.

"Why, that belongs to Howard," he was told. "You mustn't have that." And the cup was placed back with the Joneses' possessions.

The Joneses climbed in. There were the last minute goodbyes, the waving of hands, and a few tears.

Just as they were about to drive off, someone noticed Howard's cup was missing from its place again. Baby John had trotted off with it once more!

Papa drove the Jones family to the train station and checked the freight and luggage. Angie and the cousins climbed aboard the train, waved goodbye, and the train pulled out.

When the Joneses reached San Francisco, they rode on a street car. There was still rubble in the streets, although the area from the train depot at Third and Townsend to the Ferry Building was among the first to be cleared.

Buildings were still in danger of falling. Soldiers were guarding them to keep people away and prevent looting.

Safes in stores were still too hot to open. Experience had shown, the Joneses boys were told, that if the safes were opened too soon, the papers inside would burst into flames. A lot of valuable papers would be saved by waiting for the safes to cool off.

After the folks left, Grandpa rented his house to another family, also named Jones. Whenever Grandpa was in Morgan Hill, he stayed with Mama and Papa. But the arrangement didn't work too well.

Grandpa and Mama didn't get along well, and sometimes clashed. He tried to tell her how to run her house and how to raise her children, and she resented it.

And he was critical.

If he came in and found her resting, he would jump on her and accuse her of being lazy. Mama quickly learned to be busy darning socks, or picking up the baby, or doing some other job whenever she saw Grandpa coming.

Grandpa had the old idea of a patriarch--he believed he was head of the family and able to tell children, grandchildren and married-ons what to do, as long as he lived.

But Mama wouldn't kow-tow to him. She wouldn't do what he told her to do, like his own daughters would. She stubbornly insisted on doing what she believed was right or best.

Grandpa was just as determined to make her do as he wished--although deep down he admired her stubborn refusal to give in. And, on occasion, this deep admiration showed through.

For example, Mama asked him to take a little package to Berkeley with him one time, as he often did.

He slammed the package down in anger. Then he demanded that Mama pick it up.

But Mama wouldn't. Grandpa said she had to; but Mama knew she didn't.

Grandpa finally realized he couldn't get any place ordering Mama around. He stopped--hesitated--and then slipped his arms around her and hugged her.

Grandpa's deep-seated respect for her also led to heart-to-heart talks on occasion. Grandpa would sit and visit, while Mama tidied up the house or did sewing or mending.

"If I had my life to live over again," he told her one day, "I would have remarried--for the children's sake."

He also confided he didn't smoke "because it costs too much," rather than because of any deep moral reasons.

At times, he paid compliments to Mama. He said of her once, "She's always singing," and Mama was very pleased.

But he could be exasperating, too.

The doctor came to the house one day, and went inside. Grandpa saw him come, and went to see what was doing. He walked right in, without knocking. Mama was being examined.

Normally, a person would have backed out as graciously as he could. Not Grandpa. He stayed. It was a delicate situation. But Mama was equal to it.

"I'm having my examination," she said.

"What?"

"I'm having my examination," she repeated.

Grandpa stomped out.

Things grew worse after Mama's parents moved in with Mama and Papa. Grandpa was going to move out.

"No, Grandpa," Mama insisted. "My folks make no difference. There's plenty of room for all. The front bedroom is yours, whenever you want it."

"I don't want to take it away from an old woman," Grandpa grumbled. "I know when I'm not wanted."

He refused to stay there any more, and lived in his own house whenever he was in Morgan Hill.

One time he arrived unannounced, on a cold and rainy Saturday night. The family didn't know he was coming, and there was no telephone, so he had to walk out to the ranch on his own.

He stopped by at Papa and Mama's house with a bundle of meat under his arm, and knocked on the kitchen door. Mama went to open it.

"Why, come in, Grandpa!" she exclaimed. "We didn't know you were coming back tonight."

"No." Grandpa's face grew stern, his jaw set.

"Come in and have supper with us," Mama urged.

"No. I'm going on home."

"Come in for a while, and have something warm to eat."

"No." And he threw the meat across the room and stalked off into the night. When he got home, he sat down and wrote to his girls in Berkeley, telling them how much he was abused.

Grandpa Tallmon and Grandpa Shaffer were almost complete opposites. Whenever they got together, there was trouble.

Grandpa Tallmon was a staunch Republican, and Grandpa Shaffer was just as staunch a Democrat. There was no compromise. They would argue by the hour.

In physical appearance, they were almost complete opposites, too.

Grandpa Tallmon was wiry, thin, gray-haired, and always wore a long, gray beard. Grandpa Shaffer was taller, just as thin, and handsome with black curly hair, long chin and rather sharp nose.

Grandpa Tallmon was resentful, too. He kept making derogatory remarks about the Shaffers. He considered Grandpa Shaffer lazy, and not as good as the Tallmons.

"Why doesn't Shaffer get a job around here instead of going down to L.A. all the time?" he wanted to know. "Why doesn't he go to Oakland and look for work?"

Antagonism between the grandpas mounted and mounted. All the controversy was wearing on Mama. It was killing her with nervous strain.

One night she awoke in horror.

"I can't breathe," she gasped to Papa.

Papa took her outside and walked her up and down the driveway until she got her breath back. It was just nerves.

Another time she was lying, sick and upset, on the living room couch. Grandpa Tallmon and Grandpa Shaffer were arguing politics. Finally Mama couldn't stand it any longer, and called Papa over.

"That arguing has to stop!" she demanded.

So Papa told his father and father-in-law to please stop arguing, as it was bothering Emma. They stopped.

Grandpa Shaffer began doing odd jobs around Morgan Hill, and Grandpa Tallmon hired him to build a tank house and windmill on his ranch.

Mama begged Papa not to let them do it.

"There will just be trouble," she insisted.

But the Grandpas went ahead anyway, with Papa's assistance. And, sure enough, there was trouble.

A few days later Grandpa Tallmon came marching over to Papa's ranch, with fire in his eye. He went straight to Grandpa Shaffer, and demanded, "Where's my hammer?"

"What hammer?"

"The hammer you took."

Grandpa Shaffer held his temper. "I didn't take your hammer," he insisted. "What would I want with your hammer? I have all the hammers I want now. Anyway, if I was going to take a hammer, it would not be yours. It probably fell down the well or something."

Grandpa Tallmon cooled only slightly.

"Well, I can't find it. You must have taken it." Saying that, he headed for home.

Grandpa Shaffer turned to Mama, who was standing nearby.

"If it hadn't been for you being here," he told Mama, "I would have given him a piece of my mind!"

That wasn't the end of the hammer incident. For years after, whenever Grandpa Tallmon saw Grandpa Shaffer, he made some remark such as, "When are you going to bring my hammer back?"

This infuriated Grandpa Shaffer, and they almost came to blows several times over the issue.

45.

Papa, remembering the hard times when he was an officer in the Salvation Army, occasionally invited a Salvation Army family to stay at his home for a few days' rest.

Mama was willing, too, to entertain the guests, although it added an extra burden to her chores. It was even harder on her, now that she was expecting again.

Papa received a letter one day from Mrs. Cameron, head of a Salvation Army home and orphanage in San Jose.

"We have a married couple with several small children who has just completed a difficult charge in a small town in Northern California," Mrs. Cameron said in her letter. "Could they stay a week or so at your home?"

Papa wrote back and cordially invited them to come.

They proved to be a pleasant family, and seemed to enjoy the beautiful autumn days on the ranch. The children, however, were tiny and in need of constant care.

In addition to Mama's regular work, she had twice the usual crowd, to feed and care for. Having so many small children in the house naturally resulted in noise and confusion.

Mama, about half way through her pregnancy, wasn't feeling well anyway. She got through most of the week, but then began having troublesome pains.

Papa was concerned.

"They'll be leaving tomorrow. Then you must rest."

On the last day, Mama was fixing breakfast. She was standing before the hot stove, turning pancakes, when suddenly a sharp pain struck through her. She dropped everything and left the room without a word.

Papa went to see what was wrong. He returned with a worried look on his face and said: "I think she is going to lose the baby."

"Oh, I'm so sorry," the woman exclaimed. "I'm so sorry. I'm afraid our being here has caused it all. I'm so very sorry."

"I think perhaps we should go just as quickly as we can," her husband said. "We mustn't cause any more complications."

They gathered up their things and were gone.

Papa hurried back to the bedroom. Mama was weeping quietly. He sat down on the edge of her bed and took her into his arms.

"We must not give up hope mama," he said. "Perhaps everything will be all right."

"But I'm afraid, Papa," she kept repeating. "I'm afraid."

"I have to go to work," Papa said, gently. "I'll call the doctor, and he'll see what he can do."

"All right," said Mama. "All right. That will be fine."

The doctor came, examined Mama, and said there wasn't much to do except to hope and pray--time would tell. Papa worked close around the place, prayed, and frequently checked on his wife. The children--except the younger ones--were at school.

Mama didn't get better. The day passed. The pains continued. That evening, Mama took a turn for the worse.

"I think . . I think you'd better call the doctor, Papa," she said, anxiously. Papa hurried to the telephone, made the call, and returned to Mama's bed. But it was too late. By the time the doctor arrived, it was all over.

The baby was a little boy, and seemed to have developed satisfactorily to that point. Mama was crying bitterly. Papa fashioned a little coffin out of a shoe box, and sadly buried the baby out by the side of the house, under an almond tree.

It took a long time for Mama to get over the loss. She didn't feel really well again for a year.

"I was working with Mr. Boutell today," Papa said one evening, a few months later, as the family sat down at the supper table. "Mrs. Boutell's sister is missing."

"She is?" Mama asked.

"Yes. She was gone when the family got up this morning--suitcase and all. The older Brizee boy disappeared, too."

"They were keeping company, weren't they?" Mama asked.

"Yes. Sounds like they ran off and got married."

Little Edith, who was nine, took it all in. She decided something must be done about it.

So right after school next day, she asked to go home with Maxine Boutell.

"I have something important to tell your mother," she explained.

Mrs. Boutell invited them in, and Edith began:

"Mrs. Boutell, your sister ran off with Mr. Brizee to get married. That's where they are. My mama and papa were talking about it, so I know it's true."

When Edith got home, she proudly told Mama and Papa what she had done.

Mama looked at Papa, and Papa looked at Mama.

"It serves me right for talking in front of the children," Papa said. "I'll have to go and apologize."

Papa worked more or less regularly for Mr. Boutell for several years. Boutell owned the local fix-it shop, and Papa acted as an assistant, fixing bicycles and doing plumbing work and other odd jobs.

Papa did a conscientious job, and sometimes spent more time than Boutell got paid for the work. But he learned a lot about the trade.

One day J.J. Jones, a local rancher, ordered a new galvanized chimney for his prune dipper. When he arrived to pick up the finished product, he was shocked by the high price.

"I didn't expect it to be this much," he objected.

Boutell explained: "Tallmon used the best material."

"I'm sorry," said Papa, adjusting the Salvation Army cap on his head. "I thought that's what you wanted."

"Well," said Jones, good-naturedly, "it'll last longer, anyway."

Nob Hill was a little knoll at the edge of Morgan Hill. From its top, a person could look down on the town and over a wide vista of ranches and trees in the valley.

Edith kept talking of climbing to the top, and Papa promised to take her some time.

Then, Papa's work changed so that he was working downtown for Mr. Boutell. It seemed like an ideal opportunity to keep his promise. So he made arrangements to go during noon hour the next day.

Mama packed their lunches together, and Edith walked over to the fix-it shop from school.

"Are you ready to go?" asked Papa, as she came in.

"Yes!" exclaimed Edith, her eyes bright with anticipation.

Papa pulled on his coat, picked up the lunch, and they started off. At the bottom of the hill, green with grass this time of the year, they sat and ate their lunch. Then they left the lunch pails and climbed toward the top.

Edith was wide-eyed as the beautiful view began to take shape below her. They could see a long ways north of the town and a long ways south.

"Over there is the school, and over there the church," Papa pointed out. "There's Dunne Avenue. And if you look carefully, you will see our house."

"Do you mean that house over there?" she asked, pointing in the wrong direction.

"No." Papa used his finger as he spoke. "Farther out. That white house--about half way to the other side of the valley."

They stood there, looking. Edith saw it. Papa, with his arm across his young daughter's shoulders, pointed out other landmarks. Then, it was time to climb downward again.

To Edith, it was a thrilling occasion--an experience she was never to forget.

As they reached the bottom, Edith exclaimed: "Thanks, Papa, for taking me!"

"That's all right," he replied, with his usual twinkle in his eye. "I enjoyed it, too. After all, I didn't want you to go alone. And I wanted to be the first one to take you."

While working for Boutell, Papa received a letter from Mrs. Cameron, the lady Salvation Army officer who ran the orphanage and home in San Jose.

Mr. and Mrs. Henry Schilder, a former Salvation Army couple, wanted to move to Morgan Hill from Oakland, seeking a warmer climate.

She said she had promised to write to the Tallmons "and they will find you a place."

Papa rented a house on the hill back of the church. The Schilders brought their possessions to Morgan Hill via horse and wagon.

Next day at church, Papa noticed a young woman dressed in Salvation Army suit and bonnet, holding a 2 1/2-year-old boy by the hand. He went over to greet her.

"You must be Mrs. Schilder," Papa said, cordially.

"Yes, I am," she replied. "Henry stayed home with the baby." She was an attractive young woman, with reddish-brown hair, small and thin.

"Did you find the house all right?" Papa asked.

"It's fine. It seems like a nice location. We did have some visitors last night."

"What was that?"

"Some mice. They got into the food."

"Oh, that's too bad. I'm sorry. They must have come in during the winter, while the house was vacant."

"There must be a lot of them, and they must be very starved. Because when my son dropped some food, two of them came running out and fought over it."

"We must get some cats and get rid of them," Papa said.

They sat down; it was time for the service to begin.

After church, Papa said: "Would you like to come out to our house for dinner?"

"No," Mrs. Schilder said. "Your wife would not be expecting us. And there are some things I must do yet before we are settled."

"Well, then," Papa suggested. "I have to come to town this afternoon to conduct Junior League. Perhaps after that you can come out to the ranch for a visit. I know Mama would like to meet you."

"That would be fine," Mrs. Schilder replied.

Later in the afternoon, Papa stopped by the Schilders' home in his spring wagon and drove them to the ranch. Mama welcomed them in, and the adults sat down to talk.

Mrs. Schilder noticed how poorly Mama was. John tried to lean against her, but she wouldn't let him.

"I haven't felt well for some time," Mama explained.

The Tallmon girls buttoned and unbuttoned each other by backing up to one another, and also changed the boys into their old clothes. Then they made lemonade and served it with cookies.

"My, how helpful and grown-up you little girls are," Mrs. Schilder exclaimed.

When it came time to leave, Papa drove the Schilders home. Thus began a life-long friendship between the two families.

Mr. Schilder took a job handling lumber, but it was only a temporary job, lasting about 10 days. After that, Papa managed to get him a job with Mr. Boutell. Papa and Mr. Schilder spent the summer working together, doing jobs at surrounding ranches, such as pump repairs.

One of their main tasks was assembling water tanks. The tanks were made of wood lined with galvanized iron, held together with pieces of iron riveted on around the outside.

Papa worked on the outside and Schilder on the inside, making holes and putting rivets through. A lot of new people were moving into the Morgan Hill area, and they needed water before anything else.

The two men got sick doing one job. Boutell built a house for someone, and the plumbers installed the plumbing wrong, with the fall backwards. Papa and Schilder were given the job of going under the house and correcting the error.

It was hot weather, and for a week the two men lay on their backs on the cool ground, sawing all the plumbing loose, and reversing the fall. They both came down with hard colds.

While the Schilders were living in Morgan Hill, Papa did everything he could to make them comfortable. Everytime he sensed they were the least bit lonesome, he came and took them to his home for a visit.

In the fall, the Schilders decided to move back to San Jose, where Mr. Schilder could find lighter work. Papa loaned Schilder his wagon to carry their furniture and other possessions to their new home.

The Schilders came out to the ranch to say goodbye.

"You don't know how much we appreciate all you've done for us," Mrs. Schilder told Papa and Mama. "You were friends when we needed you most."

46.

Bessie left the other children at the road and headed across the orchard on her way home from first grade.

She made her way as best she could across the plowed ground, gaily swinging her lunch pail from one hand. She carried a school paper, fluttering in the breeze, in the other.

The October sun was warm and pleasant, and the autumn leaves on the fruit trees were beautiful shades of yellow and gold and brown.

Bessie, pretending she was a horse, began trotting across the rough ground, dodging in and out of the fruit trees.

Then, as she reached the back door where the quince tree grew, she stopped short. Aunt Lillie was at the door. That was strange. Why was Aunt Lillie there?

"Give me your lunch pail and paper," Aunt Lillie was saying. "You are to go over to Grandpa's house."

That was strange. Nothing like this had ever happened before. Bessie wondered why.

"Should I change my dress?" she asked.

"No," Aunt Lillie replied. "You go over there and play this afternoon."

That was even more strange. Without changing her dress? Why, Mama would never think of sending her out to play in her school clothes! But, without protest, she did as she was told, following the orchard path connecting the two ranches. She wondered all the way why she had been shuttled next door.

When she reached Grandpa's house, Raymond and John were already there, playing in the orchard dirt. She joined them, and they had fun playing. But, she kept wondering and wondering about the strange events of the afternoon.

Finally, toward dusk when the sun was setting, Grandpa came hurrying back from the other ranch. He seemed anxious to tell them something.

"You children," he announced, "have a new little baby brother. Well, I shouldn't say little. He weighs more than 10 pounds, and is 21 inches long."

Bessie jumped up. Raymond and John just went on playing.

"Oh," Bessie exclaimed. "May we see him?"

"I think maybe you can, later," Grandpa replied. "You children go on home, now. Your Grandma Shaffer has supper ready for you."

As soon as they got home, Bessie asked Papa if they could see "our new little baby brother."

Papa smiled.

"I think maybe you can," he said. "Come with me."

Three little children, their clothes still soiled from play and still dirty behind the ears, followed their father into the bedroom.

There, tucked in bed beside Mama, was a fat, red little baby, with his eyes closed up tight.

The children didn't say anything. They just looked.

"How do you like your little brother?" Papa asked, holding each of the boys up high in turn so that they could get a better look.

"Fine."

"His name is Willard Burton Tallmon," Papa explained. Then he gave Mama a sly look. "Mama named him," he added, "--for Jesse Willard, the prizefighter."

"No," insisted Mama, a little provoked. "For Frances Willard of the WCTU" (Woman's Christian Temperance Union).

"And the middle name," Papa continued, ignoring Mama's calculated reaction, "is for Uncle Burt Jones."

"It will please Angie," Mama said.

Grandma Shaffer called supper just then, and Papa and the children went to eat. Later, Grandpa came over, and said he had a surprise for Mama. He handed Mama an envelope.

When Mama opened it, she found a poem Grandpa had written just for her. It read:

To Emma
Oct. 1st, 1907

I have mingled in the battle
Where heroes brave are made,
But I yield the "crown" to womanhood--
And at YOUR feet 'tis laid!

You're the bravest little woman!
And worthy of all praise--
And that ancient, Bible promise--
Made for your stress of days!

Affly. Papa.

"Thank you, very much, Papa," Mama said to Grandpa. "That was sweet of you."

"Do you like the poem?" Grandpa asked, expectantly.

"Very much," Mama assured him.

When Grandpa was gone, Papa sat down on the side of the bed and leaned his arm across Mama, looking down on her. He kissed her--a long, sweet kiss, and said:

"You know mama I love you very much."

"I love you, too," Mama replied.

"We've been married more than 10 years," he said. "It's been a happy 10 years. We've had our troubles and trials and tribulations, but I wouldn't want to change things for all the world."

"I wouldn't, either," said Mama.

"I'm thankful to our Father for giving us each other and making us so happy," Papa continued. "I believe you are happy, aren't you dear?"

"Oh, yes," Mama replied. "I loved you with all my heart when we were married. And now, 11 years later, I can say you are ever more dear and precious. I feel ashamed that I could ever have been cross or impatient, for you have always been so much better than I. So strong and brave to bear the heavy burden and always ready to sacrifice your own personal wishes and comforts for your family."

"You are such a sweet and beautiful woman," Papa said, "and so capable. I am truly thankful to have you as my wife. Sometimes I've been hard on you darling but you are always so loving and forgiving. You are a wonderfully sweet and precious woman."

And he leaned down and kissed her again.

The next day Mama had a toothache--of all things. She suffered through it all that day and most of the next before it went away.

When the doctor came to check on her, she told him about the toothache.

"It must have been worse than having the baby," he remarked, with a smile.

"It lasted longer," Mama retorted.

The doctor looked around the room. "This place is too dark," he said. It was true. The bedroom, surrounded by other rooms, had only one window to gather in any light, and it faced the north.

"Move into the front room," he suggested. "It has more sun." So, with Grandma and Papa's help, Mama and baby changed the living room into a maternity ward.

A few days later there was a knock on the door. Mrs. Grigg, the minister's wife, and another woman, all dressed up, had come to pay Mama a social call.

Grandma invited them in, while Mama tried to look pretty and entertain them with proper social graces during their visit. Mrs. Grigg and her friend sat primly on the edge of chairs about the room and began talking with Mama.

"My, what a beautiful baby," Mrs. Grigg remarked. "And such a big little boy! How many children do you have now?"

"Five," Mama replied. She felt uneasy. She wished the house was a little neater, and that some of the baby's things had been picked up before they came.

"You have such a nice family," Mrs. Grigg continued. "We certainly are happy to have them in our church. And your husband is so dependable. My husband said he was so pleased to have Mr. Tallmon help split and stack the wood at the church last week."

Mama wished the front room had not been used as a bedroom when the preacher's wife came.

"My husband says George Tallmon is the finest layman he has ever had. A fine churchman, very noble, very loyal, willing to make a sacrifice for the sake of the church at any time."

"He's glad to do anything he can," Mama said. She was afraid some of her hairs were out of place.

Just then, there was a loud crash. The women's heads turned toward the kitchen. The kitchen stove pipe clattered about the floor.

Papa, dressed in old clothes and with soot sprinkled about his face, poked his head through the door.

"I'm sorry, ladies," he said. "I was fixing the stove pipe and it slipped."

Mama could have sunk through the floor.

Mr. and Mrs. Valchester and their three children--who lived across the road from Grandpa's house--moved away shortly after the Joneses left. They moved to an apple ranch out towards Mt. Madonna.

A few months after Mama's Willard was born, Mrs. Valchester had a little baby boy--and died of childbed fever. When Mama and Papa heard about the new little baby without a mother, they drove out to the Valchester ranch and brought the baby home.

Mama was just weaning Willard, so she thought she could nurse the little boy. He was such a scrawny, tiny little thing--not healthy nor plump and fat like her own offspring. She felt sorry for little Paul--although it was somewhat distasteful to be nursing a baby not her own.

Then she heard a rumor that Mrs. Valchester had actually died of cancer. That worried her.

"Will I get cancer if I nurse her baby?" she asked Papa.

"I don't know," he replied.

Mama was so concerned and upset that Papa decided to check with Mr. Valchester. Mr. Valchester suggested that they talk with Mrs. Valchester's doctor in Gilroy, a town 12 miles from Morgan Hill and a little larger.

The doctor advised Mama definitely against nursing the baby. In those days, doctors didn't know as much about cancer. And perhaps he thought it best for Mama not to be worried.

Another woman living on Dunne Avenue was willing to take the baby--for pay--so Mama was relieved of the responsibility.

Meanwhile, Mr. Valchester moved his motherless family back to their ranch on Dunne Avenue, in a valiant effort to keep them together. He worked again as janitor, this time at the high school.

Mama and Papa took the children under their wing, and were almost like a second mother and father to them.

Mama washed clothes and cooked meals and cleaned house. When she made a batch of bread for herself, she always remembered to fix an extra batch for the Valchesters, too.

When the children had the measles, "Aunt Emma" made sure the children were washed, fed, and remained in a dark room.

Finally, the day came when baby Paul was too old to need the nursing care of the lady down the road. He was getting close to a year old, and could sit up by himself now.

Mr. Valchester stopped by the Tallmon place one evening and came in to talk with Mama and Papa.

"I've been to Berkeley to make arrangements with a foundling home to take the baby and find a home for him," he told them.

"Oh!" said Mama. "You are going to give him away?" There was a concern, a sadness, in her voice.

"Yes," said the father. "He doesn't need the nursing care any more. And I can't take care of him and work, too."

"I wish we could take him . . " Mama said.

"No," Mr. Valchester was definite. "You have enough to do now, with your own children. You have been kind, helping as much as you have with the others. I've thought it all over, and it seems the only wise thing to do is to give him away for adoption."

"Will you know where he will go?" Mama asked.

"No. The foundling home wouldn't take the baby unless I signed an agreement never to seek to find out what happened to the baby or what kind of a home he was placed in."

"Then it will mean giving him up for good."

"That's right. But that's the way it will have to be. Now, you've been very kind and helpful. But I wonder if I can ask you to do me one more favor. Would you be willing to take little Paul up to Berkeley for me?"

"Why, yes, of course I will," Mama replied. "I'll be glad to do whatever I can."

The day came to leave with the baby. Grandpa went with Mama. He often went to Berkeley, and it was easy for him to take her. They went on the train.

It was a sad journey.

"I would adopt him myself if I didn't have my own children to take care of, and knew for sure I would not have any more," Mama told Grandpa.

Paul sat on Mama's lap, and Mama pointed out pretty things through the window as they rode along.

At the foundling home, Mama set little Paul down on the lounge.

He cried for her, and reached up his little hands toward her in desperation.

"You'd better go quickly," the matron said.

Mama took one long look at the little boy, and tears filled her eyes. Then she turned away and marched herself out of the room, with the baby's cries still ringing in her ears.

Her heart was heavy as she climbed into the waiting buggy, and she had little to say all during the trip home. All she could think about was that poor little boy, starting a new life among complete strangers. Years afterward, she often thought of how old he was, and wondered what he was doing by then.

47.

"I need a ranch in the hills," Papa said one morning as he milked the cows in the barn, "a place with some grass to pasture my animals and some trees for firewood. If I had enough trees, I could cut wood and sell it around town."

"Sounds like an excellent idea," agreed Grandpa, who was sitting on a stool nearby. "Do you know of such a place?"

"Yes," said Papa, "I've heard that the Henry place on Willow Canyon Road up in the Llagas Valley is for sale--77.4 acres."

"How much do they want for it?"

"I don't know exactly, but I understand it's a pretty good price. Amburn, a rancher who lives up that way, has first chance to buy it. If he doesn't want it, I think maybe I'll take it--that is, if you would loan me the money to buy it."

Grandpa leaned forward, his eyes shining with anticipation.

"I'll tell you what I'll do," he said. "I still feel badly about my ranch next door here; you were going to buy it and I put it in my name. I'll buy this hill ranch, and give you half interest."

Papa wasn't too pleased with the suggestion, but said nothing. Grandpa was trying to do him a favor, and maybe it would work out fine.

"Where do the owners live?"

Papa gave the cow two or three last squeezes, pulled the pail out from under the cow's udder and stood up.

"Take the Monterey Road as far as the church north of Madrone. Turn west, and follow that road to the hills. Turn right for a quarter mile, then left, and follow the creek to Saunders' place."

"Fine," said Grandpa. "I'll take your horse and buggy and go over there right now."

Papa set the milk pail down in a corner of the dusty barn, and helped Grandpa hitch up the horse. He watched Grandpa drive out of the yard. Then he picked up the milk pail, poured some of the milk for the calf, and took the rest into the house.

Several hours later, Grandpa drove into the yard, pulled old Prince to a halt, and strode over to the workshed where Papa was repairing harness.

"Well, I bought it," Grandpa beamed, holding out a paper in his hand. "Here's the bill of sale."

"Bought it?" Papa was stunned. He thought for a moment. "Did the Amburns give up their option?"

"No." Grandpa was unconcerned. "But I put up a down payment, and got it."

A surge of dismay swept through Papa, but he said nothing. He looked at the bill of sale. It was all duly signed and complete. Nothing could be done now.

He felt a little sorry for having even mentioned the place to Grandpa. He didn't think it was right nor honest for Grandpa to jump in first if the Amburns really wanted the place. He only hoped that perhaps the Amburns hadn't wanted it after all.

Grandpa recorded the deed with the county recorder: "J.H. Henry and wife, Emma, to George W. and G.A. Tallmon. Lot 127A 77.4 acres Willow Canyon Road north of Llagas Avenue and Llagas Creek. Dec. 2, 1907."

The ranch was in a beautiful spot. Near the road the land was fairly level and could be cultivated. The rest, on the side of a mountain, was quite steep and wooded.

A spring flowed from the hillside, and the area around it was green and covered with trees and brush.

Grandpa later built a small cabin on the place, and planted some eucalyptus trees in a grove. The trees grew fast and made excellent firewood. The idea of planting trees for firewood was new, and was a sign of Grandpa's progressiveness.

Even though Papa was displeased with the method of purchasing the hill ranch, he helped Grandpa take care of it and used the place as a hay field and pasture for his own animals.

Each summer he cut the hay and carried it by wagon to the home place. One day he arrived home with a load of hay just as the mailman was leaving the mailbox.

Papa stopped, pulled the letters and newspaper from the box, and gave them to Mama, who was just heading out to the mailbox herself.

Mama carried the mail into the house, opened a letter and started reading it. Then she exclaimed to Edith and Bessie:

"Why, Clara Jones is coming to visit us!"

"Oh, goodie!" Bessie clapped her hands. "Dorothy will be here!"

"No," said Mama. "Not the Joneses from Oregon. Clara Jones from Oberlin, Ohio. Her husband, Lynds, is professor of zoology at the college there."

"Oh-oh-oh!" The girls were disappointed.

"But they have a little girl just your age," Mama said. "Her name is Beth--and she is about as old as Bessie. Her brother, Harold, is coming, too. We'll have lots of fun."

Two or three weeks later, the girls were playing in the doll house and Raymond and John were out helping Papa fix fence when Grandpa drove into the yard in the buggy.

A woman with puff sleeves and long dress and two children climbed down from the buggy and brushed the dust from their clothes. Grandpa had gone to the train to meet them.

Papa strode over, his own children bashfully lagging behind.

"Clara, how are you?" he exclaimed. "You are looking fine. Come on in the house and see Emma."

But Mama was already coming out the door. Papa picked up some of the suitcases and all went into the house. The children were shy at first, but, at the adults' suggestion, went out to look around the ranch.

Soon Clara was telling all about their trip, her visit to other sisters in Berkeley, and what they had seen.

The Jones children found the ranch an interesting and exciting place. It was a novel experience to eat "plums" right off the trees out in the orchard.

The ground was dry and dusty--it was late summer and water was getting short. There were odd smells, odd trees, and a much different land than the Ohio they were used to.

It was also strange to sleep out-of-doors at night under the stars--and not have to worry about rain at any time. And so strange to wear sweaters in the evening--in Ohio it was hot all night every summer.

The next day, Papa had to go somewhere on business. He said he would be gone two or three hours, and suggested Clara go with him.

"I would like to go," Clara replied. "But wouldn't I be a bother?"

"Bother?" Papa exclaimed. "You wouldn't be a bother. If you don't go, what chance would I have for a visit with you?"

So she went.

Papa and Mama and Grandpa and the whole family took the Joneses to see the hill ranch Grandpa had purchased.

Clara found it an interesting and unusual place--full of natural wonders.

While Papa and Grandpa were loading hay onto the wagon, Mama climbed down a slope to dig up a plant Clara wanted for her garden at home.

The children were playing nearby. Bessie, Raymond and Harold pretended they were horses.

Bessie was the driver, and Raymond and Harold were crawling on their hands and knees down the path; they were the horses.

Suddenly, they heard a low, rattling sound close beside them. It sounded like a load of buckshot in a can being shaken.

Instinctively, the children reacted. Raymond and Harold half rolled, half tumbled down the hill away from the path. Bessie ran back toward the other folks.

The rattlesnake was lying coiled under a bush along the path, almost exactly where the children had been. Its tongue was darting out from its mouth, menacingly, and its fangs were protruding. Its head was erect and moving back and forth, ready to attack.

Grandpa picked up a fence post and swung at the coiled reptile. The snake jerked, stiffened, and then fell limp on the ground, its head bashed in.

Everyone gathered around the dead rattler. It lay there, its colored, diamond-shaped scales glistening in the sun.

"That was a close call," exclaimed Grandpa with a sigh. "It's a good thing those children got out of there fast. That fellow was ready to strike!"

"If the snake bit you, would you die?" asked Harold.

"Yes," said Papa. "Rattlesnakes are very deadly."

"They are attracted by the heat of your body as you pass by," explained Grandpa. "They can't strike unless they are coiled. They can lash out half the length of their body. That's why I was safe as long as the post was longer than the snake."

Grandpa picked up the snake by its tail and carried it down into a small ravine, and laid it down next to a tree.

"Can we pet it? Can we pet it?" asked the Jones children.

"Sure, go ahead if you want to," said Grandpa. So Beth and Harold petted the dead animal. But the Tallmon children--Raymond, Bessie, Edith--stayed back. They didn't want to touch a dirty, poisonous snake. They kept their distance.

The differing reaction was a commentary on the children's backgrounds. The Joneses had learned to be awed and intrigued by nature's creatures, because their father was a biologist, while the Tallmons had been taught to be cautious about creatures that might be dangerous--partly because their mother was leery of such things.

Clara wanted to take the snake home to make a belt, so Grandpa laid it on top of the load of hay. Grandpa later skinned it, and Clara took the skin when they left for Ohio.

A year or so later, Aunt Edith, Grandpa's youngest daughter, was entertaining a visitor from the East. To celebrate, the family took the friend on a moonlight picnic along Coyote Creek--across the valley from the hill ranch.

At the end of the evening, Papa and Grandpa left the group to hitch up the horses and buggies for the trip home. The womenfolk and children walked slowly up the trail, following them to where the buggies were.

Suddenly Edith's friend shied. There was a rustle in the bushes.

"What was that?" Mama exclaimed.

"Oh, nothing!" the friend replied, and continued on up the trail.

It wasn't until a couple of days later that Mama had an inkling of what the girl may have seen--and realized she may not have wanted to frighten anyone.

The next night, Jack and Harold Alexander were walking along Dunne Avenue near the Tallmon home. They spotted a dark form lying in a ditch.

At first they thought it was a drunk, and decided to toss a rock at him. But when they leaned down to pick up a rock, they saw round yellow eyes glowing in the night and knew it wasn't a man.

They headed for home as fast as they could, cutting across the orchard, not knowing when they might be attacked. They made it all right. Then, after catching their breath, curious what it was, they took a light and returned to the orchard.

Not far from their home, they spotted tracks in the soft dirt--two to three inches long, like the paws of a big cat.

A mountain lion! And it had been right behind them all the way home!

Apparently it had come out of the Dunne Woods, and was just resting along the road as the boys went by.

They realized then what a close call they had--mountain lions are vicious animals and will attack a person, if provoked.

The next day, on Monday, a pretty young Sunday school teacher named Isola Kennedy took a group of children on a picnic to Coyote Creek, to almost the same spot where the Tallmons had picnicked two days earlier. Four of the boys were from her class and one was a visitor at her home.

She had taken the lunch out of the picnic basket and had laid it out on a blanket on the ground. She called the boys to eat.

There was a rustling in the bushes.

Suddenly, a tawny-colored animal dashed out and rushed at the group, attacking the visiting boy. The boy screamed as the mountain lion struck at him with its paw and bit him on the ear.

Quickly, Miss Kennedy pulled a long hat pin from her hair--her only weapon--and leaped to the boy's defense. The boy was knocked, torn and bleeding, into the water and the lion turned on the young woman.

"Run for help!" Miss Kennedy exclaimed, trying to ward off the lion with her hatpin. The other boys dashed away in the direction of a nearby bridge where a man lived in a tent.

Not understanding just what had happened nor what kind of an animal it was, he brought a shotgun. When he got there, he didn't dare use it, for fear of hitting the teacher.

So he left her, fighting and struggling with the lion, while he went back to his tent for a rifle.

By the time he returned, the lion had gotten Miss Kennedy on the ground and was gnawing at her. Her arm, which she held over her face to keep the lion from getting to her throat, was ripped and shredded, red with blood. Her ear was almost chewed off.

The man leveled his rifle, took aim, and fired. The lion leaped with the impact, made a half motion with its paw in the air, and fell to the ground. It rolled over once, and lay motionless--shot through the heart.

Miss Kennedy lay there, bleeding profusely, her pretty face torn and bloody, her skin ashen gray, her breath coming in short gasps.

The boys rushed to the injured teacher's side.

"Miss Kennedy! Miss Kennedy!" one of them exclaimed. "Are you hurt BAD?"

The man's wife came hurrying with a bowl of warm water and cloths, and began to dress Miss Kennedy's wounds. The pretty young woman moaned and writhed in agony.

Word of the accident quickly spread to nearby ranches, and a group of men came to help. The first ones there could see pieces of a broken hatpin still protruding from the lion's skull.

Miss Kennedy was wrapped in a sheet and carefully laid in a wagonbed, then transported into town. She had been so terribly mauled and scratched--150 spots on one arm alone--that people didn't expect her to live.

A group of men scoured the hills and rocks, thinking maybe the lion had some cubs hidden someplace. They didn't find any. The lion, which measured nine feet long, nose to tail, was skinned and the pelt was made into a rug and kept for years afterward.

The entire community was shaken by the episode, and people's hearts went out to the brave young Sunday school teacher and the young boy. Nell Stone went regularly each afternoon to Miss Kennedy's bedside, and wrote letters for her.

Miss Kennedy also was president of the Tri-County Woman's Christian Temperance Union at the time. She was engaged to Morgan Hill's first dentist, young Dr. P. Otto Puck. He took the mishap very hard.

Both Miss Kennedy and the boy began to get well. But, then, after several weeks, rabies set in. Even though the boy was only scratched, he was hurt enough, apparently, to be infected. He soon died.

News of the boy's death was kept from Miss Kennedy. But, somehow, she heard. And a few days later, she also died, a victim of rabies.

The entire community was heartbroken. And the dentist, deeply grief-stricken, left town, and never returned.

A few months later, Raymond and Papa were busy at the hill ranch. Raymond said he was thirsty and Papa suggested, "There's a spring up there," pointing toward a clump of trees up the hill.

Just as Raymond got there, a cat jumped from a tree and bounded up the other side of the creek. Startled, Raymond was sure it was a mountain lion. But it was only a bobcat. The animal was as frightened as he was.

48.

By this time, Nell, the little colt born in 1904, was a full-grown, mature work horse. She was ready for a teammate, so Papa bought Prince, a three-year-old stallion, from Mr. Stone. The two horses were Papa's team for many years.

Prince was a sleek, reddish horse--a member of the rare Suffolk-Punch breed, a British coach horse. He was not as light as a carriage horse, nor as heavy as some work horses, but could be used for both.

For a while he was Papa and Mama's only buggy horse, after Dolly was sold to a minister.

Prince was big and gentle, and the children loved him. They could walk between Prince's legs without fear. Sometimes, when they rode Prince bareback, he would run under the branch of a tree and brush them off. He was not mean. He was just tired of carrying them, and gently removed them.

Nell, black with white face, was a more ornery creature. Mama was afraid of her. Papa had to deal roughly with her at times. She was big and clappity--not at all well formed.

But together, Prince and Nell made a good team. Actually, they were half brother and sister.

To the children, horses were very wonderful and important. Bessie loved horses, and often wished she were one.

Coming home from school, the girls sometimes played that they were horses. Raymond was a pack mule, and carried the lunch pails.

On occasion, the children drank out of the horse trough. Mama was shocked when she found out. The water was rich and had been standing for weeks, and the horses slobbered in it when they drank.

But, the children said, weren't they horses and didn't horses drink out of the horse trough? And how could they wipe their mouths, when horses didn't?

Mama insisted that they dispense with such realism in the future.

The Tallmon boys were taught to work when very young. Raymond guided the horses from Papa's lap almost as soon as he could walk.

Before he was much older he was plowing--all by himself. He was so small he had to reach up to the handles of the plow. At the end of rows, he couldn't turn the plow around and had to let the horses drag it around.

Mr. Hamilton, a neighbor, joked that Raymond had to pack a prune box around with him to stand on when he plowed.

Raymond was soon driving the team and wagon along the roads--often alone or with John as his only passenger.

The neighbors were astonished to see two young Tallmon boys, high up on the box of the wagon, hauling a big load of wood or hay.

The boys were so small their legs stuck straight out when they sat clear back in the seat.

But it never seemed to worry them. Nor did it worry Papa.

"You are taking a big risk," neighbor Arthur Brizee remarked to Papa one time, "or else you have a lot of faith in your horses to trust them with your small son."

"They'll do all right," replied Papa. "Anyway, you couldn't scare the horses if you tried. They're very tame."

On his sixth birthday, Raymond drove the horses and wagon to the woodlot on San Martin Avenue, all by himself.

The woodchoppers loaded the wagon for him, and Raymond drove home. He made a second trip to the woodlot and back--a total of two trips that day. It was about four and a half miles each way--18 miles altogether.

That night, Papa pulled out his enormous big snap-purse, took out a large round silver dollar, and gave it to Raymond.

"That's a birthday present and pay for doing a day's work," he smiled. "You earned a whole dollar on your sixth birthday."

Several months after selling Dolly, Papa happened to go by the place where she was sold, and stopped to see how she was doing.

He was shocked. He could hardly believe his eyes. The gentle white buggy horse that had always been so plump and well-fed was thin and sickly-looking. She was just skin and bones.

He took a little grain from under the seat of his wagon and offered it to her through the fence. She came galloping over to him, stuck her nose through the fence and nearly bit his arm off grabbing for the bit of food. She bolted it down like she hadn't eaten for a week.

She was just plain starved! Papa gave her the rest of the grain he had with him, and a little hay, and she ate just as ravenously. She nudged his hand for more.

"Sorry, old girl," he said. "I wish I had more, but it's all gone."

That night, Papa told the story to the family. They were in tears.

"Oh, poor Dolly!" wept Bessie.

"She was always so gentle and nice--a perfect driving horse," said Mama.

"Oh, Papa, you must buy her back!" Edith was insistent. "Those people will starve her to death. You must, Papa! Please!"

"But we don't need her. We have Prince now. We can't afford to care for any more horses."

"But, Papa, we can't just let her starve to death."

Papa's feelings weren't so far different from that, and he decided to buy her back. He gave the new owners a good price for her, and brought her home.

The family was overjoyed. But Dolly never did well after that. Papa fed her and nursed her, and tried to fatten her up, but she just wouldn't respond.

Finally, he gave her away to some people who promised to take good care of her, and let her roam the hills for the rest of her life. The money he had used to buy her back was never replaced, nor was the money spent to nurse her back to health.

Jack rabbits were becoming a menace on the ranch. They ran about the orchard, nibbling at the young trees. They threatened to destroy Papa's young orchard.

Papa didn't like to kill things. He'd rather pick up a snake--a harmless garter snake--on his shovel and carry it far out into the orchard than to kill it. He only killed chickens because he had to.

But the rabbits were becoming a serious threat. He decided he must try to reduce their population.

Borrowing Grandpa's .22 rifle, single shot, he waited until he spied a rabbit in the orchard, not far from the back door.

The rabbit was sitting, munching at a small tree, less than 120 feet away. Papa grabbed the gun, took aim, and fired. The rabbit started running.

"Next time, you'll get him, won't you, Papa?" Raymond piped up.

Papa tried again. The rabbit was still running.

"Next time, you'll get him, won't you, Papa?" Raymond was still undaunted.

Papa tried again.

"Next time, you'll get him, won't you, Papa?" Raymond still hadn't lost faith in his father.

Papa tried some more, but couldn't hit the rabbit. He wasn't a very good shot, anyway.

The rabbit finally got away, and Papa more or less gave up his attempts to shoot the rabbits. Other ranchers and nature eventually reduced the rabbits to the place where they were no longer a serious nuisance.

Raymond was timid as a child, but John was not.

This was graphically illustrated one day when they visited the Morgan Hill second hand store with Mama.

The young grandson of the owner, who lived upstairs, came forward with mean look and clenched fists.

Raymond, 7, backed away, but John, who was 5, stepped forward, ready to fight. Mama stopped the skirmish before it started. But it was an interesting comparison of the two personalities.

The McPhails bought milk from the Tallmons and wanted it delivered. So every day the Tallmon children had to carry a quart of milk half a mile and return, which was hardly worth 3 cents a quart. They had to walk as far as Murphy Avenue.

One night as John and Raymond were delivering the milk, they passed some boys and girls of the neighborhood out having a good time. The children included the Alexander cousins from down the road.

When the children saw Raymond and John coming, they slinked behind the hedge in front of Grandpa's place.

They might have been playing, or just hiding from the boys for the fun of it. As the boys passed by, one of the Alexander boys let out an oath from the hedge, "God damn it!"

John repeated the oath after him.

A week afterward, Mama knew all about it. Her relatives had told her, implying, "Your children aren't so perfect. John swore."

Papa and Mama were anxious for their children to be just right. Some of the relatives were jealous, because the Tallmon children were better behaved than their own.

John, for his part, got his mouth washed out with soap.

Across the road was a green house where the McGees once lived, and then the Gersons. It was a little house, two main rooms and two bedrooms, one of them a lean-to.

All of the water used on the place, including that for the horses and cow, came from a small well about four inches in diameter. It was equipped with a long bucket and windlass, and the bucket was let down into the deep well by hand and then pulled to the surface by winding the windlass.

One day after the Gersons moved away, the boys of the neighborhood were playing about the deserted ranch.

They let the bucket down into the well and then threw rocks down. They threw a good many down, enough to clog the well.

Raymond and John were there, but they were innocent bystanders. They took no real part in the mischief.

Someone found out what had happened, and all the boys in the neighborhood denied doing it.

"I saw Raymond and John over there," said Papa's sister Edith, who had come to stay with Grandpa.

"Were you there?" Papa confronted his young sons.

Raymond and John didn't know how to deny a part when they weren't directly involved.

"Yes, Papa." They spoke softly, with heads bowed.

"All right, then. We must pay for fixing it. I'll have to go over to see the owner. And John, we'll have to take $5 from your savings account at the bank to help pay for it."

Papa paid $15 for a well driller to come in and crush the rocks and force them to the bottom, in order to open up the well again.

Later the other boys admitted their part, but their parents didn't do anything about repaying Papa.

Every Saturday night Papa went downtown to pay for the San Jose Mercury and get a haircut.

He mentioned one time that even though his hair was getting thin, he still had to pay 25 cents for a haircut.

The paper agent started a custom of giving customers a cigar when they paid for the paper, as a reward for paying on time.

But Papa didn't smoke, and told the man so.

"Well, I'll give you chewing gum instead," the agent said. "Take it home for the kiddies."

To Mama, gum was almost as bad as a cigar.

"No lady chews gum," she said.

Papa and Mama had a conference: Was it all right for the children to chew gum? Mama didn't like the idea too well. Papa wasn't overly enthusiastic. In a way, chewing gum resembled chewing tobacco, although of course it was much different. Mama said, when she was a girl, she swallowed some gum one time in a train station, and choked.

The children waited expectantly, eagerness written over their faces.

"Please, Papa. Please, Mama," Edith ventured.

"Well," said Papa, "if they chew it just long enough to get the sweetness out, and then spit it out immediately."

"And if they throw it away as soon as they take it out of their mouths--even once," added Mama.

Saturday night was bath night. Soon all four children-- Edith, Bessie, Raymond and John--were sitting in a row in the bathtub--all chewing gum.

Bessie, a quiet, tearful little girl--rather shy and reserved-- was a good pupil in school and very conscientious. She always came home with wonderful marks.

She was a dead-eye in spelling. She never missed a word. Children who missed had to stay in during recess and study. This never happened to Bessie.

But one day she decided it would be fun to stay in and see what it was like. So she misspelled a word on purpose.

It wasn't the lark she expected. She could hear the other children outside playing and having a good time, while she toiled over a list of words she really knew.

She never misspelled another word again.

One day in a school composition, she talked about Papa's "watery-blue eyes." She meant "water-blue." Papa chuckled about that one for days.

Bessie's class was studying Longfellow. Bessie raised her hand.

"I'm related to Longfellow," she announced.

"That's nice," replied the teacher, amicably. "In what way?"

"Well, his name is long-fellow and my name is tall-man."

The teacher quickly changed to some other subject.

49.

Thin, short and wiry, Papa was not a husky person. His build was on the lightweight side.

His gait was a little mincing walk. He took short steps, and it was easy to keep up with him. His voice was quiet and refined.

At the same time, he was all man; a hard worker, able to direct the affairs of his family and his own life.

He had deep wrinkles, a quiet little chuckle in his voice and a wide smile. The wrinkles made three smiles around his mouth. His cheekbones stuck out quite a bit; Grandpa used to tease Grandma about being descended from an Indian princess, and there was truth to it.

Both Papa and his father were strong, active men with close-set, tight knuckles and tough, sinewy hands, but short.

Papa out-towered his father by one or two inches, and he was only 5 feet, 8 inches, and weighed 145 pounds.

Both were swarthy, too. Papa tanned a dark, dark brown when he was exposed to the sun, although his arms and chest, protected by his shirt, remained comparatively white. His body was almost completely hairless.

Papa wasn't interested in sports. The only time he went to school athletic contests was to take Edith because she wanted to go. He didn't care for competition; he felt sorry for the losers.

His main interest revolved around people--rich or poor. He liked to be with people; he loved people. He had a deep love for humanity. He was sensitive to their needs, and he didn't like to see anyone in want.

He was kindly, thoughtful of others, a sweet person with a warm, friendly personality. You certainly felt he liked you.

He was always smiling, always cheerful and pleasant. Nothing was ever too much trouble for him; he was always willing to help, and always so good-natured about it.

If he disagreed with anyone, he just grinned and let it pass. He was seldom in trouble with anyone, and had no enemies.

But his own father--out of everyone--was his biggest problem. Grandpa tried him to the utmost. If anyone was able to upset or frustrate Papa, it was Grandpa.

For one thing, he treated Papa like a little boy--and even called him Georgie. And he told Papa how to run his ranch.

Many mornings Mama could hear Grandpa's loud voice from the house: "Well, Georgie, what are you going to do today?"

Then Mama could hear Papa's soft voice, telling his father what he was planning to do, but not loud enough so she could understand what he said.

"Well," boomed Grandpa's mighty voice again, "I don't think you should." And then he told Papa to do something else. And, to keep peace, Papa did.

"Here I am nearly 40," Papa complained to Mama, "and I can't do as I please."

Grandpa not only told Papa what to do on Papa's own ranch, but he also insisted that Papa help him on Grandpa's ranch.

Often on a morning, he would walk the length of the wide dirt path beaten between the two places and tell Papa: "Georgie, I want you to haul hay for me today."

Papa had planned something else--something that needed doing on his own ranch. But he always went. He and the boys hauled load after load of hay. They pruned and cultivated and picked fruit and harvested crops.

"I'm willing to do for my father," insisted Papa, when Mama objected to the hours and hours he spent. "But it does make it hard to get my own work done."

Once in a while, Grandpa gave Papa a dollar or two. He said he had "paid for everything," but it wasn't a drop in the bucket compared with the time put in and the number of people working.

About that time, Grandpa received word from Texas that his third-to-youngest daughter, Hester, was not getting along well as teacher in a small school.

"Better call her home," a letter stated. "She's acting rather queer."

Grandpa made no mention of the letter to Mama and Papa, preferring not to reveal Hester's problem. He only said that Hester was coming home.

He made arrangements for her to live at his house and he expected her to get a job teaching school at Morgan Hill.

A week or two later, a buggy drove into Mama and Papa's yard. It continued on toward the barn, and then braked to an abrupt halt. The dust rose in a cloud and continued on in the direction it had traveled. Grandpa climbed from the driver's seat. He reached up and helped a young woman down the long steps.

She was tall and angular in appearance. Her long, straight dark brown hair was knotted in a bun at the back of her head. She was wearing a bonnet and was dressed in a flowing white skirt. But her clothes did not hide her plainness and lack of grace.

Papa came from the barn, adjusting one shoulder strap of his dirty bib overalls with his thumb, and approached his young sister with a smile.

"Welcome to Morgan Hill!" he greeted her, taking her two hands in his. "How was the trip?"

"Oh, hot and uncomfortable." Hester's voice was low and somewhat sarcastic, but she was soft-spoken. "So this is the ranch! It doesn't look like much."

"Well, we like it," said Papa, pleasantly. "It's a nice place to live. Grandpa's ranch is right over there." And he waved his hand toward the adjoining orchard. "Come and see Emma."

But Mama already was coming from the house--a host of children running before her.

"Hello, Hester," she said, as she drew close. She reached out her hand. Hester took it, but without much feeling.

"Hello," she said.

The children gathered around, all eying their unknown aunt.

Mama placed her hand on her eldest daughter's shoulder. "This is Edith," she said. "And this is Bessie . . and John . . . and Raymond. Little Willard is still in the house."

Hester turned to Grandpa.

"Don't you think we ought to go and get unpacked?" she asked.

"Yes," said Grandpa.

"Go ahead and go," agreed Mama. "And you plan to come over here for supper tonight."

Mama could feel the old resentments flaring anew--the resentments she had experienced when she first married and was living with the Tallmons at Grinnell.

Hester, even then, didn't feel Mama was good enough to be a member of the Tallmon family. To Hester, Mama was a poor little girl that big brother George had met in the Salvation Army.

She never went to college; her schooling was scattered. Her family didn't come over on the Mayflower. She just wasn't of the proper caliber for a Tallmon.

George should have married someone more his age and stature in life.

Mama felt this attitude, and resented it and was upset by it. She felt it all coming back to her once again.

Hester was speaking. "We can't come for supper tonight," she was saying. "I must unpack."

She climbed back into the buggy without further ado, and Grandpa turned the horses around and drove out of the yard to the road, turning left toward his ranch.

The dust rose in a cloud, filling the air above the driveway, and then slowly settled behind the disappearing carriage.

It didn't take long for the resentments to flare into the open. As soon as Hester learned that Mama and Papa's son was named "John Carhart Tallmon," she objected.

"They have no right to that name," she told Grandpa. "It's a family name. You tell George they can't use it."

Grandpa went over.

"You have no right to that name," he declared.

"I don't see why not," Papa replied, quietly. "My mother was a Carhartt and he's my son. Besides, my brother's name was John and Emma's father is named John."

Grandpa reported back to Hester. "They won't change his name."

"Well, he's Jackie to me," Hester retorted. "I'll not call him John." Her efforts to change his name, of course, went no further than herself.

As the weeks and months went by, relations with Grandpa and Hester grew only more and more strained.

"George doesn't treat you right," Hester would say at the breakfast table. "After all you've done for him! You'd think he would appreciate it!"

"Yes," said Grandpa.

"He makes you work for him, and then he keeps your wages."

"Yes," agreed Grandpa.

"You helped him load a car with wood, but did you ever see any pay for it?"

"No."

"You put some money in the bank, and he used it, didn't he? And he was supposed to cultivate all of your orchard in exchange for using your horse, wasn't he?"

"Yes."

"If I were you, I'd go over there and do something about it," said Hester. "I wouldn't let it go. I'd do something about it."

So Grandpa would put on his coat and go over.

He'd find Papa doing the chores, and he'd start chiding him.

"When are you going to come over and do my orchard? If it isn't pruned soon, it'll be too late and we won't have any crop this year."

"Tomorrow morning I'll start in," replied Papa.

"I want you to do it TODAY," insisted Grandpa. "It has to be done TODAY."

Papa had planned to go to town that day. He needed to fix the pen so the calf wouldn't get out. And the water pipe at the horse trough was leaking and making a big mud puddle for the animals to tramp in.

But, to keep peace, he changed his plans, put off his own duties until another day, and went with his father to do the pruning.

There was no use making an argument. It would only upset Grandpa further. The best thing was to avoid trouble. He'd forget his own plans, once again.

Another time, Hester would stir up Grandpa again.

"It's time to cultivate the orchard," she'd say. "Why doesn't George come over and do it? I'd get after him, if I were you."

So Grandpa would put on his coat and go over, and maybe this time he'd find Mama doing the baking, and he'd start berating her.

"Why doesn't George come over and do my orchard? After all I've done for him, he should have some consideration."

"He'll do it, Papa, just as soon as he gets a chance."

"What's he doing today? It can't be very important. I've helped him and helped him, many a day. And yet he can't do just a little something for me. You tell him I want him to start plowing my orchard TODAY."

And he stomped out the door. When Papa came in, he found Mama upset and near tears.

"Grandpa was over," she exclaimed. "He was nasty, and he insisted that you must go over and do his orchard TODAY."

"But I was busy fixing harness today," said Papa. "I was going to start his place tomorrow. I can't do it until I get the harness in order. It's almost ready to break."

"Oh, Papa." Mama broke into tears. "I don't think I can stand much more. Why does he have to be so mean? Can't you go over and talk to him?"

"It wouldn't do any good," said Papa. "'To forgive and forget' is the best policy. He'll feel better tomorrow."

Tomorrow, Grandpa would come back and apologize. But the next day, it was the whole story all over again.

Grandpa was ordering Papa around, or complaining, or taking advantage of Papa, or being unreasonable or stubborn.

His stubbornness was apparent one time when some men were hired to cut wood at the hill ranch. Grandpa paid the choppers. Later, when they sold the wood, Papa urged his father to take the money.

"No," insisted Grandpa. "The ranch is half yours."

"Well, then, take out what you paid the choppers, and keep half of what is left."

"No," insisted Grandpa, stubbornly. And he banked all of the money in Papa's name.

When Papa needed some cash for his family, he drew on the account, thinking little of it until one day when he saw Grandpa walking determinedly towards him across the orchard.

Papa pulled back on the reins, stopped the horses and waited for his father to reach him.

"George!" demanded Grandpa, as soon as Papa was within earshot. "I want you to get me that $19 out of the bank."

"What $19?" asked Papa, surprised.

"That money we got for selling the wood."

"But," Papa replied. "I can't. I've already used that money for something else."

"Used it?" exclaimed Grandpa. "But I paid for the choppers. It was my money."

Papa turned pale. "I know you paid for the choppers," he said. "And when we sold the wood, I wanted you to take the money. But you insisted on banking it in my name. I thought you intended it for me."

Grandpa took one long look at his son, then turned away.

"Highway robber!" he muttered.

A wall of resentment started building up inside Papa, but he swept it away. To forgive and forget, as we hope to be forgiven for our own sins--that was the best way. Whatever he might say would only build greater strife. He held back any comment, and in silence watched his father walk away.

Another day, Papa was downtown at the store. As he walked out the door, a friend accompanied him.

The friend waited until they were outside, and then drew close to Papa and asked in a low, confidential voice:

"What's this I hear about you and your father being on the outs?"

Papa was surprised. "What do you mean?"

"Well, he was telling around that you collected his wages and kept them."

"Kept them?" exclaimed Papa.

"Yes, that's what he said. It didn't sound like you. There must have been some misunderstanding. But that's what he said."

Papa was puzzled. What could Grandpa mean? He had helped Papa load a car of wood or had spent a few hours driving Papa's team when Papa was busy doing something else.

But Papa didn't suppose he expected pay for the work, any more than when he spent half a day working at Papa's woodpile as he had done a hundred times.

Papa was provoked and exasperated. What right did his father have to talk behind his back around town? But there was no use making an issue over it. It was much better to ignore the whole matter.

Mama and Papa were provoked another time when Grandpa claimed they were not keeping up yearly payments on their ranch.

"But we've made our payments regularly," Mama insisted. "I know, because I asked you to 'let me give Grandpa the $100' so I could have the thrill of making another payment on the place."

"Yes," said Papa. "We haven't missed a single payment . . "

"And some years it has been very hard to squeeze it out. I think you should go over and tell him so."

"I suppose I should," said Papa. But he didn't. It would just lead to trouble. Grandpa meant well. And he had a temper. What was the point of stirring up something, making things worse?

It would just cause more hard feelings.

Another time, Grandpa came over and found Papa in the barn.

"Are you still milking that cow?" Grandpa demanded. "It should be dried up so it can have another calf."

"I know," replied Papa, well aware of what Grandpa was saying. "But I need the milk."

"Well, if you didn't have such a large family you wouldn't need so much milk!" Grandpa retorted.

Papa got the implication, but made no reply. No use to stir up more trouble--even to pointing out that Grandpa had had an even larger family. He just let it go.

But soon Grandpa was back again, berating and accusing Mama unmercifully, and making derogatory and insulting remarks about Mama's family.

He told her Grandpa Shaffer was a "no good bum"; a lazy, shiftless man; a man who liked his liquor. Ella's husband, Callie, was no better. He was an ignorant, lazy, good-for-nothing no-account from Kentucky.

Mama was angry and upset, and deeply hurt. When Papa came home and Mama told him what Grandpa had said, he was incensed.

He was on the verge of going over and giving his father a piece of his mind. But he managed to restrain himself. It wouldn't accomplish anything.

"It would just make him all the more resentful," Papa reasoned. "It's best to just let it pass. He'll feel better tomorrow."

But that wasn't the end of it. Grandpa would apologize, but soon he was badgering Mama about something else.

"Why don't you keep those children from arguing?" he'd ask. Or, "Can't you see it's after 10 o'clock and there you are rocking the baby. Aren't you ever going to get your work done?" Or, "Don't you think it's time to cut those peaches?"

"I was up at 5:30 and I have already done the washing, cleaned the house, made the beds, fixed breakfast and got the bread made," Mama retorted. She'd talk back to Grandpa.

But it did no good. He'd be back another day and jump on her again.

Grandpa's unkind remarks about Mama also were directed through Papa. One day Grandpa noticed that Papa had a sore on his lip.

"Oh, you, too?" he asked. "Hester said Emma had syphillis. Now you're getting it."

Papa flared.

"You know that isn't true! Emma would never catch such a disease as that!"

"Well, just look at that family she comes from . . " Grandpa was haughty. "She's just that kind of a person . . "

"You know better than that!" replied Papa. "Emma always has been a sweet, pure young woman. You are completely mistaken."

Mama broke into tears when Papa told her about it.

"Grandpa knows I'm not like that!" she exclaimed. "Why doesn't he leave me alone?"

"He's just getting old," Papa said. "He doesn't realize what he's saying."

"He's just repeating what Hester tells him," retorted Mama. "She feeds him full of lies and then he comes over here and repeats them."

"No," said Papa. "I don't think so. Grandpa has always been sharp with his tongue. He made our home a hell on earth with his wicked temper, when I was a boy. That's his nature; he doesn't mean all he says. No, it's Grandpa--that's his way. Hester is fair. Hester is fair."

"She's the root of all the trouble," insisted Mama. "Everything has gone wrong since she came. Grandpa was not easy to get along with before, but he's much worse now.

"Oh, Papa!" she exclaimed, looking up into his face with tear-streaked and begging eyes, "can't we move away from here? Anywhere, I don't care. Anywhere, but not here."

Papa looked at her with compassion, and his heart was moved for her.

But he said: "I can't. We have a living and a job here. I can't hold my breath long enough to move elsewhere."

50.

When Mama's family came to visit, Grandpa carried his campaign of smears directly to them. He chided Grandpa Shaffer for being a "no good Democrat." As far as he was concerned, no swear word could be any worse.

He accused Grandpa Shaffer of not doing enough work. He wanted to know why Callie was not regularly employed in Oakland--even though Callie was working steadily as a hod carrier and making good wages.

And one thing he would never let Grandpa Shaffer forget was the hammer incident. He badgered Grandpa Shaffer about it everytime he saw him. Grandpa Shaffer usually was fairly patient, but one time he lost his temper.

Grandpa Shaffer happened to be helping Papa unload wood at the ranch that day. Grandpa Tallmon came by, and when he saw Grandpa Shaffer standing there on the wagon, his eyes blazed in a belligerent way.

"Where's my hammer?" Grandpa Tallmon demanded in a sarcastic tone. "When are you going to bring back that hammer you stole from me?"

"I didn't take your hammer!" exclaimed Grandpa Shaffer, flushing angrily. "You know I didn't take your hammer. It probably fell down the well."

"Thieves always make excuses!" declared Grandpa Tallmon, scornfully.

Grandpa Shaffer flushed and lost what little control he had left. He clenched his fists and muttered: "I'll show you whether I'm a thief or not."

Mama, who was in the house, heard the shouting and looked out the window just then. She saw her father just ready to jump off the wagon.

Papa stepped up, put his hand on Grandpa Shaffer's arm, and said, quietly: "Wait, you don't want to do something you'll be sorry for." Then he turned to Grandpa Tallmon and said: "I'm sure if Father knew where your hammer was, he'd return it to you."

"No he wouldn't," muttered Grandpa Tallmon. "He'll keep anything he can get his hands on!" And he turned his back on them and marched off towards home.

"You're nothing but a no good Democrat," he shouted over his shoulder as he went.

Papa and Grandpa Shaffer watched him go, and then began tossing pieces of wood off the wagon again.

All of this turmoil and tension was making a nervous wreck out of Mama. She couldn't sleep at night. She wept easily. She felt depressed and unhappy all day.

Her heart pounded, or seemed to stop entirely.

One night Papa awoke with a start. His arm was across Mama's chest, and she wasn't breathing. He shook her, and she sat up and asked, "What's the matter?"

"I just wanted to be sure you were all right," he said.

A few days later Hester stopped by. Mama was working in the garden next to the driveway.

"Here," said Hester. "Here is some mail. That mailman is always giving us your letters."

"Thank you," replied Mama, pushing her trowel into the ground and standing up. She brushed the dirt from her hands and accepted the mail. Glancing at the envelopes, she noticed some business letters for Papa.

Just then, Papa drove into the driveway with a load of wood. Nell's hoofs kicked up the dirt, forming small clouds about her legs. The wagon wheels, following along behind, added to the brown dust in the air.

Nell neighed, shook her head and stomped her feet as she passed. Mama shrank back, and Hester noticed her fear immediately.

"Don't you like the horse?" Hester asked.

"No," Mama admitted. "I have felt uneasy around her from the time she was a young colt and reared up over me when I tried to tie her up."

"Oh, she's quite a gentle horse!" Hester scoffed. "Besides, she's Papa's anyway," referring to her father.

"What do you mean, 'Papa's'?" Mama flared. "George bred her and raised her."

"My father pastured her and fed her," Hester replied, calmly. "He told George he wanted the colt."

"My husband gave that colt to his children as a pet long before Grandpa asked for it," Mama retorted. "Papa told Grandpa he couldn't give her up. He'd have to pay Grandpa for her, if Grandpa ever wanted to take her away."

"Oh, he doesn't want to take the horse," Hester said, still quietly. "He only wants George to help him with his work. That's small enough pay for the money my father spent on Nell when she was a colt."

"But Papa does help Grandpa with his work. He spends hours over there fixing or cultivating or picking fruit. But Grandpa never appreciates it. He just wants more and more and more. He's been that way since Papa was a boy."

Hester flushed angrily.

"What do you know about our father when George was a boy?" she demanded.

"All I know is what I read in the journals written by your mother," replied Mama, "and the little Papa has told me."

Hester looked at Mama with contempt.

"You're from a no-account, good-for-nothing family," she barked, and headed for home, without a backward glance.

Within 10 minutes, Grandpa was over, his eyes flaming and his face flushed.

"How do you know what I was like when Georgie was a boy? Who let you see those journals, anyway? You had no right to see them. They weren't true, anyway. And you know perfectly well that Nell is my horse. I fed her and raised her and paid for her keep. That's enough to make her mine. I told Georgie I must have her."

"It was Papa's colt . . . " Mama tried to say, but Grandpa kept on spilling out the words.

"After all I've done for Georgie, you'd think he'd appreciate it. I've helped him with his ranch and I've done many things for him. He's my only son, and he'll inherit the bulk of what I have when I'm gone. But it doesn't seem enough. He just wants to take advantage of me. He never helps me with my ranch work, even though he knows I can't do it myself. I put some money in the bank, and he goes ahead and takes it out. I loaned him hundreds of dollars to buy his ranch here, and he doesn't keep up the payments. Here I am, an old, old man, and have a son that abuses me, and doesn't understand me, and is too busy at his own affairs to care.

"But, then, I guess it isn't entirely his own fault. With a wife like you, a man is apt to be misled and confused. Anyone with a background like yours, what can you expect? A senile old man like your father--a lazy, good-for-nothing bum, a thief, and a drinking man. And the rest of your family is no better. Cal--I suppose that shiftless character is still doing nothing up in Oakland . . But what can you expect?"

And he kept on and on, in the same vein, until Mama broke into tears, and buried her face in her hands.

"I can't stand it. I can't stand it," she cried. Grandpa marched off home, leaving her sobbing and weeping and alone.

When Papa came home for lunch, he found Mama with tears streaming down her face. She had lunch ready, but obviously with much effort.

"What's the matter?" Papa asked, tenderly.

"Grandpa was over all morning," she said. "He scolded and berated and talked until I thought I would go out of my mind. He called Father a 'no good bum,' and a thief, and Callie no better. He said we weren't keeping up our payments on the ranch--and I knew we have. He said you never help him with his ranch work, and that I'm a bad influence on you, and that Father drinks, and that we never could be any good. Papa, I don't think I can stand any more. I just can't."

Papa's eyes blazed.

"You don't need to stand it, especially in your condition," he said. "I'll go over and tell him something."

So, leaving her there weeping, he crossed the orchards and strode into Grandpa's house. Grandpa and Hester were eating lunch.

"Emma said you were over all morning, berating her," Papa said, without anger. "This must stop. You are driving Emma out of her mind. She can't take it. You worried our mother to her death, and made our childhood home a hell on earth by your wicked temper. When you start doing the same thing in my home, it has to stop. Emma is my wife, and you leave her alone. You have no right to come over and scold my wife!"

Grandpa just looked at him, with a surprised expression on his face. George, his son, never talked this way!

Papa returned home, and found Mama in the bedroom on her knees by the bed, weeping and praying. He put his arm across her shoulders and knelt down beside her.

"Dear God," he prayed. "Forgive me for what I've done."

He also asked the Lord to be with Emma and comfort her "in this dark hour. And help my father and sister to be more understanding and sympathetic."

That should have been the end of it, but it wasn't.

A few days later Grandpa came storming over to Papa's ranch and told Papa: "Give me the deed to your half of the hill ranch."

"Fine," said Papa.

If Grandpa wanted the hill ranch, he wasn't going to argue.

"I shouldn't have given you any part of it, anyway," continued Grandpa, almost shouting. "You never appreciate the things I do for you, and you never help me with my work. We'll just cancel all business arrangements. You give me a deed to the hill ranch, and I'll give you the notes you owe me on this place, and we'll cancel all debts."

"Fine," said Papa. And he and Mama signed over to Grandpa all interest in the ranch in the hills. That was on Jan. 27, 1910.

As it turned out, Grandpa didn't even record the transfer until March 17, 1911. And he never did give Papa the notes he held.

Grandpa wrote in great detail to other members of the family. He complained that Papa was abusing him, not helping him with his ranch work, didn't understand him, and was being misled by Mama.

Back came letters of sympathy.

Burt Jones, from Portland, wrote:

"I am very sorry that anything has come up to in the slightest mar your comfort or happiness in your work with George . .

"He is at heart a dear, good, fine boy, and I think would never have a word to offer contrary to your wishes. He knows how much he owes you in every way. But when a man is shut up with his wife, and hears only one thing day after day, even if it but a fancied wrong, he gets her point of view . . I suppose he ought to, in a way.

"But Emma is not a normal woman. She is small and frail, and unusually nervous and supersensitive, and these natural deficiencies added to the strain of heavy child bearing have, in my judgement, caused all the trouble.

"I think it will all blow over if you could just be away from them a short time. Why not come up and make us a visit now and stay this summer? . . . "

Burt's wife, Angie, was considerate enough to write to Mama and ask what was wrong. Mama didn't feel like replying, so Papa wrote for her--a general letter, only touching on the problems briefly. The letter didn't satisfy Angie--only made her afraid she might have been the cause of the trouble. So she wrote to Grandpa:

> The time has come for this letter to be written for I can think of little else and you must be wondering why you didn't hear . .
>
> Well--I hope your troubles are less and less--for surely they were all mistakes or founded on mistakes. I'm glad I don't know many particulars, but I have learned enough from George to see how part of the trouble was misunderstanding--pure and simple--the part ccncerning me--and to that I only hold the key. That is why I speak

of it--for it must be explained. I am so glad to be exonerated.

When we lived in Smith Center and Emma was visiting us that summer, I gave her a book of Mama's sketches to read one or two interesting stories of Georgie and John and the little girls--their sayings and cute baby ways--true little stories which I knew she would enjoy.

How much more of the book she read I didn't know. There was nothing I would care if she saw. . . She told Hester (George says) that the most she ever learned about your early days etc. was from a 'journal' of our mother's which she read in Smith Center.

This book was not a 'journal.' It does not pretend to be a 'journal' and if she so understood she must have been astonished! There ARE stories of Grandma's brothers-in-law (horrid men), stories about 'Mrs. Smith's Canary,' 'Queer Names,' etc. etc. One little satire about 'Smart Folks' is a composite picture. It does include you but was written, as I remember, when Aunt Maggie and Mrs. John Merrill had been irritating Mama some way . . . .

Mama was clever. She wrote some very good things and I prize her writings among my choicest treasures. I know she sometimes spoke or wrote too sharply, but there is so much of sweetness and beauty and faithfulness I wouldn't give up these writings to anyone because, though I want to be unselfish, I don't care to let anyone see any of the bitter things . . .

She would want me to sort out these and that I shall do sometime . . .

You were always overworked. You were always nervous and sometimes hasty but your ideals were pure and unselfish and you were in most ways a noble man. But the weight of your displeasure--I'll never forget how heavily it fell when it fell! . . . In all those years since Mama left, you have been father and mother both to us all . . I surely understand how difficult your task has sometimes been . . . I know Mama loves you for all you have been to us and if there were, in old days, mistakes on both sides sometimes, they weigh nothing now. They should not be remembered . .

I haven't hurt you, have I? I wouldn't want to. I pity Emma and George . . I can see very dimly how misconceptions, mistakes, little sensitivenesses etc. caused it all. Too bad. I lived there too. I spent some nights in tears over some misunderstandings and hasty words but Emma never knew it and time has healed them all.

There is one way in which her disposition is way above mine (many ways perhaps). But she can forgive and forget so beautifully . . I wish I could forget everything like she can and 'start fresh' as she does . . .

I am not naturally so hasty or suspicious but I WILL remember old hurts so long. I think some of my sisters are like me. We can't understand people who would let themselves go so and are apt to fear them afterwards. But life is short. We need not worry about what others think or say of us--just so we do our best.

God is faithful and He won't let trouble come which He cannot help us bear. Some way--in His time-- we shall be set right before all the world.

Do you remember the verse which begins:

So many little faults we find.
We see them--for not blind
Is love.

Days change so many things--yes hours.
We see so differently in sun and showers.
But if you and I
Perhaps remember them some by and by
They will not seem faults then
But just mistakes, odd ways or even less--
Remembrances to bless.

I don't give it exactly--but I like the verse. I hope you are feeling well again . .

Your daughter Angie.

Grandpa laid down the letter, and there was a smile on his lips.

51.

Papa and Mama first realized something was wrong when they failed to hear from Papa's sisters. Weeks went by, with no letters.

Then, one day, Papa was downtown and saw Hester coming toward him.

"Hello, Hester," he greeted her. She made no reply, but looked the other way and passed without acknowledging him.

Papa watched as she continued on down the sidewalk. His own sister! Ignoring him!

Then, a feeling of wonderful relief swept through him. He understood. Mama was right. Now he knew where the real trouble lay. It was Hester, not Grandpa! Grandpa was only reflecting Hester's attitude.

It helped to excuse Grandpa. Papa could feel just as friendly toward him as ever in his life. Even as a boy, he had always been on Grandpa's side—not because of his wicked, cruel temper, but because he felt Grandpa wasn't always treated fair.

But now, Hester had shown her true colors. Papa was tempted to add some stronger words to his vocabulary to express his opinion of her. It really wasn't necessary.

Her name itself would be more expressive to him than a whole book of swear words. He'd pray for her with the same feeling he had for criminals and outcasts.

In spite of all this, Papa tried to continue his relationships with Grandpa and Hester as if nothing had happened. Papa helped his father as much as he ever did, and tried to be friendly.

The children were free to go over and visit Hester whenever they wanted to. Hester was pleasant enough when they visited. She let the younger children bake cookies, and she chatted with the older ones.

Edith and Bessie thought a lot of the aunties and Hester was considered one of them.

But, at the same time, Hester took advantage of the situation to pump the children and get all the information she could regarding Mama and her family.

And then she started making pointed remarks.

"All Emma has to do is ask for something and George gets it for her. He's too good for her."

The children repeated the remarks at home, which hurt Mama deeply.

Hester grabbed at every little comment that was made, and turned and twisted it to her way of thinking.

Edith happened to mention, one time, that both she and her mother liked pepper on their tomatoes.

"You inherited a liking for liquor, that's what!" Hester replied, disgustedly.

She was referring to Grandpa Shaffer's drinking, and was implying that the craving was inherited and Mama and Edith were satisfying their bent for liquor by using spice since they didn't drink. Another crack that the Shaffers weren't good enough for the Tallmons.

And that wasn't the only theme she used. Mama was pregnant again, and Hester had something new to harp upon.

"You're father's nothing but a brute," she told Edith. "Just a brute. Nothing but a brute to have so many children."

The words burned themselves into the young girl's mind. Brute—brute—nothing but a brute. She thought: they did have a large family, that was true—and babies kept coming. Hester must be right. Papa must be a brute!

Resentment filled her chest. Poor Mama! Evil Papa! The more she thought about it, the more she hated Papa. At the supper table, she looked at him, and remembered, and wondered how she ever could have loved such a despicable man.

"Edith, pass the potatoes around."

She passed them, but without a word.

"Edith, how was school today?"

She ignored him, turned the other way, and made some comment to Mama.

Papa, somewhat taken aback, let the matter pass, although it was strange for Edith to act that way. Perhaps she wasn't listening. Perhaps she was piqued about some little thing, and it would soon pass.

But when she continued to ignore him for several days, he finally asked her what was wrong.

"Nothing," she replied.

"But, there must be," insisted Papa. "Something must be troubling you. This isn't like you. Tell me, won't you? Have I done something wrong?"

"Yes . . ." Edith couldn't lie.

"What have I done?" Papa asked. "Tell me, and maybe I can change it."

His voice was soft and kind. He was understanding, not angry.

"Oh, Papa!" Edith exclaimed. "Hester says you are a brute, because Mama has so many children. You aren't, really, are you?" The tears began to roll down her cheeks.

Papa sat up straight. His face turned white, and his eyes blazed.

"Is that what she said?" he asked. "When did she tell you that?"

"The other day . . . That's why I wouldn't speak to you."

"She has no right to talk that way to my daughter!" he exclaimed. "I'm going over and tell her so!" And he marched out the door.

Edith was frightened. What would happen now?

Papa found Hester preparing supper. She turned as he entered.

He was no longer angry. But he made it clear what he had come for.

"Hereafter, you keep your opinions to yourself," he told her plainly. "It's none of your business. It doesn't make any difference to you if we have 100 children. What do you know about marriage anyway?"

The reference to her being married was just a little bit pointed, not the type of thing he would normally say.

Then he left. She didn't utter a word. But for many days, Mama and Papa saw or heard nothing from Grandpa or Hester.

For weeks, Hester wouldn't speak and Grandpa was short and aloof. Apparently Papa's confrontation of Hester had done little good, and only caused more problems. He wished he'd never gone over.

Edith cringed with fear whenever Grandpa or Hester passed by on the road. Maybe they would turn in and there would be another scene. She was weepy at school and couldn't do her work. It took a long time to get over it.

Hester spent a year as a teacher at Morgan Hill. Her teaching wasn't bad. But she was unkempt and dirty in her personal appearance, and she failed to hold the respect of other teachers and pupils. She had no discipline over her classes.

Mr. Stone, the school trustee, ws forced to tell her she would not be hired another year. Hester, for years afterward, did not forgive him for it.

Clara heard Hester had lost her job, and invited her to come to Oberlin, Ohio, to live and teach in a little school at Birmingham, a small town nearby.

Hester gladly accepted the offer, and left that summer. Relationships at Morgan Hill became more peaceful—for a while.

There was a brief flare-up when Grandpa cashed one of Papa's checks, delivered to him by mistake. When Papa found out, he objected and Grandpa returned the money.

Papa forgave him. "He reasoned ineffectively," Papa explained to Mama.

It was peach season when Mama's baby was due. Mama and Papa were feeling poor; peaches were only 20 cents a box for a 40-pound box (and nice ones, too). They felt they couldn't afford a nurse.

Mama's sister, Lillie, agreed to come and help. And Edith, it was decided, was old enough to look after the other children and keep house—with Papa's help.

One other matter must be taken care of—a name for the new little arrival.

For years Papa had wanted a little girl named Susan. To him, it was a beautiful name. His mother, his sister and a favorite Sunday school teacher all were named Susan.

But Mama didn't like the name. As a child she knew a little girl named Susie who was untidy and dirty.

When Mama and Papa had three boys in a row—and wondered if they would ever have a girl again—Mama decided it might be because she refused to use the name Susan. All right, she said, if the next baby were a girl, she would give in.

"But it must be 'Susan' and not 'Susie.' I just can't stand the name, 'Susie.'"

The day arrived. Aunt Lillie and the doctor were notiified. Papa was always with Mama during each of her deliveries.

But this one was slow. He chopped wood, waiting for things to develop. He didn't want to go off, because he wanted to be right there. Chopping wood needed doing, and yet he was close at hand.

At noon, they were still waiting. As the family gathered around the dinner table, Mama remarked to Papa, "We have no s-t-r-i-h-s for the little one."

Papa replied: "I'll go downtown and get some."

Bessie, who was 8, figured out that the word spelled "shirts" backwards, so the children wouldn't know what it was. She guessed that a baby was coming.

Edith already knew, and it was her job to take care of the little ones—keep them out of the way. After dinner, she—with Bessie's knowing help—took them all, including Aunt Lillie's children, down the orchard. The Early Crawfords were ripe, and they tasted good.

They stayed and stayed. No one came to get them. Their clothes were dirty from playing and eating peaches. They definitely were not hungry.

The shadows were getting long when finally Papa came and said, "Why didn't you come up to the house? We've been wondering where you were."

"We didn't know we were supposed to," Edith explained. "No one came to tell us."

Papa's attitude immediately softened. He smiled and then he said, his face beaming:

"You have a new little sister. Her name is Susan."

"Really? Really?" exclaimed the Tallmon children, jumping up and down with excitement. But not Edith. She was happy, but she was in on the know. A baby was not a surprise to her.

"May we see her?" the children begged. "May we see her?"

"Of course!" replied Papa.

So three little, dirty urchins ran for the house, followed by Papa, Edith and the Alexander cousins. Aunt Lillie made all of them clean up—at least the high points—before they were allowed to go into Mama's room.

Little Willard, who didn't go to the orchard because he was only three, greeted them. "Do you want to thee?" he asked, excitedly, clapping his hands. "Do you want to thee?"

There, tucked under Mama's arm, lying on the clean white bed sheet, was a little round red face peering from a tiny curled blanket, eyes closed tight—the newest of the Tallmon clan.

The children stood watching little Susan for a while, fascinated, but not saying anything. Then Aunt Lillie said supper was on the table and the food would get cold.

Reluctantly the children left the baby and went to eat. But no one ate very much. The excitement was too great.

Aunt Lillie helped get the dishes done and the younger children to bed. Then she went home, leaving Edith in charge.

She came back the next day to bathe Mama and the baby. She took the washing home, too. But the rest was up to Edith.

Edith and Bessie kept the dishes done. That was what they were impressed needed doing. The rest of the house may have been neglected, but at least the dishes were washed.

Edith was the cook, with help from Papa. The menus were very simple—boiled potatoes, fruit, canned tomatoes, macaroni and cheese—nothing Edith couldn't fix.

And they had corn flakes every morning for breakfast. Edith stacked the boxes behind the bathroom door. It seemed a good place for them.

As soon as Mama was well enough to be up and around again, everyone, with sighs of relief, gratefully handed the work back to her.

When she found the stack of empty corn flakes boxes behind the door, she was shocked. She never would have done that! She disposed of them as quickly as she could.

Having a large family meant an extra burden on family finances. Every penny counted, and Papa had to be careful about expenses and "extras."

One day Mama went downtown and bought a new pair of shiny pumps for Bessie and Edith. The girls had been looking forward to having nice shoes for a long time.

The next day was Sunday, and they eagerly put them on and went out to "surprise" Papa.

But he was more concerned than surprised.

"Who bought you those?" he asked.

Mama flared up. "I did," she replied. And, without further words, she quickly made the girls change to their old high-top shoes.

The girls were bitterly disappointed. They thought their father was very unfair. The next day Mama took the pumps back for a refund.

Later Bessie overheard Papa tell Mama that he was mostly teasing when he asked, "Who bought those?" and that he didn't expect her to take them back.

"I just feel that fancy clothes are unnecessary, and that there was plenty of wear left in the old shoes," he explained. "I thought the money spent for the pumps could be better used for some other purpose."

On another occasion, Mama put the girls' hair up in curlers, so that they would have beautiful curly hair for Sunday.

Papa wasn't particularly pleased, and when he said something about it, Mama quickly took the curlers out. She combed the girls' hair the best she could, although some waves still remained. The girls went to church that way. Papa hadn't said to take them out, but Mama was sensitive. If there were the slightest objection, she wasn't going to do it.

Papa also opposed jewelry. He didn't want his girls to appear to be showing off.

Lots of people who lived near Morgan Hill couldn't afford pumps and didn't have someone willing to take the time to put their hair up in curlers. Papa was just as concerned about the Tallmons not making a show as he was that the pumps or curls were too fancy or unnecessary.

He also questioned whether the family's small amount of money should be spent on frills when it was needed for more practical things. Frills were nice if you could afford them, but other things came first.

But Papa was a quiet man. He didn't argue. And when he said nothing, Mama and the girls got the idea he disapproved. Mama had a tendency to jump to conclusions anyway. If someone didn't express an opinion for something, or made the slightest objection, to her they were against it.

Mama insisted on one thing, though—putting ribbons in the girls' hair. Bessie was allowed to wear three ribbons—one at the top, one in the middle, and one at the end of her pigtail. Edith—who was nearing 13—wore two big bows in her pretty brown hair.

Papa made no complaint, and the girls were happy that Mama insisted on some such nicities. Otherwise, they felt, they might have missed out on a lot more than they did.

Although Papa steered away from "extras," he was progressive about providing any conveniences he could to lighten the family's chores.

He was always fixing. The family had a telephone soon after moving to Morgan Hill—long before other people had one.

And the Tallmons became one of the first families in Morgan Hill to have an indoor "patent closet." Almost no one had them in those days, especially out in the country.

It was a nuisance for Mama to have to take the little ones outdoors at night in the cold before they went to bed.

Papa installed a modern bathroom for the Coats family in town while working for Mr. Boutell.

"Well, if those folks can, I can, too," Papa said, and proceeded to take the necessary steps. When completed, the indoor bathroom was the pride of the family.

The next day at school, Bessie raised her hand during "current events." She said she had some very important news to tell.

"All right, Elizabeth," said her teacher. Bessie stood up.

"We have a brand new patent closet at our house," said Bessie, "—indoors." And then she went on to tell about it in full detail.

The pupils were fascinated. They wanted to know all about it. Two of the girls walked home with her after school, even though it meant going two miles out of their way. They were shown the new bathroom from the outside. Then they were shown from the inside. Then they walked home and told their parents all about it.

Soon word spread all over Morgan Hill that the Tallmons had a new indoor toilet!

Papa was a considerate father, and tried to find time out of his busy life to do a few things for his children. He thought of things they would enjoy, and made special plans for good times together.

Before fruit harvest that summer, Papa said one day: "Let's go to the beach on a camping trip."

The children were delighted and, although Mama didn't particularly like camping trips, she agreed to go.

Papa packed the camping equipment onto the spring wagon, and all the family—including Nilo the dog—started off toward the ocean.

There was singing and laughter as they rode down the road to town, then turned south through the foothills. Toward afternoon they reached the foot of the mountains and began climbing the steep, winding Mt. Madonna grade.

At the top of the mountain, they bedded down for the night.

When they awoke the next morning, the whole valley, toward the ocean, was a sea of fog. By the time they had eaten breakfast and packed belongings on the wagon, the fog was beginning to dissipate. And as they started down the mountain, the weather began to clear.

They reached the coastal plain and soon entered the town of Watsonville, then turned north as the sun began to burn through the fog. They drove along the edge of the coast for a few miles, but couldn't see the water, as it was hidden by trees and small hills.

Finally, Papa turned off the road and headed toward the west. They came to the edge of a cliff—and then, suddenly, there below them, was the fascinating beauty of the Pacific Ocean, stretching as far as eye could see.

The green-blue waves, white caps forming as they neared the shore, rolled one after another toward the beach, then crashed and receded.

Only a few clouds remained off-shore, remnants of the once-heavy fog. The sky was blue now, and the sun was shining bright. A seagull flapped its wings, just once, as it soared barely over the water, its eye searching for a wayward fish.

They could hear the deep-throated roar of the mighty ocean, and they could smell the salty, fishy, full-bodied aroma of the sea breezes that caressed their cheeks.

Then Papa drove on—down a road to the water's edge. The children couldn't wait to get into the surf. They jumped from the wagon, removed their shoes and stockings, and ran for the water.

The waves rolled across the sand toward them, not more than an inch or two deep. As they waded in, the foamy water swirled about their feet, and then receded.

Courage grew, and they moved farther and farther into the water, until the waves were as high as their ankles—and then their knees.

Only it was a little uncertain. The waves were not always the same. Several would be small, and the children would venture out from the shore. And then a big one would come—unexpectedly—and rise much higher on their legs than they had planned.

When this happened, the children tried to run back. But usually the wave moved too quickly. Soon they were wet about their pants legs or the bottom of their dresses.

Bessie, who was timid about going into the water in the first place, had had enough. The ocean was just too big and mighty for her. She returned to the camp to help Mama, and to play with baby Susan.

Little Willard, only 3, waded into the water, holding onto the hand of his older sister, Edith. A big wave came along, knocked him down, and then drained back to the ocean from which it had come. Willard, tears in his eyes, climbed to his feet, wet and dripping. Edith led him back to camp, and changed his clothes for him.

But no such tragedies befell John or Raymond or the dog. They had a wonderful time. When they were tired of wading, they went exploring. Soon they came back with news that the Ward family and other people from Morgan Hill were camped a short distance away. The families visited back and forth, and all had a grand time.

That night, the Tallmons bedded down. They slept on the ground in a row in front of the tent Papa had borrowed from Grandpa. Mama had brought along some wide quilts, and two or three slept under each quilt. But they didn't get much sleep. Nilo, the dog, wasn't happy with the situation. He fussed and whined and cried all night. Raymond tried to quiet him, and Papa tried to quiet him, but he just wouldn't be happy.

The next morning, Papa got up early and walked down to the beach, where some men were fishing. Some of the children went with him. They watched the men draw in a big net attached by rope to a winch on the shore.

The fishermen caught a large haul of sole and were having difficulty. Papa pitched in and helped pull the nets to shore.

Afterward, Papa bought a fish—and the fishermen charged him full price for it, 15 cents, in spite of his assistance. After all, they probably figured, they didn't ask Papa for help. Mama prepared the fish over a crude campfire, and served it for breakfast. The family sat on the gray sand around a white sheet on which the food was placed. The fish, sizzled in the big frying pan to a light brown, couldn't have tasted more delicious.

And so the time passed—a week's vacation they would never forget.

The older children played from morning to night, and were seen in camp only for meals. They went wading every day, on hikes, played ball, dug holes in the sand, and watched the fascinating waves, seagulls and far-stretching ocean.

Often Papa did things with them. He helped dig holes in the sand, and went wading. He built a little sand-dam, with a ¾-inch pipe running through as a spillway.

He went on walks with the children. One time, as they walked down a steep slope toward the beach in single file, Willard slipped and bumped into John.

"Stop it!" demanded John. Papa told him it was an accident; Willard didn't mean to.

The open-air life, with its exposure to wind and sun, gave everyone either a deep tan or a sunburn. Especially Edith. The elements were unmerciful to her pink cheeks and soft skin, and within three days, her red nose began to peel.

Little Susan celebrated her first birthday during the time they were there. But she wasn't too happy. She cried and fussed and apparently missed the comforts of home. Even at night, Mama had trouble getting her to sleep.

Johnnie was fascinated by the tall eucalyptus trees and the stately evergreens. He recalled that when he was a baby, Papa and Mama took home a eucalyptus tree from an earlier camping trip. He asked if, this time, he could take home a blue gum and a baby pine tree. Papa said he could.

When the day came to leave, Mama happily began packing. The children were sad, and Papa was sympathetic. They broke camp and soon were on the road toward home.

As they rode, they sang—old favorites and hymns at first. Then Papa began singing a song he made up as he went along, and it went like this (to the tune of Yankee Doodle):

Papa Tallmon took his tribe
To have some recreation.
The times they had both glad and sad
Exceeded expectation.

Edith Tallmon lost her looks
Just looking! I should say so!
Her face sunburned and poor nose peeled
Just like a boiled potato.

Bessie Tallmon wished to wade
Out in the great big ocean,
 But the waves they dashed and crashed and
 splashed
Until she lost her notion.

Raymond Tallmon took the dog
To guard their expedition,
But it fussed and whined and cried one night
And caused them great vexation.

Johnnie Tallmon took home trees—
A blue gum and a pine—
They make such lovely souvenirs,
I'll have them both for mine.

Willard Tallmon took a slide
While walking down the hill.
He bumped into his brother John,
Who said, "Hold on there, Bill!"

Susie Tallmon went along—
Nobody would exempt her.
The simple life was far too crude—
It nearly spoiled her temper!

Mama Tallmon fed us fine,
She cared for one and all,
And when our happy trip was o'er,
She sighed, "Home's Best of All."

52.

It was fruit season when they arrived home, and Papa took on extra work in order to provide for his expanding family.

In addition to harvesting his own crop of peaches and prunes, he accepted a job as night watchman at Cunningham's dry yard.

It meant working all day at home, and then spending long nights at the dry yard sleeping on a cot. Every hour during the night he woke up with an alarm clock and checked the premises, to guard against fruit thieves.

None ever came, but there was $10,000 worth of fruit on hand.

It was a hard and rugged six weeks, with only a few snatches of sleep as he could get them.

He stopped only on Sundays, when he was too tired even to go to church. It was the only time in his life that he ever missed regularly. He didn't even shave, and began to grow a beard.

For many years Papa had wanted to grow a beard, like his father. But Mama didn't want him to. She said, "Wait until you are 40, and then you can."

Now he was 40, and a beard was starting to grow. It had grown quite long before harvest season was over. In spite of her bargain, Mama didn't like it. Although she said nothing, Papa could feel the lack of enthusiasm.

Then, one Sunday, after church, the children went running into the house, and there was Papa--and if he didn't look like a picked chicken!

"Why, Papa!" exclaimed Edith, "What happened to your beard?"

"And your mustache," said Ray. "It's all gone!"

"I shaved them off."

"But, Papa!" objected John. "You don't look like Papa any more!"

"I don't like you without a mustache," Bessie said.

"Well," laughed Papa, "I guess I'll just have to grow it back on!"

And he did. But he never wore a beard again.

Papa hired Mr. Edmond to do some dynamiting around the ranch. Mr. Edmond dynamited an old cherry tree within five to ten feet of the house. He also removed old stumps from the orchard, and dynamited around each tree in order to "break up the soil." Later it was determined that the process did more harm than good. Although the soil immediately around the dynamite was crumbled, the blast created an inverted dome of hardness underneath.

Little Bill was very interested in what Mr. Edmond was doing, and followed him around. Mr. Edmond would set the charge, pull the cap off with his teeth, and then would move quickly to a safe spot two or three tree rows away.

He and Bill watched as the dynamite exploded and the stump shot into the air with a big cloud of dust. Bill followed Mr. Edmond around all morning. Then he went into the house and told Mama where he had been. She exclaimed: "You stay away from there."

A few days later, Papa came home with sad news.

"Mr. Edmond failed to come up to the house at quitting time while working at another job," he related. "He was found with his head blown off!"

"Oh!" exclaimed Mama, horrified. "How terrible! Poor Mr. Edmond! I'm so sorry for his family!"

"Yes," added Papa. "No one knows exactly what happened, but many people figure he used his teeth once too often."

Mama paused, her mind lost in thought. "It could have happened at our place," she said, pensively. "Little Bill could have been right there! How terrible that would have been!"

"Yes," agreed Papa. "Bill's guardian angel must have been with him!"

Hester didn't get along well in Ohio, either. The severe winters were hard on her, and she didn't take good care of herself. In March, she came down with a bad case of inflammatory rheumatism, and was in bed for two weeks.

When she got out of bed to take a sponge bath in an unheated room, she had a severe relapse. She was very ill.

To make matters worse, she could not bear to have her brother-in-law touch her. Instead, she insisted on Clara, her sister, doing everything.

This was hard on Clara. She had to lift Hester, bathe her, care for her, as well as take care of her own family. The load was almost more than she could bear.

When Clara practically collapsed and Hester was rather worse, Hester was taken to the hospital at Oberlin. But this was expensive, and as soon as she was well enough, she had to be discharged. And then the load fell on Clara again.

The situation went on for several weeks until Hester finally recovered and summer arrived again. Even then, she did little to help with the housework or meals, and the load fell heavily on Clara.

Another winter was coming, and the family couldn't go through the same difficulties again. They also felt it would not be good for Hester, either. The only sensible thing, it was decided, was for her to return to California.

But they couldn't very well say, "Hester, you go back to Morgan Hill." She must be made to feel she was wanted there-- needed there. And so a plan was worked out.

Susan, sister of Hester and Edith, was a medical missionary in China. She had been urging Edith to come to China to assist her. If Edith went to China, Grandpa would be left alone, and there would be an excuse to call Hester home.

Edith didn't want to go to China. To her, it was a bitter pill to swallow. But, if the family situation would be helped, she would go. Beside, it wouldn't be right, she felt, for two girls to be staying with Grandpa. It might as well be her to leave.

Grandpa wrote to Hester and suggested that she come home. He put it very tactfully--she didn't have to come. But Edith was leaving, and there would be no one to care for him. It would be nice if she would help out.

In spite of all the diplomacy, Hester was not very cooperative. She agreed to come--reluctantly and with a certain amount of resentment. She was pouty as she boarded the train, and her resentment grew as she crossed the continent.

She arrived in Morgan Hill at night. Without trying to contact anyone, she set out walking along the dark road toward the ranch.

Miffed and resentful, she reached Grandpa's house, and found it dark. Instead of banging on the door, or just entering on her own, she went around to the rear, climbed the narrow steps to the tankhouse, and settled down for the night there.

She spent all the next day in the tankhouse, ignoring the sounds of activity around the ranch. That night, when all was quiet, she slipped quietly out of the tankhouse, made her way around the ranch foraging for fruit from the orchard and water from the well, and then returned to her hideaway, staying there until the next night.

A week went by. Then one day the Tallmon children were visiting Grandpa and their Aunt Edith. Edith and Bessie climbed the steps to the tankhouse to get a picture from a magazine.

When they reached the top of the steps, they couldn't push the door open. It seemed to be stuck. They asked Aunt Edith to help. She tried, without success. Something was in the way.

Then a wierd thought flashed through Aunt Edith's mind. She recalled seeing signs during recent days that someone had been foraging about the ranch. The bread, for example, that was set aside for the chickens had disappeared. The heavy blanket from the clothesline that could not be found.

"Who's in there?" Edith demanded. "Hester, are you in there? You let me in."

She gave the door an extra hard shove, and it gave. Hester was standing there.

She was furious. She was red with anger.

"This is my place!" she exclaimed. "You have no right to disturb me. Why did you have to come up here, anyway?"

"But, Hester," said Edith, "why didn't you come down? We've been expecting you."

"You haven't expected me," stormed Hester. "You don't care if I come back or not. You wish I wouldn't. Well, I wish I wouldn't either. Just because I have to take care of Papa so you can go to China! What do you want to go to China for, anyway? Be nursemaid for a lot of coolies?"

"Hester," said Edith, trying to be calm, and trying to forget that she was going to China just for Hester's sake. "Hester, come down. Papa will be happy to see you. We were wondering when you would get here."

Even then, Hester refused to come down. Grandpa had to come and coax and plead and urge her to come down. Finally she descended the tankhouse steps, walked into the house, and unpacked her things.

Arrangements were completed for Edith to leave for China. The time came, her boat sailed, and Grandpa and Hester were left alone.

Hester wasn't very helpful to her father. She didn't get his meals on time, didn't keep up the house. She had her own interests, and did very little to help with family chores.

She did teach at the Morgan Hill Grammar School for awhile on a substitute basis, when another teacher was unable to complete her year. But, generally, she did little work, and spent most of her time in leisure activities, or in fooling around with the horse, cow or other farm animals.

And that was the situation in Morgan Hill when Mama and Papa learned that they were expecting another baby.

By the time summer arrived, Mama was beginning to show the effects of six months of pregnancy. She and Papa made a trip to Berkeley for a few days to visit relatives, and while there, Papa decided to attend a local Salvation Army service. He always enjoyed going when he got the chance. Mama didn't go; she preferred not to be seen in public under the circumstances.

When Papa returned, he exclaimed: "You'll never guess who I saw at the meeting. Do you remember the Stanleys?"

"Yes. The people who lived across the hall from us at Des Moines, when Bessie was a baby."

"Well, they're stationed out here now. Captain Stanley is manager of the Salvation Army store in Oakland. They invited us over to their house for supper tomorrow and to stay all night."

"But I can't go," objected Mama. "In my condition--I'd rather not."

"Oh, that's all right," Papa assured her. "Mrs. Stanley is expecting a baby, too."

They went--and spent a fascinating evening talking over old times. They compared children, discussed the Army now and then, and reviewed the lives they had lived for 12 years. How things had changed!

Mama remarked about the nice furnishings in their home. "As manager of industrial work, I have first claim to articles coming in," Mr. Stanley explained. "The children are dressed almost completely, too, from the clothing we receive."

The meal Mrs. Stanley served was meager and plain--just soup. In the pantry she had nice food, but did not use it, even though the Tallmons were there as guests. Mama was very surprised. Mrs. Stanley served supper--the better food was for noon meals.

After that, the Tallmons and Stanleys kept in touch with each other. The Stanley girls--close to the ages of Edith and Bessie--visited Morgan Hill that summer. Mr. Stanley sent lots of clothes to Morgan Hill. They weren't always the latest style, although Mama sometimes made them over.

Edith went to school that fall pretending they were up to date. Her clothes were always neat, and hung beautifully. Mama saw to that. But when the other girls' dresses were hobble, hers were straight. And when hers were hobble, the others were straight.

She never would admit it to anyone, not even to Mama. And the materials from which the dresses were made were much finer than Papa and Mama could ever afford.

Mr. Stanley also sent down some furniture, but not much. The Tallmons didn't have room for much furniture; their house was too full already.

As the time neared for the baby to be born, the old problem of a name arose again.

"Whose turn is it to pick the name this time?" asked Mama, diplomatically. "You know, we were going to take turns."

"Oh, you're having the babies," replied Papa. "You name them."

Mama suggested several names and Papa--in spite of his announced indifference--said he didn't like them. But when she proposed Donald as a name, there was no objection, and Donald it was, for a boy.

Then came the question of a middle name. Stanley--the name of their new-found friends--seemed appropriate.

They hired a housekeeper to be there when the baby was born. But she came too soon, and slept with Mama the first night. All night, she talked about cases she had had, and Mama was worn out.

The baby didn't come that night nor the next day. The next evening, the time seemed to be near. The children were sent off to bed--the younger ones in bedrooms downstairs and the two oldest girls in the unfinished attic room, up a narrow flight of stairs from the middle bedroom where Mama and Papa slept.

Still the baby didn't come. The hours of the night slowly slipped by. Mama had a hard time, and Edith, from her bed upstairs, heard more than she wanted to hear, although she covered her head with a pillow.

Finally, toward midnight, the time arrived--and little Donald Stanley was born. As soon as the first preliminaries were over, the doctor told Papa: "You'd better check to see what time he was born."

Papa looked at the clock in the living room. It said 10 minutes to midnight. The clock in the kitchen read 10 minutes after midnight. Which day should it be? November 1 or November 2?

"It could be either day," said the doctor. "Why don't you choose?"

"Well," Papa chuckled, "he has an Aunt Lucy whose birthday is November 2. It would be nice if he was born on the same day." So November 2, 1912, it was.

Papa climbed the stairs and whispered to Edith that she had a new little baby brother. And then the house grew quiet until morning.

The next day Papa had to do some hauling to San Jose. As he was leaving, he told Mrs. Johnson, the housekeeper:

"When my sister Lucy was a little girl, she always had oyster soup on her birthday, as a special treat. I'll bring some oysters back from San Jose, and we can have oyster soup on little Donald's birthday!"

Mrs. Johnson thought oyster soup would be a treat for Mama, so she kept saying, "Now, there's going to be something special tonight. Mr. Tallmon's going to bring something special from San Jose."

When supper was served, Mama was a little disappointed, as oyster soup was not her favorite dish.

They kept the tradition going for several years. But Donald didn't especially care for oyster soup either, and the custom died out.

Papa was a kind, patient, understanding father, vitally concerned with his children's welfare and character. Although he was a strict disciplinarian when necessary, he was lenient and forgiving, if there were a good reason.

Take for example the time John heaped salt and pepper and sugar on the dish of food he was eating. He took one bite, made a bitter face, and refused to eat it.

"Children must eat everything on their plates," Papa reminded him. "That's the rule. We mustn't waste food."

"But I won't eat it," John balked. "It's just too awful!"

"Hand it to me." John passed his plate, and Papa took one bite. The highly-seasoned food almost burned his tongue.

"You don't have to eat it," he said.

To Bessie, sweet potatoes were a very special treat. The family didn't have them very often, but when it did, Bessie was especially pleased.

One night, she decided to eat everything else first, and save her sweet potatoes until last. All during the meal, she looked forward to the luscious, special taste she would enjoy.

Papa noticed that she was leaving the sweet potatoes to one side. He thought she didn't want them. So, just as Bessie was finishing everything else, he reached over and took them from her plate, and ate them himself.

Papa never knew how disappointed she was.

On another occasion, John suddenly pointed his finger across the table and announced: "Willard stuck his tongue out at Mama."

Now this was a very serious thing to do--to be so disrespectful toward Mama or Papa. Willard groped for an answer.

"No, I wasn't sticking out my tongue at anybody," he replied quickly. "I--I--I was sticking my tongue out BETWEEN Mama and Susan."

Papa suggested that he should not stick his tongue out at all in the future.

One day Ray and John carefully carved their initials in the wall of the new indoor toilet. They worked hard, making beautiful, fancy letters--but amatuerish.

They were just finishing their job when Mama happened to come to the back porch and see what was going on. She was furious. The toilet was only rough boards, but to her, defacing any part of the house was wrong--especially her new indoor toilet--her pride and joy.

"What are you doing?" she demanded, ready to scold them good and proper. Papa happened by just then.

"No doubt they were just following the prevailing fashion," he said, with a laugh. Nothing more was said, and the matter was dropped.

When the older boys didn't get punished, Willard decided to add his bit, too. With Ray's help, he carved "WBT" below the other boys' initials. Then he asked Mama to come and see what he had done.

She didn't say anything at first. Finally she offered, with a toss of her head: "You made a poor B--for Burton; it looks like W--for wet."

Papa's attitude was a little different a short time later under different circumstances.

Ray was old enough to sit with the older boys in the back row at church. But one day he got carried away and carved a design on the back of the pew with his jackknife.

When Papa found out, he reproved Ray and took the knife away for a specified length of time "until you learn how to use it."

One of the Tallmons' greatest joys was their horses. They always had a number of them. But the team they owned the longest and knew the best was Prince and Nell.

Nell was ornery and tricky, and the children were warned to stay away from her. But they loved Prince. He was a family pet. His big, broad back had plenty of room for them to ride.

Often, after Papa unharnesssed the horses, he'd let one of the children ride on Prince bareback from the dipper to the barn, or across the yard. They loved that.

Mama complained, "They might fall off."

"But," said Papa, "they never have."

Prince and Nell hated to go any place. But when started toward home, no one had to drive them. They knew the way.

The boys would climb up on the wagonload--way up into the hay--and go to sleep, knowing the horses would turn into the driveway when they got there.

Often neighbors would notice the hay wagon being pulled down the road and wonder where the driver was.

One time Papa had a meeting and didn't have time to take the horses home after delivering a load of wood in town. So he drove them as far as the railroad tracks and set them loose, letting them go home by themselves.

They did just fine until they got to the driveway. There they turned the corner too close and got hung up on the cypress hedge. They were not at all excited about it, but waited patiently until Ray came and freed them. He drove them on into the barn.

Papa's blacksmith shop was located in a lean-to alongside the barn next to the eucalyptus tree. It contained an old forge and other blacksmithing equipment, along with an assorted and jumbled collection of old tools and junk.

Papa did his own blacksmithing--at night. He would have made a good shoemaker; he liked the work. He put his own boxing in the wagon, and changed the beddings on the wagon-- all blacksmithing operations.

Shoeing horses was a difficult job. First of all, Papa had to heat the coals in his portable forge and fan them with the blower until they were white hot.

Then he had to lift one leg of the horse and hold the foot between his own legs in a half-sitting position. The horse usually was lazy and leaned on Papa, until Papa would be supporting perhaps 300 pounds of the horse's total weight of 1300 pounds.

Then, while trying to keep the horse steady, Papa placed the iron shoe in position and tried to hammer the red-hot nails into the hoof.

It was ticklish business, because if the horse jerked back at the wrong time, he could tear Papa's leg muscles. Also, the nail had to be driven into the hard hoof and out the side. It stuck out an inch or more.

Until that nail was twisted off with the claw of the hammer, Papa was in constant danger from the sharp edge of the nail.

It was exacting work, and demanding, and full of frustrations. But Papa was very patient. If something didn't work, or went awry, he'd quietly try it over again. His patience was limitless.

Occasionally, though, the job was particularly trying, and he'd become a little agitated. Sometimes the horse wouldn't cooperate properly, and he'd have to whack him one on the ribs with the flat of the hammer--always the FLAT of the hammer.

Ray often held the lantern for Papa and they would work until nine or ten o'clock at night. Mama held the lantern, too, upon occasion.

One night Papa was having some real trouble. Mama, more concerned about what was going on than how she was holding the light, kept forgetting to hold it properly.

Finally Papa said: "Hold the lantern so YOU can see. And then I'll be able to see."

Papa was a good blacksmith. But, like anyone else, he sometimes made mistakes.

He was shoeing Nell. As was customary, he drove the nail in at an angle. Ever so often he checked on the side of the hoof to see if the nail were corning out where it should be.

He thought he felt it coming out, and gave two more big whacks, driving the nail right into Nell's foot. Nell jerked back sharply, nearly knocking Papa down.

Papa, chagrined, pulled the nail out and applied some linament to the sore foot. Nell was lame for several days.

One of Papa's rainy day chores was to cobble shoes, and he did it in the house. He had to soak the leather to soften it, and that sent a pungent odor wafting throughout the house. To Mama, the smell was horrible, and she didn't like those days.

Papa was an expert horseman. He knew how to train and handle horses.

If Papa had a young colt he was breaking, he'd hitch it as a third member of a team, in such a way that it could pull if it wanted to, but didn't really have to. That way, it got the idea it was helping.

Also, he often adjusted the evener to cause an older horse to pull most of the load while breaking in a new colt. That made it easier on the young horse and yet gave it a chance to get the feel of pulling.

Nell was one of the stubbornest horses Papa ever owned. She was never mean as a colt. But she cut herself on a fence as a young mare, and she was mean after that.

Mama was deathly afraid of her--especially after Nell reared over her when Mama tried to tie her up. This was while Nell was recovering from her leg cut. Papa could handle Nell, but he had to be careful.

Even out in the barn, Nell was a menace. Ray was afraid of her. She had an ornery way of waiting until he was between her and the wall in the horse stall. Then she would start leaning against him and pushing with her feet.

One evening Papa told Ray to go throw down some hay. In order to reach the barn loft, Ray had to pass through the box stall where the horses were. Usually Prince was on the wall side, but this particular evening, Nell was there.

"But Nell will crush me," Ray objected.

"Do as I say," Papa replied.

Ray did. Nell waited until Ray was clear in, between her and the wall. Then she started laying against him and pushing.

Ray hollered and Papa stabbed against Nell's back with a pitchfork. She got the idea, and released Ray.

Another night Ray was up in the haymow, pitching hay down to the animals. Papa was down below, working. Suddenly Ray slipped, slid 12 or 14 feet, and fell between the horses. As Ray landed, one of his feet hit Papa's overalls pocket, ripping it wide open. Papa grabbed him up quick before the horses stomped on him.

Nell wasn't the only ornery horse Papa owned. There was "Old Nick." Papa and Ray were driving along one day, enroute to a plumbing job, with Old Nick (his real name was Nicholas Nickleby, a Dickens character) pulling the wagon.

They met an automobile. Nick was "feeling his oats" anyway and started kicking. He put on quite a show. As he kicked, he got his foot over the singletree and couldn't get it down. There he was, like a wheelbarrow, practically helpless. He kicked a little more, aimlessly, and then gave up and lay down.

Papa started to take off the harness, then noticed that Ray wasn't helping.

"Sit on the horse's head!" Papa chided him. "Don't you know a horse is helpless when you sit on his head?"

Ray didn't know any better and, besides, Papa hadn't ordered him to do so. He was a little provoked that Papa scolded him. Papa, on the other hand, had his hands full and needed some help.

With Ray's assistance, Papa managed to get the reins off the horse and get it loose from the wagon. Then he hitched Old Nick up again and drove on without further incident.

A family that lived near Madrone, a small town north of Morgan Hill, had an ornery and balky mare. Whenever she was hitched up, she just stood there and wouldn't move. Papa offered to try to break her of it.

He took her home, and when she wouldn't move, he tied one of her legs up under her. After she got tired and was willing to go on, he'd unstrap her. If she balked again, he'd tie her up once more.

After several weeks of work like this, she had considerably improved. She was ready to go back to her owners.

Papa decided to take the family for a little drive and return the mare at the same time. He used one of his three-year-old colts to lead the mare on the road.

They delivered the mare and started back. But Jack was unhappy about leaving his "gal friend." He started acting up and putting on a show.

He kicked and kicked, his hoofs flashing out over the front of the surrey. He kicked so hard his hoofs went right through the dashboard. And then his hoofs began flying right into the seat where Papa, Mama and the two tiniest children were sitting.

Papa kept shouting, "Whoa! Whoa! Whoa!" and pulling back on the reins, trying to prevent a runaway. He pulled so hard he broke his finger. And one of the hoofs struck baby Donald on the forehead.

The family was badly frightened.

"Oh, Papa, he's killed the baby!" Mama exclaimed. She turned around and handed Donald to 14-year-old Edith in the rear seat.

The children jumped over the back of the surrey, or out the side opening. Mama jumped over the wheel--the only way she could get out--and tore her dress. The horse reared and thrashed and neighed loudly.

Papa pulled and shouted and pleaded with the horse. Jack finally calmed down, and Papa was able to get him under control once more.

Then he paused to take stock of his frightened family. Donald was not killed. But he had a nasty gash on the forehead and it was to leave a scar the rest of his life.

Papa's own hand was swollen and sore from the tightness of the reins and his broken finger.

And Mama was embarrassed about her ripped dress because a man was out in the orchard nearby.

Papa calmed everyone down and got them back into the surrey. Then they drove home.

Ray was there, waiting. He had been disking an orchard near Nob Hill and didn't go along. When he heard what had happened, he had some big brother's advice to offer in return.

"Why didn't you jump over the back?" he demanded of his younger brother, Bill. "If the surrey had tipped over, it would have fallen right on top of you! You should never jump out the side!"

53.

Troubles with Hester and Grandpa continued to be strained. Papa worked on his father's place and tried to keep normal relations going. But Grandpa seldom came over any more, and Hester only rarely.

The only time they got together, as a rule, was when some of the aunties were visiting. The conversation on those occasions usually was of a general nature, although once in a while indirect comments were made regarding the problems, or of how much Grandpa was being neglected.

Papa said nothing, preferring not to make matters worse. He'd rather let others be witness, judge and jury, than to cause any more controversy.

One time, though, when Clover and Lucy were down, Clover said something about Grandpa "buying the place" for Papa and Papa couldn't restrain himself.

"Yes," he said, "he bought my place for me before I came to California, and 10 years have proved that it is a gold brick. Income has not been enough to pay for the work, interest and taxes."

"But Papa often sent down things to help out," said Lucy.

"That's right, and I appreciated them. He felt worse than I did over the place. He wanted me to sell out, and was going to give up his ranch next door on which he owned a mortgage. But I saw a way where I could buy a home and pay for it without being under obligation to him or anyone."

The sisters stirred uncomfortably, but Papa continued on. "By selling off the rear six acres of my property, I was able to raise $500. I asked to borrow $400 from him, to raise the necessary $900 to pay off the mortgage and buy his place. He agreed and offered to do the business for me. But then I found out he had bought the place for himself."

"Why, I'm sure he intended--" said Clover. The sisters seemed agitated and unwilling to listen. They stirred and figeted uneasily.

"Of course his intentions were good," Papa continued. "I'm sure he intended for me to have the place eventually. But I might have owned a place with twice the income of the one I am on for less than the amount I put into this one--to say nothing of $500 or $600 I have given him in interest and rent."

"I'm sure Papa was doing the best he could for you," insisted Lucy. "I think you'd appreciate all he's done for you. . "

Papa gave up. He didn't try to carry the subject any further. They weren't willing to listen.

Papa needed an extra horse that year during the plowing and cultivating season. He asked to borrow Grandpa's mare, in exchange for plowing Grandpa's orchard. Papa used the horse 25 days during the season on his own work, and also plowed Grandpa's orchard--a job that required $27 worth of work according to the going rates. A dollar a day for a horse was considered proper.

Hester came over when Mama was home alone, walked into the house without knocking, and demanded:

"When is George going to cultivate Papa's orchard as he promised?"

"What are you talking about?" asked Mama, stopping her sweeping and turning toward her sister-in-law, broom in hand.

"He was to cultivate Papa's orchard in exchange for use of Papa's mare," Hester retorted. "All he has done is to plow the orchard. Is that fair?"

"I'm sure he's done all he should--and more," replied Mama. "George wouldn't take advantage of anyone!"

"He's taken advantage of his father, many times!" Hester's voice was icy. "All Papa has done for him! You'd think he would appreciate it!"

Mama bristled inside. Of course Papa appreciated it! Mama began to think of some of the ways in which Grandpa had taken advantage of Papa, and they were many. But she held her tongue and said nothing.

Hester continued: "He's used Papa's mare all season. You tell him that he's to come over and cultivate the orchard right away." Then she stormed out the door.

Mama broke into tears and buried her face in her hands. Why did Hester have to act that way? Why couldn't they get along together? Why was Hester so unreasonable?

She was still in tears, preparing supper, when Papa came in. He wanted to know what was wrong, and she told him. He put his arm across her shoulder tenderly.

"I'm sorry, mama." He said. "There's no reason for her to act that way." Then he exclaimed, turning away: "If it was necessary I'd divide my last dollar with him. But he can hire help as cheap as I and why should he ask charity from me?"

Although Papa was fighting mad inside, he didn't go over to talk with Hester and Grandpa. He didn't want to make matters any worse. He only wished he knew what the answer was.

That night Mama awoke and sat up, gasping for breath. Papa, alarmed, sprang out of bed, helped her to her feet, and led her about the room. He talked softly, trying to comfort her. Gradually she calmed down, and finally was able to go back to bed.

Just a bad nervous heart condition, brought on by all the strain, Papa was sure.

New Year's morning, 1914, was a cold, stormy day. Mama and Papa hated to get up. Papa's sister, Clara, and her boy, Lynds Jr., were visiting from Ohio, and everyone had sat up late the night before playing games.

Papa scrambled out of bed, pulled on his cold clothes, and went to the kitchen to start a fire in the stove.

Mama awakened the children, then took little Donald to the living room to get him dressed. Susan, who was 3 1/2, sat on the couch, dressing herself.

"It's a rather poor fire," called Papa as he went out the door to do the chores.

Soon they could hear a loud crackling sound from the kitchen.

Mama thought: That's an awful lot of noise for a poor fire. She got up and looked.

The sight that greeted her was chilling. Huge orange flames were shooting up from behind the stove. The whole wall was on fire!

Dish towels, hung over the back of the stove, had ignited when the stove pipe grew red hot. They, in turn, ignited the wall.

Running to the door, Mama screamed to Papa: "The house is on fire!" Then she grabbed a pan and threw water on the flames, while Susan jumped up and down and yelled. The fire sizzled and grew weaker.

By the time Papa rushed back, it was out.

"Oh!" exclaimed Mama, weakly, collapsing in a chair. "We came so close to losing our little house. What would we have done!"

Papa shook his head solemnly. "Yes," he agreed, "such a stormy day is no time to be burned out of your home."

Susan looked at the water all over the floor.

What a mess! she thought, then, childlike: But I don't have to clean it up!

Grandpa Shaffer was not at all well after he and Grandma moved back to Morgan Hill a second time. He had trouble keeping food in his stomach, and was thin and failing.

Nevertheless, it came as a shock when Mama's sister Lillie phoned one morning.

"Father's gone," she told Mama. "He died in his sleep last night."

Mama caught herself. The tears began to flow. Although somewhat expected, it was hard when the news finally did come.

"He went very easily," Lillie continued. "Mother didn't know until this morning. She noticed his arms were out when she got up, and she covered them over with a blanket. When he didn't come for breakfast, she went back and checked. . "

"Thank you," Mama managed to say on the phone. "I'll tell George."

She hung up, then turned to one of the children. "Go tell Papa that Grandpa Shaffer has died," she said.

Papa was out at the barn. He was ready to take the calves to the hill pasture. When he heard the news, he put the calves away and came on into the house.

A short time later the phone rang. Papa answered.

"Hello," he said. ".. Oh, yes, hello, Dave."

Mama knew it was Lillie's husband.

"Yes, Dave, I think that would be fine. The funeral? Yes, tomorrow will be fine. All right. If there's anything we can do, please let us know. All right. Goodbye."

Mama was dismayed. Burying her father the next day? That seemed awfully soon.

"But," replied Papa, "the undertaker said tomorrow was all right with him, and Dave's lodge was willing to work it out that way. Tomorrow is all right."

To Papa, death was not the great tragedy it seemed to many people. It was merely the passing from this life to the next. Once a person has died, the funeral and burial was a necessary part of life and might as well be completed as expeditiously as possible. But to Mama it seemed less respectful.

The next day dawned cold and clear. By time for services to begin, a weak sun was trying to bring a little warmth.

The funeral--from the Shaffers' home--was simple but appropriate. Afterwards, a long procession of buggies and cars followed the hearst to the cemetery.

It was January, and the ground was moist from recent rains. As the coffin, inside a protecting box, was being lowered into the ground, the side of the grave caved in, and dirt and water fell into the grave. The lid of the box was still open, and the dirt and water fell into the box and around the coffin. But the coffin itself was closed and protected.

Some of the men in the back made on-the-side comments about "he was soaked in life; he might as well be soaked in death."

But the undertaker jumped into the grave, quickly removed what he could of the mud, and closed the box.

That night, Mama awoke, unable to catch her breath. Papa walked her about the room and talked quietly to her. Finally she calmed down, and they went back to bed.

It took Mama a long time to get over her father's death. She missed him and she kept thinking that he would not go to Heaven--because of his drinking problem.

Then she realized: drinking alone does not make a wicked man. Deep down, her father was a good man. He was kind and considerate, respectful to women, sweet to children, and never anything but a true gentleman. He had a fault--just as most of us have faults. God would forgive. She felt better after that.

An exciting and different experience came to the boys that summer--a chance to see new places and interesting sights they had never seen before.

Mr. Voorhes, the grammar school principal, had been transferred to Niles, north of San Jose and about 40 miles from Morgan Hill. He hired Papa and the boys to help him move.

Papa loaded up two wagons with Mr. Voorhes' possessions, and early the next morning they set out on the trip.

The horse plodded along the road through prune ranches to San Jose, then skirted San Francisco Bay. The road led for mile after mile through farming country and little villages.

At Centerville, Papa stopped and looked at a vegetable dealer's wares. The man had large, prickly-looking fruit on sale, and Papa bought one as a treat for the boys. It was a pineapple, and the juicy yellow tart fruit made the chills run up and down their spines.

By mid-afternoon, they reached Niles and found Mr. Voorhes' new home. Unloading the cargo took the rest of the day and the sun was setting when they said goodbye to Mr. Voorhes and headed towards home.

Papa drove a short distance out of town and stopped in a grove of trees. He built a fire and soon he and the boys were eating a supper prepared over the campfire. They were hungry and the meat, roasted in the out-of-doors, tasted delicious.

After supper, Papa bedded down the two older boys in the spring wagon and fixed a bed for Bill up front with him in the farm wagon. Then he fed the horses.

It was pitch dark, as Bill lay there, waiting for Papa to come. All he could hear was the chomp! chomp! of the horses eating.

All of a sudden, he became panicky, and called out. Papa came right over and comforted him.

"Don't be frightened, son," he said, softly. "I'm right here. Everything is all right. I'll come to bed soon."

Papa loved children, and understood them. Little Bill, 7, snuggled down in bed. He felt secure now. And soon Papa climbed in under the covers, too.

They awoke in the morning just as the sun was peaking over the eastern hills. There was a chill in the air, and the boys lay in bed while Papa got up and started a fire.

Bill's eye felt funny and sore. He put his hand up to his face, and felt about his eye. It was big and swollen.

The others noticed it, too, as soon as they got up. "What happened to you?" they asked.

Papa examined Bill's eye.

"Something bit you during the night," he told Bill. "It was a mosquito or a bee--probably a mosquito, because I saw some of them buzzing around last night."

Soon breakfast was ready. It tasted good, cooked over a campfire on a crisp, cool morning. After doing the dishes, they packed up and started out once again on the road toward home.

They took a different way back--through Mission San Jose--just for fun.

Soon they came to a field where some men were thrashing grain with a stationary threshing machine. Papa was anxious for the boys to see the machine, so stopped and let them look. For mechanically-minded boys, it was a fascinating experience. They didn't want to leave. Finally, Papa said they must go.

The road continued on, winding through the foothills and along the valley close to the bay, until they reached San Jose.

Papa stopped at a watermelon stand on North 13th Street and bought two melons, a large one and a smaller one.

As he handed them up to Bill on the wagon, Bill slipped and dropped the larger one. It fell against the wagon bed and split wide open.

"Oh, pshaw!" exclaimed Papa, a little exasperated. "I was going to take that one home. Now we'll have to eat it for lunch and take the smaller one home."

Bill felt badly about it as they plodded along on the last leg of their journey. Papa seldom was impatient, and Bill hated to do anything to displease him.

When they arrived home, everyone wanted to know what had happened to Bill's eye. He had to explain. "A mosquito bit me during the night."

He was destined never to forget it.

The next day, which was Sunday, family pictures were taken. Bill, on tiptoes in his Sunday best, stood sideways so that his swollen eye would not show. Everyone else faced forward.

Ever after that, whenever the pictures were shown to someone new, the question came up as to why Bill was standing sideways. So the story of Bill's swollen eye had to be re-told.

The McNaughts were a distinguished family. In age, they were a generation ahead of Papa and Mama; they were old folks when Papa and Mama were just raising their family.

John McNaught was editor of a prominent New York paper and nationally-known. He married a wealthy woman from San Jose. Among her possessions was a 40-acre ranch at Morgan Hill. It was located just west of the Tallmons', and extended all the way from Dunne Avenue to Diane Avenue.

William McNaught, John's brother, came to live as a bachelor in a shack on the Morgan Hill ranch. He had been a newspaper executive with the San Francisco Call, and retired to the ranch as a place to stay and to oversee its operation.

William was used to wealth and luxurious living, and ranch life in a vine-covered shack, way back in an orchard, was a rude awakening for him.

But he thought a lot of the Tallmons. He was impressed with Mama's large family, and marvelled at the babies that kept coming with regularity.

"My, you're a wonderful woman, wonderful lady, to have all these children," he often said to her.

He enjoyed the little ones, and often made over them. But Bessie was his favorite. He was captivated by her sweet, quiet way, and by her serious response to his casual questions.

When the Lycum lectures tour came to town, Mr. McNaught bought tickets and took the children with him. He only had two tickets, and took one child at a time, including some of the neighbor children. Mama went, sometimes, too.

The Lycum series brought culture and intellect to a small town, and to attend was a great treat. Lectures were given once a week for several weeks.

Papa did Mr. McNaught's orchard work under contract. He was paid well, but part of the deal was that he had to work on McNaught's place whenever he was called. That meant that at times he had to neglect his own work or Grandpa's in order to do McNaught's orchard first.

This led to complaints from Grandpa. He couldn't see why Papa couldn't do HIS place first. Why should Mr. McNaught get top priority? He often grumbled about it. And Papa did the best he could, working long hours in an effort to get all of the work done.

Mr. McNaught lived on his Morgan Hill ranch for several years. But it was obvious he was growing more and more restless. He missed the luxury he had been used to during his earlier life. And financial difficulties worried him. He was lonesome.

One day Papa heard that Mr. McNaught had boarded the train and had left town, carrying a suitcase. Papa thought this was strange--Mr. McNaught usually informed him when he went away, and asked him to watch after the place. He always made clear when he expected to return.

Papa walked over to Mr. McNaught's house. The sight that greeted him was alarming. The door was open and the place was in disarray. Dresser drawers were open and contents pulled out as if in a hurry. The stove was still warm. Dirty dishes were left on the table. The carpet was worn in one spot, as if Mr. McNaught had paced back and forth, back and forth. Papa was puzzled.

Days passed, and then weeks. Mr. McNaught didn't return. There was no word from him. Papa kept an eye on the place, and did the necessary chores.

Finally, he decided to write to Mr. McNaught's brother in New York, telling him of the situation and asking him what to do about the ranch.

Within a few days, Papa received a very nice and courteous letter explaining that Mr. McNaught had had a nervous breakdown, and had left Morgan Hill.

"Go into the house and take as much of the furniture as necessary to pay for the work you have done on the place," the letter read. "Take everything, if you want to, except the typewriter--that is to be sold separately."

Mr. McNaught owed Papa quite a bit--it added up to about $100. So Papa and the family went over and picked out some things.

Papa took a big roll-top desk, which he kept for the rest of his life. Other treasures were an old dresser, one or two antique chairs, a cane-bottom rocking chair, a dozen good books including some from the 17th Century, and an autographed edition of the "Life of Theodosius."

Edith looked over some other books and discarded them as not the best reading for the family. Papa took some packages of typing paper home for the children to use.

The family tried some cans of caviar which they found, but they didn't like it.

The typewriter was sold through Papa to his sister Hester. Papa sold some of the other furnishings, and sent the money to Mr. McNaught's brother.

A short time later, Mr. McNaught himself wrote and apologized for leaving without a word. He said he just had to get away, and was not coming back.

Later, while traveling in Canada, he mailed some cuttings from a Tallman Sweet apple tree. The family was thrilled, because of the name. Mama had known of the variety of apples before--she had seen some trees in Colorado while engaged to Papa.

The cuttings looked dried and lifeless, and Mama was sure they would not grow. But Papa graphed them onto an apple tree in the family orchard. And, in time, they budded out and took hold.

Eventually the family had a branch of Tallman Sweet apples growing in their very own orchard!

54.

Papa's sister, Margaret, frequently came from her home in Illinois to visit Grandpa for a week or two. She always dropped over to say hello to Emma and George.

But one time the children brought word that Margaret, unknown to Papa and Mama, had been visiting next door for two or three days.

Mama was surprised. "I wonder why she hasn't come over to see us?" she pondered.

Just then, there was a knock on the door. It was Robert, Margaret's oldest boy. He handed Mama a letter.

"Thank you, Robert," she said, looking at the letter to see who it was from. Apparently it had been placed in Grandpa's mailbox by mistake.

She closed the door, and Robert turned and ran back to his grandfather's ranch.

That night, when Papa came in for supper, Mama told him that Margaret was there.

"That's strange," Papa said. "She always comes over and sees us as soon as she gets here."

Right after supper, Papa went over to Grandpa's house to see what was the matter. Margaret was polite but cool.

"We heard you were visiting," Papa said as Margaret ushered him into the parlor. "We wondered why you didn't come over and say hello."

"I sent Robert, but Emma didn't even invite him inside."

"I'm sorry," said Papa. "He brought over a letter, didn't he? Emma probably thought he was just running an errand. I'm sure it was all a misunderstanding. Won't you stop by and say hello?"

"I don't know if I'll be able to or not. We won't be here long. We are leaving next Tuesday . . "

Margaret never had acted this way before. She always was most friendly and cordial. What was the matter? Had she been influenced, too, by Hester's and Grandpa's tales of the trouble between them? Papa decided to try to explain.

"I don't know what Hester and Papa may have told you," he said, "but . . ."

"I know all about it," Margaret snapped. "We heard about you coming over and talking harshly to Papa, and starting all the trouble. Was that right?"

"Are you talking about the time I came over and told Papa he had no right to scold my wife?"

"Yes."

"The trouble didn't start with that," Papa replied, quietly. "Ever since Papa moved down here from Berkeley, we have been having problems. Papa has come over and had tantrums. Sometimes he jumps on Emma with some grievance, and sometimes he only sulks and pouts. I don't know what the purpose was but he had an insane idea that Emma hated him and after Hester was keeping house for him . . "

"Papa has only the highest regard for your welfare," Margaret retorted. "He spent a lot of time enlargening your house and doing things for you, didn't he? I should think you'd appreciate it."

"Yes, I do appreciate it. But if Papa had done 10 times as much for us as he intended to do he has no right to ask me to uphold him in false charges against Emma or help him browbeat her. Please, if I seem ungrateful. . "

"You kept his horse after it was raised, and after he had paid for its feed and pasture. Was that right?"

"Hester said he didn't want to take the horse, only wanted me to do his work," George explained. "Wouldn't $50 worth of work a year be pretty big interest to pay him for $15 he spent on a little colt I had given to my children before he asked the privilege of claiming it?"

Margaret made no reply, and George continued:

"I have always treated him fair and have done the best I could in every way. If he were left alone he would be real decent, but plagued like he is it isn't in him to do very different."

Margaret seemed agitated and unconvinced. George felt a wall of distrust and doubt rising between them. Margaret hesitated for a moment, then demanded:

"Papa bought you one place, and then you said you should have the other. Is that fair?"

"Yes, he picked out the first ranch," George started to explain. "He paid $2,750 for it, and I took it off his hands, giving him my note for $1,500 with interest at 5 per cent. But the place has proven to be a gold brick. The income has not been enough--"

"But that wasn't Papa's fault--"

"He felt worse than I did, that's right," George agreed. "He did a lot of work for me and sent down things so I could make both ends meet. He wanted me to sell out but then I saw where I could buy a home and pay for it without being under obligation to him or his estate if anything should happen. He agreed and offered to do the business for me. And then--wait, I'll get the letter he sent to us at the time. It tells in his own words just what he had done. Wait, I'll be right back."

George strode out the door, crossed the orchard, and walked into his own home. He went to the roll-top desk, pushed the corrugated cover into the recesses of the back, and thumbed through papers in the pigeon-holes.

"What happened?" Mama asked, coming to his side with a dish towel in her hands.

"Margaret's upset by the things she's been hearing," Papa explained. "I came to get that letter Papa sent to us after he put the place next door under his name."

"Are you going to show it to her?" asked Mama, somewhat dubious.

"Yes," Papa replied. "I want her to see for herself what he said."

"Do you think you should?"

"Yes, maybe it'll clear up some of her doubts."

Papa finally found the letter under some other papers in a bottom drawer of the desk. He slipped it into his pocket.

"I won't be long," he called as he went out the door. He crossed the orchard again to his father's house.

Margaret was still in the sitting room. He handed her the letter, and she glanced at it quickly, reluctantly.

"He had bought the place for himself," George offered. "He put the place in his name. "

"I know, I know," Margaret replied, a little impatiently. "I know all about it."

Margaret's attitude and her insistence that she knew the whole story preyed on Papa's mind after he started back across the orchard toward home.

For three years he had said nothing about the troubles. The family only had heard the other side.

"I know all about it," Margaret had said. "I know all about it." But she didn't.

When Papa got home, he went to his desk, got out paper and pen, and sat down to write. He'd lay it all out for Margaret-- and for Susie, too. Susie was understanding. And maybe the letter could be passed around to all.

March 22,1914.

Dear Margaret and Susie,

I started to talk to Margaret about our trouble and since none of you girls ever talked about it to ME except a word with Clover and Lucy similar to what I had with Margaret and a letter to Angie once, I believe I ought to say a little more.

For three years I have let others be witnesses, jury and judge and if Margaret hadn't said she knew ALL ABOUT IT I wouldn't have a word to say now.

The trouble didn't start with my going over and telling Papa he had 'no right to come over and scold my wife.' That was when the worm turned.

He worried our mother to her death and made our childhood home a Hell on Earth by his wicked temper and when he got to doing the same things in my home it had to stop. He apologized more than once for his meanness but afterward would be just as ugly again.

Sometimes he would only sulk and pout, then again jump onto Emma with some real or fancied grievance that was more than she could stand or should be asked to stand. You were made a cats-paw in similar style, Margaret.

We were provoked and exasperated time and again but were able to overcome our anger. To forgive and forget as we hope to be forgiven.

I didn't say a single word more than the circumstances warranted, not half what he deserved, nor one tenth what I would if I had it to do again.

Every one of you girls should have given me your moral support in the hardest, most painful thing I ever had to do.

I was not angry at the time. (I have been fighting mad since.) When I came home to lunch and found he had been over having a tantrum I told Emma she didn't need to stand it (in her condition). I would go over and tell him something. She was on her knees while I was over talking to him and was no more responsible for what I said than her unborn baby.

That any one of my sisters would think I was too hard or unjust to him never entered my head until I failed to hear from you and Hester passed me on the street with her nose in the air . .

If Papa had done 10 times as much for us as he intended to do he had no right to ask me to uphold him in false charges against Emma . .

Please if I seem ungrateful remember I give him all the credit I can for intending to do the handsome thing by me.

I asked him to let me have four hundred dollars to put with the five hundred I could raise and he agreed and offered to do the business for me. (Then he wrote the letter I showed you Margaret.) He had bought the place for himself.

Of course his intentions were still good and I let things go on as I had before. But I might for $900 have got a place that has always given more than twice the returns of this $2,700 place. .

I asked to borrow money from him again to buy a wood-lot and pasture. His conscience hurt him so over taking the other place that he bought the little ranch and gave me half interest in it. .

We got some wood cut he paying the choppers and then when we sold it I wanted him to take the money but he banked it in my name. He has since called me a highway-robber or something of the kind for using it . . .

But what's the use of going over all this?

I have always treated him fair and have done the best I could in every way . . I was never in sympathy with any idea of his in giving me a larger share of his money than any of the other children and will be glad to pay the heirs any amount I may have received above my share but to pay what he thought he was giving me would take all the entire property would bring on the market.

I ought not to be responsible for the thousand and more dollars he wasted here any more than the three thousand he lost in mining stock when I was a boy.

Now the question is: What am I to do? My work and living are here. I can keep my family fairly well on my wages and I have planted young trees that will soon make a good income property but Emma had a bad nervous heart trouble brought on by the strain three years ago and lately it is worse partly on account of her father's death .

I ought to have told you all about this long ago but hoped it would get better with waiting. This constant irritation is bad for all of us concerned but killing to Emma.

What am I to do? Your advice is earnestly requested.

With love, Geo.

P.S.--This letter is for Angie and Burt too if it is not too disturbing to pass around. I suppose I ought to write to Clara Lucy and Clover too but one letter like this is enough for me.

Papa picked up the letter, put it in an envelope, and started for the door. He would give it to Margaret right away.

Then he paused, glanced over it, opened the top of the desk, and slipped the letter into a pigeon-hole.

Maybe he'd better not give it to Margaret right now. It might just cause more hard feelings. He didn't want to do that.

Years later , the letter still lay in a deserted corner of his desk.

55.

Mama couldn't understand why Margaret would not stop by, even for a short visit. When she didn't, Mama was hurt even more deeply. Margaret still hadn't come over when she left for home a few days later.

In the days and weeks that followed, Mama's nervous strain grew even more intense. Often her heart would jump and then slow down, jump and then slow down. There were many nights when she awoke with shortness of breath.

"I just don't think I can take any more," she exclaimed one night. "Papa, can't we move away?"

But Papa replied, "I don't dare." And all Mama could do was to bear up under it, as best she could.

Her condition was complicated by an additional factor-- she was pregnant again. She didn't mind another baby, but pregnancies made her feel so miserable. And she would have been even more miserable, if her mind hadn't been occupied by the many family chores that kept her so busy.

One day she was sewing baby clothes and little Susan, who was 4, was curious.

"Who are those for?" she wanted to know.

"We are going to have a new baby," Mama explained, then cautioned: "But we don't tell anyone." In those days, it was considered indelicate to discuss a coming child until birth.

A short time later a lady from the church came to call.

As soon as Mama ushered her in, little Susan piped up, proudly: "We're going to have a new little baby!"

Mama squirmed and Susan could sense her embarrassment. But the lady didn't seem to understand.

"Yes, you're a nice little baby," she replied. Nevertheless, Susan felt badly. She had violated her mother's trust.

Papa picked out the baby's name. Alice it would be, if it were a girl. He always was fond of that name. He knew several people who had it, including an old Sunday school teacher in Iowa. And, for a middle name, Marjorie seemed just right.

If it were a boy? That was simple. Ellis would be a natural substitute. Besides, Aunt Susie knew some friends in China by that name.

It was Saturday night--time for the family's weekly baths --when Mama began to feel labor pains. In fact, when the doctor came, the boys were still bathing, and they had to pass through Mama's room to the hallway in order to go upstairs to bed.

As always, Papa was right there with Mama during the childbirth. He was a gentle person. Viewing physical pain and blood disturbed him. But he loved Mama deeply and was determined to be there with her.

And he was more or less philosophical about the naturalness and necessity of the pain of childbirth. That was part of it, he believed.

It also helped, no doubt, that he was busy. Usually he and the doctor were the only ones present, and there was plenty for him to do.

Alice was born at 9 o'clock that Saturday night--"just in time for a bath," as Papa often said afterwards. .

Soon Mama was cuddling her new little daughter in the warmth of her arms--their ninth child.

Susan slept that night with Edith and Bessie--a very special treat. In the morning she was allowed to go into Mama's room so she could kiss the little hand, covered with a woolen mitten for warmth.

Papa was so thrilled about having a new little daughter that he sat right down and wrote to his old Sunday school teacher. He never received a reply.

Alice was born just two years and 12 days after Donald— on Nov. 14, 1914.

The baby was only two weeks old, and Mama was just getting back on her feet, when it happened.

The children were leaving for school. Mama was busy sweeping the living room. The last child went out the door, and Mama noticed suddenly that Hester was there.

"Why, Hester!" Mama exclaimed. "What do you want?"

Hester seemed agitated, upset, and Mama didn't like the hard look on her face.

"I want my typewriter paper!" she declared. Her voice was low and quiet, but it carried a cutting edge.

"What typewriter paper?" asked Mama, surprised. "I don't know what you mean."

"Yes, you do." Hester was firm, caustic. "The typewriter paper that goes with the typewriter I bought from Mr. McNaught. You know that paper is mine."

"Oh, you mean the paper that was in Mr. McNaught's house?" Mama stopped her sweeping and stood with the broom upright. "Why, I didn't know that was to go with the typewriter. I guess Papa just brought it home, along with the rest of the things from the McNaughts' place. I would gladly give it to you, but I think the children have used it all up."

"Used it up?" demanded Hester. "That typewriter paper is mine. I bought it along with the typewriter. You give it back to me! You're nothing but a thief and a cheapskate!"

"The paper wasn't worth more than 10 cents," said Mama. "You would be more than welcome to it if it was still here." But Hester would not be satisfied.

"No, I'll stay right here. I'll stay until I get my typewriter paper. When are you going to give me my typewriter paper?"

"I'm sorry," Mama tried again to explain. "I think it's all gone . . "

"You know it's not all gone. You have hidden it here some place. You give it to me. You stole it, just as you stole Papa's rocking chair, and the set of drawers for the kitchen, and the cream can . ."

"No, we didn't steal any of those things," Mama insisted.

"You know you stole them. You know the rocking chair was just loaned. You tried to keep it."

"No," said Mama. "Grandpa gave us the rocking chair."

She remembered several occasions when Grandpa had accused her of taking something. Often it was something he had given her and then, like a child, he would want it back. So she would let him have it rather than cause any problems.

"You tried to keep it," Hester continued. "You're nothing but a cheat and a sinner. You cheated Papa by overcharging him for the milk. You even stole this ranch. You don't have any right to this place. It belongs to Papa."

"Why, Hester, what do you mean?"

"Papa bought this place and let George have it. It wasn't his. But does George appreciate it? He won't even help his father with the orchard work. And he's collected Papa's wages and kept them. Is that fair?"

"George never did anything of the kind--"

But Hester didn't let Mama finish. She raged on.

"George has neglected his father ever since he joined the Salvation Army and left Papa alone at home. Papa had to do all the farm work, and George should have helped him. Instead, George was off gallivanting about the country. Was that right?"

"George was doing what he thought was right. . "

"If he hadn't been associating with all that trash, he wouldn't have gotten involved with you. Drunkards, sinners, outcasts. Just a lot of good-for-nothing people. But when you get down in the gutter, what can you expect?"

Mama blanched. Her family may not have been as well educated as the Tallmons, but they weren't THAT bad . .

"You're a sinner and a cheater, that's what you are. You're downright good-for-nothing--you and all the Shaffers. You're just a cheat!" .

"Hester, come on in and sit down," implored Mama.

"All of the Shaffers are no good," Hester ranted on, paying no attention to Mama's invitation. "You're no good. George should never have married you. You have no right to be part of this family. You have no right to any recognition whatsoever. You had no right to use the name, 'John Carhart.' That's our family name. You stole that name. That was a sin!"

Mama thought: John is Papa's son, and Papa is a Tallmon. Papa had as much right to the name as anyone else in the family. Resentment, anger and bitterness filled her heart.

She couldn't take Hester's accusations and torment any longer. She had to get out of there. But what could she do? She didn't want to be rude, but she couldn't take any more.

She moved into the kitchen, leaving Hester in the doorway. But Hester wouldn't be ignored. She abandoned her self-appointed post by the door. She followed right behind Mama, continuing her spew of bitter denunciation.

"When you first moved to Morgan Hill, Papa tried to help out," she hammered, as Mama began collecting the breakfast dishes. "But did you appreciate it? He brought down staples and supplies from Berkeley. But did you care? When he came to the door late at night, you wouldn't even let him in. You made him stay out in the cold. He had to go home and fix his own cold supper. Were you too good for him?"

Mama cringed as she filled the dishpan with hot water. She remembered how she had begged Grandpa to come in that night, how she implored him, and offered a warm meal. But he threw the meat across the room and stalked away in the darkness --piqued, apparently, because Mama's folks were there.

Hester was continuing on, without respite.

"Your family is not to be trusted. Look at your father--he stole Papa's hammer and never gave it back--and even denied that he ever took it. And Callie. He sat around, doing nothing. He wouldn't get a job. An ignorant, shiftless, no-account from Kentucky. Your father, a no-good man, a man who liked his liquor. But it runs in the family. You like your food highly spiced, and so do your children.

"George got a sore on his lip, too. Got it from you. Got it from the kind of trash he lives with."

Mama was near tears. It wasn't true. It wasn't true. Hester was telling lies, the same lies she had been repeating and repeating through the years, and which Grandpa had been passing along.

"My family is a good family," she tried to say, as she swished the dishes through the sudsy water.

"Did your family come over on the Mayflower?" Hester demanded. "Did they go to college? Are any of them teachers? You just aren't worthy of being a Tallmon. I can't understand why George ever married you. He should have married someone more his age and stature in life. You aren't worthy of being his wife."

Mama didn't think she could stand it. She just couldn't stand it. Hester's words cut right through her, piercing to the bone. Why did Hester have to be so cruel? Why did she have to torment her so? Why didn't she leave? If Papa had been home that day, Mama would have rushed outside to him. But he was not there.

Hester, tall and slender, her dark hair absolutely straight and worn in a bun at the upper back, never raised her voice. She had a soft, low voice. But it was very accusatory. Her words cut to the quick.

"It was all George's fault," Hester declared in scathing denunciation, her finger stabbing the air to emphasize her point.

"If he had stayed home and helped his father on the farm, it wouldn't have happened. He would have met and married some fine local girl. But he insisted on going off and joining the Salvation Army. What can you expect? Even now, he doesn't appreciate what Papa has done for him.

"Papa bought this ranch, and later he bought the hill ranch for George. But George didn't keep up his payments and Papa had to take it back. Papa did a lot of work for George, and George never paid him. In fact, he collected Papa's wages and kept them.

"George had no right to borrow Papa's mare and then not do Papa's orchard as he promised. Papa helped raise the little colt. But do you think George would do his work? Don't you think that was rather thoughtless?"

All of this was distorted. Hester was repeating the same old falsehoods that had been circulating among the family for years. It just wasn't true. Mama was furious. It just wasn't true.

Hester continued on and on, never once ceasing her verbal harangue. As Mama moved from chore to chore around the house, Hester followed, repeating the same accusations over and over.

Mama tried to ignore her, tried not to listen, tried to avoid baiting her. The worse thing that Mama said during all that long, black day was: "We always had to handle you with kid gloves, Hester."

But it made no difference. Hester kept on and on, endlessly. Mama was near the breaking point. She couldn't take much more.

"Papa helped George load a car with wood, but did he ever get paid for it?" Hester demanded. "Papa chopped wood for George many, many times, but did George appreciate it? Was that right? Papa needed help with his work so badly, but did George help? Why not?"

Mama couldn't take any more.

"He did help; he helped a lot," replied Mama, collapsing into a chair. "But George has his own family to think about, too. We have a lot of children--"

"Yes," retorted Hester. "And whose fault is that? George is a beast to have so many children. Any man who has that many children must live like an animal!"

Mama was in tears. She buried her face in her hands. She kept repeating: "No! No! No!" Tears filled her eyes and dropped down her cheeks. It was such a short time since she delivered her baby. She was near total collapse. The room was spinning and she was dizzy.

Across her mind jabbed the sharp memory of what Papa had once told her: if anything should ever happen to her, he'd ask Hester to care for the children.

Mama shuddered. I mustn't let Hester get them, she vowed. I must not die. I must live for my children. I mustn't let Hester get my children.

"Let me alone! Please let me alone!" Mama exclaimed, tearfully. "We're all in the same family. Can't we be friends?"

But Hester paid no attention. She kept harping on Mama's "sins" and shortcomings endlessly.

Finally Mama implored: "Please, Hester, please! Let's live in peace! We both hope to go to Heaven someday. Why can't we get along together now?"

Hester retorted: "I don't want to be in Heaven if some people I know are there."

 Mama was shocked.

Then Hester turned on her heels and strode out the door and down the path, heading for home. It was 2 o'clock and the children were just getting home from school. She had been there all day.

Mama rushed to her room, threw herself across the bed, and broke into sobs. She sobbed long and hard, from the depths of her being.

Why did Hester have to be so mean? Why did Hester have to be so cruel? Mama was heartsick. She couldn't take this any longer!

When Papa came home that night and learned that Hester had been there all day, he turned white, then flushed with rage. He didn't hesitate once, but headed straight for Grandpa's house.

Grandpa was sitting at the kitchen table, reading a book. Hester was preparing a meal for her dog. George's face was ashen, his fists clenched.

"You were cruel to come over and do what you did," he told Hester. "Leave her alone; you're driving her insane. She can't stand any more of this. Don't you ever, ever come over to my house again! Don't you ever speak to her again! Don't you bother her any more in any way!"

To Grandpa he said: "You made our home a hell on earth, but you aren't going to make my home a hell on earth. Hester has to stay away."

Grandpa and Hester were silent. George was very, very seldom like this. They had no stomach to argue with him.

Papa left, and the die was cast.

Hester never set foot in her brother's house again. Grandpa also remained away. The children were forbidden to go next door.

Relations between the two households were effectively severed, except for business dealings between Papa and Grandpa. Papa continued to assist his father in the ranch work. Otherwise, his only contact came occasionally when relatives from elsewhere visited both ranches.

It was good for Mama to be rid of the torture she had endured for so many years. It was good not to have that trouble, that bitterness. It was a load off her shoulders and a weight off her soul. She never thought she would ever see the day when it would be gone--but that day had come!

56.

Mama would have been glad to have moved--anywhere. She dreamed of a place that was not so dry--like the coast over near Watsonville or Santa Cruz, where she could grow pretty flowers.

But Papa couldn't see his way clear. They were settled there. It would be expensive to move. This was not a good time for a change.

He did make a trip with Howard Sweet, Floyd Stone and two other Morgan Hill friends to Lake County north of San Francisco in Howard's new automobile.

They looked over the ranches there with the idea of maybe buying. The ranches in Lake County specialized in stock, grain, hay and some fruit, especially pears. Upper Lake raised and hauled out more string beans than any other place in California at that time.

That kind of ranching appealed to Papa more than prune growing. He was tempted to make the move. But none of the men--including Papa--found just what they wanted to buy. Papa pretty much gave up the idea.

On the way home the car lights burned out, and they slept overnight in the car before driving on to Morgan Hill.

About that time the old McNaught ranch was sold and subdivided. Five acres immediately adjacent to Papa's ten acres-- on the other side from Grandpa's place—became available for $1,000. Papa decided to buy it, in order to expand his holdings and provide a larger base of income. That pretty much settled the matter of moving.

In order to finance the purchase, Papa mortgaged the home place and borrowed the money from the sister of J.J. Jones, another rancher. Mama didn't like the idea too well--and the children reflected her feelings. Papa explained that he was just putting up the old ranch as a promise to pay, but Mama worried about what would happen if they couldn't pay--would they lose even the original ranch?

The financial burden proved to be difficult. The additional property didn't produce much profit, and Papa had to struggle to keep up just the interest payments and taxes. He never did pay a cent on the principal. It was a drag on Papa's finances all the rest of his life.

Even though automobiles were beginning to enter American life, they were beyond the financial means of most families, and horses still were the main mode of transportation. Papa depended upon his teams for many years.

By this time, Prince and Nell were his standbys. Nell had been a colt out of Polly, an earlier horse owned by the family. Nell had several colts, but none lived. They would die shortly after birth. Finally, Papa bred Nell to a donkey. The colt, when it was born, turned out to be just fine.

So Papa bought the unborn foal of a pregnant mare—in order to have another mule colt to match the first one. When they grew up they would form a new team.

As Papa led the expectant mare into the yard, the children gathered around excitedly.

Papa had a twinkle in his eye.

"Do you know who this is?" he asked. "This is Alice."

It didn't take long for word to reach the house--that the visiting mare had the same name as the Tallmons' little girl.

Papa was just putting the mare into the corral--he had a little trouble getting the well-rounded animal through the gate-- when 2-year-old Alice came running out to the barn.

"Papa! Papa!" Alice exclaimed. "Is that me?"

Kate and Fan--as the colts were called--were true mules, stubborn and mean from birth. But they showed great promise as potential work animals.

People couldn't tell them apart, they looked and acted so much alike. Whenever they got a chance to run off, they moved swiftly--they were light and agile.

For several years, Papa operated a free lance freight service to San Jose. He hauled fruit to the cannery or wood to sell, and on the way back he brought merchandise for Morgan Hill stores.

Generally he would load up the wagon the night before, then leave Morgan Hill at 2 or 3 in the morning. This would get him to San Jose by 8 or 9. It was 20 miles, but a slow 20 miles by horse and wagon. A horse could only travel about three or four miles an hour.

Some other men in the same business, taking a load of goods to San Jose and leaving at 3 in the morning, could get to the outskirts of San Jose by 7 or 8. But they had to alternately walk and trot the horses, pressing them as hard as they could, in order to make it that soon.

After Papa delivered his load, he went around town buying some things or picking up merchandise, and then started home late in the afternoon.

Every two or three miles along the highways there were water tanks and watering troughs for horses. Papa would stop at Edenvale or Coyote, about half way home, and feed and water his horses. Then he would bed down for the night and continue on the next day. That afternoon, he loaded the wagon in preparation for an early start the next day.

One year during the height of the peach season Papa attempted a double-take delivery service to San Jose. One wagonload had been loaded with boxes of fruit the night before, and was waiting at the ranch. Another was placed during the night in Morgan Hill, waiting for him to pick it up as he came by.

He was up very early in the morning--1 or 2 a.m.--and on the road, stopping in Morgan Hill to get the second wagon. After arriving in San Jose at 8 a.m., he unloaded the peaches and turned the horses around, returning to Morgan Hill. They would arrive about 12 or 1 p.m. At about 4 he'd go out and load up another wagonload for the next day.

The horses, as a result, really rested only from about 6 p.m. to 2 a.m. It was pretty hard on them. The job lasted for about three weeks, until peach season was over. Papa was nearly exhausted by that time--and the horses were tired out, too.

Papa delivered turkeys to San Jose for the Barretts for awhile. The birds were raised on a ranch near San Martin, south of Papa's place and in the opposite direction from San Jose. They were killed and dressed when he picked them up.

Papa had to leave even earlier with the turkeys--as early as 1 a.m.--in order to get to San Jose by the time the free market opened. He sold all he could there, then hawked others on the streets. Any turkeys left over were sold to a butcher. The wagon was extra long, and it was clear full, so Papa had a big load.

During another period Papa delivered firewood to San Jose and brought back mill feed to a local store.

Sometimes Raymond, as a small boy, went along. He found it was cold early in the morning. At the Tennant Avenue station, where Papa was loading up the wagon, a woman noticed Raymond standing there, shivering as the men worked. She invited him inside, where it was warm. He stood looking out the kitchen window, warm and comfortable, watching the wagon being loaded.

When it was time to go, Raymond left the house and climbed up on the wagon. Papa wrapped a blanket around him, and they started off. Papa wound the lap robe around his own legs and put the lantern under their feet, to keep warm.

They rode along, past the dark farm houses and the trees, fields and orchards, under the starlit sky. After awhile the sky began to redden above the mountain range to the east.

Then gradually the sky grew lighter and lighter and soon the round red sun peeked over the hilltops.

They spent the day delivering and selling the wood, and stayed overnight at a hotel, putting the horses in the livery stable for the night. Papa didn't make much money after paying for the hotel and livery stable out of profits from the trip.

On another of the trips, to San Jose and out Park Boulevard, Ray saw a bum pick up a horseshoe, spit on it, and throw it over his shoulder for good luck. As Ray watched, the bum took two steps, bent over, and picked up a snipe (cigar butt). As far as the bum was concerned, good luck had really come to him--fast. He crumpled up the butt, put it in his pipe, and smoked it.

Once in awhile Papa brought back something from San Jose when he made a trip there.

On one occasion he and Mr. Beach attended an auction and purchased a number of buggies, wagons and a surrey. The surrey was for Papa--as well as a wagon that was to be his No. 1 work vehicle for several years until an unfortunate accident occurred.

Two or three days after buying the surrey and wagon, Papa went back to take delivery on the things they had purchased. Raymond and John went along. They rode in Papa's old spring wagon.

Coming home, Papa hitched all the vehicles together and pulled them with one team. He put the heaviest article first--the wagon--and then, behind that, the surrey, the spring wagon and the other vehicles. There were seven in all, one behind the other.

The boys had lots of fun. They would ride on one vehicle for awhile, then get off and go up and try another.

Another time Papa returned from San Jose with four bicycles--one for each of the boys and one for Bessie.

Ray's (blue) was a good bicycle. John's (black) was not so good, and Bill's (red) was big and heavy and only cost $5. It had inch-and-a-half pipes for framework and was hard to pump, but Bill rode it to school anyway for a year and a half. He never learned to ride with no hands, though, because the frame was out of line. As soon as he let loose of the handlebars, the bike would veer sideways.

John's was the one Papa already owned and had gotten repaired. Ray's was light and very nice. It cost about $30 which was a lot in those days. Raymond and Papa both got a lot of use out of it. Whenever Papa needed a bicycle, that was the one he used.

Having a bicycle made it possible for Papa to send Raymond ahead with the team, headed for San Jose, while Papa stayed behind and finished up the chores. Then Papa would catch up on the bicycle, relieve Raymond, and send Raymond back to school on the bike.

One day something went wrong and Papa didn't show up. Raymond kept driving farther and farther. He was passing the Burnett School--another school on the way to San Jose--when the 9 o'clock bell rang and Papa finally came.

Papa was upset and Raymond was upset. It was five miles back to Morgan Hill and Raymond never forgot how madly he pedalled. He never had been late to school before.

Raymond was unhappy. And Papa was concerned more with the situation than anything else. They had missed connections or Papa had miscalculated. Papa never intended for Raymond to get so far, and his 10-year-old son didn't know what else to do but to keep going.

Bessie was in high school when she owned her bike. The bike had an unfortunate ending. Papa warned her that the bar was weak, and said if were broken, he couldn't fix it.

A girl wanted to borrow Bessie's bike; Bessie hated to turn her down. The girl used it once a week. One day Bessie came and found the bike abandoned and the bar broken. She never said anything to Papa; she walked after that.

Use of the bicycles was not confined to the older children. The younger ones took their turns, also. They'd throw their leg under the bar and ride that way, partly off to one side, and whiz around the yard.

This was not surprising, since the Tallmon children could ride anything that could be ridden--bike, horse, wagon. They were not afraid. They climbed right up. Their cousin Leroy Smith was amazed. He had always been taught to be careful.

One or more of the Tallmon boys learned to ride a single buggy wheel. They put a crank on it and rode it like a monocycle. One of the boys learned to ride a bicycle on the rear wheel only, with front end up in the air.

Often on a trip to San Jose Papa stopped at the Salvation Army salvage store and brought home something interesting.

It might be an old book or an old piece of music. One time it was an aged folio of pictures and paintings--big, beautiful artwork.

Once he purchased a complete set of Dickens' works in magazine form--a rarity that would have been worth hundreds of dollars in later years. It was a first edition, but Papa didn't know this. He purchased it for almost nothing. The type was fine and hard to read. Eventually the family burned the edition--unaware of its value--since they had most of Dickens' writing in book form.

By this time, Dickens had become a family favorite. Papa had enjoyed Dickens' stories for years. He would sit up far into the night, forgetting chores the next morning, while the tears rolled down his cheeks and his shoulders heaved and shook at the touching spots. Tenderhearted and compassionate, he was easily moved.

Mama used to josh him.

"You are unruffled by things that happen in real life," she said. "But over stories you go to pieces . . . "

Papa's love of reading dated back to his childhood, when his mother read to her children. Mama didn't have the same kind of background, although Papa often read aloud to her early in their marriage while she sat darning or sewing.

Edith, when she was old enough to read, enjoyed all the drama and emotional suspense of Dickens' tales. Often she and Papa would sit around the table, reading, with tears rolling down their cheeks when the tale grew sad.

"You two!" exclaimed Mama, half joking, as she sat mending clothes.

Papa kept urging Mama to try reading "David Copperfield." He had enjoyed it when younger and said he would like to re-read it, too. While in Gilroy, Mama bought a copy of the book and gave it to Papa as a present. She wasn't interested in reading it herself.

But, shortly after that, she was sick and, without anything "better" to read, decided to try to get interested in "David Copperfield"--just to please Papa.

She was fascinated and couldn't lay the book down. She read day and night until she had read the last chapter. After that, she read every Dickens book she could lay her hand on, and was a confirmed Dickens enthusiast. She also became an avid reader of other books.

Papa loved to recite passages from Dickens. He was always quoting, "More, more!" and other gems from Oliver Twist and Mr. McCauber.

To him, Little Nell and the Old Curiosity Shop, Oliver Twist, David Copperfield and all the rest were almost like real people.

He named many of his animals after personalities in Dickens' books. A big, white old sow was named Sairy Gamp.

Not only Dickens, but other famous authors were enjoyed by Papa. Reading was one of his favorite recreations. Besides Dickens, he especially liked, "The Forsythe Saga"; Thackeray's works, and others. He also enjoyed the stories in "Classmate," the church youth magazine.

One night Bessie was crying over the climax of "Lorna Doone." It appeared the heroine would die. Papa came by and commented: "Pretty sad story, isn't it?" Bessie found the ending was happy after all. Then she went to bed.

Next morning, Papa remarked: "I had forgotten everything turned out happy." He had stayed up and read the book after Bessie went to bed.

Papa could be touched by humor as well as pathos. He saw a story in a magazine and was so tickled he read it out loud to the rest of the family. They all laughed and were able to repeat it years later.

It was the story of a little girl who had gone to her first wedding. She was very much impressed and wrote a poem while the wedding party was still there. She asked her mother if she could read the poem. Her mother, who hadn't read it, said she could.

The little girl got up before the assemblage and proudly read:

Some had pug noses, Some had Roman.
But all wore a red ribbon Around their abdomen.

Mama had always been interested in music. She loved to sing. For years she had wanted a piano but the family budget wouldn't allow it.

Then one summer a crop of cling peaches was offered to Papa for nothing. The owner didn't want to bother with the fruit because it was so hard to cut. The stones clung so tightly they had to be dug out with a special spoon before drying.

Papa told Mama and the girls that if they wanted to cut the peaches, any money they made could go toward a piano. They agreed enthusiastically.

Papa brought home boxes and boxes of ripe, yellow fruit. Mama, Edith and Bessie worked at tables set up under the trees-- out of the hot sun. The peaches were sliced in half and pit removed, and each half was laid out on a tray, cut side up.

The trays full of fruit were slid into sulphur houses--small sheds where sulphur was burned for several hours or overnight, in order to bleach the fruit and prepare it for drying in the sun.

Mama and the girls would sing by the hour, or tell stories or talk, while the smaller children played around the cutting tables. One of the girls or Mama would go in about 11 o'clock and get lunch for the family. They took turns. They worked hard, but had fun.

The boxes of fresh fruit brought by Papa and the boys went slowly, but after many hours and days of work, the season was over and the peaches were all laid out to dry. And when they were sold, the family had earned $125--enough money for the piano, to the dollar!

Papa couldn't be depended upon to buy the finest merchandise. He was too trusting and sometimes was taken by a foxy merchant.

Papa brought the piano home from San Jose on the gravel wagon. As he neared the ranch, he expected to receive a thrilling reception. He was surprised when the family didn't come down the road to meet him; he thought they would dance with joy.

But the girls, who were beginning to grow up, felt too dignified for that.

Nevertheless, an atmosphere of excitement prevailed about the ranch as Papa unloaded the paino and, with help of some other men, moved it into the house.

As the family gathered around, Mama sat down to try it out. She played a few chords and sang a song--and pronounced the instrument excellent--a fine, old piano of high quality.

After that, music from the piano often filled the air at the Tallmon household. Mama played and sang in the evenings after the children were in bed and the older ones were studying--this was the only time she had. The girls didn't mind. They could study better when she was singing--it made a peaceful, homey atmosphere.

57.

For many years Mama had wanted a new sleeping porch. Each year, as the family grew larger in size and number, the situation grew more acute. But a sleeping porch cost money and, besides, Papa didn't have time to do the job, with all his other responsibilities.

Since buying the piano had worked so well, Mama and the girls decided to use the same method the next year to earn money for a sleeping porch. Papa obtained some more peaches and they worked hard, all during the season, cutting boxes and boxes of fruit out in the yard.

Finally, when the summer was over, they had reached their goal--once again they had earned $125. It was enough to buy the materials and to hire a neighbor, Mr. Greenslade, to do the work.

The sleeping porch was added onto the house to the west, behind the bedrooms. It was just a porch with heavy curtains that could be rolled down at night to close it in.

The boys couldn't wait for the addition to be completed. Mr. Greenslade hardly had the floor down when they started sleeping out there. Gradually, the roof and walls were built around the spot where their beds stood.

Finally, the project was completed and with great joy the family moved in. It gave a lot more room. For many years, almost the entire family slept on the porch, using the regular bedrooms for dressing and other purposes.

Raymond took all the prerogatives of being an older brother. He was a natural-born leader, anyway, and Bill and John both were more of the retiring type. They would just as soon follow along with what Ray said--most of the time.

Ray could enforce his prerogatives, too. When John and Bill weren't getting along, Ray sometimes took Bill's side, sometimes John's. But the side he was on always won out.

There was a story (denied by Ray) that he made the other boys cut their toenails. He kept his long so that in bed he could control them. John also kept Bill in his place, so Bill usually had the short end of the stick. At least he thought so.

There was a rough place at one end of the old zinc bathtub, where Papa had soldered a leak and hadn't smoothed it off. When all the boys bathed together, Bill had to sit on the bad spot, by the law of the rule of the "jungle" because he was the smallest.

At first, the boys slept three in a bed--a double bed. At Ray's suggestion, they rotated positions by the week, so that each boy slept in the middle only once every three weeks.

Later they had two double beds, and Bill slept with whomever would have him.

Papa was an understanding father, but he was strict. When he felt punishment was in order, it was administered soundly, and with dispatch.

Typical was one night when the three boys were making a fuss after they had gone to bed. John was making the most noise, although the other two were quarreling some, too. Finally Papa came in and administered a good spanking--to John.

Sometimes Papa made a mistake in his discipline, usually through some kind of misunderstanding.

Edith and Bessie were "handy" with their hands. The boys were bothering them one evening and the girls hit them.

"This hitting has gone far enough," Papa said, and the boys didn't hit back.

Later, in bed, Ray, John and Bill got to hitting each other, just for fun. Out of a spirit of fun, Ray went out to Papa and Mama and said, "I hit John." He said it in terms of play and expected to have it taken that way.

But Papa, who wouldn't stand for any nonsense and probably was influenced by the earlier episode, took it seriously.

He got down his rawhide buggy whip and gave Ray one of the severest lashings he ever got.

As far as Papa was concerned, Ray's honesty in reporting the battle was commendable. But it was not a mitigating circumstance to reduce or eliminate the punishment. If someone did something wrong, he had to accept the consequences.

Usually the spankings were fully justified, and Papa was completely aware of the facts.

Bill received the hardest spanking he ever got while he was in the second grade. His report card was graded "u" in deportment--under "remarks" it said, "Willard whispers too much."

Bill knew he would be in trouble when he got home. But he said to the other children as they were walking along, "I don't care."

That evening, after supper, Papa took him into the back room and got down a long strap.

"This is for whispering," Papa said, and struck Bill a good many times on the spot where most spankings are administered.

"This is for deportment," Papa said, and struck Bill a good many more times.

"And this is for, 'I don't care!'" and Papa really poured on the heat.

Bill could still see the marks from that spanking while he was taking a bath two weeks later. And you can bet your boots he didn't whisper in class any more.

He had been whispering because he wanted attention--perhaps because he wasn't getting enough notice at home in such a large family. The teacher put children that whispered in the corner but that was no punishment, just a chance for more attention.

But with Papa it was different. He expected his sons to toe the mark always--to obey the rules without exception. If they did not, they could expect to be punished.

For example, one time the boys were riding their horses through someone's orchard on the way to go swimming in the Mick Hole along Coyote Creek. It seemed an innocent thing, but the owner stopped them and gave them a talking to about trespassing.

Papa didn't punish them. But he had no sympathy. His comment was, "They should have been talked to."

Generally speaking, the Tallmon boys were good, reliable, straight-forward youngsters. Some of the neighbor children were not, particularly one wild boy who often got into trouble for a variety of reasons.

One Halloween he accused Raymond of dumping boxes of grapes at a neighboring ranch. It was true that Ray had ridden by the ranch on his bike at about the time the vandalism occurred. (Unfortunately, Ray had seen an auto accident downtown and had stopped to look at it; otherwise he might have arrived home sooner.)

When the boy got into trouble he remembered seeing Ray ride by. He decided to point the finger at Ray to shift the blame off himself.

The ranch owner came over to the Tallmons'. Her face flushed and her eyes darting with anger, she demanded to see Raymond.

"He's not here right now," said Mama.

"Well, he upset my grapes last night!" the neighbor denounced. "The boxes were overturned, and it caused a lot of damage!"

"I'm certain Raymond didn't do it," Mama replied. "Not one of our boys. They wouldn't do anything like that!"

"Well, the boy down the road said Raymond did it. He saw Raymond turn over the grapes. Halloween 'fun' is one thing, but causing damage is something else. I'm really angry about this!"

And the neighbor woman turned and, without a backward glance, marched off toward home.

When Raymond got home, he was upset with the charges.

"I didn't do it," he told Papa and Mama. "I wouldn't do anything like that. What shall I do?"

"Go tell her you didn't do it," Papa replied.

Raymond was shaking and frightened, but he went. He faced her. At first she was dubious. But when he explained what had happened, how the boy had seen him and shifted the blame, she was understanding.

"That's all right," she said. "I believe you. I'm glad you weren't the one."

Raymond went home feeling much relieved.

Edith was about 12 or 13 when she learned to milk--quite involuntarily. The family was discussing milking and Edith made the off-hand remark: "That's one thing I'll never do--learn to milk!"

"Young lady," replied her father, "we'll see about that. Come out to the barn."

And out to the barn she went. He set her down on a stool in front of the cow, and she proceeded to milk. He showed her just how to hold her hands and pull on the teats, so that the milk would flow into the bucket.

And that wasn't all. She had to go out and do it several times, until she learned--although she didn't milk after that.

Papa was never too tired to transport the children when they went to some doings in the evening. He never grumbled nor complained, even if it meant staying up until 11 o'clock or later to bring them home even though a busy day lay ahead. In fact, he seemed to enjoy it.

Papa made a rule against getting the horses out after they had been put away for the night, so it was a case of walking to town, returning home, and then walking to meet his youngsters when it was time to come home.

Edith was the one he walked with most, before she was old enough to have boy friends to accompany her, although he escorted the other girls, too.

"I'll beau you home," he would say. And he would meet the girls and walk home, arm-in-arm, through the starlit night.

Epworth League was the big event of the week--every Sunday night at the church. A league party once a month was about the only other social outlet the young people had. There were no movies, no cars.

Epworth League was an organization of young people-- from high school through young married couples. As the married couples began to have children, they dropped out of the league because of family responsibilities, and new teen-agers, entering high school, joined the group.

The representatives of such a wide age span got along surprisingly well together; the younger ones learned from the older ones and the married couples didn't seem to resent the high schoolers being there.

Papa sometimes walked Edith to town on Sunday night, and then stayed for the league meeting, usually a worship service and discussion period. He sat in the back--unusual for him because his custom was to sit in the front of any group he attended.

He and the preacher usually were the only older adults present. As a rule, Papa never said much and left the meeting to the young folks, whose meeting it was. But if the discussion wasn't going well, or the leader was unprepared, he would speak up with some very appropriate thoughts. And he was always one of the ones to pray when the group was saying spontaneous prayers.

On other occasions Papa would walk with Edith to town, leave her there, and then come for her after the affair was over. Sometimes he would ride a bicycle to town and then push it along, walking beside her, on the way home.

Those walks were a highpoint in life's experiences, a sweet memory never to be forgotten. They did more to mold Edith's character and outlook on life than almost anything else. She and Papa became very close.

Papa knew a lot about astronomy--picked up from his father and a course he took in college--and he talked about the stars that twinkled and glowed like little jewels in the dark sky. Astonomy was so much more interesting when the real sky stretched overhead and the stars and constellations and movements were explained by an ardent father.

"Look at all the stars in the sky," Papa would say, as they scanned the blue-black heavens, punctuated by little bits of light of all sizes and intensities. "How many do you think there are?"

"There must be thousands and thousands," Edith replied.

"Scientists estimate that there are more than 2,000 stars visible to the naked eye," Papa agreed. "But there are many more than that--those that can be seen with powerful telescopes. Scientists say there are millions of stars in the universe--and perhaps many, many more than that. In fact, the Bible says there are as many stars in the sky as sands in the sea--and you can imagine how many grains of sand there are in all the oceans. Our sun is only one of many suns--but they are so far away they look like tiny pin-pricks of light."

They had reached the edge of town by this time and were crossing the railroad tracks. The long, thin rails lay silent and deserted as they disappeared into the darkness. Dunne Avene, a narrow road between rows of budding fruit trees, stretched out ahead. The darkness was penetrated only by the faint glow of lights in the town behind them and a single bit of light flickering through the prune trees from a far-off ranch house.

Papa held his daughter's arm so she wouldn't stumble in the darkness.

"Auriga is clear and bright tonight," Papa continued, pointing to a cluster of stars in the northern sky. "See? That brightest star close to the North Star, in line with the Big Dipper? The bright star is Capella. To the left and a little higher is another star, and then three other ones in a sort of circle. They represent Auriga the Charioteer. According to the Greek myth, Aurgia was a crippled Athenian king who invented a horse-drawn chariot so that he could ride. The gods were so delighted that they honored Auriga with a place in the sky."

As Papa's daughter watched the cluster of stars, their significance grew for her.

"You know how to find the North Star, don't you?" Papa asked and she nodded.

"You sight along the outer stars of the Big Dipper," Edith said, "and you see the North Star or Pole Star about half way up the sky in the direction of the North Pole."

"Ancient mariners used to chart their courses while crossing the ocean, far from any land, by the North Star," Papa said. "If the North Star was always to their right, they knew they were headed west.

"See the Milky Way, there, stretched across the heavens? Actually, it is composed of many stars, or suns, all within our galaxy. The galaxy is a group of stars of which our sun is a part. And there are many other galaxies, and suns, and planets, even farther away, just as our Earth and other planets revolve around our own sun."

"Do you think there is life like ours on other planets?" Edith asked. "Are there people on some other world who live in houses and ride on horses and go to school? Is there some other father and some other daughter walking home, arm-in-arm, looking up at the stars, right now, too?"

"We don't know," replied Papa, looking down on his daughter lovingly, "but chances are good that there is. Maybe not on the planets that revolve around our sun--they may be too hot or too cold or don't have enough atmosphere. But it doesn't seem reasonable that God would form such a vast and wonderful universe and create human life such as he did on this one isolated planet alone and nowhere else." And Papa gave her arm a little squeeze.

"It's a wonderful world and a wonderful universe that God has created," he continued. "The vastness of the universe shows his greatness. His greatness is beyond our comprehension. All of this--so well organized and so well planned--could not have happened just by itself."

They could hear sounds in the night--a dog barking far off, horses stomping in a nearby corral, the hoot of a night owl.

Papa turned toward his daughter.

"Do you think that a God who created such a wonderful universe wouldn't, at the same time, care very much about his creatures--people like you and I?" he asked. "Do you think we are important to him?"

"Oh, yes," she replied. "I don't think he would have created us unless he loved us. I think he is concerned about everything we do and say."

Papa nodded his head in agreement.

"Jesus proved this to us," he said. "Jesus revealed God as a loving Father. He told us that each one of us is as important to God as if we were the only person in the whole world--and yet God loves everyone else in the same special way. All he asks is for us to love him and follow his way."

The night was chilly, and Papa put his arm around his daughter's waist and held her close, to keep her warm.

Papa asked: "What do you think God expects us to do?"

"To follow our ideals," she replied. "To be good Christians. To accept a Christian's responsibility in the world."

"That is very important," agreed Papa. "It's true that everything we do has an influence on others--for good or evil. If you live a good Christian life and do what is right, you influence others in ways that you may never realize. If you do things that are not right, even little things that don't seem bad, you may influence people for wrong without knowing it.

"Take smoking, for example. You may think that smoking is your own business--if you want to acquire a bad habit and subject yourself to the harm that can result to your body, that's up to you. But someone else, seeing you do it, may start smoking, too.

"You may think, 'I can drink in moderation.' But someone else, following your example, may be a person who drinks to excess. Then he might not be a good husband and father, and cause a lot of unhappiness.

"'If meat causes my brother to stumble,'" Papa quoted from the Bible, "'I will eat no meat. '"

"Is the same thing true of dancing?" asked his daughter.

"Yes," replied Papa. "Here we are, making Christianity a profession. As a family we stand for certain ideals. If you go to dances and are seen by someone not of moral background, aren't they apt to say, 'The Tallmons do it, it must be all right'? But they may not have the moral background you do, and things could go wrong. 'Abstain from all appearance of evil' is the best rule."

Papa didn't preach; he just expressed his ideas in a quiet way that couldn't offend anyone. Nevertheless, he was firm and definite about what he believed. And the girls respected and loved him for it.

They were nearing the Tallmon ranch now, making their way along the narrow dirt road. Clumps of green grass sprouted in the middle strip and on each side of the well-worn ruts. Branches of the trees were silhouetted against the dark sky, while tiny stars peeked through the rustling leaves.

"One of these days," said Papa, "you will have a boy friend to beau you home—or maybe you have one already?" and his daughter blushed in the moonlight.

"When you do," continued Papa, "it will be wonderful. But you must be careful it is the right boy, someone you truly admire. Do you know why this is so important?"

"Because it would be too bad if you fell in love with the wrong kind of person and wanted to marry him," she replied. "But isn't it all right to be just friends?"

"It's fine to be friends," agreed Papa. "but to go with a boy or girl you do not truly admire is questionable. Because if you go around with the wrong crowd, you'll become like them. You'll marry the kind of people you go with.

"You start out and think you will be careful; you don't admire them too much but you'll be friends. Then you fall in love and it's too late. Remember: 'First pity, then endure, then embrace.' So it's best to think first."

They turned into the driveway leading to the Tallmon ranch, and Papa gave her arm an extra squeeze. They reached the front porch and entered the house. Inside, Mama was sitting in a chair mending clothes. Some of the other children were reading.

Papa headed for his chair, picked up a book, and soon was dozing over its contents.

His daughter went off to bed—her thoughts on the things he had said. Neither realized that before long his comments regarding boy-girl relationships would have deep meaning.

58.

Edith plopped down on the bed and, leaning back, doubled up her legs, arms knotted around them, and rocked back and forth, her face radiant. A dreamy look filled her eyes.

"Do you know that handsome boy I was telling you about?" she asked Bessie. "You know, the one with the sweet blue eyes and strong shoulders who looks something like Papa? Well, he SMILED at me today. He was walking down the hallway and we passed and he actually LOOKED and. . "

Bessie, curled up in a chair across the room, glanced up only momentarily from the book she was absorbed in.

"Oh, Edith!" she exclaimed. "Do you always have to be talking about boys?"

"He's a senior," Edith continued, oblivious to her younger sister's disinterest. "I don't know if he even knows I exist . ." And she bounced from her perch on the bed and lightly tripped in circles across the room, her arms swinging and her body turning in gay, carefree spins.

"He's the most handsomest boy in the whole school!"

Bessie's eyes continued to follow the lines of printing down the page, one after another.

Edith went on, even if only for her own benefit. "I guess ANY girl would just love to have him interested in her, and he SMILED at me."

Edith was older than the rest of the children, enough older to have developed interests unknown to them. She was beginning to have stirrings that would eventually take her away from the family and into her own independent life.

Soon she would be given a chance to take a first plunge out into the world on her own--a job as helper at Gould's Department Store. Mrs. Gould, wife of the owner, wanted a "good, honest girl" and reliable. Mama and Papa said it would be all right and Edith was hired for the job.

Her responsibility was to wait on customers, run errands, and do odds and ends in caring for the store. She worked after school and during vacations. Mr. Gould operated a watch repair shop and barber shop as part of the business.

The Goulds had a son, Vernon, who was just older than Edith and who also worked at the store. He helped clerk and deliver packages.

At first, Mr. Gould took Edith home if it were late, or Edith would walk home, often with her friend Jeannette. But one day, after Edith had worked at the store for awhile, Vernon mentioned he had a package to deliver in the neighborhood and soon was walking beside Edith as she left for home.

She thought he had come along because of her friend Jeannette, but Jeannette said no. "He's interested in you."

Often after that Vernon walked home with her. Edith fell hard for him. He was such a nice boy and all she could think about day and night was the thrill of knowing that he liked her. Vernon was a little shy, but good company as they walked along and talked while he pushed his bicycle beside him.

One day she and Vernon and a number of other boys and girls were invited to a taffy pull at the Estes' home. The party started after school and lasted until after 8 o'clock.

When it was all over, Vernon asked if he could drive her home. Thrilled! My, she was thrilled! But a boy had never driven her home before, and she knew she would have to ask permission. So she phoned Mama.

"This certain boy wants to drive me home."

"Well, I don't know," Mama said.

"Pleeeease, Mama."

"I don't know about that."

"Oh, pleeeeease, pleeeeeeease, Mama!"

Edith had never been on a date alone with a boy before; it was hard for Mama to let her go. But Edith, who was 15 and a sophomore in high school, was growing up.

"Oh, pleeeease, pleeeease."

Mama finally gave in. "All right. You may go. But come right straight home."

Vernon went to hitch up the buggy. Thrilled! Thrilled! Edith didn't say two words all the way home. All she could think about was--the joy of the occasion. The idea of a man liking her--enthralled her.

After that, they had more dates together. They were sweethearts and whenever possible they were together--at church, at school and at the store.

When he came to get Edith for a date, Vernon usually was invited in. Papa would sit and talk with him, until Edith was ready.

Vernon always was reticient to talk and felt jittery speaking with an older man. Papa had to carry on the conversation. They talked about the news of the day, or school. Papa would ask Vernon what he was doing in school-- Papa was trying to be friendly--and Vernon would reply in answers as short as possible.

One night when Vernon came, Papa wasn't home and Vernon sat in a chair by the door and waited. Susan stood and just looked at him. He was very uncomfortable. He winked at her because he didn't know what else to do, but she just kept on looking. So, for want of something better to do, he winked at her again. The impasse might have gone on forever, if Edith hadn't come.

For dates, Edith and Vernon didn't have a lot of choice. There wasn't much social life in the small town of Morgan Hill. Mostly it was church affairs or school affairs and they were limited.

Live Oak was a non-dancing high school, and Edith wouldn't have been allowed to go to a dance, anyway. The only athletic event was basketball played on outdoor courts. A major activity for young people was parties at friends' homes.

Vernon attended several parties at Edith's house. All of the young people from Epworth League were invited. They played games--guessing games and similar activities--and had refreshments.

Gradually, Vernon and Edith grew apart. Vernon became interested in another girl, and Edith had other boy friends. But their romance was not over yet. Suddenly it blossomed once again, in very serious manner.

By then, their friends were old enough to drive cars and a favorite date was going to San Jose to the show. A group from Epworth League would go--Harold and Agnes Ward, Ed Acton, and others. Ed Acton drove his parents' car.

The rule was: home by midnight or else. Vernon and Edith were always home by that deadline, even on nights when they went to San Jose.

But Papa didn't always let Edith go. Vernon never knew why--only that her folks didn't think she should go. Perhaps her father thought she was going too much. Edith would act as the go-between. Vernon would ask her and then she would check with her parents. If her father said no, Vernon went alone with the other young people.

Papa and Mama thought Vernon was a nice boy, and were pleased to have Edith go with him. Edith adored him. And Vernon's mother was very serious about the romance, too.

After they had an automobile, Vernon's folks sometimes went for rides on Sunday afternoons and invited Edith along.

Once they went to Gonzales, a 60-mile trip each way. Another time they drove to Pacific Grove, near the ocean, and had a picnic at Point Lobos. Because the Goulds were remaining for a visit there, Edith returned home by herself on the train. It was a thrilling experience for her, traveling alone on a train.

When Vernon was able to drive, he took Edith on rides in his father's Model T Ford. Early one Sunday morning in the spring, they drove out the Redwood Retreat Road where the wildflowers were in full bloom--mariposa, petunias, columbine.

They gathered flowers by the armful, and took them home to Vernon's mother and Mama. The young people were to be home in time to dress for Sunday school. It was a delightful experience and they did it again the next week and the next.

Then Mrs. Gould said maybe some people might not understand, and maybe they'd better not do it any more. So they gave it up.

But they never did anything wrong--often they were far apart, both gathering wildflowers. Mama and Papa always said: "We know we can trust you." With an attitude like that, how could she let them down?

One night Edith came home, overflowing with joy. Mama and Papa were still up--Mama doing some darning and Papa snoozing in a chair.

"I have the most wonderful news to tell you!" she exclaimed, her eyes shining. "Vernon and I are engaged!" She was fairly dancing about the room.

"Why, that's wonderful!" replied Mama. "Vernon is a nice boy." And Papa said: "I'm very happy for you."

"Of couse, we can't get married until Vernon gets through school. But, isn't it wonderful? Mama, can we have Vernon over for dinner this Sunday?"

"Certainly, I think that would be very nice."

Edith was jittery and wanted everything just right. After church, Vernon and Edith drove to the Tallmon ranch together, and Edith bustled around the kitchen helping to prepare the meal, while Papa talked with his prospective son-in-law.

It was a typical family meal--with Papa at the head of the table, Mama at the foot, and the children lined up on either side.

Papa said grace, and then began serving the plates. Edith sat there, sometimes fidgeting, sometimes dashing to the kitchen for something extra, as dishes were passed around and plates filled.

The food was delicious, a traditional Sunday dinner with meat, potatoes, vegetables and all the trimmings. Things went reasonably well, with none of the great crises that Edith had feared.

Edith and Vernon, now seniors in high school, had many dates. Often they would come home and stand outside the door and Vernon would kiss her good night.

Little Susan, watching them and noting how Edith looked up at him with big, calf eyes, thought to herself, "How silly!"

But, to Edith, her life was now complete.

59.

The highlight of the year 1915 was an excursion the Tallmon family made to visit relatives in Berkeley and Walnut Creek--and, at the same time, to enjoy the excitement and awe-inspiring sights of the fabulous World's Fair in San Francisco.

Howard Jones, one of the Oregon cousins, had come to visit in Morgan Hill for a week or more that summer. Already guests at the Tallmon home were Dorothy and Edith Stanley, daughters of Mama and Papa's old Salvation Army friends from Oakland.

Howard, who was 15, was working with Uncle Dee at Berkeley, and had taken time out for the visit.

Howard wore his hair combed straight back--a new and popular fad--and Raymond, three years younger, had to try it. For a year afterward, Raymond wore it that way.

It was a gay occasion for the girls to have a teen-age boy around and Howard, for his part, was enthralled with one of the Stanley girls--Edie. The young people had lots of fun together.

One day they decided to do something--go on a picnic or see someone--and needed transportation. Papa said Howard could take the team.

"But don't let the horses run," Papa warned Howard. "They just ate green corn and they'll get the colic."

Out on the road, the horses wanted to run, and Howard let them go. He didn't make them run, but neither did he hold them back.

When the young people got to where they were going, one of the horses came down with the colic. Papa, summoned by telephone, got there with another man as soon as possible.

They poured kerosene down the animal's throat and worked with him for some time before he began to show signs of recovery.

And although the horses might have died, and although Howard had done exactly what Papa told him not to do, never once did Papa say a word to Howard about it nor rebuke him in any way. Howard was amazed, thankful--and regretful for what he had done.

Howard, while staying at the ranch, went to a camp meeting with the Tallmons. A young evangelist was conducting the services.

Howard attended as a visitor, along with Mama, who had a baby in her arms. Edith Stanley, whom Howard was sweet over, was with them. They were sitting there, in the tent, while the red-haired minister gave a speel about how he used to be a booze fighter (Howard didn't know what that was and didn't care, too much).

At the end of the service, the evangelist urged all those who wanted to be saved to come forward to the weeping bench. Howard was not going to go. He considered himself just a bystander, a visitor.

But Mama turned to him and whispered, "Aren't you a Christian?"

"Yeh," Howard replied.

"Then you'd better go up there," she said.

So Howard had to go. He looked back. The only people remaining in the seats were Mama, with her baby, and two "atheists" in the back.

Papa decided that Howard's visit was a good time for a family excursion. Taking Howard back to Berkeley--and the Stanley girls as well--provided a good opportunity to visit Aunt Clover and Aunt Lucy and, while there, to attend the World's Fair across the bay.

Papa fixed up the old hay wagon so that the children could both ride and sleep on it. The wagon bottom dipped in the middle, providing a good place for the feet, and Papa attached sideboards for the children to lean against. Underneath, he fastened wagon springs.

At night the children slept on beds spread out on the wagon bed. It was sort of like a bus, not bad at all, really quite comfortable.

When all was ready, and the wagon was packed with provisions, the family got up at 2 a.m. and was off. The children were expected to sleep the rest of the night on the wagon, but they were too excited. They couldn't.

The two-horse vehicle drove to town, then followed the highway to San Jose. It skirted the city and headed north along the east side of San Francisco Bay. Papa drove all the way to San Lorenzo that day--about 50 miles, which was exceptional with horses.

Their stopping place was at the end of the Oakland streetcar line. At that point the Stanley girls, the two older Tallmon girls and Howard boarded the streetcar, rode into Oakland, and stayed with the Stanleys that night.

The rest of the family bedded down near a blacksmith shop. Papa looked around until he found a farmer with a cow so that he could buy fresh milk for baby Alice. The farmer insisted that Papa not pay. Papa and Mama were disappointed to find out later the farmer had given them skimmed milk.

The next day, Papa drove on as far as the Stanleys, where they stayed that night, and then left the next morning for Aunt Clover's house, east of Berkeley.

The Stanley boys went along, to show Papa the way to Berkeley. Papa drove around Lake Merritt and right down Broadway, while the Stanley boys tried to identify the few autos they met. Raymond considered they were trying to show off, attempting to act as sophisticated "city boys."

From Berkeley, someone told them about a "short cut" through the back hills. But they got on the wrong road and drove 10 miles out of their way, along windy, dusty, deserted, hilly roads--while Mama worried and the children wished they were already to their destination.

Finally, they made it to Clover's place and that's where they stayed for almost a week. They camped out on a flat just below the Smiths' home and slept there, though they ate meals with Clover, Uncle Dee and family.

Prince and Nell, the Tallmons' horses, were put into Dee and Clover's pasture. They didn't get along well with the Smith horses.

Prince, in the past, had been an invincible fighter, but he met his match in King, Uncle Dee's horse. The men and boys watched. King was punishing Prince until King, while chasing Prince, fell into a gopher hole. Then they were separated.

Three days during the week, the family--or part of it--took a train to the waterfront, and then a ferry across the bay to San Francisco, to visit the fair.

Even five-year-old Susan went along, as Mama said: "Susan has to go at least once, so she can say, 'I went to the 1915 fair.'"

The family watched eagerly as the San Francisco shoreline grew close as they crossed the bay. The ferry slid into its V-shaped dock and was tied to its mooring. The pilings along each side creaked and groaned.

They boarded a cable car, and after clanging up and down San Francisco's hilly streets, found themselves at the fairgrounds. The excitement was intense. Crowds of people were hurrying here and there, anxious to see all they could of the fair's exhibits and features.

A mother was kneeling down, fixing the bonnet of her little girl. Two lovers strolled hand-in-hand along the main promenade. The Tallmons, country folk, had never seen such sights.

The buildings were filled with strange exhibits—art forms, paintings, household wares, and revolutionary gadgets such as radios and high, rugged, fine-built automobiles.

Susan was awed by a wax figure representing a child with measles. She was kind of embarrassed because the child had no clothes on (to show he had red measles all over).

And she was intrigued by a moving figure of a nurse in a home, going from the sick room to the family room, carrying a tray and not washing her hands. The exhibit was supposed to show how germs are spread. Susan noted that the nurse wore a blue and white apron.

The family took a streetcar to Golden Gate Park to eat lunch. They had trouble finding a place to spread out their food. Mama wanted to stop where they were, but Papa insisted on looking farther for a better place.

"Oh, this is all right," Mama said.

"No, we can find something better," replied Papa.

"But it's time to eat."

"We'll look farther."

"You never care about eating on time." Mama was provoked. "You wouldn't mind if we waited for another hour or two."

Papa retorted: "We'll eat soon--but not here."

The children were much surprised, because their parents almost never were cross with each other.

Soon Papa found a nice spot in some flower gardens near a lake, and before long the family was enjoying a hearty lunch. When it was finished and everything was cleaned up they returned to the fair for an afternoon of further sightseeing.

Papa bought the children some ice cream--the first time Willard had ever eaten chocolate ice cream. That was a real treat. It was so cold and delicious, and slid down the throat so nicely!

As the afternoon waned, they caught a streetcar and headed toward the waterfront again. Soon they were crossing the choppy, wind-swept bay. The sun was setting over the Golden Gate behind them.

As they passed Yerba Buena Island, the ferry rocked and swayed. Bill began to feel sick, pale and greenish about the throat. The more the ferry swayed, the more pallid he became.

They reached the Oakland shore all right, and soon caught the electric train that carried them across town. Bill tried to retain control. But finally he could hold back no longer. All over the floor of the train went the remnants of a day's unusual diet-- candy, popcorn, chocolate ice cream, cake.

"Oh, Willard," exclaimed his father, the slightest bit of very unusual irriation on the edge of his voice. "Couldn't you have waited until we got off the train?"

Well, Bill couldn't have waited--not any longer. He had tried. Didn't Papa understand? It was so unusual for Papa to show any signs of displeasure. Bill didn't WANT to be sick. Perhaps Papa didn't realize how hard he had been trying.

Papa went to get a conductor and helped clean up the mess. The next day, while some of the family returned to the fair, Bill had to stay at home. But on the third day he went again.

When the week's visit was over, the Tallmons said goodbye to Clover and Dee and journeyed on across the hills to Walnut Creek. There they visited Papa's sister Lucy and her husband, Harry--and their family--for several days. While at the ranch, all of the men and boys slept in the hay mow. The women and children slept in the house.

Harry had an almost-new double-moldboard plow, painted blue, that caught Papa's eye.

"That's the best-looking plow I've ever seen," remarked Papa.

"How would you like to have it?" asked Uncle Harry. "I don't want it any more. I'm going to have to get rid of it. I paid more than $50 for it originally, but you can have it for $10 if you want it."

"I do need a plow," said Papa. "That one's very nice. But are you sure you don't want to keep it?"

"No." Harry waved his hand toward the nearby fields. "I don't have any use for it any more. I'm raising a different kind of crop now. You're welcome to it, if you want it."

The blue plow went home in the wagon along with the children and everything else. It had wheels on it. Papa and Uncle Harry used some planks and they and the boys ran the plow up onto the wagon to load it. Papa tied it on securely.

On the way home, as they were riding through Danville, a gust of wind suddenly caught Mama's prized Panama hat. The wind carried it up and over some fences and out of sight. "Oh, Papa! My hat!" exclaimed Mama.

"That's a shame," replied Papa, but he didn't stop. By that time, the hat had flown over several fences, and he didn't think it was worth chasing. Mama was sick about losing it. It was several years before she was able to have another one.

60.

The wind was whistling through the trees, whipping the rain as it pelted down on the driveway and clattered on the rooftops. A knock came at the Tallmons' door.

Mama, surrounded by a host of children, went to see who it was. Standing on the porch, drenched by the rain, were a short, chunky, dark-haired woman and a little 4 1/2-year-old girl clutching a doll as big as she was.

"I Mrs. Guglielmetto," the woman said, as Mama looked at her in amazement. "We moved into house across the road. I . . I . . sorry bother you. You sell us eggs?"

"Come on in, out of the rain," Mama urged. "It's cold and wet out there!"

Mrs. Guglielmetto and her little girl walked into the warm and dry room. The little girl was afraid, and she clung close to her mother's side.

"Oh, thank you! Thank you!" the visitor exclaimed. "We come here tonight. Need eggs for supper."

"I'm sorry," Mama replied, regretfully. "We have no eggs. But perhaps Hester next door has some."

"Next door?"

"Yes, that way." And Mama pointed to the house across the orchards down the road to the east. The little girl snuggled even closer to her mother and clung tight to her doll.

Mrs. Guglielmetto started to turn to go. Mama was concerned.

"Why don't you leave the little girl here with us and save her from the long muddy walk over there?" she asked. "She can play with the children."

Mrs. Guglielmetto spoke to her daughter in Italian.

"Lena, you like to stay here while I go next door for eggs?"

Lena took one look at all those eyes staring at her. A spark of fear swept across her face. She tightened. She pressed against her mother's leg.

"Oh, no!" she cried, in alarm. "No! No! They might hurt my dolly!"

The Gugielmettos, immigrants from Italy, had purchased the ranch across the road. They lived for 18 months in the Italian colony in San Francisco, and before that in Sonora, California.

Mrs. Guglielmetto and Lena took the train to Morgan Hill, and the father rode along in the moving van that was carrying their furniture and other personal belongings.

When Mrs. Guglielmetto and her daughter arrived at the Morgan Hill train station, Mr. Guglielmetto wasn't there yet. So they started for the ranch on foot. They took the wrong road, then had to return and finally found the right road. The February rain was pouring down, and the unpaved roads were sloshy and wet.

They reached the ranch about the time Mr. Guglielmetto arrived there. It was late, so Mr. Guglielmetto and the moving van driver unpacked just the stove and beds, and left the rest until morning. There was nothing to eat, so Mrs. Guglielmetto headed for the nearest ranch to try to buy some eggs. The nearest ranch was the Tallmons'.

The little girl had clung to her precious doll on the train ride and all the way out to the ranch.

Lena was shy at first, afraid to go play with the children. Finally Mrs. Tallmon went over one day and asked her mother: "Why don't you let Lena come over? We are cutting down the eucalyptus trees in the grove, and the children are having fun playing around the fallen branches."

Lena went over, and had so much fun she begged to go back when she had to go home in the middle of the afternoon. After that, she played with the Tallmon children every day.

Shortly after the Guglielmettos moved to Morgan Hill, Papa and Mama took Mrs. Guglielmetto and Lena for a ride to see the country around Morgan Hill. Lena was delighted, but the winding roads through Paradise Valley were too much for Mrs. Guglielmetto, and she got "horse and buggy" sick.

She was very embarrassed, because she wanted to make a good impression on her new neighbors. But Mama and Papa were very sweet and understanding about it.

Although the Guglielmettos were Italian, and although their beliefs (such as smoking, drinking, working on Sunday) differed, they were always well respected by the Tallmons. Some people in the community considered Italians as a lower class, and called them "wops" and "dagos." But the Guglielmettos never felt that the Tallmons considered them in any way inferior.

The Tallmons always treated them well. They were friendly, helpful, good neighbors. Papa helped Mr. Guglielmetto with his ranch work, and showed him how to care for the prune and peach trees. Mama sometimes took cookies over to the Guglielmettos, or visited for awhile.

The Tallmons accepted people for what they were. The fact that they were Italian, Catholic, and drank liquor did not phase them at all. It didn't make any difference. They liked them as people.

Mr. Tallmon was strongly against liquor. Yet that did not keep him from associating with people who believed in using it. He could consider them as warm friends.

But Edith was the one who was very close to Mrs. Guglielmetto. They weren't that far apart in age. Mrs. Guglielmetto considered Edith almost as a sister.

Shortly after the Guglielmettos moved to Morgan Hill, Mr. Guglielmetto wanted to cultivate his ranch on Sunday. Now, he had no scruples against it. The Catholic church did not object.

Papa was going to do the work for Mr. Guglelmetto, but hadn't had time, and hadn't gotten around to it. Mr. Guglielmetto asked Papa if he could use his mules and do the work himself, on Sunday. But Papa declined, saying it was against his principles for even his animals to work on Sunday.

After that, the Guglielmettos respected Papa's beliefs on the subject. But, if you don't know, you don't know until you find out.

One time the Guglielmetto's cow became sick with milk fever, caused by a cow producing so much milk she robbed her body of necessary calcium.

The Guglielmettos had made the mistake of not feeding the cow much when it was dry, then feeding it heavily when the calf came. They called Papa, and he took care of the cow and got her over her illness.

The families helped each other. The Guglielmettos gathered manure for their vegetable garden from the Tallmon barnyard, and in turn gave vegetables to the Tallmons. Mr. Guglielmetto used an old barrel cut in half on wheels to haul the manure.

Lena couldn't speak a word of English. She would have started school that way, but, being around the Tallmon children, she began to pick up their language.

She tried to teach them Italian—including some Italian songs—but, except for a few words here and there, never had much success.

She and Donald, just six months older than she, were special pals. They played together all summer. When time came for Donald to start school that fall for the first time, Lena saw him start off, a woolen cap with tassel on top of his head.

She wanted to go, too, and cried and cried. Why shouldn't she go with him? But she wasn't old enough quite yet.

As it turned out, Donald stayed back one year in the first grade because he couldn't speak clearly. They attended school in the same class after that.

Lena's life was influenced by knowing the Tallmons. She became "óne of the family." They took her wherever they went—church, social doings, picnics, etc.

She attended Sunday school with the Tallmon children for a while, and later Junior League—her father wasn't a strong Catholic and didn't object. Her character was enriched by the contact she had with them. Many of the principles and morals she had, came from them.

Papa was a typical citizen of the early 1900's--even to wearing a mustache. He didn't impress people as being different. He had the same beliefs generally as other church people. He tried to guide his children in the proper life.

And yet he held those beliefs most sincerely. He was vitally concerned about the training of his children and with living as Jesus taught people to live.

His godliness was a godliness handed down from generation to generation, a golden thread of faith and belief. He prayed a great deal for his family--for each child--as he rode along in his wagon and did his work.

He taught his children to be proud of their family--not false pride, but a thankfulness for belonging to a family of high ideals--a thankfulness for possessing that wonderful jewel or "Pearl of Great Price" that made them better than they would be otherwise, and held them together. That pearl of great price, to a great extent, later was handed down to his children and grandchildren and great-grandchildren--just as he wanted it to be.

Papa's beliefs were based upon the Golden Rule and upon the teachings of Jesus as written in the Bible. He strove always to do things for other people, to do good toward his fellow man, to further anything that was for the good.

One of his favorite songs--and he had many--was a simple, but potent, little piece about, "A Little Talk with Jesus." It went:

> Tho' dark the night and clouds
> Look black and stormy overhead,
> And trials of almost every kind
> Across my path are spread;

How soon I conquor all,
As to the Lord I call.
A little talk with Jesus
Makes it right, all right.

Papa lived his faith. He made a decision to live only for Jesus when he was a boy- -and never faltered.

Money was not important to him, but character and morals definitely were. Kindness and unselfishness, as well as the love of God, were, to him, the Christian life. He had a creed, but he felt that acts were much more important than creed. Papa believed a person should show his religion through good works and unselfishness. He believed in giving his life completely to God, without reservation.

He favored few sacraments and religious ceremonies and symbolism. He even considered baptism and communion not too important. He allowed his children to be baptized, but mostly to humor Mama, not that he thought it really so necessary. Bessie wasn't baptized until she was seven years old. Papa didn't go in for robes, refinement, candles and pageantry. The emphasis, he felt, should be on God's Word.

Papa believed that being converted and following God's way was most vital. Living the life of a Christian, day-by-day, was all that was important to get to Heaven, in his opinion.

And he believed in a Hereafter. He believed in Heaven and Hell and believed that a person's life here determined where he was going after death. Only people who lead a good life on Earth or, if not, repented before death, could go to Heaven, he believed.

He would quote Jesus' remarks in regard to Heaven: "In my Father's house there are many mansions. I go to prepare a place for you. If it were not so, I wouldn't tell you." Papa never "fell" for the controversial theory of evolution. He never worried about man descending from monkeys or about finding "the missing link." There were plenty of people of his generation that did. He believed God created the world, but just how God did it wasn't important to his faith.

Papa believed in a strict interpretation of the Bible and accepted the Bible as it was, but he did so in an intelligent way.

He realized that the Bible had been translated through a number of languages and that it might have lost some of the meaning of the words along the way.

He didn't worry about the world being made in a week-- what the Bible terms a day might have been a thousand years or a million years. The important thing, in his opinion, was that it was made by God. He didn't throw out the whole Bible because he didn't understand something.

If a statement was in God's book, it had some reason for being there, he was sure, even if it were hard to understand. Some acquaintances took pleasure in teasing Papa about his faith. How could Noah be swallowed by a whale with a throat no bigger than a cow?

But it didn't worry Papa. He was confident there was some explanation--for one thing, the Bible didn't say whale but "large fish." And the story could have been only symbolic. He felt the beliefs the Bible taught were more important than any puzzling discrepancies in the text.

The worst sin, in his view, was rejecting God.

Papa's motto was: "What can I do for Jesus today?" Not, "What can I do for Jesus during my whole life?" but, "What can I do TODAY?"

His life was filled with the love of God. He put God first before everything else.

Papa believed people should live up to their religion-- "have the courage of your convictions," he often said. It was worse, in his opinion, to have a principle and ignore it than not to have a principle at all.

Papa didn't go around expounding on his beliefs. But when asked or the subject came up he was not afraid to state his views.

He stood up for what he thought, his ideals, no matter who was on the opposing side. On the other hand, no one else could dictate to Papa what was right or wrong. He had to make the decision himself.

And people respected Papa, because they knew he was sincere. They knew he was not professing religion just because he went to church every Sunday. He believed it and lived it. His whole life was God. People could tell.

Often when some question came up during a conversation, Papa would answer by quoting some passage from the Scriptures. He knew his Bible well.

One time a neighbor youth who was studying for the ministry was showing off how much he knew. He liked to argue about the Bible, and he gave the impression that no one in the world could tell him anything about theology or the Holy Book.

It took Papa only two or three questions to stump him.

Papa was considerate of others' religious beliefs. He said one time that as long as a person is sincere in what he believes, that is what is important. But he didn't always agree with them.

He felt especially strongly about Catholicism. He distrusted the Catholics' heirarcy and he did not agree with their theology, especially such things as adoration of the Virgin Mary. It was a very strong feeling with him.

Papa came in contact with various Indians and Mexicans around Morgan Hill who were Catholic. One man was living in a common law marriage. He told Papa he had finally saved up enough money so he could get married. He and his wife already had six or eight children.

Papa felt it was not right for a couple like that not to be legally married, just because they didn't have the money to pay the priest. Papa thought it was wrong for the church to insist on people paying for a ceremony when they couldn't afford it, to the point where people lived without marriage instead--if that were the situation.

When Mama's sister, Ella, was considering joining the Catholic faith, Papa tried to talk her out of it. It was one campaign he lost. He pointed to some of the problems of becoming a Catholic. But Ella was of an argumentative mind. The more Papa talked, the more determined she was to join anyway.

After becoming a Catholic, Ella did not change anything but her mode of worship. For example, she would not let her husband play cards, something that Catholics allowed but her Protestant church did not. Her ideas about religion remained much the same.

Papa had just as strong feelings about Seventh-day Adventists. One man who was a member of the Seventh-day

Adventist church lived on the road to town. On Sunday mornings, he invariably was out plowing or cultivating in his orchard while the Tallmons were passing by, on their way to church. His wife's snow-white laundry was on the line.

"Why do they have to show off all the time so?" Papa asked. He felt they shouldn't have made such a spectacle of their religion--as if trying to show the Tallmons that they were Seventh-day Adventists and worked on Sunday.

But Papa got along well with all those he disagreed with, as individuals; he did not run them down and always was friendly. He was critical of such people only as a group.

His own beliefs were very strong and he stuck closely to them. And he expected his family to do likewise. Usually his family agreed with him and followed suit, but there were times when they balked.

On the other hand, Papa talked about the Bible and Christianity and practiced his beliefs so faithfully that his children knew in their hearts he was right, even before they accepted Jesus for themselves.

Some people said Papa was a good family man and husband because he put his family first. But he was a good husband and family man because he didn't put his family first--he put God first.

And his dependence on Christ and his loyalty to God led him into some compelling circumstances and absorbing experiences.

61.

It was Saturday night. The hands of the big clock were closing in on midnight. A hammer, screwdriver, saw and chisel lay on the floor, along with other tools.

Papa was busy installing a swinging door between the kitchen and dining room. It was a big job and, although he was nearing completion, there was a question whether he would be done that evening.

"I'll work until midnight and then if I'm not done, I'll quit," he said. All the family stood and watched as the hands of the clock neared 12.

The new door fit fine and Papa was installing the hinges-- about the last part of the job. Drilling of screw holes and a few turns on the screws was all that remained.

But when midnight came and the clock in the living room chimed out its twelve tones, the job wasn't finished. And Papa quit. The door installation wasn't completed until the next week. A little more work and it would have been done. But after midnight was Sunday and Papa didn't believe in working on Sundays.

This little episode was typical of Papa. He believed in rest on the Sabbath--rest and church. He used to quote the saying,

> One day in seven
> We learn the way to Heaven.

But then he would quickly caution his children that they should not restrict their religious growth to Sunday but should be good Christians every day of the week.

Papa never worked on Sunday except to help someone.

Only necessary chores were done. Papa didn't even work in the fruit on Sunday at picking time. The fruit may be so ripe it was dropping from the trees, or in danger of burning from the hot rays of the sun. But he would let it be. The only exception was stacking trays of cut and drying fruit when a storm threatened.

One Sunday when the Tallmons drove home from church, they saw a number of neighbors out in the orchards picking prunes.

"They won't gain anything working on Sunday," Papa remarked to the family. "The prunes may be burning a little, but one day won't make that much difference." Then he added: "A person who works on Sunday doesn't get any more done in the long run. He needs that rest."

It was Papa's custom to get up on Sunday morning and milk the cow, then dress and go to church. On Sunday afternoons, he slept and read in the easy chair and the children played outside. In the evening, he milked and then dressed up again and went down to church.

When Willard was quite young, it seemed to him that Papa was two people. Weekdays Papa was a corduroy cap with earmuffs buttoned down across the top and work overalls. On Sundays he was a derby hat and his best suit, and sat around all day all dressed up.

It was customary for people in Morgan Hill to go visiting on Sundays--no one had time during the week because they had to work--or go riding through the countryside on a Sunday afternoon.

That is, other families did, so prettily dressed in their surries as they drove past. But the Tallmons didn't. The children wanted to, but Papa said they shouldn't--not on Sundays.

He wasn't opposed to visiting or riding as such but, as he explained, "the horses work all week and on Sundays they deserve their rest."

Later, when the Tallmons had a driving horse, they did--sometimes. That was all right, since the driving horse was used only sparingly during the week. But not a work horse--not if it could be helped and only in an emergency.

Papa often said that teams of horses that work seven days a week can't work nearly as well by spring as those that work six.

One exception to the rule was transportation to church. As long as the Tallmons had a driving horse, it was no problem. But after Nellie had been sold, Papa had no choice but to use one of the work animals. He said he always felt guilty about it. He rotated the horses so that the same one wouldn't have to take them to church every week.

Although Sunday was a day of family relaxation, a big Sunday dinner was always a special event. It was the gourmet highlight of the week--with meat and potatoes and all the trimmings.

Papa used to joke about that, although he was sympathetic. He quoted from the Fourth Commandment: "Six days thou shalt labor . . but the seventh day . . thou shalt not do any work, thou, nor thy son, nor thy daughter, nor thy man servant, nor thy maid servant, nor the stranger than is within thy gates. ."

And then he pointed out that the Bible didn't mention anything about "thy wife." He said the wife was omitted so that she could prepare Sunday dinner! And then he would look at Mama with a twinkle in his eye.

Mama and Papa did not encourage their children to read the funny papers on Sundays, either.

One Sunday the boys asked if they could go on a bike ride, but Papa said no.

"Why not, Papa?" asked Raymond. "That's not working."

"No, it's not," Papa agreed, "and a lot of people do go on bike rides and long hikes on Sunday. I don't believe that it's wrong. But Sunday is supposed to be a day of rest in preparation for the next week."

"Would it be all right if we rode our bikes just a short ways?"

Papa thought for a moment, then said, "Well, yes, as long as you ride close to home."

One Sunday afternoon Ray and John and Bill rode their bikes to visit the Pillow family, about a mile away. They were friendly with the Pillow boys, Bill and Sedley.

During the afternoon, the Tallmon boys and the Pillow boys started riding their bikes around the corner of the Pillows' house and onto a three-inch-thick plank laying on the ground. The object was to see if they could ride the entire 14 or 15-foot length without slipping off.

Bill Pillow was looking back and not watching where he was going, and ran headon into an old stove. The impact bent his bicycle forks way back.

So the boys pulled the forks off the bike and Ray pumped Bill back to the Tallmon ranch, where Papa had a big old blacksmith's vice. They straightened the forks so they looked all right and then took them back and put them on Bill's bike again.

The bike rode better than ever before. For the first time, Bill could ride without hands. The forks had been "out of true" and now they were just right!

The Tallmon and Pillow boys had some other good times on Sunday afternoons. They'd go off somewhere or do something together.

The Tallmons had to get home in time to do the chores. The Pillows, rather than continuing on to their own home, often stayed at the Tallmons' house for supper, and then accompanied the Tallmons to Epworth League.

The family's chief activity in life was church. Every week Papa faithfully attended services. He was either sick or laid up if he weren't there.

And all the children always went with him. They got there, usually on time, looking as nice as anyone--the girls dressed in their neat dresses, little shoes and white stockings, and the boys in white Sunday suits.

Every Sunday morning, Papa would get down his round, hard black shoes and polish them carefully. Then he would get dressed and all the family would start off to church in the surrey with fringe on top.

Or, if the family couldn't go to church, he rode his bicycle. Or the boys went on bicycles. Or Grandpa drove the surrey.

The mode of transportation varied during the years, and the whole family didn't always ride together. But they all got there. That was an essential family rule.

For a while, Papa gave Mrs. Cooper, a neighbor woman, a ride to church. Even though she was lame, she walked over to the Tallmon home, if the weather was good, to save Papa having to come for her. If the weather was bad, Papa picked her up.

When the family got too big, plus neighbor children, it was sometimes necessary to make two trips to Sunday school with the surrey and Prince and Nell.

For many years, Mama didn't go. She stayed home with the baby. She was busy and, really, she didn't feel she had the proper clothes to wear. And, then, so often she was pregnant and felt embarrassed.

For a time, Papa went on Sunday mornings and Mama in the evenings. But it meant hitching up the buggy and Mama driving down to church by herself. She didn't like it so didn't go for long.

There were a few times, though, when for a few months the whole family went regularly. That was when she was not sick, had no tiny child, nor one coming.

When she didn't go, she often had Sunday dinner ready when the family arrived at home. Usually she did a lot of the preparations the night before.

The children always were good in church--no trouble, well behaved. They sat all in a row, in stair-steps, beside Papa.

Once in a while, one would wiggle a little. But Mr. Kimball used to say the Raney and Tallmon children "all together did not make as much noise as one ordinary kid."

The Tallmons usually sat in the front row if late, because by that time the rest of the pews were taken. And the family was inclined sometimes to be late. Papa didn't mind but it bothered Mama.

One time when Mama didn't go along, the family was late leaving the house. And she asked, when they got home, "Did you get there on time?"

"Yes, we certainly did," Papa replied. "--just in time for the collection!"

Usually, though, the family sat in the back pews, and their customary spot was just inside the door next to the wall.

For a while a large and offensive woman, who had a sickness and was smelly, also sat there. Papa didn't mind sitting next to her, although most people avoided it. He was used to sitting near worse-smelling people than that in the Salvation Army--bums, drunks, etc.

As the years went by, there were more children, until finally the Tallmon family occupied two full rows of pews in church. Or they extended all along one pew and across the aisle to the side section.

Then the older ones began to want to sit with their friends, or by themselves.

An early morning "class meeting" was started at church--a sort of Sunday prayer meeting before services. Papa went to that, leaving before the family and usually walking to town.

Papa usually had the team hitched to the surrey and all ready to go before he left, so that the family could get to church.

Often Mr. and Mrs. Weller, neighbors, picked him up and gave him a ride as he strode along the road.

At the class meeting, people gave testimonies on how they had become Christians, or how God effected their lives-- how they placed their faith and trust in the Lord.

The meeting included songs--stirring, joyous songs-- prayers and Bible readings. The whole structure resembled Salvation Army meetings, and therefore appealed to Papa.

Papa wondered if maybe he shouldn't go back to the Salvation Army, but he never did.

And that is only part of the story of George A. Tallmon. He lived another 15 years, dying in 1931 at age 62 of prostate cancer.

He had three more children, Dorothy, born in 1916, Evelyn, born in 1918, and Melvin, born in 1923.

Throughout his remaining years, he remained the same considerate, patient, loving, kind father and husband, neighbor and friend.

He lived his life in dedication to the Lord, following Jesus' commandments, and helping others as he could.

That story is yet to be told. There are more family stories, more happiness and sadness, more heart-rending tales.

If I live long enough, I'll write that story. But, it may well be that someone else, another of his descendants, perhaps, can add the sequel. The notes are there; the time is not.

Hopefully, this book has made George Albert Tallmon one of your most cherished friends—as it has mine.

INDEX